Manual of Online Search Strategies

Third Edition
Volume III: Humanities and Social Sciences

Edited by
C.J. Armstrong
and
Andrew Large

Gower

First edition 1988
Second edition 1992

Published by
Gower Publishing Limited
Gower House
Croft Road
Aldershot
Hampshire GU11 3HR
England

Gower Publishing Company
131 Main Street
Burlington VT 05401–5600 USA

The authors of this book have asserted their rights under the Copyright, Designs and Patents Act 1988 to be identified as the authors of this work.

British Library Cataloguing in Publication Data

Manual of online search strategies. – 3rd ed.
    Vol. III: Humanities and social sciences
    1.Online bibliographic searching – Handbooks, manuals, etc.
    2.Information storage and retrieval systems – Humanities –
    Handbooks, manuals, etc. 3.Information storage and
    retrieval systems – Social sciences – Handbooks, manuals,
    etc.
    I.Armstrong, C. J. (Christopher J.) II.Large, J. A.
    025.5′24

ISBN 0 566 08305 1

Library of Congress Cataloging-in-Publication Data

Manual of online search strategies / edited by C.J. Armstrong and Andrew Large.– 3rd ed.
    p. cm.
    Includes bibliographical references and index.
    ISBN 0–566–07990–9 (set) – ISBN 0–566–08303–5 (v. 1) – ISBN 0–566–08304–3 (v. 2)
    – ISBN 0–566–08305–1 (v. 3)
    1. Online information resource searching–Handbooks, manuals, etc. 2. Online
information resource searching–United States–Handbooks, manuals, etc. I. Armstrong,
C.J. II. Large, J.A.
    ZA4060.M36 2000
    025.5′24–dc21

                                                                                00–025154

Typeset in Times by Bournemouth Colour Press, Parkstone and printed in Great Britain by MPG Books Limited, Bodmin.

Contents

List of figures   vii
Notes on contributors   xiii
Preface   xv
Acknowledgements   xvii

1   Search strategies: some general considerations   1
     Chris Armstrong and Andrew Large
     Information seekers   1
     Technologies   4
     Database differences between vendors   10
     Controlled versus natural-language searching   11
     Interfaces   13
     Search evaluation   14
     Database evaluation   17

2   Citations   23
     David Bawden
     Introduction   23
     The nature and principles of citation searching   24
     Citation indexing in practice   26
     Comparison of access media   28
     The Web of Science   29
     Techniques of citation database searching   30
     Applications of citation searching   46
     Citation searching and the Internet   94
     The significance of citation searching   96

3   Social and behavioural sciences   99
     Mark Watson
     Introduction   99
     Background   100

Major bibliographic databases in the social and behavioural sciences   102
Social welfare databases   110
Journals on CD-ROM and online   115
Citation indexes   117
Statistical databases   119
Internet subject gateways as databases   120
Research databases   122
Conclusion   123

4 Humanities   **125**
Vince Graziano
Introduction   125
Overview and history   126
The nature of humanities research   127
Information-seeking practices   129
Databases   132
Bibliographic databases   150
Prospects   210

5 Education resources   **213**
Lynne Lighthall and Linda Dunbar, with assistance from Brenda Smith
Introduction   213
Factors affecting the search   214
Steps in the search process   222
The resources   227
Internet resources   244
Resources for students   256
Search strategies for students   274
Developing the search strategy   275
Conclusion   284
Searches   285
Database details   327

Database index   335
Subject index   349

List of figures

1.1	Opening directory on YAHOO!	6
1.2	Excerpt from the opening screen of the AUSTRALIAN BIOLOGICAL RESEARCH NETWORK	7
1.3	SOCIAL SCIENCE INFORMATION GATEWAY (SOSIG)	8
1.4	Failure of controlled language	12
1.5	French-language interface to EXCITE	18
1.6	SYSTRAN translation software on ALTAVISTA	19
2.1	Variant of cited reference	31
2.2	Citations to works of art	34
2.3	Example of searching for co-citations	36
2.4	Further example of searching for co-citations	38
2.5	Following developments to a publication on a simulation technique	47
2.6	Following developments to a publication on galactic clusters	49
2.7	Identifying the latest developments	51
2.8	Finding applications of techniques	59
2.9	Information comprising a small part of a publication	75
2.10	Searching for reviews (a)	84
2.11	Searching for reviews (b)	86
2.12	Reference verification	89
3.1	SOCIOLOGICAL ABSTRACTS on DataStar Web	103
3.2	ASSIA CD-ROM	106
3.3	IBSS on BIDS	108
3.4	SOCIAL SCIENCES ABSTRACTS FULL TEXT Web interface	110
3.5	CAREDATA database search on educational attainment of children in care	113
3.6	SOCIAL SCISEARCH citation search	118
3.7	ESRC REGARD record	122
4.1	Sample search in the WWWEBSTER DICTIONARY on the Internet	134
4.2	Sample record in the WWWEBSTER DICTIONARY on the Internet	134

4.3	ARTFL Project at the University of Chicago: *Dictionnaires d'autrefois* on the Internet	136
4.4	Sample record from the OXFORD ENGLISH DICTIONARY ON COMPACT DISC, 2nd edition, 1992	136
4.5	Searching for quotations in the OXFORD ENGLISH DICTIONARY ON COMPACT DISC, 2nd edition, 1992	137
4.6	Sample record from the QUOTATIONS DATABASE on DIALOG	138
4.7	Humanities information in other fields: INSPEC on DIALOG	139
4.8	Humanities information in other fields: INSPEC on DIALOG	140
4.9	Humanities information in other fields: MEDLINE on the Internet – medicine in art search	140
4.10	Humanities information in other fields: MEDLINE on the Internet – medicine in art and neoplasms search	141
4.11	Humanities information in other fields: MEDLINE on the Internet – examples of documents retrieved by medicine in art and neoplasms search	141
4.12	LEXIS-NEXIS *Don Giovanni* search	142
4.13	LEXIS-NEXIS *Don Giovanni* retrieved documents	142
4.14	PROJECT GUTENBERG listings by author	144
4.15	PROJECT GUTENBERG search form	144
4.16	The University of Pennsylvania's ON-LINE BOOKS PAGE	145
4.17	The University of Pennsylvania's ON-LINE BOOKS PAGE search form	145
4.18	Sample record from the ELECTRONIC TEXT CENTER at the University of Virginia	146
4.19	An Index of Poets in Representative Poetry at the University of Toronto	147
4.20	Sample record from the WEBMUSEUM	149
4.21	Homepage of the AMERICAN MEMORY PROJECT	149
4.22	Search options on SIRIS	151
4.23	Sample record from the Archives and Manuscripts Catalog on SIRIS	151
4.24	Sample record of a 'citation classic' in ARTS & HUMANITIES SEARCH on DIALOG	153
4.25	Sample record from ARTS & HUMANITIES SEARCH on DIALOG	154
4.26	Searching for implicit citations in ARTS & HUMANITIES SEARCH on DIALOG	155
4.27	Finding cited references for *The English Patient* as a film or literary work in ARTS & HUMANITIES SEARCH on DIALOG	156
4.28	Sample record from ART INDEX	158
4.29	Sample record from HUMANITIES ABSTRACTS	158
4.30	Sample thesaurus entry in ART INDEX	159
4.31	Using the **Neighbor** command in HUMANITIES ABSTRACTS	160
4.32	Truncating descriptors in HUMANITIES ABSTRACTS	160
4.33	Reproductions in ART INDEX	161

4.34 Record types in ART INDEX   162
4.35 Record types in HUMANITIES ABSTRACTS   162
4.36 Physical descriptor codes used in ART INDEX   162
4.37 Illustrations and art reproductions in ART INDEX   163
4.38 Searching by medium in ART INDEX   163
4.39 Using the CT qualifier to identify creative works in HUMANITIES
      ABSTRACTS   164
4.40 Record from CT qualifier search in HUMANITIES ABSTRACTS   164
4.41 Publication years in RILA on DIALOG   165
4.42 Sample record from BHA on DIALOG   166
4.43 Searching for exhibitions in the Exhibition and Descriptor fields in
      BHA on DIALOG   168
4.44 Partial exhibition record retrieved by searching the Descriptor
      field in BHA on DIALOG   168
4.45 Example of the classification schedule in BHA   169
4.46 Searching section headings in BHA on DIALOG   169
4.47 Record retrieved by searching section headings in BHA on DIALOG   171
4.48 Sample record from ARTBIBLIOGRAPHIES MODERN
      (Web-based version)   172
4.49 General search screen and searchable fields in
      ARTBIBLIOGRAPHIES MODERN on disc   173
4.50 Essay entry in ARTBIBLIOGRAPHIES MODERN
      (Web-based version)   174
4.51 Partial list of subheadings for 'Iconography' in
      ARTBIBLIOGRAPHIES MODERN on disc   175
4.52 Sample record of an exhibition catalogue in
      ARTBIBLIOGRAPHIES MODERN (Web-based version)   175
4.53 Searching the gallery index in ARTBIBLIOGRAPHIES MODERN
      on DIALOG   176
4.54 Name variations in the gallery index on ARTBIBLIOGRAPHIES
      MODERN on DIALOG   176
4.55 Sample 'old' record in AMERICA: HISTORY AND LIFE on
      DIALOG   179
4.56 Sample record with 'new' fields in AMERICA: HISTORY AND
      LIFE on DIALOG   179
4.57 Sample 'old' record in HISTORICAL ABSTRACTS on DIALOG   180
4.58 Sample record with 'new' fields in HISTORICAL ABSTRACTS
      on DIALOG   180
4.59 General search screen on AMERICA: HISTORY AND LIFE on disc   181
4.60 Specific fields screen on AMERICA: HISTORY AND LIFE on disc (a)   181
4.61 Specific fields screen on AMERICA: HISTORY AND LIFE on disc (b)   182
4.62 Parenthetical descriptor subdivisions in HISTORICAL
      ABSTRACTS on disc   183
4.63 General descriptors in HISTORICAL ABSTRACTS on disc   183
4.64 Using controlled vocabulary and free text in HISTORICAL

	ABSTRACTS on DIALOG	184
4.65	Record retrieved with controlled vocabulary in HISTORICAL ABSTRACTS on DIALOG	185
4.66	Record retrieved with free text in HISTORICAL ABSTRACTS on DIALOG	185
4.67	Free text versus controlled vocabulary in AMERICA: HISTORY AND LIFE on disc	186
4.68	Searching time periods in HISTORICAL ABSTRACTS on DIALOG	187
4.69	Sample record from ATLA RELIGION DATABASE on CD-ROM	188
4.70	Person as Subject field in ATLA RELIGION DATABASE on CD-ROM	190
4.71	Biblical figures in ATLA RELIGION DATABASE on CD-ROM	190
4.72	Dates as subject subdivisions in ATLA RELIGION DATABASE on CD-ROM	191
4.73	Criticism of the books of the Bible in ATLA RELIGION DATABASE on CD-ROM	191
4.74	Scripture Reference field in ATLA RELIGION DATABASE on CD-ROM	192
4.75	Sample literature record from MLA INTERNATIONAL BIBLIOGRAPHY (a)	193
4.76	Sample language record from MLA INTERNATIONAL BIBLIOGRAPHY (b)	193
4.77	Sample pre-1981 record from MLA INTERNATIONAL BIBLIOGRAPHY	194
4.78	Sample pre-1981 record from MLA INTERNATIONAL BIBLIOGRAPHY showing character names but not title of work	195
4.79	Example of thesaurus entry in MLA INTERNATIONAL BIBLIOGRAPHY	196
4.80	The SilverPlatter Explode feature of the MLA thesaurus	197
4.81	Subfield descriptor codes in MLA INTERNATIONAL BIBLIOGRAPHY	198
4.82	Example of searching subfield descriptors in MLA INTERNATIONAL BIBLIOGRAPHY	199
4.83	List of role indicators in MLA INTERNATIONAL BIBLIOGRAPHY	200
4.84	Example of the use of role indicators in MLA INTERNATIONAL BIBLIOGRAPHY	201
4.85	Sample record from LINGUISTICS AND LANGUAGE BEHAVIOR ABSTRACTS	202
4.86	Searching Descriptor fields in LINGUISTICS AND LANGUAGE BEHAVIOR ABSTRACTS	203
4.87	Sample entry in the *Thesaurus of Linguistic Indexing Terms*	204
4.88	Descriptor terms and codes in LINGUISTICS AND LANGUAGE BEHAVIOR ABSTRACTS	204
4.89	Searching for place names in LINGUISTICS AND	

	LANGUAGE BEHAVIOR ABSTRACTS	205
4.90	Partial listing from the LLBA Classification Scheme	206
4.91	Searching subject headings and classification codes in LINGUISTICS AND LANGUAGE BEHAVIOR ABSTRACTS	206
4.92	Sample record from PHILOSOPHER'S INDEX	207
4.93	Positive and negative descriptor terms in PHILOSOPHER'S INDEX	209
4.94	Abbreviations in descriptors in PHILOSOPHER'S INDEX	210
5.1	Search (conducted November 1998) on the relationship between class size and student achievement in Australian primary schools	286
5.2(a)	DIALOG search on the pros and cons of 'accelerating' gifted elementary school students	293
5.2(b)	ERIC search on the pros and cons of 'accelerating' gifted elementary school students (SilverPlatter disc)	296
5.2(c)	ERIC search on the pros and cons of 'accelerating' gifted elementary school students (World Wide Web)	306
5.3	ERIC search on appropriate strategies for teaching problem-solving to K-12 students with learning disabilities (SilverPlatter disc)	309

Notes on contributors

Chris Armstrong is Managing Director of Information Automation Ltd (IAL), a consultancy and research company, established in 1987 in the library and information management sector. Prior to this, he worked as a Research Officer at the College of Librarianship Wales/Department of Information and Library Studies, University of Wales, Aberystwyth. In 1993, following several projects which indicated a need for action in the area of database quality, IAL set up the Centre for Information Quality Management (CIQM) on behalf of The Library Association and the UK Online User Group; the Centre continues to monitor database quality and work towards methodologies for assuring data quality to users of databases and Internet resources. The company's Web site can be found at <URL http:/www.i-a-l.co.uk/>. Chris Armstrong publishes in professional journals and speaks at conferences regularly. He is a Fellow of the Institute of Analysts and Programmers and a member of the Institute of Information Scientists, the UK Online User Group and The Library Association. He maintains close contact with the Department of Information and Library Studies and is currently Director of its International Graduate Summer School.

David Bawden is Senior Lecturer in the Department of Information Science at City University, London, where he is Course Director for the MSc in Pharmaceutical Information Management. He also conducts training courses for a number of organizations, including the British Library, Aslib and the Soros Foundation Network Library Program.

Linda Dunbar is a graduate of the School of Library, Archival and Information Studies at the University of British Columbia (UBC), Canada. Until 1997 she managed the Teachers' Professional Library where she provided reference services, online searching and information retrieval for the Vancouver School District. Since 1997 she has worked as a Reference Librarian in the UBC Education Library where she instructs students in database and online searching, and in public libraries where she conducts Internet training for individuals and groups. She has published a children's literature review column and educational bibliographies in local and national periodicals.

Vince Graziano has an MLIS from McGill University in Montreal, Canada and a Masters degree in history from York University in Toronto, Canada. He is a Reference/Selection Librarian at the Webster Library of Concordia University in Montreal. He has selected materials for the Fine Arts and is currently the Selection Librarian for English Literature. His responsibilities also include designing and conducting workshops on databases and designing Web pages for the Library's Web site.

Andrew Large is the CN-Pratt-Grinstad Professor of Information Studies at the Graduate School of Library and Information Studies, McGill University in Montreal, Canada. As well as editing earlier editions of the *Manual of Online Search Strategies* and Unesco's *World Information Report* (1997), he has authored several books, the most recent being *Information Seeking in the Online Age* (1999). He is also joint editor of the quarterly *Education for Information*. He has published widely on a variety of information science themes and acted as consultant for both national and international organizations.

Lynne Lighthall is Associate Professor and Graduate Advisor in the School of Library, Archival and Information Studies at the University of British Columbia (UBC) where she teaches introductory and advanced courses in bibliographic control. For nine years prior to her appointment at UBC she was Manager of Library Services for the Vancouver School Board, overseeing technical services and the implementation of a district-wide automation project. Her research interests include school library automation and the effective organization of learning resources – topics on which she has spoken and written widely. More recently, her interests in library and information studies education have prompted her to explore alternative modes of delivery, particularly via the World Wide Web. Professor Lighthall is co-author, with Marilyn Kogon, of *The Canadian Library Handbook: Organizing School, Public and Professional Libraries* as well as editor/compiler of *Sears' List of Subject Headings: Canadian Companion*.

Brenda Smith is in the second year of the Master of Library and Information Studies Program at the School of Library, Archival and Information Studies, University of British Columbia.

Mark Watson is Director of Information at the National Institute for Social Work (NISW). He has been responsible for the development of the NISW Web site and is currently leading a Managing Information and Knowledge module on the NISW/University of Sheffield Diploma/MA in Managing Practice in Social Work and Social Care. He is taking the lead in the development of the electronic Library for Social Care.

Preface

Despite the development of more friendly, attractive and helpful interfaces, a declining emphasis on time-related charges that placed a premium on familiarity and expertise, and more imaginatively packaged information, the need remains for know-how if the numerous and expanding electronic information resources are to be exploited effectively. This third edition of the *Manual of Online Search Strategies*, as with the earlier editions, sets itself the task of offering to the searcher – whether an information professional or otherwise – sound advice on database selection, search service selection and search strategy compilation in order to maximize the chances of finding the best information available for a given task. In a range of subject fields, experienced searchers pass on to the reader the benefits of their daily familiarity with electronic information resources, whether available from dial-up online services, CD-ROMs or the Internet.

This third edition of the *Manual of Online Search Strategies*, unlike its predecessors, has been divided into three separate volumes rather than appearing as a single entity. This decision has been necessitated by the growth in size of the contents – itself a reflection of the continued information explosion. This volume contains five chapters: Citations, Social and Behavioural Sciences, Humanities, and Education, together with an introductory chapter on Search Strategies. Volumes I and II deal with the Sciences (Chemistry, the Biosciences, Agriculture, the Earth Sciences and Engineering and Energy), and with Business, Law, News and Current Affairs and Patents, respectively.

The inclusion of Citation Index databases in this volume requires brief explanation. Like Patents, covered in Chapter 2 of Volume II, Citation Indexes have a wide potential application across many subject disciplines, and are certainly not confined to the Humanities and Social Sciences. Indeed, a strong argument could be made for their inclusion in either of the other two volumes. In this case, the principal reason for their inclusion in this volume was the prosaic, but nevertheless weighty, argument to equalize as far as possible the sizes of the three volumes.

The most obvious differences between the third and second editions of the *Manual*, apart from the breakdown into multiple volumes, are the slightly amended chapter divisions and the inclusion of Internet-based information resources alongside dial-up online and CD-ROM services. The latter requires little explanation, so dramatic has been the impact especially of the World Wide Web since the publication of the last edition in 1992. The only change to humanities and social science coverage in this edition has been the addition of a chapter dealing with the important area of education and resources for children.

Similar provisos regarding content must be made about the third edition as were offered for the earlier two editions. This is not an introductory textbook on information retrieval; apart from some advice offered in the opening chapter it is assumed that readers will have a basic familiarity with accessing and finding information from electronic sources (skills, in any case, somewhat less necessary with today's more user-friendly systems). Authors have been given free rein to select information sources and services for their chapters, guided by their familiarity with them. It has never been the intention to list absolutely every source or service that might conceivably be used in a search (itself an impossible task if the *Manual* is to be confined to realistic dimensions). The authors of this volume are drawn from North America and the UK, and this inevitably influences their selections. Nevertheless, sources and services from elsewhere are by no means ignored in the following pages. Perhaps the most thorny issue with publications of this type is currency: it would be pointless to deny the rapid rate of change in the electronic information sector. Every effort has been made by the authors, editors and publisher to ensure that the content is as up-to-date as possible on publication.

Information sources, let alone information services, cannot neatly be compressed into the chapter division used by the *Manual* (or any other subject division, for that matter). Inevitably, many databases and services are mentioned in more than one chapter. It is hoped that the indexes in each volume will enable the reader to pursue specific titles across the chapters and volumes.

It is never simple to compile a book involving two editors, one publishing editor and 17 authors scattered across two continents and several countries. Notwithstanding the marvels of modern telecommunications, at times one dreams of a real meeting around a non-virtual table. It is to the credit of the many people involved in the production of this book that it has seen the light of day without that particular dream being realized. We remain very grateful for the promptness and courteousness unfailingly exhibited by all the authors. Special thanks must be offered to Suzie Duke of Gower Publishing, who did all and more than could be expected of a publishing editor.

While this *Manual* was struggling to emerge, another battle was being waged. Kathy Armstrong, who had followed with a lively interest work on all the editions of the *Manual*, was fighting her own battle with a courage and fortitude that none of her family or friends will ever forget. This edition is dedicated to her memory.

Chris Armstrong, Bronant, Wales, UK
Andy Large, Montreal, Quebec, Canada
September 2000

Acknowledgements

We should like to acknowledge the support of the various information providers and services who have kindly given permission to reproduce their content in the third edition of the *Manual of Online Search Strategies*. Copyright over all figures and searches remains with the individual producers.

Chapter 1

Search strategies: some general considerations

Chris Armstrong and Andrew Large

The subsequent chapters in the *Manual of Online Search Strategies* discuss in detail the strategies that can successfully be used to retrieve digitized information in a wide range of subject areas. However, more general topics common to all areas are assembled in this opening chapter, rather than being duplicated throughout the book. The objective here, then, is to provide introductory comments on the users of information systems – the information seekers – and the variety of technologies that can now be used to offer digitized information to those seekers. It also reminds seekers that the same database may differ in content or structure from platform to platform or even from vendor to vendor. Subsequent chapters discuss the specific indexing characteristics of many databases; in this chapter some general points are made about the relative merits of searching on assigned controlled terms as against natural-language terms as found in the database documents themselves. The interface to any retrieval system is a crucial determinant both of user satisfaction and success, so interface design criteria are very briefly reviewed. Finally, the chapter discusses the important topics of search and database evaluation.

Information seekers

There is a tendency to discuss information seekers as if they are a homogeneous group. In reality, of course, each seeker is an individual who brings to the workstation a particular set of personal characteristics, subject knowledge and retrieval skills as well as a unique information need; all of these influence the search outcome. Nevertheless, it is both practical and useful to sort them into categories according to certain broadly defined characteristics.

The most common characteristic relates to the seekers' level of experience in information retrieval. Applying this measure, seekers can broadly be categorized as novice or experienced. Unfortunately, no generally accepted criteria have been formulated to assist in this distinction. Borgman (1996) suggests that an information seeker requires three layers of knowledge:

- conceptual – to convert an information need into a searchable query
- semantic – to construct a query for a given system
- technical – to enter queries as specific search statements.

An experienced searcher, therefore, would be someone possessing such knowledge and able to implement these three actions. This begs the question, of course, as to *how* such tasks might be assessed and judged as well or badly performed. Hsieh-Yee (1993) offers more specific criteria: novice searchers are non-professional searchers who have little or no search experience and have not taken courses in online searching or attended relevant workshops provided by librarians or system vendors; experienced searchers are professional searchers who have at least one year of search experience and have either taken courses on online searching or attended workshops provided by system vendors. This definition, equating novice with non-professional (or end user) and experienced with professional, suggests that only the latter can become experienced. While user studies do indicate that many non-professionals are not especially effective when searching, it is a sweeping statement to suggest that only professional searchers can attain expertise, and that this is achieved only by taking courses or attending workshops. Extensive information seeking on the World Wide Web, and discussion of this activity in popular magazines and on radio and television, is providing a level of familiarity (if not always expertise) with information retrieval among diverse user groups regardless of formal instruction. Despite the definitional problems, the terms 'novice' and 'experienced' recur in discussions of information seeking.

A related distinguishing characteristic is between an information professional (or information intermediary) – the person who conducts a search on behalf of a client – and an end user – the person who actually wants the information to answer a specific need (as we have just seen, Hsieh-Yee uses this characteristic to distinguish between the novice and the experienced). This distinction was especially valid when most online searching was conducted by intermediaries – librarians or other information specialists – rather than by the actual information requester. Information professionals were considered experienced users, as was generally the case, and end users were novices who conducted searches rarely and with little or no preliminary training (often also true). Much searching is now undertaken by end users – a consequence in large part of simpler retrieval interfaces and a wider range of accessible information on CD-ROM and the World Wide Web.

Information seekers can also be categorized by a variety of other criteria. Do they have a thorough knowledge of the subject in which that search is to be conducted (whether novice or experienced, end user or intermediary)? The subject specialist's search is likely to be different from the non-specialist's because, for example, the former will have a greater awareness of the subject's terminology, and therefore be better placed to select suitable search terms. The specialist should be better at selecting the most suitable sources for the search, which has become increasingly difficult as electronic information resources proliferate. The specialist should also be able to judge the relevance of retrieved information and adjust a search strategy if this seems appropriate.

Many user studies have investigated young adult information seekers in the context of a university library. Most researchers are located in university departments, and the most obvious and accessible subjects for their studies are to be found on their own doorsteps. It would be difficult to argue, however, that university undergraduates necessarily represent a cross-section of information system users in general. More recently, greater interest has been shown in other user groups. A prime example is children, who increasingly use online information systems both in school and from their homes. Do systems that have been designed for adults work just as effectively for children, or do the different cognitive skills and knowledge bases of children demand information systems that have been specially designed with this specific user group in mind? The same might be said of users at the opposite age spectrum. Elderly citizens are likely (for the time being, at least) to be less familiar with computers, to have poorer eyesight and less precise hand movements than their juniors. Should this make a difference, for example, to the kinds of interfaces provided by the OPAC or Web site?

Seekers might also be differentiated by their search objective: are they trying to find absolutely everything that is available on a topic, even if only tangentially linked to it, or only a little information directly on the topic? These distinctions will almost certainly affect the search strategy, and perhaps the choice of database.

Finally, psychological factors such as attitude, motivation and cognitive style can differentiate users (or even the same user on different occasions), although attempts to measure their impact on search outcome have proved far from conclusive. As in other types of human performance, it is extremely difficult reliably to isolate individual characteristics that can then be tested for an effect on searcher performance. Fidel and Soergel (1983), for example, identified over 200 variables that could come into play when investigating searching.

Some studies have failed to find a clear, positive relationship between search experience and search results. Lancaster *et al.* (1994), for example, compared CD-ROM searches on a bibliographic database by graduate student end users and skilled university librarian intermediaries. The librarians were able to find, in total, more relevant records on the database than the students, but a higher percentage of the records retrieved by the students were judged relevant by them. The greatest problem encountered by the students was failure to identify and use all the terms needed to perform a more complete search; they were less successful in identifying synonyms than the librarians. Hsieh-Yee (1993) found, however, that search experience positively affected search behaviour, especially when the experienced searchers had some subject knowledge relevant to the topic of the search. They used more synonyms and tried more combinations of search terms than novices.

Many studies have commented on the positive evaluations typically made by end users of their own search results, and questioned whether such optimism is really justified (see, for example, Lancaster *et al.*, 1994; Martin and Nicholas, 1993). Sanderson (1990) considered that no matter how user-friendly the system, end users need clear directions to help them get the best results; training programmes should emphasize system capabilities and the kind of information that can be obtained, and should include hands-on sessions in which users are taught how to do basic searches.

Technologies

Digital (or electronic) information can now be found using several related, but distinct, technologies. Remote online information systems, accessible via dial-up telecommunication networks (typically only to users who have signed a contract with the system) remain important purveyors of databases. Examples of such systems are DIALOG, DIMDI and STN. The first public demonstration of such an interactive retrieval system was made by the System Development Corporation in 1960, and until the late 1980s these online systems dominated the digital information market.

In the 1980s libraries began to replace their card catalogues with Online Public Access Catalogues (OPACs). Unlike the traditional online systems, whose use was largely confined to information professionals, OPACs were intended for all library users. Another development of the late 1980s was the CD-ROM, an optical rather than a magnetic data storage medium. Although data could not be deleted from or added to a CD-ROM (as is the case with magnetic storage media), the CD-ROM proved to be a cheap and efficient medium for publishing digital information, thereby extending the market from the institutional to the domestic setting. Increasing numbers of CD-ROMs are purchased to be used on home-based personal computers for recreational purposes (in many cases the CD-ROMs contain games rather than 'information' *per se*).

Technology developments have continued into the 1990s. In their early days, CD-ROMs could not be networked, or if this was possible then response times were severely degraded. Institutional exploitation of CD-ROM technology was greatly facilitated by the emergence of networked versions of many CD-ROM titles. CD-ROMs also have been joined by related optical storage devices that greatly extend the quantity of data that can be stored on a single disc (the Digital Video Disc/Digital Versatile Disc or simply DVD-ROM, for example, can accommodate around seven times more data than a CD-ROM); data can now be added to a disc so it is not just read-only (the introduction of CD-R – CD Recordable – for example, allowed institutions or individuals to create their own CDs and therefore to store locally created data on this medium).

Undoubtedly, the most dramatic development of the 1990s, however, has been the rapid growth of the Internet, and especially the World Wide Web that makes statistics outdated by the time they are collected. In late 1999, however, one Web search engine – ALTAVISTA – claimed to index 250 million pages (Notess, 2000) while INKTOMI, in January 2000, had over 1 billion documents in its database, each relating to a unique page (Inktomi, 2000). And not even the largest engines are able to index anything like the entire Web.

Web search engines can either be general, such as ALTAVISTA <URL http://www. altavista.digital.com/> or NORTHERNLIGHT <URL http://www. northernlight.com/>, attempting to provide access to the Web as a whole, or specialized, such as AL IDRISI <URL http://www.alidrisi.com> (in this case, Arabic-language pages) or WAITER.COM <URL http://www.waiter.com/cgi-bin/SCMMOS/RegSys/AutoRegHome.cgi> dealing with take-out food delivery. An increasing number of search engines cover a specific country or region, such as SEARCHUK <URL http://www.searchuk.com/> or NZ EXPLORER <URL http://nzexplorer.co.nz/> (for over 250 000 Web pages in New Zealand).

At the other extreme, meta search engines like DOGPILE <URL http://www. dogpile.com/index.html> or METACRAWLER <URL http://www.metacrawler.com/ index.html>, search simultaneously on multiple regular search engines (useful because no single engine, including the very largest general ones, in practice indexes more than a part of the entire Web). Hock (1999) advises that these meta-engines are most useful when searching for a single, very rare word or when it is not important that all the relevant records are found (because most of the meta-engines only return between ten and 30 pages from each target engine, and do not employ sophisticated search syntax such as Boolean term matching, even if the user enters them),

Web search engines should be distinguished from Web directories, the best known of which is YAHOO! (see Figure 1.1). These directories provide hierarchical menus of subjects that can be used to narrow a search, but will only give access to a fraction of the Web.

The Web has made digital information an everyday fact of life for millions of people across the globe. In part, it has provided an alternative platform for the kinds of databases that previously were only found on traditional online systems, OPACs or CD-ROMs. But it has also extended the type of information that can be accessed digitally by enabling practically any institution or individual to create a Web site from which information can be disseminated around the world. Virtual libraries such as the AUSTRALIAN BIOLOGICAL RESEARCH NETWORK (ABREN) Virtual Library <URL http://abren.csu.edu.au/abren/library/Organisation.html> and gateways such as the SOCIAL SCIENCE INFORMATION GATEWAY (SOSIG) <URL http://sosig.ac.uk/> are just two examples (see Figures 1.2 and 1.3).

It is interesting to see these changes mirrored in the various editions of the *Manual of Online Search Strategies*. The first edition, appearing in 1988, was confined to traditional dial-up online systems. By the second edition, in 1992, CD-ROMs also occupied a prominent place in most of the chapters. The most casual perusal of this third edition will reveal the central role now being played by the World Wide Web, alongside traditional online systems and CD-ROMs.

Many databases are now available on more than one technology – dial-up online system, CD-ROM and the Web, as well as other possibilities such as diskette or magnetic tape – and from more than one supplier. For example, the MEDLINE database is found on several online systems (including LEXIS-NEXIS, OCLC FirstSearch, Ovid Online, DIALOG, DataStar, and STN), as CD-ROMs from, for example, SilverPlatter, and in at least two Web versions (PUBMED

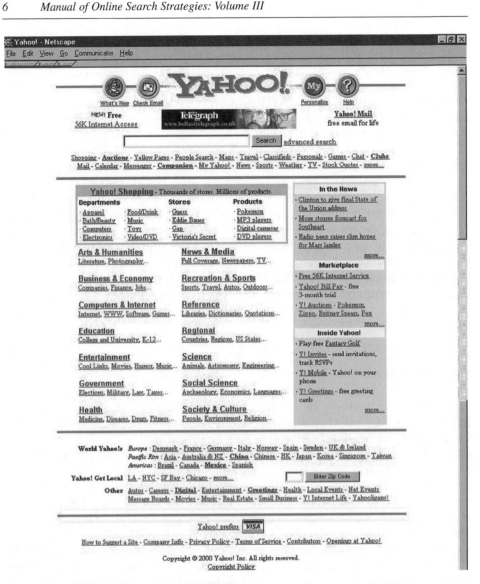

Figure 1.1   Opening directory on YAHOO!

and INTERNET GRATEFUL MED), as well as being available on tape for local installation. Some database producers, such as the National Library of Medicine, have long made their products available themselves over dial-up routes or on CD-ROM; the Web has encouraged many more, like the Institute for Scientific Information (ISI), to follow suit.

When a database is available via several technologies, how should a choice between them be made? Both the traditional online systems and the World Wide Web require the use of a data transmission network to connect the user's workstation with the database server. Response times can be variable depending

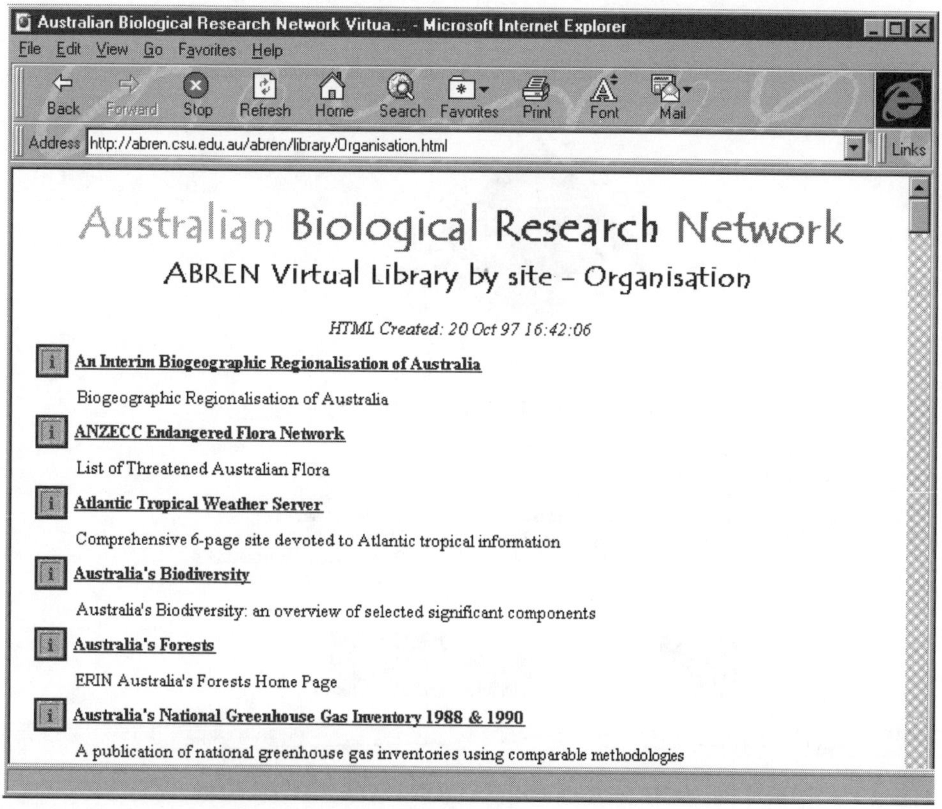

Figure 1.2   **Excerpt from the opening screen of the AUSTRALIAN BIOLOGICAL RESEARCH NETWORK**

on network use (for example, from Europe the use of North American-based hosts tends to be faster in the morning – when most North Americans are in bed rather than hunched over their computers – than in the afternoon or early evening). The use of graphics on Web versions of databases can enhance database content compared with traditional online versions, but also slow down data transmission. CD-ROMs and leased tapes (as well as OPAC searching within the OPAC's home library) normally eliminate the need for long-distance data transmission.

Although interface dialogue modes – command languages, menus of various kinds, and direct manipulation or an object-oriented interface (an interface that provides a visual environment for the dialogue between user and computer) – are not strictly related to individual technologies, in practice command searching has been associated with traditional systems, whereas menus and direct manipulation techniques have been more common with CD-ROMs and now the Web. Vendors such as The Dialog Corporation do offer menus on their traditional online version as well as commands, and commands on their Web version as well as menus, but experienced command-mode users may still find the online version preferable to the Web version because it is easier to view the search developing in a linear

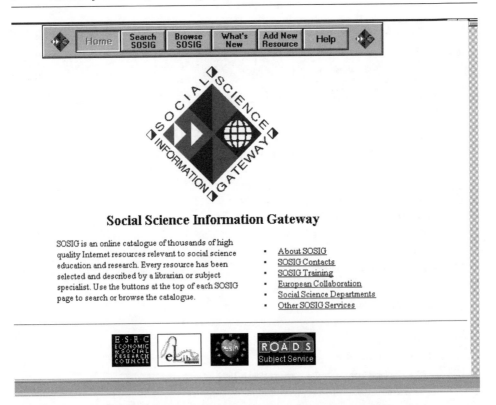

Figure 1.3   SOCIAL SCIENCE INFORMATION GATEWAY (SOSIG)

sequence (although it must be conceded that familiarity also plays a big part – searchers who have learned their skills in one mode will tend to cling to it through habit and familiarity).

Pricing structures differ between the various platforms, which in turn can encourage somewhat different search strategies. Traditionally the online systems charged largely according to connect time – the duration of a search from an initial system log-on to a final system log-off. This pricing structure placed a premium on short searches, which in turn favoured experienced, professional searchers who could quickly find the desired information, and a command-driven interface which in the hands of such an experienced searcher is faster than a menu-driven or even a direct manipulation interface. In contrast, CD-ROMs incurred no incremental costs when a search was undertaken. Like a book or a serial, the CD-ROM was obtained either by direct purchase or by subscription independently of the number of times used. CD-ROMs were therefore more hospitable to novice or occasional searchers and could employ user-friendly menus even if these proved much slower than commands. Although Web searching does involve a connect charge (in the form of a charge for an agreed number of hours connect time over a given period of time – typically a month), this is so small in practice as to be largely or entirely discounted, and therefore, as with CD-ROM searching, professional expertise is less needed. In the case of certain vendors that offer Web services, such as DIALOG, a connect charge is incurred to the vendor as well as the Internet provider. Such connect time, however, is only measured when the host computer is actually occupied with the search; as the client workstation logs on and off the host server, the counter is switched on and off, thus allowing the searcher to pause for thought within a search at no connect cost – a luxury never afforded by the traditional online systems.

A major drawback with the CD-ROM is that its data cannot be updated except by issuing a new disc. A new CD-ROM disc cannot really be updated more frequently than every three months or so. This poses no problems for databases containing rather static information that does not require frequent updating, such as encyclopedias. Where more regular updating is required – monthly, weekly, daily or even real-time – online and Web services have a clear advantage. For example, someone searching to establish whether a particular invention has already been patented will want to ensure that the database is as up-to-date as possible (Volume II, Chapter 2). For this reason, a CD-ROM may be searched for retrospective information, but its online equivalent searched for the most recent updates. Increasingly, hybrid CD-ROMs are appearing that allow an initial disc search to be updated from a dial-up online or Web connection. Examples include Microsoft's ENCARTA and World Books' MULTIMEDIA ENCYCLOPEDIA.

Dial-up online systems and CD-ROM search engines typically offer similar options: Boolean term matching, stem truncation (usually only right-handed – masking the end of the word so that all words beginning with that word stem will be found – although DIMDI also offers left-hand – to find all words *ending* in the search term), embedded truncation (to mask letters within words in order, for example, to find both 'woman' and 'women'), adjacency (or proximity) searching (to locate words next to or close to each other as phrases), and field searching. Increasingly, the Web search engines are also providing these features, although fields are much less formally defined on a typical Web page. One advantage that remains with the online systems is the ability to store and re-use if necessary sets retrieved earlier in the search, although some Web interfaces to an existing online service (for example, Ovid) also now offer this option. The Web search engines offer an additional feature – ranking of retrieved documents. Whereas the online systems and CD-ROMs have normally displayed any retrieved data records in chronological sequence – the last ones to have been added to the database in any retrieved set will be the first displayed on the screen – Web engines attempt to rank by probable relevancy (to the initial query) the most relevant retrieved documents being displayed first. Such ranking typically relies on various techniques such as word frequency occurrences in the query, the retrieved documents and the Web as a whole (Stanley, 1997), location of words on the page and the number of links to the page.

The World Wide Web, with its intra- and interdocument hypertext links, provides a navigational tool that facilitates database browsing in contrast to database searching. Boolean-driven retrieval systems are not hospitable to browsing. They are designed to divide a database into two parts – one that contains those records matching the search statement, and the other which contains all the other non-matching records in the database. Yet many users do not begin with such a clear view of their information requirements that they can formulate a sharp search statement. For these users it can prove very productive to browse the database (or a part of it), looking for potentially interesting material. Hypertext allows this to take place. The danger in such systems, as exemplified by the Web, is that the browser becomes disorientated – lost, so to speak – in a tangle of linked sites. Navigational aids such as the back, forward, bookmark and search history facilities on a Web browser are intended to minimize such problems.

Traditional online systems, unlike CD-ROMs or the Web, cannot provide multimedia graphics, still images, video, animation, or sound clips. Such graphic capabilities are invaluable in many information fields.

Database differences between vendors

This diversity of delivery leads to a very important observation, and one that is explored much more fully in the following chapters: database content and/or structure can differ from one medium to another, or one vendor to another. It is therefore important that the user be aware of the different configurations of the same database title that might be encountered in the market.

Tenopir and Hover (1993) have established seven criteria by which to compare differences between the same database mounted by different vendors:

- The first criterion is update frequency. INSPEC, for example, was then updated weekly on Orbit but bi-weekly on DataStar; PSYCINFO was updated quarterly on the SilverPlatter CD-ROM but monthly by several online vendors.
- Second, database time coverage can vary. CAB ABSTRACTS was then available from DIALOG since 1972 but on DataStar only since 1984.
- Third, pricing formulae for the same database can vary greatly: connect time, flat fee charge, payment per retrieved record, and so on.
- Fourth, a database may be searchable as one big file or as several files. MEDLINE, for example, was then available on DIALOG as one huge file (and therefore easier to search in its entirety), while on NLM it was broken down by date into several separate files (making it therefore easier to search for, say, records only appearing in the most recent few years).
- Fifth, database content can vary. For example, although the CHEMICAL ABSTRACTS database is available on several online systems, only the version on STN includes abstracts as well as the bibliographical citation. Dissertations are to be found in the online versions of PSYCINFO, but not on the PSYCLIT CD-ROM equivalent. A full-text omnibus news database may include items from different source publications in its various versions; if a vendor already offers a newspaper title as a separate database, then records from that paper may not be added to the omnibus version carried by that vendor.

- Sixth, value-added support features like online thesauri, document delivery, cross-file searching and so on, will not be available from all vendors.
- Seventh, records in the same database may be structured and indexed differently by various vendors.

On the Web, the search engines index pages according to different principles as well as offering different search capabilities. For example, ALTAVISTA, EXCITE and NORTHERNLIGHT attempt to index every page on a site while INFOSEEK, LYCOS and WEBCRAWLER only index sample pages. Several offer truncation, but WEBCRAWLER and LYCOS, for example, do not. Sullivan (1998) has compiled useful comparative data for seven major search engines, and Hock (1999) offers tips on searching eight major Web engines.

Controlled versus natural-language searching

Many databases continue to offer the information seeker a choice between conducting a search using the words found in the records themselves – titles, abstracts or complete texts – or using index terms that describe the content of the record while not necessarily using the natural-language words found within it. In most cases such index terms have been assigned by a human indexer and have been chosen from a list of controlled terms representing the subject area of the particular database. Web sites (other than those few that contain organized databases which utilize controlled vocabulary) do not include controlled index terms, although in some instances the site creator may have added metadata at the beginning of the document, which can include uncontrolled keywords that seek to encapsulate its content. As this is not uniformly or exclusively used by search engines for indexing purposes it is currently of questionable benefit. Furthermore, an unscrupulous site developer can deliberately add keywords of little or no relevance to the site's content just so as to attract users (a practice termed 'spamming'). The absence of indexing on most Web sites is considered by many information professionals, at least, as a grave weakness and one reason why large numbers of irrelevant documents are so often retrieved in a Web search.

When a database does offer the choice between a search on the natural-language terms found within the records themselves, and a search limited only to the index terms assigned to those records (often called descriptors), which option should the searcher choose? Natural-language searching offers the opportunity to search for the actual words and phrases employed by the author. It also provides more words on which to search, as typically a record will not be assigned more than a handful of descriptors whereas the words in a full-text article may number in the thousands. In subject areas where the vocabulary is volatile, controlled vocabulary cannot keep pace with change; only by searching on natural language can the latest terminology be applied.

From the database producer's point of view, indexing is an expensive proposition. The benefits therefore must be considerable to justify the extra work

Title	Journal	Issue	London (Eng)	Fires	Subways	Fires-Great Britain	Great Britain
UK police doubt arson caused fatal subway fire	Calgary Herald	Nov 21,1987	■	■	■		
Reports say (London) subway fire warnings were ignored	Calgary Herald	Nov 22,1987	■	■	■		
Full inquiry ordered into (London subway) tragedy	Calgary Herald	Nov 20,1987	■	■	■		
Fire safety on subway questioned	Globe and Mail	Nov 20,1987	■	■	■		
Swift spread of flames in station baffles London subway officals	Globe and Mail	Nov 20,1987	■	■	■		
London subway bans smoking, tobacco ads	Globe and Mail	Nov 25,1987	■	■	■		
Raging fire claims 32 in (London) subway	Calgary Herald	Nov 19,1987	■	■	■		
Police don't suspect arson in subway fire	Montreal Gazette	Nov 21,1987	■	■	■		
"Coctail" of gases suspected in subway fire	Globe and Mail	Nov 21,1987	■	■	■		
35 killed, 80 hurt in UK subway fire	Globe and Mail	Nov 19,1987	■		■		
Killer fire (in London subway) sparks ban on smoking	Calgary Herald	Nov 25,1987			■		
Subway inferno kills 32:"catastrophe" strikes London underground	Halifax Chronicle Herald	Nov 19,1987	■				
(London) subway fire inquiry announced	Winnipeg Free Press	Nov 20,1987	■	■	■		
Britain to hold public inquiry into subway fire that killed 30	Montreal Gazette	Nov 20,1987	■	■	■		
32 dead in London subway blaze	Montreal Gazette	Nov 19,1987	■	■	■		
Escalator carried commuters into inferno of flames, smoke	Toronto Star	Nov 19,1987	■	■	■		
UK fire chief says blaze began on subway escalator	Toronto Star	Nov 20,1987	■	■	■		
Escalator problems cited in subway fire	Toronto Star	Nov 21,1987	■	■	■		
Flaming horror in London subway (King's Cross)	Macleans	Nov 30,1987			■	■	■
An inferno in the London Underground	Newsweek	Nov 30,1987			■	■	■
Escalator to an inferno: panic and death in London's Underground	Time	Nov 30,1987			■	■	■
Total occurrence of each descriptor			17	15	20	3	3

Source: Jacsó (1992). Reproduced by permission.

Figure 1.4   Failure of controlled language

involved in preparing the database. The greatest advantage offered by indexing is the control that it imposes over the inconsistencies and redundancies in natural language. The synonyms (and near synonyms) so frequently encountered in all languages can be represented by just one index term, thus removing the searcher's need to enter all possible synonyms in order to be certain that the actual word used by the author has been entered. A few carefully chosen controlled terms can also summarize the main subjects dealt with in a record, thereby allowing the searcher to find records that are central to a particular subject rather than minor referents (the words chosen for the title may also accomplish this objective, but titles, especially in the humanities and social sciences, are not always descriptive of the actual content). A list of controlled terms may also be very helpful to a searcher who is unfamiliar with the subject area of the database and finds it difficult to formulate a search unaided using natural-language terms. Controlled terms from a well-organized thesaurus can help with hierarchical or generic searches. For example, someone looking for information on dogs might expect that all records dealing with individual breeds will have been indexed with the generically higher term 'dogs'; a natural-language search, to be comprehensive, might have to include the names of individual breeds in case the authors themselves only mentioned the breed and not the species. Of course, if the searcher opts for controlled language then confidence is placed in the reliability and the consistency of the database's indexers. It is not an easy task to take an article and determine which, say, ten terms from a controlled list should be chosen to represent the subject matter of the article. Figure 1.4 shows that controlled languages are still at the mercy of the human indexer.

Interfaces

Most of the interfaces discussed in the following chapters rely on graphical devices: windows, pull-down and pop-up menus, buttons and icons. A dwindling number of CD-ROMs and OPACs, as well as traditional online systems, rely on non-graphical, DOS-based interfaces. Shneiderman (1998) lists several benefits for the user of graphical interfaces:

- control over the system
- ease of learning the system
- enjoyment
- encouragement to explore system features.

At the same time, unless designed with some care, graphic devices can seem little more than gimmicks, and their initial novelty value can soon dissipate. Furthermore, users unfamiliar with graphical interfaces can find them confusing and forbidding. It is all too easy to produce cluttered and confusing screens containing too much visual information. Careful screen layout, restrained use of colour and consistency in the application of graphical devices will all help to produce an effective, rather than a baffling, interface. Many guides to sound interface design are available (see, for example, Galitz, 1997; Mandel, 1997; Shneiderman, 1998), but unfortunately, as in other areas of human endeavour, it is often easier to propose, than to follow, guidelines. Head (1997) provides a useful discussion of graphical interfaces specifically directed at online information services.

Search evaluation

The *Manual of Online Search Strategies* provides guidance on how to conduct most effectively searches for information in a variety of subject areas. It is therefore important to discuss how a successful search might be measured, so as to differentiate it from an unsuccessful search. How can search performance be evaluated?

The first large-scale tests of information retrieval systems began in the late 1950s at the Cranfield College of Aeronautics in England. The Cranfield Projects employed two measurements for an information retrieval system: recall and precision. The assumption behind these measures is that the average user wants to retrieve large amounts of relevant materials (producing high recall) while simultaneously rejecting a large proportion of irrelevant materials (producing high precision).

Recall and precision

Recall is a measure of effectiveness in retrieving all the sought information in a database – that is, in search comprehensiveness. A search would achieve perfect recall if every single record that should be found in relation to a specific query is indeed traced. It is normally expressed in proportional terms. The recall ratio in any search can theoretically be improved by finding more and more records; in fact, 100 per cent recall can always be achieved by retrieving every single record in the database, including all the irrelevant alongside the relevant ones, although this defeats the purpose of a retrieval system. Clearly, a parallel measure is required to work alongside recall, which will take account of the false hits produced. This measure is called precision. It assesses the accuracy of a search – that is, the extent to which the search finds only those records that should be found, leaving aside all records that are not wanted. A search would achieve perfect precision if every single record retrieved in relation to a specific query were indeed relevant to that query. Precision, like recall, is normally expressed in proportional terms.

The Cranfield tests found an inverse relationship between recall and precision. As attempts are made to increase one, the other tends to decline: higher recall can only be achieved at the expense of a reduction in precision. As a strategy is implemented to retrieve more and more relevant records there is a tendency also to retrieve growing numbers of irrelevant records; recall is improved but precision worsened. As a strategy is implemented to eliminate irrelevant records there is a tendency also to eliminate relevant ones; precision is improved but recall worsened. There is a common sense logic to this inverse relationship that has been demonstrated in many, but not all, evaluation tests.

Criticisms of recall and precision measures

Despite the widespread use of recall and precision as measures of search effectiveness, a number of criticisms can be made. First, recall and precision offer an incomplete evaluation of information retrieval, at least from the average searcher's point of view. Searchers may want to maximize both recall and precision, but what about other factors such as the expense involved in completing the search, the amount of time taken, and the ease of conducting it? A retrieval system might give impressive recall and precision ratios yet be costly, slow and frustrating.

Secondly, recall depends on the assumption that a user wishes to find as many relevant records as possible. In practice, users may not always want a search that finds everything, but instead opt for a search that retrieves just a few highly relevant items. In such cases, precision alone is the only measure of retrieval effectiveness. Many Web searchers, for example, are likely to find themselves in this situation; high recall in many cases will simply overwhelm the searcher.

Thirdly, to measure recall it is necessary to know the total number of relevant records in the database, retrieved and not retrieved. But how can the number of relevant non-retrieved records in the database be established? In the case of the very small test databases sometimes used for evaluation experiments, it is feasible to examine all the documents and thus to determine which are, and which are not, relevant to any particular search query. Considerable doubt has been expressed, however, about the validity of extrapolating search results from these test databases to the much larger databases typically encountered in real searches. The constantly changing content on the Web, as well as the vast size of the 'database', make recall measurement especially problematic. Clarke and Willett (1997) have proposed, however, a methodology for measuring recall, as well as precision, in order to evaluate the effectiveness of search engines.

The most serious criticisms of precision and recall measures, however, concern the reliability of the crucial concept underlying both – relevance. How is relevance to be determined, and by whom? Experimentally, relevance judgements have typically been based on a match between the subject content – the 'aboutness' – of a retrieved record and the initial query that stimulated the search. In the Cranfield tests, for example, the subject content of the query and the subject content of the records were compared by subject experts to decide whether a retrieved record was relevant or not. Many searches are now conducted by end users and not, as in earlier days, by information intermediaries. This means that the person judging the retrieved results as they are displayed is the ultimate user of the information, who may bring various subjective elements into play. A bibliographic record, for example, might be judged relevant on the basis of its author, the series in which it appears, its recency, local availability and so on, as well as on its subject content. On the other hand, would a retrieved document that the seeker has already read be considered relevant, even if directly related to the subject? Lancaster and Warner (1993) prefer to distinguish between relevance and a related concept – pertinence. They define pertinence as the relationship between a document and a request, based on the subjective decision of the person with the information need. They argue that pertinence decisions are essential to the evaluation of operating (rather than trial) information retrieval systems serving real users who have real information needs. Harter (1992) proposes the term 'psychological relevance' for records that suggest new cognitive connections, fruitful analogies, insightful metaphors or an increase/decrease in the strength of a belief. He argues that records about a topic may in fact prove less important to the user than relevant records which are not on the topic but that allow new intellectual connections to be made or cause other cognitive changes in the user. Furthermore, he believes that such a view of psychological relevance is inconsistent with the notion and utility of fixed relevance judgements and with traditional retrieval testing as exemplified by the Cranfield tests and their successors.

Nevertheless, most information retrieval experts do agree that subject aboutness is still the principal criterion used in judging relevance. A search system can only be judged in terms of whether it is able to match the user's information need as expressed in the search strategy with the stored data. The additional facility to screen out from the retrieved records those that the user has already read may well be a highly valuable feature, but the failure of a system to undertake this extra step cannot reasonably be invoked to judge the performance of the system at *retrieving* relevant information.

Another problem with relevancy is that judgements about one record may be influenced by other records that have already been examined. After examining nine totally irrelevant documents, a tenth one might be considered relevant, but had this tenth record been viewed after seeing nine highly relevant ones it might have been judged irrelevant. This emphasizes, of course, the binary nature of relevancy judgements for recall and precision purposes: there is no place for the fairly relevant, or the marginally relevant, or even the extremely relevant. A record is accepted as relevant or rejected as irrelevant.

Spink and Greisdorf (1997) argue that researchers should question the assumption that users always even need the most highly relevant items. At the outset of an information-seeking process a user's information problem is often ill-defined. The retrieved items considered highly relevant may well provide users with what they already know: as they are likely to equate strongly with the current state of the user's information problems, they may only reinforce the current state of the information problem. Items that are only 'partially relevant' may then play a greater role in shifting the user's thinking about the information problem, providing new information that leads the user in new directions towards the ultimate resolution of the information problem.

Unfortunately, the critics of recall/precision measures are unable to proffer any alternative quantitative evaluation technique. Yet everyone does agree that the ability to evaluate information retrieval is crucial. All this suggests that recall and precision ratios as reported in experimental studies should be treated as relative, rather than absolute, indicators. The measures of recall and precision based on estimates of relevance remain valid evaluation parameters even if their precise measurement in experimental studies is problematic. In evaluating strategies and reacting to preliminary results during an interactive search, for example, the concepts of recall and precision are extremely useful to help the searcher decide on strategy adjustments. A small number of hits may suggest a need to broaden the search to improve recall, even if this adversely affects precision. A search with higher recall but a large percentage of irrelevant records is a prime target for strategy adjustments to improve precision, even if at the expense of lower recall.

Making judgements during a search on the relevance of intermediate results and then using these judgements to revise the search strategy is termed 'relevance feedback'. Some information retrieval systems do not simply rely on the searcher to initiate such feedback. The system itself may automatically search, for example, to find more records that share index terms with records already retrieved and judged relevant by the user.

Database evaluation

No matter how sophisticated is the information seeker or powerful the retrieval system, the resulting information from a search will ultimately depend on the database quality: the accuracy, completeness, authority and currency of its information, and the reliability of its indexing. Unfortunately, database quality cannot be taken for granted. Information stored in electronic format is inherently no more nor less reliable or accurate than other kinds of information. A few years ago, when much electronic information had been transcribed at the keyboard from hard copy originals, many typographical errors were detected in all kinds of databases. These errors not only affected data use but also data retrieval; only by similarly misspelling the term in the search would the record containing the misspelled word be found. More data are now generated at the outset electronically, and scanning equipment is more reliable, but errors are still to be found in databases.

Technically, electronic data can be updated more easily and quickly than, say, printed information. Many databases are updated monthly, weekly, daily or even in real time. Nevertheless, it should not be assumed that electronic information is always current. A number of online encyclopaedias, for example, contain data long since superseded even by print sources. Typically, online or Web-based sources are updated more frequently than CD-ROM or print equivalents (if these also exist), but occasionally technical problems have reversed this dictum.

The Internet, in particular, has highlighted the problems of data reliability. There is no umbrella organization to ensure data accuracy, currency or consistency, or to vouch for the authority of the data. Now that anyone can create a Web site there is no longer an established publishing process to ensure some kind of quality control through, for example, market pressures or academic refereeing. It can be difficult to assess the validity of much data available on the Web, although some search engines claim to exercise judgement when deciding whether

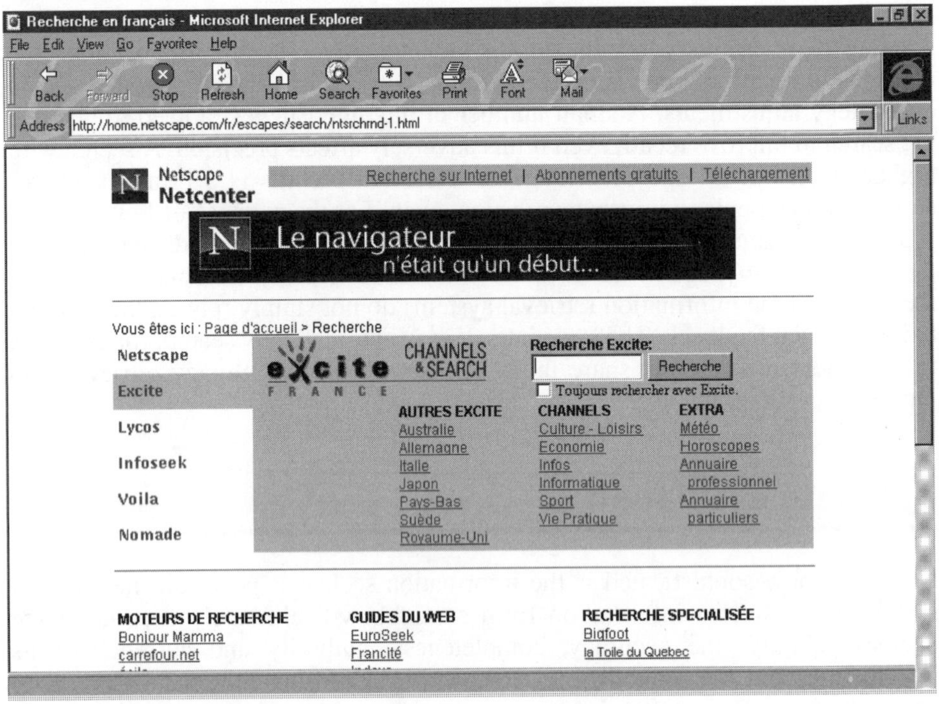

Figure 1.5   French-language interface to EXCITE

or not to provide access to sites from their hierarchical indexes, and some provide evaluation scores based on an assessment of 'quality'. The ephemeral nature of much Web material also means that what can be found today may have vanished or been transformed by tomorrow. In Volume I, Chapter 5 on the biosciences, for example, Frank Kellerman cites the example of the GENOME database from Johns Hopkins School of Medicine which had a short-lived life on the Web before being withdrawn. The ephemeral nature of much Web content is now posing very considerable bibliographic problems.

Although the Web is dominated by English-language information, pages in other languages are now being added proportionately faster than the English-language sites. Many problems remain in accessing, on the Web, information in a language unknown to the searcher (Large and Moukdad, 2000) but the reality of a truly worldwide service, free from language barriers, is getting a little closer. The provision, by many Web search engines, of interfaces in languages other than English, for example, is a welcome sign. Figure 1.5 shows the French-language interface from EXCITE. It is now possible to input search terms in other languages and to confine the resulting search either to sites in that language or to sites originating in a country using that language. ALTAVISTA goes one step further by allowing a search term in one language to be translated automatically into the corresponding term in a second language (although currently only between

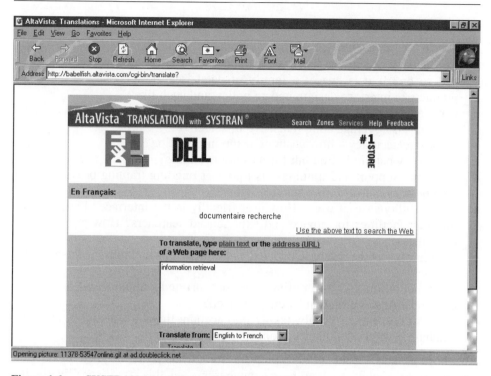

Figure 1.6   SYSTRAN translation software on ALTAVISTA

English, on the one hand, and French, German, Italian, Portuguese or Spanish on the other) prior to a Web search. In Figure 1.6 the term 'information retrieval' has been translated into French by SYSTRAN, the machine translation software employed by ALTAVISTA: the correct French phrase requires an inversion of word order from the English original: 'recherche documentaire' rather than 'documentaire recherche' as SYSTRAN has it (although this does not matter in a Web search unless the two words are to be searched together as a phrase).

The recurrent issues concerning pornography and hate literature further complicate discussions concerning Internet content. This is likely to prove especially controversial where certain user groups, and especially children, are involved. Some libraries have experimented with various proprietary site-blocking software, but the results generally prove unsatisfactory, failing to block some material deemed unacceptable while excluding other material to which exception is not taken.

Evaluation criteria

Evaluation criteria for databases have been proposed by a number of authors, and there is a large measure of agreement about these. One influential evaluation checklist was formulated in 1990 by the Southern California Online User Group (Basch, 1990):

- Consistency – does the database maintain consistency in coverage, currency and so on? If it is one of a family of databases, how consistent are these products in interface design, update policy and such like?
- Coverage/scope – does the coverage/scope match the stated aims of the database; is coverage comprehensive or selective?
- Error rate/accuracy – how accurate is the information?
- Output – what kind of output formats are available?
- Customer support and training – is initial or ongoing training provided? Is a help desk available during suitable hours?
- Accessibility/ease of use – How user-friendly is the interface? Does it have different facilities for novice and experienced searchers? How good are the error messages? Are they context-sensitive?
- Timeliness – is the database updated as frequently as it claims, and as the data warrant?
- Documentation – is online and/or printed documentation clear, comprehensive, current and well-organized?
- Value to cost ratio – finally, taking into account the above features, does the database give good value for money?

Anagnostelis and Cooke (1997) propose somewhat more detailed evaluation criteria to be applied to Web-based databases – in this case, specifically for comparison of various MEDLINE database services on the Web:

- authority of the service provider as well as the database
- content – coverage and currency
- retrieval mechanism – general search features, free-text searching, natural-language queries, thesaurus searching, command searching, display and output
- ease of interface use
- unique features
- help and user support.

Similar evaluation criteria can be found in Tenopir and Hover (1993) who specifically discuss comparison of the same database available on different systems, and from the Organising Medical Networked Information (OMNI) Consortium (1997), which is involved, among other tasks, with the evaluation of MEDLINE Services on the Web. The SOCIAL SCIENCE INFORMATION GATEWAY has prepared a detailed list of criteria used by various eLib Gateway projects (including OMNI as well as SOSIG itself), while Bartelstein and Zald (1997), and Tillman (1997) also provide valuable insights. A longer discussion can be found in Cooke (1999).

References

Anagnostelis, B. and Cooke, A. (1997), 'Evaluation criteria for different versions of the same database – a comparison of Medline services available via the World Wide Web', *Online Information '97: Proceedings of the 21st International Online Information Meeting, London, 9–11 December 1997*, Oxford: Learned Information, 165–179.

Bartelstein, A. and Zald, A. (1997), *Unwired R545: Teaching Students to Think Critically about Internet Resources: A Workshop for Faculty and Staff.* Available at <URL http://weber.u.washington.edu/~libr560/NETEVAL/index.html>.

Basch, R. (1990), 'Measuring the quality of data: report of the Fourth Annual SCOUG Retreat', *Database Searcher,* 6 (8), 18–23.

Borgman, C. L. (1996), 'Why are online catalogs still hard to use?', *Journal of the American Society for Information Science,* 47 (7), 493–503.

Clarke, S. J. and Willett, P. (1997), 'Estimating the recall performance of Web search engines', *Aslib Proceedings,* 49 (7), 184–189.

Cooke, A. (1999), *A Guide to Finding Quality Information on the Internet: Selection and Evaluation Strategies*, London: Library Association Publishing.

Fidel, R. and Soergel, D. (1983), 'Factors affecting online bibliographic retrieval: a conceptual framework for research', *Journal of the American Society for Information Science,* 34 (3), 163–180.

Galitz, W. O. (1997), *Essential Guide to User Interface Design: An Introduction to GUI Design Principles and Techniques*, New York: Wiley.

Harter, S. P. (1992), 'Psychological relevance and information science', *Journal of the American Society for Information Science,* 43 (9), 602–615.

Head, A. J. (1997), 'A question of interface design: how do online service GUIs measure up?', *Online* 21 (3), 20–29.

Hock, R. (1999), *The Extreme Searcher's Guide to Web Search Engines: A Handbook for the Serious Searcher*, Medford, NJ: CyberAge Books. Updated at <URL http://www.onstrat.com/engines/>.

Hsieh-Yee, I. (1993), 'Effects of search experience and subject knowledge on the search tactics of novice and experienced searchers', *Journal of the American Society for Information Science,* 44 (3), 161–174.

Inktomi (2000), Inktomi WebMap. Available at <URL http://www.inktomi.com/webmap/>.

Jacsó, P. (1992), *CD-ROM Software, Dataware and Hardware: Evaluation, Selection, and Installation*, Englewood, Colorado: Libraries Unlimited.

Lancaster, F. W., Elzy, C., Zeter, M .J., Metzler, L. and Low, Y. M. (1994), 'Searching databases on CD-ROM: comparison of the results of end-user searching with results from two modes of searching by skilled intermediaries', *RQ,* 33 (3), 370–386.

Lancaster, F. W. and Warner, A. J. (1993), *Information Retrieval Today*, Arlington: Information Resources.

Large, A. and Moukdad, H. (2000), 'Multilingual access to Web resources: an overview', *Program*, **34** (1), 43–58.

Mandel, T. (1997), *The Elements of User Interface Design*, New York: Wiley.

Martin, H. and Nicholas, D. (1993), 'End-users coming of age? Six years of end-user searching at the Guardian', *Online and CDROM Review*, **17** (2), 83–89.

Notess, G.R. (2000), *Search Engine Statistics: Database Total Size Estimates*. Available at <URL http://www.notess.com/searchstats/sizeest.shtml>.

OMNI Consortium. (1997), *Medline on the Internet*. Available at <URL http://www.omni.ac.uk/general-info/internet_medline.html>.

Sanderson, R. M. (1990), 'The continuing saga of professional end-users: law students search Dialog at the University of Florida', *Online*, **14** (6), 64–69.

Shneiderman, B. (1998), *Designing the User Interface: Strategies for Effective Human–Computer Interaction*, (3rd edn), Reading: Addison-Wesley.

Social Science Information Gateway (nd), *Quality Selection Criteria for Subject Gateways*. Available at <URL http://sosig.ac.uk/desire/qindex.html>.

Spink, A. and Greisdorf, H. (1997), 'Partial relevance judgements during interactive information retrieval: an exploratory study', in C. Schwartz and M. Rorvig (eds), *ASIS '97: Proceedings of the 60th ASIS Annual Meeting, Washington, D.C., November 1–6, 1997*. Volume 34. Medford: Information Today, 111–122.

Stanley, T. (1997), 'Search engines corner: moving up the ranks', *Ariadne*, **12**. Available at <URL http://www.ariadne.ac.uk/issue12/search-engines/>.

Sullivan, D. (2000), *Search Engine Features for Webmasters*. Available at <URL http://searchenginewatch.com/webmasters/features.html>.

Tenopir, C. and Hover, K. (1993), 'When is the same database not the same? Database differences among systems', *Online*, **17** (4), 20–27.

Tillman, H. N. (1997), *Evaluating Quality on the Net*. Available at <URL http://www.tiac.net/users/hope/findqual.html>.

Chapter 2

Citations

David Bawden

Introduction

This chapter differs from others in the volume as it deals with a general way of searching, applicable across many subject areas, and dependent on a rather unusual type of indexing. Citation searching deserves a separate treatment, since it provides a uniquely valuable means of finding certain kinds of information, while also offering a useful complementary approach to 'conventional' subject searching. The advantages offered by citation searching are often not well understood, even by experienced searchers, although databases supporting this approach have been available for many years.

This chapter focuses on the citation indexes available online and in CD-ROM format from the Institute for Scientific Information (ISI), as these are the main generally available bibliographic citation indexes. The DIMDI host system has a useful additional facility – an ability to identify all citations to an author, from the ISI files, in a single search statement, without the need to select each citing reference separately. The inclusion of citation data in the chemical literature databases produced by Chemical Abstracts Service was announced in mid-1999. This is the first example of citations being made available for searching in a major literature file other than those of ISI.

Although primarily aimed at describing the concept and application of citation indexing and searching *per se*, the chapter also acts as a primer in the use of the ISI files. This enables the value of citation searching to be demonstrated across a wide subject area, including science and technology, social sciences, and arts and humanities. The particular value of citation searching in cross-disciplinary, multidisciplinary and interdisciplinary areas is emphasized. The references at the end of the chapter give both discursive treatments of the nature and value of citation indexing and searching in general, and also accounts of its application to particular subject areas and types of information.

Citation indexing and searching is of particular importance for two specific types of information: legal information, particularly case law, and patents information.

These are not dealt with here, being covered elsewhere in these volumes (see Volume II, Chapters 2 and 5). This chapter focuses on bibliographic citation databases.

While citation indexing, strictly speaking, is not possible or meaningful on the Internet, there is an analogous form of linkage between material on the World Wide Web. While this has not yet led to the introduction of searching services analogous to the ISI databases, these developments are interesting in their own right and as a possible pointer to the future, and are discussed at the end of the chapter.

The nature and principles of citation searching

The basic concept of citation indexing and searching is simple. Virtually all 'scholarly' or professional documents – articles in journals, newsletters and magazines, books and chapters in them, reports, and so on – include references to earlier related work, in the form of footnotes or bibliographies. These references, or citations, are usually bibliographic descriptions of other documents in which related material may be found, although they may sometimes be incomplete or informal – for example, 'personal communication' or 'in press'. Obviously, they must be older than, or possibly contemporary with, the citing document.

Citations are of most obvious value in referring the reader to relevant older material; 'following up references' is perhaps the most common technique of bibliographic information retrieval. Citation indexing, in a sense, inverts this process by making possible the opposite process: a search for documents that have cited the original. These citing documents must be more recent than, or perhaps contemporary with, the cited document.

So if author A refers to an article by author B in the bibliography of a paper, it will be straightforward for the reader of A's paper to find B's work by consulting the list of references. A citation index makes it possible for a reader, knowing of and interested in B's article, to find A's paper; the bibliographic reference to B's article, the cited reference, is used as the starting-point – a kind of index term.

A citation index is therefore a list of bibliographic references, sorted initially by author's name (usually, for practical reasons, this is limited to the first author of the cited article), and then by date, volume and similar identifiers, so that each cited article is uniquely identified. Alongside that document's identification, which acts as an index entry point, are listed details of those documents that have cited it, in a manner analogous to any 'conventional' subject index.

It should be noted that the time coverage of a citation index is that of the publication dates of the citing papers. The dates of the cited documents are unrestricted, since authors can and do – albeit more in some subject areas than in others – cite work of any earlier date. A citation index may, and usually does, include as entry points – that is, index terms – documents ranging in age from the most up-to-date, which may be contemporary with the citing documents, to the oldest works recognized as 'citable' scholarly documents. Humanities authors, in particular, frequently cite very old material: Socrates and Herodotus, Aristotle and

Plato all feature extensively among the cited references in ISI's ARTS AND HUMANITIES SEARCH database.

It is also worth noting that citation indexes generally record only that a document has been cited, but give no reason for the citation. Obviously, there must be some form of semantic linkage – that is, some subject matter in common – but quite what this is will become evident only from a reading of the citing document. There have been proposals for the creation of citation indexes which would include such information, as a kind of refinement of indexing specificity, but this approach has never been adopted in a practical, operational citation index.

A good deal of research has been carried out on the nature of, and reasons for, citing, and on the citation practices of authors in different subject areas, in order to attempt a clarification of different types of citation. This work is summarized and discussed by, *inter alia*, Oppenheim (1978), Cronin (1984), Cano (1989), Sen (1990), Garfield (1989), Liu (1993), and Baird and Oppenheim (1994).

Weinstock (1971), in an early description of bibliographic citation indexes, lists 15 principal reasons for citations; his list remains valid, and much of the more recent work constitutes essential variants and refinements of this categorization. His reasons, not in order of importance or frequency of occurrence, are:

1. paying homage to pioneers
2. giving credit to related work
3. identifying methods, equipment, and so on
4. providing background reading
5. correcting one's own work
6. correcting the work of others
7. criticizing previous work
8. substantiating claims
9. alerting readers to forthcoming publications
10. providing leads to poorly disseminated work
11. authenticating data and facts
12. identifying the original publication in which an idea was discussed
13. identifying an original publication describing an eponymic concept or term – for example, Hodgson's disease
14. disclaiming work or ideas of others
15. disputing priority claims by others.

There are therefore many valid reasons for one document to cite another. A more cynical view of human nature, supported by sociological research, suggests that authors often include inappropriate citations, and/or omit appropriate ones, for a variety of less valid reasons (Cronin, 1984). These reasons may include:

● inclusion of irrelevant citations to impress readers with the author's breadth of knowledge
● citation of irrelevant work by respected authors to add spurious validity to an argument
● citation only to works by an author's friends, colleagues or compatriots
● failure to cite relevant work through ignorance, forgetfulness or laziness.

Citation practices of authors, both individually and *en masse*, are obviously of importance for the use of citation indexes for retrieval. Inclusion of irrelevant citations, and omission of relevant ones, will affect the precision and recall of searches respectively. They are also of particular importance in the somewhat controversial use of citation analysis in such areas as the mapping of scientific disciplines, the sociology of science, and assessment of research quality (see, for example, Garfield, 1983; Lindsey, 1989; White and McCain, 1989), but these issues are not considered here. Their only relevance to the use of citation databases by 'ordinary' searchers is that the number, and nature, of citations to a given publication, author and so on may be a crude measure of 'influence' or 'importance', which may, in some circumstances, be useful.

The searcher must therefore be aware of the lack of rigour and consistency in citation practice, which will affect the performance of citation databases. This is hardly a unique problem when one considers the well-known deficiencies and inconsistencies of other access points to bibliographic databases, particularly human intellectual indexing. As with other searching techniques, searchers must allow for the problems, and develop sufficiently flexible strategies to allow for them. As Synge (1990) puts it:

> ... [citation indexing] depends for intellectual content on citations by authors, who are sometimes prodded by editors and referees. Its patchiness is therefore not surprising, but frequently it gives access to relevant and up-to-date documents not easily accessible by other means.

On the other hand, being able to search for documents related in some way (as shown by the citation link), without needing to specify the nature of the link, still less worry about indexing policies and so on may be valuable. In particular, this can lend an element of serendipity to a search, with the prospect of uncovering unexpected relationships between concepts and subjects.

In summary, we can say that, used in the right way to answer the right sort of question, citation indexing can prove uniquely useful. It is also a very valuable complement to other forms of searching, and other types of database.

Citation indexing in practice

The history of the development of citation indexing and indexes, though an interesting topic in itself, will not be dealt with here, having been well covered elsewhere (Weinstock, 1971; Garfield, 1983; Garfield, 1985). The earliest practical example of a citation index was *Shepard's Citations*, an American legal reference tool based on citations to precedents in case law. Another early application area was in statistics, well suited to citation indexing because of the high proportion of 'method' papers being referred to in descriptions of their applications. A number of citation indexes covering various aspects of statistics were produced from the 1950s onwards, but none is commercially available today (Bawden, 1984). As noted earlier, patents citation indexes are also of importance. A few other citation indexes, mainly to bibliographic records, have been produced on an experimental basis, some in computerized form, but none became commercially available.

Bibliographic citation databases are therefore now synonymous with the products of ISI. The availability of these databases, as of mid-1998, is given below. Further information can be found from ISI's Web site at <URL http://www.isinet.com/prodserv/citation>.

Multidisciplinary databases

SCIENCE CITATION INDEX

Print from 1961.
Tape service from 1974. Updated weekly.
CD-ROM from 1980. Published monthly.
Online SciSearch from 1974. Updated weekly.

- DIALOG 1974 to date
- DataStar 1980 to date
- DIMDI 1974 to date
- STN 1974 to date.

SOCIAL SCIENCE CITATION INDEX

Print from 1969.
Tape service from 1972. Updated weekly.
CD-ROM from 1981. Published monthly.
Online Social SciSearch from 1972. Updated weekly.

- DIALOG 1972 to date
- DataStar 1972 to date
- DIMDI 1973 to date.

ARTS AND HUMANITIES CITATION INDEX

Print from 1976.
Tape service from 1975. Updated weekly.
CD-ROM from 1990. Published triannually.
Online ARTS AND HUMANITIES SEARCH from 1980. Updated weekly.

- DIALOG 1980 to date
- DataStar 1980 to date
- OCLC 1980 to date.

Specialized databases

COMPUMATH

Computer science and mathematics literature, with selected material from a wide subject range (described in ISI's literature as multidisciplinary).
Print from 1981.
CD-ROM from 1993. Published quarterly.

Speciality Citation Indexes

Biochemistry and Biophysics
Biotechnology
Chemistry
Materials Science
Neuroscience
All these are CD-ROM only and are published bi-monthly.

Comparison of access media

As will be clear from the above, ISI's citation databases are available in several formats: print, online, tape and CD-ROM. The Internet may be used as a convenient means of telecommunications access to the online files, and is also offering new search facilities in its own right, via the Web of Science discussed later.

Print sources continue to have a place, particularly where frequent access is required by large numbers of users – for example, in a college library. It is true to say, however, that the nature of citation databases is not particularly well suited to the browsing of printed products. There is little chance for serendipitous findings in the tightly structured layout, and complex or extensive searches soon become tedious. (Searchers of more mature years will remember that the printed annual citation indexes came with a free magnifying glass.) Electronic searching is therefore the preferred form of access for most users.

Tape products, for those large organizations with the need and resources to deal with them, offer integration of citation data into familiar in-house systems, but this is not an option available to the great majority of users.

Until Web-based access becomes the norm, users of citation databases will choose between online and CD-ROM access. CD-ROM is the only choice for the smaller 'speciality' databases, and a choice has therefore to be made only between the three major multidisciplinary files. The criteria are essentially the same as for other forms of online database. Online access offers pay-as-you go access, suitable for those whose usage is small, or unpredictable, while CD-ROMs require a single payment followed by unlimited use. Unless the discs are networked, however, access is limited to one user at any one time. Online offers the more up-to-date information, while CD-ROMs are necessarily limited to a less frequent updating schedule. The search interface of the CD-ROM products has a more modern appearance, being Windows-based and menu-based, by comparison with the DOS-like command line approach of the online services. Experienced users still claim that more precise and sophisticated searches can be done in command mode; hence the lack of popularity for the 'friendly front end' introduced by some of the online hosts.

As a rule of thumb, therefore, CD-ROMs are preferred where there is a large user group of end-user searchers, where demand is likely to be high, and particularly where these databases are among a small number of preferred sources. Online access will be favoured where these databases are used primarily by experienced searchers, where usage is relatively low and infrequent, and where these databases are used as part of a large portfolio of possible sources.

The Web of Science

The Web of Science is ISI's system for providing Web access to the three large ISI multidisciplinary citation indexes: SCIENCE CITATION INDEX, SOCIAL SCIENCE CITATION INDEX, and ARTS AND HUMANITIES CITATION INDEX. The system is available free of charge to subscribers to ISI's tape services, and on a subscription basis to others.

In essence, Web of Science uses hypertext linkages to create a browsable 'web' using the citation linkages present in all forms of the citation databases. Its originators claim that it is, at the same time, designed for the novice searcher yet also able to offer retrieval features not present in other formats, and hence appeal to expert searchers. Separate Quick Search and Full Search modes are provided for the two groups. Boolean logic and proximity operators can be used in the latter mode.

Its capabilities include:

- navigation, by hypertext link, forward and backward through time, following citation links
- direct link to information on a cited document from the citation (for those documents included in the database)
- searching on secondary authors in cited references
- convenient access to citation counts over time
- use of the Related Records feature to find articles sharing one or more cited references
- search of databases singly or in combination
- export of information from the databases into bibliographic retrieval software
- link to local holdings information

- document ordering electronically from the ISI document delivery service
- links to publishers' homepages from retrieved documents
- links to authors' e-mail addresses for reprint requests.

At the time of writing, Web of Science is newly introduced, and little user reaction has emerged. Initial reviews indicate that the system, while requiring considerable refinement, is capable of adding new dimensions to the effectiveness of the ISI databases, particularly in the integration of different information formats (bibliographic and citation data, full text, e-mail, and so on), while not improving the effectiveness of citation searching *per se* (see, for example, Atkins, 1999; Rosenberg, 1998; Wiley, 1998). Cawkell (1998) gives an example of the use of the Web of Science for bibliographic research on the topic of image retrieval by shape matching.

This system, like its equivalents being made available by other database producers, has the potential of presenting the best features of the online and CD-ROM implementations – primarily, sophisticated flexible searching and ease of use respectively. It can also add to them the integrative capabilities of the Web, linking to e-mail and to homepages.

Information on Web of Science can be found at <URL http://www.isinet.com/prodserv/citation/wosprev.html>.

Techniques of citation database searching

In this section, some of the more important general ways in which citation databases may be searched online or as CD-ROM are outlined. Five main approaches are distinguished, but in practice there may be overlap and the opportunity for the inventive searcher to devise hybrid techniques. The main approaches are:

- 'simple' citation searching
- searching for combinations of citations; co-citations
- combining citations with other access points
- iterative citation searching
- forward and backward citation searching; cycling.

'Simple' citation searching

This is the most straightforward application of a bibliographic citation database: finding documents which cite a known 'starting-point' document. This is done, in principle, by searching directly for the full cited reference description. In practice, this is not a good idea. The full cited reference (author, year, volume and so on) is a long string to type, and the searching systems are unforgiving of minor errors such as misplaced commas, so that it can be difficult to know whether a null result means that there are no such citations, or simply that a typing error has been made. Perhaps more significant is the variability in the description of the cited reference, which is generally carried over from the original publication without standardization. Different practices in inclusion of authors' second initials, as well as simple errors, mean that some variant of the citation is likely to be missed by any precisely specified search statement. The problem of errors, as well as simple variant practice in citation, is a problem of long standing (Sweetland, 1989; Brown, 1998). It is therefore always a good idea to examine the index around the required citation (for example, by the **EXPAND** command in DIALOG), and then select the entries required. This should enable the searcher to identify variations in authors' initials, and in bibliographic details. Beyond this, the searcher should be aware of the need to allow for variations in authors' names, especially if the family name is hyphenated or multiple; this is the same thought process as is necessary for comprehensive author searches.

Figure 2.1 shows an example of this: the many variant ways in which Ed Krol's well-known *Whole Internet Guide* appears as a cited reference. Brown (1998) gives other examples.

Although E41 is the most usual form of citation to Krol's book, E4-6, 17-26, 30-31, 35-43 and 46 all appear to be variants.

Truncation can, of course, be used to widen a citation search, as shown in the following example (using DIALOG syntax):

```
File  34:SciSearch(R) Cited Ref Sci  1988-1997/Oct W3
      (c) 1997 Inst for Sci Info

    Set  Items  Description
    ---  -----  -----------
?e cr=krol e


Ref   Items  Index-term
E1      1    CR=KROL DS, 1987, P35, VESTN OFTALMOL
E2      1    CR=KROL DS, 1991, P98, AKTUALNYE PROBLEMY S
E3      0 *  CR=KROL E
E4      1    CR=KROL E, INTERNET USERS GUIDE
E5      1    CR=KROL E, WHOLE INTERNET USER
E6      5    CR=KROL E, WHOLE INTERNET USERS
E7      1    CR=KROL E, 1984, HITCHHIKERS GUIDE IN
E8      1    CR=KROL E, 1985, V10, P105, BIOL
E9      1    CR=KROL E, 1985, V10, P105, ZESZ NAUK FILII
E10     1    CR=KROL E, 1985, V10, P105, ZESZ NAUK FILII UW 4
E11     1    CR=KROL E, 1985, V21, P70, ACTA ORN
E12     1    CR=KROL E, 1989, E COMMUNICATION

     Enter P or PAGE for more
?p
```

Figure 2.1   Variant of cited reference

```
Ref   Items  Index-term
E13     2    CR=KROL E, 1989, HITCHHIKERS GUIDE IN
E14     1    CR=KROL E, 1991, V46, P614, POL TYG LEK
E15     1    CR=KROL E, 1992, E COMMUNICATION
E16     1    CR=KROL E, 1992, P1, THESIS JAGIELLONIAN
E17     1    CR=KROL E, 1992, P11, WHOLE INTERNET USERS
E18     1    CR=KROL E, 1992, P127, WHOLE INTERNET GUIDE
E19     1    CR=KROL E, 1992, P155, WHOLE INTERNET USERS
E20     3    CR=KROL E, 1992, P189, WHOLE INTERNET USERS
E21     1    CR=KROL E, 1992, P212, WHOLE INTERNET USERS
E22     4    CR=KROL E, 1992, P227, WHOLE INTERNET USERS
E23     1    CR=KROL E, 1992, WHOL INTERN US GUID
E24     4    CR=KROL E, 1992, WHOLE INT USERS GUID

        Enter P or PAGE for more
?p


Ref   Items  Index-term
E25     8    CR=KROL E, 1992, WHOLE INTERNET
E26    49    CR=KROL E, 1992, WHOLE INTERNET USERS
E27     1    CR=KROL E, 1993, E COMMUNICATION
E28     1    CR=KROL E, 1993, FYI WHAT IS INTERNET
E29     1    CR=KROL E, 1993, P1, FYI20 U ILL GOPH COM
E30     1    CR=KROL E, 1993, P227, WHOLE INTERNET USERS
E31     5    CR=KROL E, 1993, WHOLE INTERNET USERS
E32     1    CR=KROL E, 1993, 1462 RFC
E33     1    CR=KROL E, 1994, E COMMUNICATION
E34     1    CR=KROL E, 1994, IN PRESS J COMP PH B
E35     1    CR=KROL E, 1994, INTERNET USERS GUIDE
E36     2    CR=KROL E, 1994, P227, WHOLE INTERNET USERS

        Enter P or PAGE for more
?p


Ref   Items  Index-term
E37     1    CR=KROL E, 1994, P247, WHOLE INTERNET USERS
E38     1    CR=KROL E, 1994, P65, WHOLE INTERNET USERS
E39     1    CR=KROL E, 1994, WHOLE INTENET USERS
E40     1    CR=KROL E, 1994, WHOLE INTERNET
E41    28    CR=KROL E, 1994, WHOLE INTERNET USERS
E42     1    CR=KROL E, 1994, WORLE INTERNET USERS
E43     1    CR=KROL E, 1995, WHOLE INTERNET USERS
E44     1    CR=KROL E, 1996, V22, P13, MINER ELECTROLYTE ME
E45     1    CR=KROL EC, 1989, P311, ACT POL HIS
E46     1    CR=KROL ED, 1992, P155, WHOLE INTERNET USERS
E47    19    CR=KROL ES, 1991, P118, J CHEM SOC CHEM COMM
E48     1    CR=KROL ES, 1991, 74TH ANN CAN CHEM C
```

Figure 2.1   concluded

S CR=BLUE A, 1997?	Citations to all A. Blue's 1997 publications
S CR=BLUE A, 199?	Citations to all A. Blue's publications from the 1990s
S CR=BLUE A,?	Citations to all A. Blue's publications

It is worth reiterating that only the first author named on a publication will appear as an entry point in a citation index. To find citations to all of an author's work, including publications in which they may not have been first author, it will be necessary to do an initial author search to find all documents which may have been cited, then search on each of these references using the first-named author rather than the sought author.

It will be evident that one or more key papers must be known to act as a starting-point for a cited reference search. If not, then one must be identified by a search using other access points – for example, subject indexing or title words, either in an appropriate ISI database or in another source. (At this point, it is worth recalling that the cited reference itself need not be a record in the citation database, so long as the citing reference is included.)

If the search is for a subject, albeit one represented by a single key reference, rather than for citations to a particular document, then it is necessary to consider alternative citations which could be made; authors do not necessarily choose to cite the same document, even to make essentially the same point. In particular, original papers are often no longer referenced, having been replaced for citation purposes by later expositions, review articles and the like, or simply having passed into 'common knowledge'. Newton's *Principia*, although it remains the inarguable first publication on the force of gravity, is not usually cited except by historians of science. This so-called 'obliteration' phenomenon is more marked in science than in other subject areas, and within science it is more obvious in experimental disciplines than in those reliant on observation or theory.

Although the ISI citation databases generally deal with bibliographic references, other 'documents' may be cited. Some of these are 'implicit citations', not formally referenced in the original document and added to the record by ISI indexers. The ARTS AND HUMANITIES CITATION INDEX, for example, includes paintings, musical scores, photographs, architectural drawings and literary reviews. Figure 2.2, as an example, shows citations to the Renaissance painter Sandro Botticelli; all are references to specific works of art. Some are denoted as being illustrations, and these can be specifically searched for – cr=illustation – as can other unusual forms of 'document'.

Searching for combinations of citations; co-citations

A search for documents citing a combination of references can be a powerful means of identifying information on very specific topics, especially in interdisciplinary areas. The strategy is simple. Citation searches are carried out for documents reflecting each subject concept of interest and the results ANDed

```
File 439:Arts&Humanities Search(R)  1980-1997/Oct W4
   (c) 1997 Inst for Sci Info

   Set  Items  Description
   ----  -------  ---------------
?e cr=botticelli s


Ref   Items  Index-term
E1     1   CR=BOTTICELLI G, 1992, P88, METODOLOGIA RESTAURO
E2     1   CR=BOTTICELLI G, 1994, RESTAURO MADONNA DEL
E3     0  *CR=BOTTICELLI S
E4     1   CR=BOTTICELLI S, ADORATION DE MAGES, ILLUSTRATION
E5     2   CR=BOTTICELLI S, ADORATION DES MAGES, ILLUSTRATIO
E6     1   CR=BOTTICELLI S, ADORATION OF CHRIST, ILLUSTRATIO
E7     1   CR=BOTTICELLI S, ADORATION OF MAGI
E8     5   CR=BOTTICELLI S, ADORATION OF MAGI, ILLUSTRATION
E9     1   CR=BOTTICELLI S, ADORATION, ILLUSTRATION
E10    1   CR=BOTTICELLI S, ANDATA AL CALVARIO, ILLUSTRATION
E11    1   CR=BOTTICELLI S, ANNONCIATION, ILLUSTRATION
E12    1   CR=BOTTICELLI S, ANNUNCIATION

       Enter P or PAGE for more
?p


Ref   Items  Index-term
E13    2   CR=BOTTICELLI S, ANNUNCIATION, ILLUSTRATION
E14    1   CR=BOTTICELLI S, BIRTH OF SPRING
E15    3   CR=BOTTICELLI S, BIRTH OF VENUS
E16    1   CR=BOTTICELLI S, BIRTH OF VENUS ( ILLUSTRATION )
E17    5   CR=BOTTICELLI S, BIRTH OF VENUS, ILLUSTRATION
E18    1   CR=BOTTICELLI S, CALUMNY OF APELLES, ILLUSTRATION
E19    1   CR=BOTTICELLI S, CALUNNIA
E20    1   CR=BOTTICELLI S, CHASSE INFERNALE
E21    1   CR=BOTTICELLI S, COURONNEMENT DE LA V, ILLUSTRATI
E22    1   CR=BOTTICELLI S, CRATERE DE LENFER ( SIMPLE IMPLI
E23    1   CR=BOTTICELLI S, CRISTO CONDOTTO AL C, ILLUSTRATI
E24    1   CR=BOTTICELLI S, DANTE DIVINE COMEDIE

       Enter P or PAGE for more
?p


Ref   Items  Index-term
E25    1   CR=BOTTICELLI S, DANTE GOTTLICHE KOME
E26    1   CR=BOTTICELLI S, DERELITTA
E27    1   CR=BOTTICELLI S, EARLY LIFE AND FIRST, ILLUSTRATI
E28    1   CR=BOTTICELLI S, ENFER, ILLUSTRATION
E29    1   CR=BOTTICELLI S, GIOVANNI DE PIERFRAN, ILLUSTRATI
```

Figure 2.2   Citations to works of art

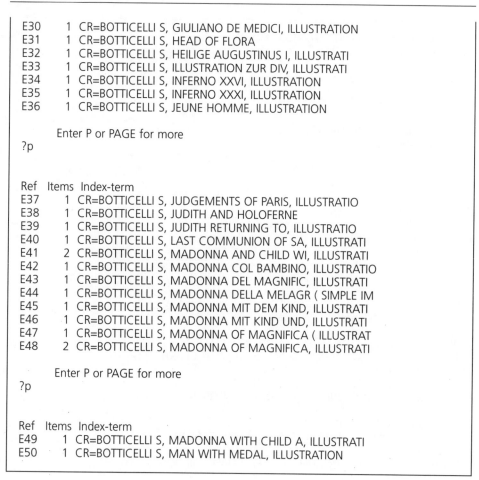

```
E30   1 CR=BOTTICELLI S, GIULIANO DE MEDICI, ILLUSTRATION
E31   1 CR=BOTTICELLI S, HEAD OF FLORA
E32   1 CR=BOTTICELLI S, HEILIGE AUGUSTINUS I, ILLUSTRATI
E33   1 CR=BOTTICELLI S, ILLUSTRATION ZUR DIV, ILLUSTRATI
E34   1 CR=BOTTICELLI S, INFERNO XXVI, ILLUSTRATION
E35   1 CR=BOTTICELLI S, INFERNO XXXI, ILLUSTRATION
E36   1 CR=BOTTICELLI S, JEUNE HOMME, ILLUSTRATION

         Enter P or PAGE for more
?p


Ref  Items Index-term
E37   1 CR=BOTTICELLI S, JUDGEMENTS OF PARIS, ILLUSTRATIO
E38   1 CR=BOTTICELLI S, JUDITH AND HOLOFERNE
E39   1 CR=BOTTICELLI S, JUDITH RETURNING TO, ILLUSTRATIO
E40   1 CR=BOTTICELLI S, LAST COMMUNION OF SA, ILLUSTRATI
E41   2 CR=BOTTICELLI S, MADONNA AND CHILD WI, ILLUSTRATI
E42   1 CR=BOTTICELLI S, MADONNA COL BAMBINO, ILLUSTRATIO
E43   1 CR=BOTTICELLI S, MADONNA DEL MAGNIFIC, ILLUSTRATI
E44   1 CR=BOTTICELLI S, MADONNA DELLA MELAGR ( SIMPLE IM
E45   1 CR=BOTTICELLI S, MADONNA MIT DEM KIND, ILLUSTRATI
E46   1 CR=BOTTICELLI S, MADONNA MIT KIND UND, ILLUSTRATI
E47   1 CR=BOTTICELLI S, MADONNA OF MAGNIFICA ( ILLUSTRAT
E48   2 CR=BOTTICELLI S, MADONNA OF MAGNIFICA, ILLUSTRATI

         Enter P or PAGE for more
?p


Ref  Items Index-term
E49   1 CR=BOTTICELLI S, MADONNA WITH CHILD A, ILLUSTRATI
E50   1 CR=BOTTICELLI S, MAN WITH MEDAL, ILLUSTRATION
```

Figure 2.2   concluded

together. The resultant set comprises those documents that are cited by both documents. It is rare, in practice, to find any answers when trying to combine three or more specific citations, unless they are unusually heavily cited or correspond to a tight subject topic.

This restriction of co-citations for pairs, or larger numbers, of actual documents may often be too restrictive in practice, unless a particularly important pair of documents, which would very commonly be cited as representing a particular topic or concept, can be identified. It is therefore more usual to use authors, rather than particular documents, as the starting-points. In fact, this simply means that *all* of an author's work, rather than just exemplifying documents, is used; this will usually be effective, unless both authors write on many different subjects.

A simple example is shown in Figure 2.3. S.E. Robertson and P.H.A. Sneath are well-known authors in information retrieval and numerical taxonomy respectively.

```
File   7:Social SciSearch(R)  1972-1997/Oct W4
      (c) 1997 Inst for Sci Info

    Set  Items  Description
    ----  -------  --------------
?s cr=robertson se?

    S1    424  CR=ROBERTSON SE?
?s cr=sneath pha?

    S2    762  CR=SNEATH PHA?
?c 1 and 2

         424  1
         762  2
    S3     4  1 AND 2
?t3/3/1-4



 3/3/1
DIALOG(R)File   7:Social SciSearch(R)
(c) 1997 Inst for Sci Info. All rts. reserv.

01922513  GENUINE ARTICLE#: Q4140   NO. REFERENCES: 119
TITLE: RECENT TRENDS IN HIERARCHIC DOCUMENT CLUSTERING - A
CRITICAL-REVIEW
AUTHOR(S): WILLETT P
CORPORATE SOURCE: UNIV SHEFFIELD,DEPT INFORMAT
 STUDIES/SHEFFIELD S10 2TN/S
   YORKSHIRE/ENGLAND/
JOURNAL: INFORMATION PROCESSING & MANAGEMENT, 1988, V24, N5,
P577-597
LANGUAGE: ENGLISH   DOCUMENT TYPE: REVIEW, BIBLIOGRAPHY



 3/3/2
DIALOG(R)File   7:Social SciSearch(R)
(c) 1997 Inst for Sci Info. All rts. reserv.

01870400   GENUINE ARTICLE#: N0501   NO. REFERENCES: 174
TITLE: RETRIEVAL TECHNIQUES
AUTHOR(S): BELKIN NJ; CROFT WB
CORPORATE SOURCE: RUTGERS STATE UNIV, SCH COMMUN INFORMAT &
LIB STUDIES,4
   HUNTINGTON ST/NEW BRUNSWICK//NJ/08903; UNIV
MASSACHUSETTS,DEPT COMP &
   INFORMAT SCI/AMHERST//MA/01003
JOURNAL: ANNUAL REVIEW OF INFORMATION SCIENCE AND
TECHNOLOGY, 1987, V22, P
   109-145
```

Figure 2.3   Example of searching for co-citations

```
LANGUAGE: ENGLISH   DOCUMENT TYPE: REVIEW, BIBLIOGRAPHY


 3/3/3
DIALOG(R)File   7:Social SciSearch(R)
(c) 1997 Inst for Sci Info. All rts. reserv.

01301335   GENUINE ARTICLE#: RY044   NO. REFERENCES: 16
TITLE: SIMILARITY COEFFICIENTS AND WEIGHTING FUNCTIONS FOR
AUTOMATIC
   DOCUMENT CLASSIFICATION - AN EMPIRICAL-COMPARISON
AUTHOR(S): WILLETT P
CORPORATE SOURCE: UNIV SHEFFIELD,DEPT INFORMAT
STUDIES/SHEFFIELD S10 2TN/S
   YORKSHIRE/ENGLAND/
JOURNAL: INTERNATIONAL CLASSIFICATION, 1983, V10, N3, P138-142
LANGUAGE: ENGLISH   DOCUMENT TYPE: ARTICLE


 3/3/4
DIALOG(R)File   7:Social SciSearch(R)
(c) 1997 Inst for Sci Info. All rts. reserv.

00739934   GENUINE ARTICLE#: GY548   NO. REFERENCES: 19
TITLE: AUTOMATIC CLASSIFICATION IN INFORMATION-RETRIEVAL
AUTHOR(S): VANRIJSBERGEN CJ
CORPORATE SOURCE: UNIV CAMBRIDGE,COMP
LAB/CAMBRIDGE//ENGLAND/
JOURNAL: DREXEL LIBRARY QUARTERLY, 1978, V14, N2, P75-89
LANGUAGE: ENGLISH   DOCUMENT TYPE: ARTICLE
?
```

Figure 2.3   concluded

A search for documents citing at least one document for which each of them is first author gives four references: these are all review articles dealing with applications of numerical taxonomy to information retrieval, and would give a good entry point to the literature of this specialized area.

Figure 2.4 shows a similar search, using G. Salton as a representative of information retrieval research rather than S.E. Robertson. The rather larger set of co-cited references retrieved includes the review (record 7) found, but also brings in a set of much more diverse material, showing the potential use of this method for investigating the influence of ideas across a wider area.

The general method of co-citation searching, then, involves searching for co-cited authors, rather than particular documents; the method has been described in detail, with examples, by Knapp (1984) and White (1981). In essence, it involves a search for documents citing any publication by each one of two authors. Although citations to each of the authors may cover a wide area, combination of the two usually leads to a set of items that are quite tightly defined in subject

```
File   7:Social SciSearch(R)  1972-1997/Oct W4
       (c) 1997 Inst for Sci Info

    Set Items  Description
    ----  -------  --------------
?s cr=salton g?

    S1  1305  CR=SALTON G?
?s cr=sneath phsa?

    S2   762  CR=SNEATH PHA?
?c 1 and 2

        1305  1
         762  2
    S3    18  1 AND 2
?t3/3/1-18


 3/3/1
DIALOG(R)File   7:Social SciSearch(R)
(c) 1997 Inst for Sci Info. All rts. reserv.

02971381   GENUINE ARTICLE#: VR673   NO. REFERENCES: 22
TITLE: A UNIFIED SIMILARITY COEFFICIENT FOR NAVIGATING THROUGH
    MULTIDIMENSIONAL INFORMATION
AUTHOR(S): TUDHOPE D; TAYLOR C
CORPORATE SOURCE: UNIV GLAMORGAN,DEPT COMP
    STUDIES/PONTYPRIDD CF37 1DL/M
    GLAM/WALES/; DK MULTIMEDIA/LONDON//ENGLAND/
JOURNAL: PROCEEDINGS OF THE ASIS ANNUAL MEETING, 1996, V33, P67-70
ISSN: 0044-7870
LANGUAGE: ENGLISH   DOCUMENT TYPE: ARTICLE  (Abstract Available)


 3/3/2
DIALOG(R)File   7:Social SciSearch(R)
(c) 1997 Inst for Sci Info. All rts. reserv.

02885160   GENUINE ARTICLE#: UG010   NO. REFERENCES: 13
TITLE: THE USE OF CO-NOMINATION TO IDENTIFY EXPERT PARTICIPANTS
FOR
    TECHNOLOGY FORESIGHT
AUTHOR(S): NEDEVA M; GEORGHIOU L; LOVERIDGE D; CAMERON H
CORPORATE SOURCE: UNIV MANCHESTER,PROGRAMME POLICY RES
ENGN SCI
    &TECHNOL/MANCHESTER/LANCS/ENGLAND/
JOURNAL: R & D MANAGEMENT, 1996, V26, N2 (APR), P155-168
ISSN: 0033-6807
LANGUAGE: ENGLISH   DOCUMENT TYPE: ARTICLE  (Abstract Available)
```

Figure 2.4   Further example of searching for co-citations

3/3/3
DIALOG(R)File   7:Social SciSearch(R)
(c) 1997 Inst for Sci Info. All rts. reserv.

02618286   GENUINE ARTICLE#: NQ281   NO. REFERENCES: 49
TITLE: ON THE CREATION OF HYPERTEXT LINKS IN FULL-TEXT
DOCUMENTS -
   MEASUREMENT OF INTER-LINKER CONSISTENCY
AUTHOR(S): ELLIS D; FURNERHINES J; WILLETT P
CORPORATE SOURCE: UNIV SHEFFIELD,DEPT INFORMAT
STUDIES/SHEFFIELD S10 2TN/S
   YORKSHIRE/ENGLAND/; UNIV SHEFFIELD,DEPT INFORMAT
STUDIES/SHEFFIELD S10
   2TN/S YORKSHIRE/ENGLAND/
JOURNAL: JOURNAL OF DOCUMENTATION, 1994, V50, N2 (JUN), P67-98
ISSN: 0022-0418
LANGUAGE: ENGLISH   DOCUMENT TYPE: ARTICLE (Abstract Available)

3/3/4
DIALOG(R)File   7:Social SciSearch(R)
(c) 1997 Inst for Sci Info. All rts. reserv.

02531949   GENUINE ARTICLE#: LW521   NO. REFERENCES: 21
TITLE: THE MEASUREMENT OF INTERNATIONAL SCIENTIFIC
COLLABORATION
AUTHOR(S): LUUKKONEN T; TIJSSEN RJW; PERSSON O; SIVERTSEN G
CORPORATE SOURCE: ACAD FINLAND,POB 57/SF-00551
HELSINKI//FINLAND/; LEIDEN
   UNIV,CTR SCI & TECHNOL STUDIES/2300 RB LEIDEN//NETHERLANDS/;
INST
   STUDIES RES & HIGHER EDUC/N-0260 OSLO 2//NORWAY/; UMEA
UNIV,INFORSK
   GRP/S-90187 UMEA//SWEDEN/
JOURNAL: SCIENTOMETRICS, 1993, V28, N1 (SEP), P15-36
ISSN: 0138-9130
LANGUAGE: ENGLISH   DOCUMENT TYPE: ARTICLE (Abstract Available)

3/3/5
DIALOG(R)File   7:Social SciSearch(R)
(c) 1997 Inst for Sci Info. All rts. reserv.

02339547   GENUINE ARTICLE#: HJ490   NO. REFERENCES: 57
TITLE: SHRIF, A GENERAL-PURPOSE SYSTEM FOR HEURISTIC RETRIEVAL
OF
   INFORMATION AND FACTS, APPLIED TO MEDICAL KNOWLEDGE
PROCESSING
AUTHOR(S): FINDLER NV; MAINI S; YUEN AFM
CORPORATE SOURCE: ARIZONA STATE UNIV,DEPT COMP
SCI/TEMPE//AZ/85287; ARIZONA

Figure 2.4   cont'd

STATE UNIV,ARTIFICIAL INTELLIGENCE LAB/TEMPE//AZ/85287
JOURNAL: INFORMATION PROCESSING & MANAGEMENT, 1992, V28, N2,
P219-240
LANGUAGE: ENGLISH   DOCUMENT TYPE: ARTICLE (Abstract Available)

 3/3/6
DIALOG(R)File   7:Social SciSearch(R)
(c) 1997 Inst for Sci Info. All rts. reserv.

02006142   GENUINE ARTICLE#: AB438   NO. REFERENCES: 13
TITLE: SIMILARITY MEASURES IN SCIENTOMETRIC RESEARCH - THE
JACCARD INDEX
    VERSUS SALTON COSINE FORMULA
AUTHOR(S): HAMERS L; HEMERYCK Y; HERWEYERS G; JANSSEN M;
KETERS H; ROUSSEAU
    R; VANHOUTTE A
CORPORATE SOURCE: KATHOLIEKE IND HOGESCH W
VLAANDEREN,ZEEDIJK 101/B-8400
    OOSTENDE//BELGIUM/
JOURNAL: INFORMATION PROCESSING & MANAGEMENT, 1989, V25, N3,
P315-318
LANGUAGE: ENGLISH   DOCUMENT TYPE: ARTICLE

 3/3/7
DIALOG(R)File   7:Social SciSearch(R)
(c) 1997 Inst for Sci Info. All rts. reserv.

01922513   GENUINE ARTICLE#: Q4140   NO. REFERENCES: 119
TITLE: RECENT TRENDS IN HIERARCHIC DOCUMENT CLUSTERING - A
CRITICAL-REVIEW
AUTHOR(S): WILLETT P
CORPORATE SOURCE: UNIV SHEFFIELD,DEPT INFORMAT
STUDIES/SHEFFIELD S10 2TN/S
    YORKSHIRE/ENGLAND/
JOURNAL: INFORMATION PROCESSING & MANAGEMENT, 1988, V24, N5,
P577-597
LANGUAGE: ENGLISH   DOCUMENT TYPE: REVIEW, BIBLIOGRAPHY

 3/3/8
DIALOG(R)File   7:Social SciSearch(R)
(c) 1997 Inst for Sci Info. All rts. reserv.

01870400   GENUINE ARTICLE#: N0501   NO. REFERENCES: 174
TITLE: RETRIEVAL TECHNIQUES
AUTHOR(S): BELKIN NJ; CROFT WB
CORPORATE SOURCE: RUTGERS STATE UNIV,SCH COMMUN INFORMAT &
LIB STUDIES,4
    HUNTINGTON ST/NEW BRUNSWICK//NJ/08903; UNIV

Figure 2.4   cont'd

MASSACHUSETTS,DEPT COMP &
   INFORMAT SCI/AMHERST//MA/01003
JOURNAL: ANNUAL REVIEW OF INFORMATION SCIENCE AND
TECHNOLOGY, 1987, V22, P
   109-145
LANGUAGE: ENGLISH   DOCUMENT TYPE: REVIEW, BIBLIOGRAPHY

 3/3/9
DIALOG(R)File   7:Social SciSearch(R)
(c) 1997 Inst for Sci Info. All rts. reserv.

01609282   GENUINE ARTICLE#: C9067   NO. REFERENCES: 105
TITLE: DIFFERENTIAL ORDERING OF OBJECTS AND ATTRIBUTES
AUTHOR(S): SUTCLIFFE JP
CORPORATE SOURCE: UNIV SYDNEY,DEPT PSYCHOL/SYDNEY/NSW
2006/AUSTRALIA/
JOURNAL: PSYCHOMETRIKA, 1986, V51, N2, P209-240
LANGUAGE: ENGLISH   DOCUMENT TYPE: ARTICLE

 3/3/10
DIALOG(R)File   7:Social SciSearch(R)
(c) 1997 Inst for Sci Info. All rts. reserv.

01590412   GENUINE ARTICLE#: C0765   NO. REFERENCES: 34
TITLE: THE SYNTHESIS OF SPECIALTY NARRATIVES FROM CO-CITATION-
CLUSTERS
AUTHOR(S): SMALL H
CORPORATE SOURCE: INST SCI INFORMAT,3501 MARKET
ST/PHILADELPHIA//PA/19104
JOURNAL: JOURNAL OF THE AMERICAN SOCIETY FOR INFORMATION
SCIENCE, 1986, V37
, N3, P97-110
LANGUAGE: ENGLISH   DOCUMENT TYPE: ARTICLE

 3/3/11
DIALOG(R)File   7:Social SciSearch(R)
(c) 1997 Inst for Sci Info. All rts. reserv.

01410921   GENUINE ARTICLE#: TT749   NO. REFERENCES: 81
TITLE: HIERARCHIC AGGLOMERATIVE CLUSTERING METHODS FOR
AUTOMATIC DOCUMENT
   CLASSIFICATION
AUTHOR(S): GRIFFITHS A; ROBINSON LA; WILLETT P
CORPORATE SOURCE: UNIV SHEFFIELD,DEPT INFORMAT
STUDIES/SHEFFIELD S10 2TN/S
   YORKSHIRE/ENGLAND/
JOURNAL: JOURNAL OF DOCUMENTATION, 1984, V40, N3, P175-205
LANGUAGE: ENGLISH   DOCUMENT TYPE: ARTICLE

Figure 2.4   **cont'd**

3/3/12
DIALOG(R)File   7:Social SciSearch(R)
(c) 1997 Inst for Sci Info. All rts. reserv.

01301335   GENUINE ARTICLE#: RY044   NO. REFERENCES: 16
TITLE: SIMILARITY COEFFICIENTS AND WEIGHTING FUNCTIONS FOR AUTOMATIC
    DOCUMENT CLASSIFICATION - AN EMPIRICAL-COMPARISON
AUTHOR(S): WILLETT P
CORPORATE SOURCE: UNIV SHEFFIELD,DEPT INFORMAT STUDIES/SHEFFIELD S10 2TN/S
    YORKSHIRE/ENGLAND/
JOURNAL: INTERNATIONAL CLASSIFICATION, 1983, V10, N3, P138-142
LANGUAGE: ENGLISH   DOCUMENT TYPE: ARTICLE

3/3/13
DIALOG(R)File   7:Social SciSearch(R)
(c) 1997 Inst for Sci Info. All rts. reserv.

01245039   GENUINE ARTICLE#: RA171   NO. REFERENCES: 28
TITLE: A COMPARISON OF SOME HIERARICHAL MONOTHETIC DIVISIVE CLUSTERING
    ALGORITHMS FOR STRUCTURE PROPERTY CORRELATION
AUTHOR(S): RUBIN V; WILLETT P
CORPORATE SOURCE: UNIV SHEFFIELD,DEPT INFORMAT STUDIES/SHEFFIELD S10 2TN/S
    YORKSHIRE/ENGLAND/
JOURNAL: ANALYTICA CHIMICA ACTA, 1983, V151, N1, P161-166
LANGUAGE: ENGLISH   DOCUMENT TYPE: ARTICLE

3/3/14
DIALOG(R)File   7:Social SciSearch(R)
(c) 1997 Inst for Sci Info. All rts. reserv.

00949584   GENUINE ARTICLE#: LF159   NO. REFERENCES: 13
TITLE: THE RELATIONSHIP OF INFORMATION-SCIENCE TO THE SOCIAL-SCIENCES - A
    CO-CITATION ANALYSIS
AUTHOR(S): SMALL H
CORPORATE SOURCE: INST SCI INFORMAT,3501 MARKET ST,UNIV CITY SCI
    CTR/PHILADELPHIA//PA/19104
JOURNAL: INFORMATION PROCESSING & MANAGEMENT, 1981, V17, N1, P39-50
LANGUAGE: ENGLISH   DOCUMENT TYPE: ARTICLE

3/3/15
DIALOG(R)File   7:Social SciSearch(R)
(c) 1997 Inst for Sci Info. All rts. reserv.

00772825   GENUINE ARTICLE#: HL569   NO. REFERENCES: 35
TITLE: CITATION STUDY OF COMPUTER-SCIENCE LITERATURE

Figure 2.4   cont'd

AUTHOR(S): SALTON G; BERGMARK D
CORPORATE SOURCE: CORNELL UNIV,DEPT COMP SCI/ITHACA//NY/14853;
ITHACA
    COLL,DEPT MATH/ITHACA//NY/14850
JOURNAL: IEEE TRANSACTIONS ON PROFESSIONAL COMMUNICATION,
1979, V22, N3, P
    146-158
LANGUAGE: ENGLISH   DOCUMENT TYPE: ARTICLE

 3/3/16
DIALOG(R)File   7:Social SciSearch(R)
(c) 1997 Inst for Sci Info. All rts. reserv.

00739934   GENUINE ARTICLE#: GY548   NO. REFERENCES: 19
TITLE: AUTOMATIC CLASSIFICATION IN INFORMATION-RETRIEVAL
AUTHOR(S): VANRIJSBERGEN CJ
CORPORATE SOURCE: UNIV CAMBRIDGE,COMP
LAB/CAMBRIDGE//ENGLAND/
JOURNAL: DREXEL LIBRARY QUARTERLY, 1978, V14, N2, P75-89
LANGUAGE: ENGLISH   DOCUMENT TYPE: ARTICLE

 3/3/17
DIALOG(R)File   7:Social SciSearch(R)
(c) 1997 Inst for Sci Info. All rts. reserv.

00291443   GENUINE ARTICLE#: AV698   NO. REFERENCES: 49
TITLE: SIMILARITY AND TYPICALITY OF TAXA
AUTHOR(S): KRISHNAMURTHY EV
CORPORATE SOURCE: INDIAN INST SCI/BANGALORE//INDIA/
JOURNAL: JOURNAL OF THE INDIAN INSTITUTE OF SCIENCE, 1975, V57,
N10, P
    358-374
LANGUAGE: ENGLISH   DOCUMENT TYPE: ARTICLE

 3/3/18
DIALOG(R)File   7:Social SciSearch(R)
(c) 1997 Inst for Sci Info. All rts. reserv.

00103596   GENUINE ARTICLE#: R1355   NO. REFERENCES: 11
TITLE: METHOD FOR AUTOMATIC CLASSIFICATION OF CHEMICAL
STRUCTURES
AUTHOR(S): ADAMSON GW
CORPORATE SOURCE: SHEFFIELD UNIV,POSTGRAD SCH LIBRARIANSHIP &
INFORMATION
    SCI,WESTERN BANK/SHEFFIELD S10 2TN//ENGLAND/
JOURNAL: INFORMATION STORAGE AND RETRIEVAL, 1973, V9, N10, P561-
568
LANGUAGE: ENGLISH   DOCUMENT TYPE: ARTICLE

Figure 2.4   concluded

terms. These subjects may be difficult to identify with accuracy by conventional subject indexes; examples given by White and Knapp include voting behaviour in critical elections, curiosity and exploration in animals, organizational boundary spanning, the socialization of women physicians, and the geographical diffusion of innovation.

The simplest form of co-citation searching (which was exemplified above) involves the linking of a single pair of authors. More complex is the systematic pairing of cited authors from a small group of three, four, five or six authors, or the linking of three or more authors from such a grouping. White gives an example of a set of six authors writing on social indicators. Combining all possible pairs gives a general bibliography of the area, while searching on particular pairs gives a specific slant – for example, mathematical modelling.

A third co-cited author strategy is a free pairing of many related authors from two or more separate lists: the so-called 'Chinese menu' strategy. This is done by ORing together the sets of cited references for the authors in each list separately and ANDing the results. White gives an example of this method using one list of authors regarded as specialists in the history of science and a second list of sociologists, historians and information scientists. The result was an extensive bibliography reflecting the breadth of methodologies applicable to the history of science studies.

Co-citation searching can be used to find material at very different levels of self-similarity, according to the particular method used. It is subject to the usual limitations of citation searching, particularly the restriction to first named author, and the vagaries of specification of form of name. Problems in the amount of material retrieved can arise with two particularly highly cited authors, and can be overcome by inclusion of publication year, an intermediate stage between co-cited authors and documents.

Combining citations with other access points

Although the majority of publications receive few, if any, citations, it may sometimes happen that a citation search retrieves more documents than can conveniently be scanned, so that the output must be reduced in some way.

This can most obviously be done by searching on other access points in the database – author name, institution, subject terms from title, abstract or indexing, source, or year of publication are obvious examples. Although this has always been a valid search technique, its usefulness has increased with the relatively recent inclusion of abstracts (usually original author abstracts) in the ISI files. Other access points specific to the ISI citation databases are number of references (to identify reviews and papers with extensive bibliographies), document type, journal subject category and research front.

Iterative citation searching

This is a way of systematically examining the influence of an initial document and thereby producing a bibliography of a given topic.

One or more starting-point documents, which will need to be several years' old, are initially identified and all the documents citing them are retrieved. Any of these judged not relevant or useful for the subject under consideration are discarded. The remaining citations are used as starting-points for a new iteration; documents which cite them are retrieved. This process continues until no useful new material is found, or until the search has been brought to the present time, so that the only remaining references are too recent to have been cited. Usually, this should not take more than three or, at most, four iterations. It is usually necessary to be stringent in rejecting documents as irrelevant in order to avoid the sets produced becoming too large and too unfocused to be useful. The process can, in any event, become tedious and time-consuming if many citations are involved.

Garfield (1983) describes an example of this technique: a three-iteration search, resulting in a bibliography of 16 journal articles dealing with the antibiotic compound trimethoprim. A starting reference is cited ten times. When each of these ten documents is used as the starting-point of a citation search, one gives three new useful references, two give one useful item each, while the remaining seven have no useful citations. The five newly found documents give no further useful references in a third iteration. This is an unusually 'neat and tidy' example; the references cover a timespan of nine years.

Forward and backward citation searching: cycling

Like the previous iteration technique, with which it has a good deal in common, cycling is a method for thoroughly exploring the literature of a topic through its citation linkages.

A starting document, which must be several years' old and central to the topic of interest, is chosen, and documents which cite it are found. The reference lists in these citing documents are examined to find older relevant material, and these documents are used as the starting-points for further citation searches. The search can move backwards in time (by following up references in relevant documents) and forward (by iterative citation searching). The process continues until no further useful material is being found or, in the case of large citing sets, until the searcher's patience is exhausted.

This technique cannot usually be carried out entirely online, since relevance judgements cannot usually be made from the limited information in reference lists, and the cited documents may not be in the online database. Stringent rejection of peripheral material is necessary in order to keep the exercise within the bounds of practicality. It is likely always to be a time-consuming method, best reserved for compilation of definitive bibliographies, when it will be used in conjunction with other searching techniques and sources.

Garfield (1983) illustrates the use of this technique in the compilation of a bibliography of serum measurement of iron and ferritin, while Synge (1990) gives examples of its use in the literature of natural product chemistry.

Applications of citation searching

In this section some of the more important applications of citation searching are described. There is, inevitably, some overlap between the categories, with some searches failing to fit neatly into exclusive categories. The ordering of the categories does not indicate any order of importance.

To identify subsequent developments to a publication

New information, directly related to material already published, will generally appear in print with a reference to the earlier work. A citation search on the older document will lead directly to identification of the newer work. This is, arguably, the most evidently valuable application of a citation database.

New information may take several forms, among them:

- corrections, retractions, errata and amendments
- criticism and refutation
- support and confirmation
- provision of new data
- comparison with equivalent work
- inclusion in a review, setting the work in context.

Citation searching is the most effective way of finding this sort of 'updating' information, and online searching of the frequently updated ISI online files is the best method. A citation search should be carried out as a matter of course on any publication which is of particular significance, to avoid the possibility of basing a report, publication, proposal, research project and so on on outdated, erroneous or incomplete information.

To give an example, albeit perhaps an extreme one, a citation search on a paper dealing with metal cluster ions, and published in the *Journal of the American Chemical Society*, reveals a number of citing references. One of these is a correction by the authors of the original paper, beginning 'We wish to retract this paper. What we believed to be Sc_4+ has been shown subsequently to be $Ta+$'.

Garfield (1983) gives an example of the use of the SCIENCE CITATION INDEX to check whether a published idea has been confirmed or not. A paper by P.M.M. Rae in the *Proceedings of the National Academy of Sciences* predicted the existence of repetitive DNA sequences. To seek confirmation or otherwise of this idea, a citation search was carried out, using this paper as the starting-point. Among the citing documents were several papers with titles indicating that they described just such repetitive sequences in the DNA of various organisms, thus directly answering the question.

Two examples of this kind of search are given in Figures 2.5 and 2.6. Figure 2.5 shows a citation search on a paper describing a simulation technique: of the two citing documents, the first gives a correction to the conditions stated in the original paper, and comments on the significance of the correction for the results; the

---

Title: SIMULATION OF FREE SURFACES IN 3-D WITH THE ARBITRARY
LAGRANGE-EULER
    METHOD
Author(s): SZABO P; HASSAGER O
Corporate Source: TECH UNIV DENMARK,DEPT CHEM ENGN/DK-2800
LYNGBY//DENMARK/
Journal: INTERNATIONAL JOURNAL FOR NUMERICAL METHODS IN
ENGINEERING, 1995
, V38, N5 (MAR 15), P717-734

?e cr=szabo p, 1995

Ref   Items Index-term
E1   2   CR=SZABO P, 1994, V20, P324, GENOMICS
E2   1   CR=SZABO P, 1994, V235, P1873, PHYSICA C
E3   0   *CR=SZABO P, 1995
E4   1   CR=SZABO P, 1995, P280, HUMAN CHROMOSOMES PR
E5   1   CR=SZABO P, 1995, UNPUB EXPRESSION CAR
E6   1   CR=SZABO P, 1995, V24, P3097, GENE DEV
E7   2   CR=SZABO P, 1995, V270, P10212, J BIOL CHEM
E8   4   CR=SZABO P, 1995, V270, P212, J BIOL CHEM
E9   2   CR=SZABO P, 1995, V38, P717, INT J NUMER METH ENG
E10   4   CR=SZABO P, 1995, V9, P1857, GENE DEV
E11   1   CR=SZABO P, 1996, INT J NUM METH ENG
E12   1   CR=SZABO P, 1996, V36, P179, J ANAL APPL PYROL

        Enter P or PAGE for more
?s e9

     S4   2 CR="SZABO P, 1995, V38, P717, INT J NUMER METH ENG"
?t4/5/1-2

4/5/1
DIALOG(R)File 434:Scisearch(R) Cited Ref Sci
(c) 1997 Inst for Sci Info. All rts. reserv.

15796654   Genuine Article#: XG821   Number of References: 2
Title: Simulation of free surfaces in 3D with the arbitrary Lagrange Euler
    method: Erratum

Figure 2.5   **Following developments to a publication on a simulation technique**
© 1996 Elsevier Science Ltd

Author(s): Szabo P (REPRINT) ; Hassager O; Rasmussen HK
Corporate Source: TECH UNIV DENMARK,DEPT CHEM ENGN/DK-2800
LYNGBY//DENMARK/
   (REPRINT)
Journal: COMMUNICATIONS IN NUMERICAL METHODS IN ENGINEERING,
1997, V13, N6
 (JUN), P511-513
ISSN: 1069-8299   Publication date: 19970600
Publisher: JOHN WILEY & SONS LTD, BAFFINS LANE CHICHESTER, W
SUSSEX,
   ENGLAND PO19 1UD
 Language: English   Document Type: ARTICLE
Geographic Location: DENMARK
Subfile: CC ENGI--Current Contents, Engineering, Computing & Technology
Journal Subject Category: MATHEMATICS, APPLIED; ENGINEERING
Abstract: A correction to the free interface condition given in P. Szabo
   and O. Hassenger (Int. J. Numer. Meth. Engng, 38, 717-734 (1995)) is
   presented. The corrections to the computations in the paper are found
   to be within numerical accuracy. (C) 1997 by John Wiley & Sons, Ltd.

   4/5/2
DIALOG(R)File 434:Scisearch(R) Cited Ref Sci
(c) 1997 Inst for Sci Info. All rts. reserv.

15291357   Genuine Article#: VX309   Number of References: 19
Title: DISPLACEMENT OF ONE NEWTONIAN FLUID BY ANOTHER - DENSITY
EFFECTS IN
   AXIAL ANNULAR-FLOW
Author(s): SZABO P; HASSAGER O
Corporate Source: TECH UNIV DENMARK,DEPT CHEM ENGN/DK-2800
LYNGBY//DENMARK/
Journal: INTERNATIONAL JOURNAL OF MULTIPHASE FLOW, 1997, V23, N1
(FEB), P
   113-129
ISSN: 0301-9322
Language: ENGLISH   Document Type: ARTICLE
Geographic Location: DENMARK
Subfile: SciSearch; CC ENGI--Current Contents, Engineering, Technology &
   Applied Sciences
Journal Subject Category: MECHANICS
Abstract: The arbitrary Lagrange-Euler (ALE) finite element technique is
   used to simulate 3-D displacement of two immiscible Newtonian fluids in
   vertical annular welts. For equally viscous fluids the effect of
   distinct fluid densities is investigated in the region of low to
   intermediate Reynolds numbers. Comparison with a simple theory for
   drainage of thin films is performed. It is found that recirculations
   deform the fluid-fluid interface significantly in situations dominated
   by buoyancy forces. Also, a deviation from the concentric annular
   geometry is shown to induce azimuthal transport of fluid. Finally, the
   efficiency of the displacement is analysed for Various flow situation.

Figure 2.5   concluded

3/7/1
DIALOG(R)File 434:Scisearch(R) Cited Ref Sci
(c) 1997 Inst for Sci Info. All rts. reserv.

13177899   Genuine Article#: NV138   Number of References: 21
Title: THE APM GALAXY SURVEY .4. REDSHIFTS OF RICH CLUSTERS OF
GALAXIES
Author(s): DALTON GB; EFSTATHIOU G; MADDOX SJ; SUTHERLAND WJ
Corporate Source: UNIV OXFORD,DEPT PHYS,KEBLE RD/OXFORD OX1
3RH//ENGLAND/
Journal: MONTHLY NOTICES OF THE ROYAL ASTRONOMICAL SOCIETY,
1994, V269, N1
 (JUL 1), P151-165
ISSN: 0035-8711
Language: ENGLISH   Document Type: ARTICLE
Abstract: present redshifts for a sample of 228 clusters selected from the
    APM Galaxy Survey, 188 of which are new redshift determinations.
    Redshifts are listed for 365 galaxies, and non-cluster galaxy redshifts
    have been rejected from this sample using a likelihood ratio test based
    on the projected and apparent magnitude distributions of each cluster
    region. We test this technique using clusters for which redshifts have
    been measured for more than 10 galaxies. Our redshift sample is nearly
    complete and has been used in previous papers to study the
    three-dimensional distribution of rich clusters of galaxies. 156 of the
    clusters in our sample are listed in the Abell catalogue or supplement,
    and the remainder are new cluster identifications.
?e cr=dalton gb, 1994

Ref   Items   Index-term
E1   1   CR=DALTON GB, 1992, V399, L1, APJ
E2   1   CR=DALTON GB, 1993, V390, L1, APJ
E3   0   *CR=DALTON GB, 1994
E4   1   CR=DALTON GB, 1994, V263, P151, MNRAS
E5   1   CR=DALTON GB, 1994, V269, P151, MNRAS
E6   16   CR=DALTON GB, 1994, V269, P151, MON NOT R ASTRON
E7   1   CR=DALTON GB, 1994, V271, L47, APJ
E8   1   CR=DALTON GB, 1994, V271, L47, MNRAS
E9   13   CR=DALTON GB, 1994, V271, L47, MON NOT R ASTRON S
E10   6   CR=DALTON GB, 1994, V271, PL47, MON NOT R ASTRON
E11   1   CR=DALTON GB, 1995, IN PRESS MNRAS
E12   1   CR=DALTON GB, 1995, V273, PD258, MNRAS

      Enter P or PAGE for more
?s e4,e5,e6

      1   CR=DALTON GB, 1994, V263, P151, MNRAS
      1   CR=DALTON GB, 1994, V269, P151, MNRAS
   16   CR=DALTON GB, 1994, V269, P151, MON NOT R ASTRON
S4   18   E4,E5,E6

Figure 2.6   **Following developments to a publication on galactic clusters**

?t4/7/1-18

4/7/15
DIALOG(R)File 434:Scisearch(R) Cited Ref Sci
(c) 1997 Inst for Sci Info. All rts. reserv.

14107294   Genuine Article#: RQ441   Number of References: 3
Title: ABELL IDENTIFICATIONS OF APM CLUSTERS OF GALAXIES
Author(s): EBELING H; MADDOX SJ
Corporate Source: INST ASTRON,MADINGLEY RD/CAMBRIDGE CB3
0HA//ENGLAND/;
    ROYAL GREENWICH OBSERV/CAMBRIDGE CB3 0EZ//ENGLAND/
Journal: MONTHLY NOTICES OF THE ROYAL ASTRONOMICAL SOCIETY,
1995, V275, N4
 (AUG 15), P1155-1159
ISSN: 0035-8711
Language: ENGLISH   Document Type: ARTICLE
Abstract: We present identifications of Abell/ACO clusters of galaxies with
    APM clusters using the metric separation between the APM clusters'
    coordinates and the nominal Abell cluster positions at both the APM and
    the (measured or estimated) Abell cluster redshift. Wherever available,
    we also take into account the positions of the APM galaxies which have
    redshift measurements. Finally, chance alignments of physically
    unrelated APM and ACO clusters at discordant redshifts are removed
    after inspection of the corresponding optical UK Schmidt plates.

    Our compilation contains only truly physical identifications, and
    so supersedes the identifications listed by Dalton et al. and also
    their subsequent erratum, which both contain a significant fraction of
    chance coincidences between clusters at different distances that appear
    close together in projection on the sky.

4/7/17
DIALOG(R)File 434:Scisearch(R) Cited Ref Sci
(c) 1997 Inst for Sci Info. All rts. reserv.

13770284   Genuine Article#: QP149   Number of References: 1
Title: THE APM GALAXY SURVEY .4. REDSHIFTS OF RICH CLUSTERS OF
GALAXIES
    (VOL 269, PG 151, 1994)
Author(s): DALTON GB; EFSTATHIOU G; MADDOX SJ; SUTHERLAND WJ
Journal: MONTHLY NOTICES OF THE ROYAL ASTRONOMICAL SOCIETY,
1995, V273, N2
 (MAR 15), P528
ISSN: 0035-8711
Language: ENGLISH   Document Type: CORRECTION, ADDITION

Figure 2.6   concluded

second describes an application. Figure 2.6 shows a citation search on a paper
dealing with galactic clusters; there are 18 citing references (note the variant forms

of citation, requiring care in selecting from the index expansion), mostly dealing with related studies. Numbers 17 and 15, which are shown, are respectively a note by the original authors presenting additions and corrections to the original work, and a further paper presenting results apparently superseding both of these.

To identify the latest developments in a topic

Citation databases, by their very nature, lead the searcher forward in time, from older publications to more recent. It is a useful way of acquainting oneself with new developments in a subject area, provided only that the topic can be associated with one or more key documents to be used as starting-points for citation searching.

These key documents may be books (particularly in the humanities and social sciences), classic journal articles (often the first substantial article to deal with a topic) or review articles. The latter have a particularly significant status for citation searching, since they not only provide many references but are themselves cited relatively frequently, since a reference to a review article encapsulates and summarizes a large volume of literature. Reviews and surveys of progress are therefore good starting-points for citation searches to find the latest developments.

An example is given in Figure 2.7. A citation search is carried out on a review article dealing with musculo-skeletal problems resulting from work with visual display units. The eight citing references provide an overview of more recent developments in various aspects of this general topic.

13476699   Genuine Article#: PP968   Number of References: 81
Title: MUSCULOSKELETAL PROBLEMS IN VDT WORK - A REVIEW
Author(s): CARTER JB; BANISTER EW
Corporate Source: SIMON FRASER UNIV,SCH KINESIOL,INST HUMAN
      PERFORMANCE/BURNABY V5A 1S6/BC/CANADA/
Journal: ERGONOMICS, 1994, V37, N10 (OCT), P1623-1648
ISSN: 0014-0139
Language: ENGLISH   Document Type: ARTICLE
Abstract: This paper discusses the possible causes of musculoskeletal pain
   in VDT workers and outlines strategies to minimize it. The paper
   reviews workstation, chair, and keyboard design, and makes
   recommendations to improve user comfort. Also discussed is worker
   selection, training, posture, conditioning, and rest breaks. Short
   term musculoskeletal discomfort is experienced by many VDT operators in
   the telecommunications industry and chronic disability may result in
   the long term. It is important that the ergonomist and office manager
   work together to improve the working conditions in this important
   occupational area.
?e cr=carter jb, 1994

Figure 2.7   Identifying the latest developments

```
Ref   Items  Index-term
E1       1   CR=CARTER JB, 1993, V11, P1302, J VAC SCI TECHNOL
E2       1   CR=CARTER JB, 1993, V4, P1301, J VAC SCI TECHNOL
E3       0   *CR=CARTER JB, 1994
E4       1   CR=CARTER JB, 1994, ACM T COMPUTER SYSTE
E5       1   CR=CARTER JB, 1994, P152, P 13 ACM SIGOPS S OP
E6       8   CR=CARTER JB, 1994, V37, P1623, ERGONOMICS
E7       1   CR=CARTER JB, 1995, ACM TOCS AUG
E8       1   CR=CARTER JB, 1995, P 5 WORKSH HOT TOP O
E9       1   CR=CARTER JB, 1995, P171, P 5 ANN S INJ PREV B
E10      6   CR=CARTER JB, 1995, V13, P205, ACM T COMPUT SYST
E11      1   CR=CARTER JB, 1995, V29, P219, J PARALLEL DISTR C
E12      3   CR=CARTER JBH, 1970, THESIS U READING

       Enter P or PAGE for more
?s e6

     S5      8  CR="CARTER JB, 1994, V37, P1623, ERGONOMICS"
?t5/7/1-8


   5/7/1
DIALOG(R)File 434:Scisearch(R) Cited Ref Sci
(c) 1997 Inst for Sci Info. All rts. reserv.
```

16069184   Genuine Article#: YB033   Number of References: 41
Title: Musculoskeletal complaints in the Netherlands in relation to age,
   gender and physically demanding work
Author(s): deZwart BCH (REPRINT) ; Broersen JPJ; FringsDresen MHW; vanDijk
   FJH
Corporate Source: UNIV AMSTERDAM,ACAD MED CTR, CORONEL INST OCCUPAT &
   ENVIRONM HLTH, MEIBERGDREEF 15/NL-1105 AZ AMSTERDAM//NETHERLANDS/
   (REPRINT)
Journal: INTERNATIONAL ARCHIVES OF OCCUPATIONAL AND ENVIRONMENTAL
HEALTH,
   1997, V70, N5 (NOV), P352-360
ISSN: 0340-0131   Publication date: 19971100
Publisher: SPRINGER VERLAG, 175 FIFTH AVE, NEW YORK, NY 10010
Language: English   Document Type: ARTICLE
Abstract: Objectives: This cross-sectional study was performed in order to
   elucidate the relationship of musculoskeletal complaints with age,
   gender and physically demanding work in the Netherlands.

   Methods: Questionnaire data of male (n = 36756) and female (n =
   7730) employees, gathered as part of periodical occupational health
   surveys among active workers in the Netherlands, were stratified for
   age, gender, and type of work demands. For each stratified group
   prevalence rates (PR) were calculated for complaints of the back, neck,
   upper and lower extremities. Moreover, prevalence rate differences
   (PRD) were estimated as an absolute effect measure of exposure to
   various types of physical work demands, with active employees in
   mentally demanding work acting as a reference population.

Figure 2.7   cont'd

Results: Musculoskeletal complaints among workers in physically demanding occupations were found to increase with age for both sexes. For several complaints, substantially higher rates were reported for women than for men, with a relatively high number of complaints observed among the older female workers (around 40% for complaints of back, upper and lower extremities). Significant PRDs were present in particular for employees in heavy physically demanding occupations and in jobs with mixed mental and physical work demands.

Conclusions: With the ageing of the workforce in mind, these findings stress the need for implementation of preventive measures. Special attention towards the susceptible group of female employees, the elderly age groups in particular, seems justified. In order to clarify the combined effects of age and physical work demands on musculoskeletal complaints, additional studies are required.

5/7/2
DIALOG(R)File 434:Scisearch(R) Cited Ref Sci
(c) 1997 Inst for Sci Info. All rts. reserv.

15910993   Genuine Article#: XQ791   Number of References: 54
Title: Cumulative trauma disorders in the upper extremities: Reliability of
    the postural and repetitive risk-factors index
Author(s): James CPA; Harburn KL (REPRINT) ; Kramer JF
Corporate Source: UNIV WESTERN ONTARIO,SCH OCCUPAT THERAPY, ELBORN
    COLL/LONDON/ON N6G 1H1/CANADA/ (REPRINT); UNIV WESTERN ONTARIO,SCH
    OCCUPAT THERAPY, ELBORN COLL/LONDON/ON N6G 1H1/CANADA/; UNIV
WESTERN
    ONTARIO,SCH PHYS THERAPY, ELBORN COLL/LONDON/ON N6G 1H1/CANADA/
Journal: ARCHIVES OF PHYSICAL MEDICINE AND REHABILITATION, 1997, V78, N8 (
    AUG), P860-866
ISSN: 0003-9993   Publication date: 19970800
Publisher: W B SAUNDERS CO, INDEPENDENCE SQUARE WEST CURTIS CENTER, STE
    300, PHILADELPHIA, PA 19106-3399
Language: English   Document Type: ARTICLE
Abstract: Objective: This study addresses test-retest reliability of the
    Postural and Repetitive Risk-Factors Index (PRRI) for work-related
    upper body injuries. This assessment was developed by the present
    authors.

    Design: A repeated measures design was used to assess the
test-retest reliability of a videotaped work-site assessment of
subjects' movements.

    Subjects: Ten heavy users of video display terminals (VDTs) from a
local banking industry participated in the study.

    Setting: The 10 subjects' movements were videotaped for 2 hours on
each of 2 separate days, while working on-site at their VDTs.

Figure 2.7   cont'd

Main Outcome Measure: The videotaped assessment which utilized known postural risk factors for developing musculoskeletal disorder, pain, and discomfort in heavy VDT users (ie, repetitiveness, awkward and static postures, and contraction time), was called the PRRI. The videotaped movement assessments were subsequently analyzed in 15-minute sessions (five sessions per 2-hour videotape, which produced a total of 10 sessions over the 2 testing days), and each session was chosen randomly from the videotape. The subjects' movements were given a postural risk score according to the criteria in the PRRI. Each subject was therefore tested a total of 10 times (ie, 10 sessions), over two days. The maximum PRRI score for both sides of the body was 216 points.

Results: Reliability coefficients (RCs) for the PRRI scores were calculated, and the reliability of any one session met the minimum criterion for excellent reliability, which was .75. A two-way analysis of variance (ANOVA) confirmed that there was no statistically significant difference between sessions (p <.05). Calculations using the standard error of measurement (SEM) indicated that an individual tested once, on one day and with a PRRI score of 25, required a change of at least 8 points in order to be confident that a true change in score had occurred. The significant results from the reliability tests indicated that the PRRI was a reliable measurement tool that could be used by occupational health practitioners on the job site. (C) 1997 by the American Congress of Rehabilitation Medicine and the American Academy of Physical Medicine and Rehabilitation.

5/7/3
DIALOG(R)File 434:Scisearch(R) Cited Ref Sci
(c) 1997 Inst for Sci Info. All rts. reserv.

15791711   Genuine Article#: XG649   Number of References: 24
Title: Team-managed rest breaks during computer-supported cooperative work
Author(s): Henning RA (REPRINT) ; Bopp MI; Tucker KM; Knoph RD; Ahlgren J
Corporate Source: UNIV CONNECTICUT,DEPT PSYCHOL/STORRS//CT/06269 (REPRINT)
Journal: INTERNATIONAL JOURNAL OF INDUSTRIAL ERGONOMICS, 1997, V20, N1 (JUL), P19-29
ISSN: 0169-8141   Publication date: 19970700
Publisher: ELSEVIER SCIENCE BV, PO BOX 211, 1000 AE AMSTERDAM, NETHERLANDS
Language: English   Document Type: ARTICLE
Abstract: Team management of frequent, discretionary rest breaks was tested as an alternative to forced rest breaks. Two-person work teams (N=30) performed a cooperative computer mediated task for 46 min under laboratory conditions. Teams were instructed to take 1 min of discretionary break time for every 10 min of work. Forced breaks were administered whenever discretionary breaks were insufficient. In the parallel condition, both team members received feedback about their discretionary break behavior. In the serial condition, only one team member received feedback. In the control condition, neither team member received feedback. Team measures of break management, work performance, user acceptance, musculoskeletal discomfort, mood, and

Figure 2.7   cont'd

psychophysiological response were collected. As expected, teams that received feedback in the parallel and serial conditions managed discretionary breaks better than controls. While teams reported more comfortable working relationships in the serial condition than in the parallel condition (strong trend), they also showed trends for increased impatience and lower productivity. Musculoskeletal discomfort and psychophysiological responses were unaffected. These results indicate that computer-generated feedback information can help two-person work teams manage discretionary rest break behavior. Trends suggest that the parallel mode of rest break management can benefit productivity and lower impatience but may increase the demand for work coordination.

5/7/4
DIALOG(R)File 434:Scisearch(R) Cited Ref Sci
(c) 1997 Inst for Sci Info. All rts. reserv.

15347260   Genuine Article#: WB219   Number of References: 24
Title: FREQUENT SHORT REST BREAKS FROM COMPUTER-WORK - EFFECTS ON
    PRODUCTIVITY AND WELL-BEING AT 2 FIELD SITES
Author(s): HENNING RA; JACQUES P; KISSEL GV; SULLIVAN AB; ALTERASWEBB SM
Corporate Source: UNIV CONNECTICUT,DEPT PSYCHOL/STORRS//CT/06269
Journal: ERGONOMICS, 1997, V40, N1 (JAN), P78-91
ISSN: 0014-0139
Language: ENGLISH   Document Type: ARTICLE
Abstract: Computer operators at two work sites (n = 73, n = 19) were
    prompted to take three 30-s and one 3-min break from computer work each
    hour in addition to conventional rest breaks. Some operators were asked
    to perform stretching exercises during the short breaks. Mood state and
    musculoskeletal discomfort were assessed at each work site over a 2- or
    3-week baseline period and a 4- or 6-week treatment period,
    respectively. Operator productivity measures were obtained from company
    records. Operators complied with about half of the added breaks but
    favoured 3-min breaks over 30-s breaks. No improvement in productivity
    or well-being was found at the larger work site. At the smaller work
    site, productivity, eye, leg and foot comfort all improved when the
    short breaks included stretching exercises. These results provide
    evidence that frequent short breaks from continuous computer-mediated
    work can benefit worker productivity and well-being when the breaks
    integrate with task demands.

5/7/5
DIALOG(R)File 434:Scisearch(R) Cited Ref Sci
(c) 1997 Inst for Sci Info. All rts. reserv.

15142087   Genuine Article#: VL802   Number of References: 21
Title: EFFECTS OF KEY STIFFNESS ON FORCE AND THE DEVELOPMENT OF
      FATIGUE WHILE TYPING
Author(s): GERARD MJ; ARMSTRONG TJ; FOULKE JA; MARTIN BJ

Figure 2.7   **cont'd**

Corporate Source: UNIV MICHIGAN,CTR ERGON/ANN ARBOR//MI/48109
Journal: AMERICAN INDUSTRIAL HYGIENE ASSOCIATION JOURNAL, 1996, V57, N9 (
    SEP), P849-854
ISSN: 0002-8894
Language: ENGLISH   Document Type: ARTICLE
Abstract: An experiment was conducted to investigate the effect of key
    stiffness on the development of fatigue, keyboard reaction forces, and
    muscle electromyography (EMG) responses. Six subjects typed
    continuously for 2 hours on each of two keyboards (0.28 N or 0.83 N
    resistance keys, presented in random order). Keyboard reaction force
    and root mean square finger flexor and extensor EMG were recorded for 2
    minutes at 250 Hz for every 10 minutes subjects typed. After typing for
    2 hours subjects were given a 2-hour rest break and then typed on the
    remaining keyboard for an additional 2 hours. Fifty-four percent more
    peak force, 34% more peak finger flexor EMG, and 2% more peak finger
    extensor EMG were exerted while using the 0.83 N keyboard. Peak and
    90th percentile values showed similar trends and were well correlated
    for force and finger flexor and extensor EMG. Subjects typed much
    harder than necessary (4.1 to 7.0 times harder on the 0.28 N keyboard
    and 2.2 to 3.5 times harder on the 0.83 N keyboard) to activate the
    keys. Fatigue was observed on the 0.83 N keyboard during 2 hours of
    continuous typing, but the trends were mild. It appears that the ratio
    of typing force to flexor EMG may not be a sensitive enough indicator
    of fatigue for low-force high repetition work.

    5/7/6
DIALOG(R)File 434:Scisearch(R) Cited Ref Sci
(c) 1997 Inst for Sci Info. All rts. reserv.

15022186   Genuine Article#: VD101   Number of References: 22
Title: CONTINUOUS FEEDBACK TO PROMOTE SELF-MANAGEMENT OF REST
BREAKS DURING
    COMPUTER USE
Author(s): HENNING RA; CALLAGHAN EA; ORTEGA AM; KISSEL GV; GUTTMAN JI;
    BRAUN HA
Corporate Source: UNIV CONNECTICUT,DEPT PSYCHOL/STORRS//CT/06269
Journal: INTERNATIONAL JOURNAL OF INDUSTRIAL ERGONOMICS, 1996, V18, N1 (JUL
    ), P71-82
ISSN: 0169-8141
Language: ENGLISH   Document Type: ARTICLE
Abstract: Short rest breaks at regular intervals can reduce musculoskeletal
    discomfort and the risk of repetitive strain injury during intensive
    computer work, but may seriously disrupt some tasks. As an alternative,
    two laboratory experiments tested if application of ergonomic
    principles of feedback control could improve worker self-management of
    discretionary rest breaks. Undergraduate typists (N = 31, N = 30)
    entered lines of randomized words for about 1 h. Typists received
    scheduled breaks unless their discretionary breaks reached a target
    level of 30 s every 10 min. Typists in treatment conditions received
    continuous feedback indicating how their discretionary breaks compared

Figure 2.7   cont'd

to the target level, but typists in control conditions did not.
Feedback in one experiment was task-integrated to reduce distractions.
Typists in the feedback conditions controlled discretionary breaks
better than controls, and also responded favorably to the continuous
feedback. Typists receiving task-integrated feedback reported less task
disruption and back discomfort than controls. Mood and cardiac response
were unaffected in both studies, but error rates were lower in the
feedback condition of one experiment. These results indicate that
computer users can utilize continuous feedback about rest break
behavior to improve self management of discretionary rest breaks, with
no untoward effects on performance, well-being, or user acceptance.

5/7/7
DIALOG(R)File 434:Scisearch(R) Cited Ref Sci
(c) 1997 Inst for Sci Info. All rts. reserv.

14813840   Genuine Article#: UN331   Number of References: 14
Title: ANALYSIS OF OCULAR SURFACE-AREA FOR COMFORTABLE VDT WORKSTATION
   LAYOUT
Author(s): SOTOYAMA M; JONAI H; SAITO S; VILLANUEVA MBG
Corporate Source: NAGOYA UNIV,SCH MED,SHOWA KU,65 TSURUMAI
CHO/NAGOYA/AICHI
   466/JAPAN/
Journal: ERGONOMICS, 1996, V39, N6 (JUN), P877-884
ISSN: 0014-0139
Language: ENGLISH   Document Type: ARTICLE
Abstract: This paper proposes a comfortable visual display terminal (VDT)
   workstation layout based on an analysis of ocular surface area (OSA). A
   large OSA induces eye irritation and eye fatigue because the eye
   surface is highly sensitive to various stimuli. The authors considered
   that OSA must be one of the useful indices of visual ergonomics and
   applied it to evaluate VDT workstation layout. Each subject was asked
   to perform a word processing task using four different VDT workstation
   layouts. It was found that the main factor affecting OSA was not
   cathode ray tube (CRT) height itself but the distance between the CRT
   and keyboard. Thus the following workstation layout is recommended to
   realize comfortable VDT operation:
      (1) the desk height should be adjusted to the user's height; and

      (2) the CRT display should be set closer to the keyboard to provide
   a smaller OSA.

5/7/8
DIALOG(R)File 434:Scisearch(R) Cited Ref Sci
(c) 1997 Inst for Sci Info. All rts. reserv.

14418332   Genuine Article#: TL129   Number of References: 23
Title: COMPUTER MOUSE USE AND CUMULATIVE TRAUMA DISORDERS OF THE UPPER
   EXTREMITIES

Figure 2.7   cont'd

Author(s): FOGLEMAN M; BROGMUS G
Corporate Source: LIBERTY MUTUAL RES CTR SAFETY & HLTH,71 FRANKLAND
    RD/HOPKINTON//MA/01748; LIBERTY MUTUAL RES CTR SAFETY &
    HLTH/HOPKINTON//MA/01748
Journal: ERGONOMICS, 1995, V38, N12 (DEC), P2465-2475
ISSN: 0014-0139
Language: ENGLISH   Document Type: ARTICLE
Abstract: The computer mouse is now present in virtually every office
    environment because of the recent adoption of the graphical user
    interface. However, Karlqvist et al. (1994) pointed out that there
    still remains a paucity of work on the musculoskeletal problems
    associated specifically with computer mouse use. Likewise, there have
    been no published data on the magnitude of upper extremity
    musculoskeletal disorders associated with computer mouse use. In order
    to ascertain this magnitude, claims data from the Liberty Mutual Group
    were reviewed for the years 1986 to 1993, inclusive. Count, total cost
    and average cost per claim for all claims associated with computer use
    and computer mouse use were determined for the years in question. It
    was concluded that although there are few claims related to computer
    mouse use, it appears to be a growing problem, and therefore, perhaps,
    deserves more research and intervention attention. However, the present
    magnitude is less than for other musculoskeletal disorders.
?

Figure 2.7   concluded

It should be noted that, because of vagaries of citation practice, searches of this sort are not likely to be comprehensive, particularly if only one starting-point document is used. However, this method is a good way of obtaining a quick overview and would form an important part of a comprehensive search strategy.

To find applications of techniques and methods

Finding information on applications of methods – scientific laboratory procedures, statistical analysis techniques, use of software packages, psychological profiling techniques and management techniques, to give just a few examples – is generally difficult. Unless the technique is a central topic within a document, which will not usually be the case, it will not be mentioned in the title, and probably not the abstract, nor will it be indexed by secondary services. However, it is usual for a reference to be given whenever a specific technique or procedure is mentioned; the reference may be to a research paper describing the technique, or perhaps to a supplier's documentation. If there is a 'standard' document which is usually referenced, then a citation database search can hope to provide a reasonably complete bibliography of applications which would be virtually impossible to find in any other way.

An example is shown in Figure 2.8, based on a citation search on R. M. Belbin's well-known book on team roles. The 45 references found (note the varied forms

```
?e cr=belbin rm, 1980


Ref   Items  Index-term
E1       1   CR=BELBIN RM, 1976, PRACTITIONERS GUIDE
E2       1   CR=BELBIN RM, 1976, V3, P23, J GEN MANAGE
E3       0   *CR=BELBIN RM, 1980
E4       6   CR=BELBIN RM, 1981, MANAGEMENT TEAMS
E5       4   CR=BELBIN RM, 1981, MANAGEMENT TEAMS THE
E6      31   CR=BELBIN RM, 1981, MANAGEMENT TEAMS WHY
E7       2   CR=BELBIN RM, 1981, MANAGEMENT TERMS WHY
E8       1   CR=BELBIN RM, 1981, MANGEMENT TEAMS WHY
E9       1   CR=BELBIN RM, 1981, P10, MANAGEMENT TEAMS WHY
E10      1   CR=BELBIN RM, 1983, HDB MANAGEMENT DEV T
E11      1   CR=BELBIN RM, 1983, MANAGEMENT TEAMS WHY
E12      4   CR=BELBIN RM, 1993, TEAM ROLES WORK

        Enter P or PAGE for more
?p


Ref   Items  Index-term
E13      5   CR=BELBIN RM, 1993, V66, P259, J OCCUP ORGAN PSYC
E14      1   CR=BELBIN RM, 1994, INTERPLACE 4 HUMAN R
E15      1   CR=BELBIN RM, 1996, MANAGEMENT TEAMS WHY
E16      1   CR=BELBIN, 1950, V2, P163, Q J EXP PSYCHOL
E17      1   CR=BELBIN, 1969, P32, IND GERONTOLOGY OCT
E18      1   CR=BELBIN, 1979, V32, B BR PSYCHO
E19      1   CR=BELBOT B, 1995, UNPUB ASSESSING CURR
E20      2   CR=BELBOT BA, 1991, V37, P135, CRIME DELINQUENCY
E21      1   CR=BELBY J, 1987, P415, UFAW HDB CARE MANAGE
E22      1   CR=BELC, 1977, DOC OR BRUT DANS CLA
E23      1   CR=BELCAMP JV, 1651, P13, CONSILIUM VOTUM PRO
E24      1   CR=BELCARI P, 1974, V237, P371, J PHYSL LON

        Enter P or PAGE for more
?s e4e8,-e8,

?s e4-e9


       6   CR=BELBIN RM, 1981, MANAGEMENT TEAMS
       4   CR=BELBIN RM, 1981, MANAGEMENT TEAMS THE
      31   CR=BELBIN RM, 1981, MANAGEMENT TEAMS WHY
       2   CR=BELBIN RM, 1981, MANAGEMENT TERMS WHY
       1   CR=BELBIN RM, 1981, MANAGEMENT TEAMS WHY
       1   CR=BELBIN RM, 1981, P10, MANAGEMENT TEAMS WHY
   S1  45   E4-E9
?t1/6/t1/3/1-45
```

Figure 2.8   Finding applications of techniques

1/3/1
DIALOG(R)File   7:Social SciSearch(R)

03087337   GENUINE ARTICLE#: XU521   NO. REFERENCES: 29
TITLE: Team roles and team performance: Is there 'really' a link?
AUTHOR(S): Senior B
CORPORATE SOURCE: NENE COLL HIGHER EDUC,PK
CAMPUS/NORTHAMPTON NN2
    7AL//ENGLAND/ (REPRINT)
JOURNAL: JOURNAL OF OCCUPATIONAL AND ORGANIZATIONAL
PSYCHOLOGY, 1997, V70,
    ,3 (SEP), P241-258
PUBLISHER: BRITISH PSYCHOLOGICAL SOC, ST ANDREWS HOUSE, 48
PRINCESS RD
    EAST, LEICESTER, LEICS, ENGLAND LE1 7DR
ISSN: 0963-1798
LANGUAGE: English   DOCUMENT TYPE: Article (ABSTRACT AVAILABLE)

1/3/2
DIALOG(R)File   7:Social SciSearch(R)

03082077   GENUINE ARTICLE#: XQ947   NO. REFERENCES: 36
TITLE: A case study of strategic engineering decision making using
    judgmental modeling and psychological profiling
AUTHOR(S): Naude P; Lockett G; Holmes K
CORPORATE SOURCE: MANCHESTER BUSINESS SCH,/MANCHESTER M15
    6PB/LANCS/ENGLAND/ (REPRINT); UNIV LEEDS,SCH BUSINESS & ECON
    STUDIES/LEEDS LS2 9JT/W YORKSHIRE/ENGLAND/
JOURNAL: IEEE TRANSACTIONS ON ENGINEERING MANAGEMENT, 1997,
V44, N3 (AUG)
, P237-247
PUBLISHER: IEEE-INST ELECTRICAL ELECTRONICS ENGINEERS INC, 345 E
47TH ST,
    NEW YORK, NY 10017-2394
ISSN: 0018-9391
LANGUAGE: English   DOCUMENT TYPE: Article (ABSTRACT AVAILABLE)

1/3/3
DIALOG(R)File   7:Social SciSearch(R)

02984900   GENUINE ARTICLE#: VY188   NO. REFERENCES: 28
TITLE: An assessment of the construct validity of the Belbin
    Self-Perception Inventory and observer's assessment from the
    perspective of the five-factor model
AUTHOR(S): Broucek WG; Randell G
CORPORATE SOURCE: HURON UNIV,SCH BUSINESS, 333 9TH ST

Figure 2.8   cont'd

SW/HURON//SD/57350
   (REPRINT); UNIV BRADFORD,CTR MANAGEMENT/BRADFORD BD7 1DP/W
   YORKSHIRE/ENGLAND/
JOURNAL: JOURNAL OF OCCUPATIONAL AND ORGANIZATIONAL
PSYCHOLOGY, 1996, V69,
   ,4 (DEC), P389-405
PUBLISHER: BRITISH PSYCHOLOGICAL SOC, ST ANDREWS HOUSE, 48
PRINCESS RD
   EAST, LEICESTER, LEICS, ENGLAND LE1 7DR
ISSN: 0963-1798
LANGUAGE: English   DOCUMENT TYPE: Article (ABSTRACT AVAILABLE)

   1/3/4
DIALOG(R)File   7:Social SciSearch(R)
(c) 1997 Inst for Sci Info. All rts. reserv.

02929722   GENUINE ARTICLE#: VA527   NO. REFERENCES: 39
TITLE: LEARNING IN SMALL-GROUPS IN UNIVERSITY GEOGRAPHY
COURSES - DESIGNING
   A CORE MODULE AROUND GROUP PROJECTS
AUTHOR(S): HEALEY M; MATTHEWS H; LIVINGSTONE I; FOSTER I
CORPORATE SOURCE: CHELTENHAM & GLOUCESTER COLL HIGHER
EDUC,DEPT GEOG &
   GEOL,FRANCIS CLOSE HALL,SWINDON RD/CHELTENHAM GL50
4AZ/GLOS/ENGLAND/;
   NENE COLL HIGHER EDUC/NORTHAMPTON//ENGLAND/; COVENTRY
UNIV/COVENTRY/W
   MIDLANDS/ENGLAND/
JOURNAL: JOURNAL OF GEOGRAPHY IN HIGHER EDUCATION, 1996, V20, N2
(JUL), P
   167-180
ISSN: 0309-8265
LANGUAGE: ENGLISH   DOCUMENT TYPE: ARTICLE (Abstract Available)

   1/3/5
DIALOG(R)File   7:Social SciSearch(R)
(c) 1997 Inst for Sci Info. All rts. reserv.

02926715   GENUINE ARTICLE#: UZ537   NO. REFERENCES: 31
TITLE: NETWORKING FOR TRUST IN TRIBAL ORGANIZATIONS
AUTHOR(S): MCMURDO G
CORPORATE SOURCE: QUEEN MARGARET COLL,DEPT COMMUN &
INFORMAT
   STUDIES,CLERWOOD TERRACE/EDINBURGH EH12
8TS/MIDLOTHIAN/SCOTLAND/
JOURNAL: JOURNAL OF INFORMATION SCIENCE, 1996, V22, N4, P299-314
ISSN: 0165-5515
LANGUAGE: ENGLISH   DOCUMENT TYPE: ARTICLE (Abstract Available)

Figure 2.8   cont'd

1/3/6
DIALOG(R)File   7:Social SciSearch(R)
(c) 1997 Inst for Sci Info. All rts. reserv.

02915015   GENUINE ARTICLE#: UU058   NO. REFERENCES: 4
TITLE: SOURCE AND SURFACE TRAITS - STRUCTURE AND
INTERPRETATION
AUTHOR(S): TYLER B
CORPORATE SOURCE: MILLER & TYLER LTD,PSYCHOL ASSESSMENT &
COUNSELING,96
   GREENWAY/LONDON N20 8EJ//ENGLAND/
JOURNAL: EUROPEAN REVIEW OF APPLIED PSYCHOLOGY-REVUE
EUROPEENNE DE
   PSYCHOLOGIE APPLIQUEE, 1996, V46, N1, P57-63
ISSN: 1162-9088
LANGUAGE: ENGLISH   DOCUMENT TYPE: ARTICLE (Abstract Available)

1/3/7
DIALOG(R)File   7:Social SciSearch(R)
(c) 1997 Inst for Sci Info. All rts. reserv.

02907196   GENUINE ARTICLE#: UQ423   NO. REFERENCES: 18
TITLE: RESEARCH UNIT ON WORK AND ORGANIZATIONAL-PSYCHOLOGY
(WORK AND
   ORGANIZATION RESEARCH-CENTER), TILBURG-UNIVERSITY, THE
NETHERLANDS
AUTHOR(S): VANDENBERG PT; ROE RA; SCHALK R; TAILLIEU T; ZIJLSTRA F
CORPORATE SOURCE: TILBURG UNIV,DEPT WORK & ORG PSYCHOL,POB
90153/5000 LE
   TILBURG//NETHERLANDS/
JOURNAL: INTERNATIONAL JOURNAL OF SELECTION AND ASSESSMENT,
1996, V4, N2 (
   APR), P106-109
ISSN: 0965-075X
LANGUAGE: ENGLISH   DOCUMENT TYPE: ARTICLE

1/3/8
DIALOG(R)File   7:Social SciSearch(R)
(c) 1997 Inst for Sci Info. All rts. reserv.

02884295   GENUINE ARTICLE#: UF627   NO. REFERENCES: 18
TITLE: FURTHER EVIDENCE CONCERNING THE BELBIN TEAM ROLE SELF-
PERCEPTION
   INVENTORY
AUTHOR(S): FISHER SG; MACROSSON WDK; SHARP G
CORPORATE SOURCE: UNIV
STRATHCLYDE/GLASGOW/LANARK/SCOTLAND/
JOURNAL: PERSONNEL REVIEW, 1996, V25, N2, P61&
ISSN: 0048-3486
LANGUAGE: ENGLISH   DOCUMENT TYPE: ARTICLE (Abstract Available)

Figure 2.8   cont'd

1/3/9
DIALOG(R)File   7:Social SciSearch(R)

02883211   GENUINE ARTICLE#: UE976   NO. REFERENCES: 7
TITLE: ORGANIZING STUDENT-CENTERED GROUP FIELDWORK AND
PRESENTATIONS
AUTHOR(S): KNEALE P
CORPORATE SOURCE: UNIV LEEDS,SCH GEOG/LEEDS LS2 9JT/W
YORKSHIRE/ENGLAND/
JOURNAL: JOURNAL OF GEOGRAPHY IN HIGHER EDUCATION, 1996, V20, N1
(MAR), P
   65-74
ISSN: 0309-8265
LANGUAGE: ENGLISH   DOCUMENT TYPE: ARTICLE (Abstract Available)

1/3/10
DIALOG(R)File   7:Social SciSearch(R)

02857496   GENUINE ARTICLE#: TU895   NO. REFERENCES: 60
TITLE: PARTICIPANTS PERCEPTIONS ON THE ROLE OF FACILITATORS
USING GROUP
   DECISION-SUPPORT SYSTEMS
AUTHOR(S): ACKERMANN F
CORPORATE SOURCE: STRATHCLYDE BUSINESS SCH,DEPT MANAGEMENT
SCI,26RICHMOND
   ST/GLASGOW G1 1XH/LANARK/SCOTLAND/
JOURNAL: GROUP DECISION AND NEGOTIATION, 1996, V5, N1 (JAN), P93-112
ISSN: 0926-2644
LANGUAGE: ENGLISH   DOCUMENT TYPE: ARTICLE (Abstract Available)

1/3/11
DIALOG(R)File   7:Social SciSearch(R)

02811767   GENUINE ARTICLE#: RZ984   NO. REFERENCES: 2
TITLE: MEASURING TEAM ROLES
AUTHOR(S): PARKINSON M
JOURNAL: PSYCHOLOGIST, 1995, V8, N10 (OCT), P467
ISSN: 0952-8229
LANGUAGE: ENGLISH   DOCUMENT TYPE: NOTE

1/3/12
DIALOG(R)File   7:Social SciSearch(R)

02792757   GENUINE ARTICLE#: RQ556   NO. REFERENCES: 18

Figure 2.8   cont'd

TITLE: SELECTING FOR DIVERSITY
AUTHOR(S): KANDOLA B
CORPORATE SOURCE: PEARN KANDOLA DOWNS,76 BANBURY RD/OXFORD OX2
  6JT//ENGLAND/
JOURNAL: INTERNATIONAL JOURNAL OF SELECTION AND ASSESSMENT, 1995, V3, N3 (
  JUL), P162-167
ISSN: 0965-075X
LANGUAGE: ENGLISH   DOCUMENT TYPE: ARTICLE (Abstract Available)

  1/3/13
DIALOG(R)File   7:Social SciSearch(R)
(c) 1997 Inst for Sci Info. All rts. reserv.

02763675   GENUINE ARTICLE#: RC678   NO. REFERENCES: 20
TITLE: A VALIDATION OF BELBINS TEAM ROLES FROM 16PF AND OPQ USING BOSSES
  RATINGS OF COMPETENCE
AUTHOR(S): DULEWICZ V
CORPORATE SOURCE: HENLEY MANAGEMENT COLL/HENLEY ON THAMES RG9
  3AU/OXON/ENGLAND/
JOURNAL: JOURNAL OF OCCUPATIONAL AND ORGANIZATIONAL PSYCHOLOGY, 1995, V68,
  JUN (JUN), P81-99
ISSN: 0963-1798
LANGUAGE: ENGLISH   DOCUMENT TYPE: ARTICLE (Abstract Available)

  1/3/14
DIALOG(R)File   7:Social SciSearch(R)
(c) 1997 Inst for Sci Info. All rts. reserv.

02735679   GENUINE ARTICLE#: QR211   NO. REFERENCES: 16
TITLE: A BEHAVIORAL-APPROACH TO THE CONDUCT OF AUDITS OF QUALITY
  MANAGEMENT-SYSTEMS IN CONSTRUCTION APPLICATIONS - A SUMMARY OF
  PSYCHOLOGICAL EFFECTS UPON INDIVIDUALS BEING ASSESSED OR AUDITED
  AGAINST THE REQUIREMENTS OF BS-EN-ISO-9000
AUTHOR(S): GUNNING JG
CORPORATE SOURCE: UNIV ULSTER,SCH BUILT ENVIRONM/BELFAST BT37
  0QB/ANTRIM/NORTH IRELAND/
JOURNAL: BUILDING RESEARCH AND INFORMATION, 1995, V23, N2 (MAR-APR), P
  114-118
ISSN: 0961-3218
LANGUAGE: ENGLISH   DOCUMENT TYPE: ARTICLE (Abstract Available)

Figure 2.8   cont'd

1/3/15
DIALOG(R)File   7:Social SciSearch(R)
(c) 1997 Inst for Sci Info. All rts. reserv.

02700786   GENUINE ARTICLE#: QA404   NO. REFERENCES: 8
TITLE: USING TEAMS EFFECTIVELY
AUTHOR(S): TAGIURI R
CORPORATE SOURCE: HARVARD UNIV,GRAD SCH ENGN SCI,ADV
MANAGEMENT
    PROGRAM/CAMBRIDGE//MA/02138; HARVARD UNIV,GRAD SCH ENGN
SCI,SENIOR
    MANAGERS PROGRAM/CAMBRIDGE//MA/00000; HARVARD UNIV,GRAD
SCH ENGN
    SCI,OWNER MANAGER PROGRAM/CAMBRIDGE//MA/00000
JOURNAL: RESEARCH-TECHNOLOGY MANAGEMENT, 1995, V38, N1 (JAN-
FEB), P12-13
ISSN: 0895-6308
LANGUAGE: ENGLISH   DOCUMENT TYPE: EDITORIAL

1/3/16
DIALOG(R)File   7:Social SciSearch(R)
(c) 1997 Inst for Sci Info. All rts. reserv.

02598419   GENUINE ARTICLE#: NG818   NO. REFERENCES: 17
TITLE: IS YOUR CIO ADDING VALUE
AUTHOR(S): EARL MJ; FEENY DF
CORPORATE SOURCE: LONDON GRAD SCH BUSINESS STUDIES,CTR RES
INFORMAT
    MANAGEMENT/LONDON//ENGLAND/; TEMPLETON COLL,OXFORD INST
INFORMAT
    MANAGEMENT/OXFORD//ENGLAND/
JOURNAL: SLOAN MANAGEMENT REVIEW, 1994, V35, N3 (SPR), P11-20
ISSN: 0019-848X
LANGUAGE: ENGLISH   DOCUMENT TYPE: ARTICLE (Abstract Available)

1/3/17
DIALOG(R)File   7:Social SciSearch(R)
(c) 1997 Inst for Sci Info. All rts. reserv.

02589804   GENUINE ARTICLE#: MY796   NO. REFERENCES: 107
TITLE: A THEORY OF THE VALIDITY OF PREDICTORS IN SELECTION
AUTHOR(S): SMITH M
CORPORATE SOURCE: UNIV MANCHESTER,INST SCI &
TECHNOL,MANCHESTER SCH
    MANAGEMENT/MANCHESTER M60 1QD/LANCS/ENGLAND/
JOURNAL: JOURNAL OF OCCUPATIONAL AND ORGANIZATIONAL
PSYCHOLOGY, 1994, V67,
    MAR (MAR), P13-31
ISSN: 0963-1798
LANGUAGE: ENGLISH   DOCUMENT TYPE: ARTICLE (Abstract Available)

Figure 2.8   cont'd

1/3/18
DIALOG(R)File   7:Social SciSearch(R)
(c) 1997 Inst for Sci Info. All rts. reserv.

02577766   GENUINE ARTICLE#: MT996   NO. REFERENCES: 7
TITLE: GROUP EFFORT AS A METHOD OF CONSTRUCTIVE SOCIOLOGY .2.
AUTHOR(S): MAKAREVICH VN
CORPORATE SOURCE: MOSCOW MV LOMONOSOV STATE UNIV,FAC
SOCIOL/MOSCOW//RUSSIA/
JOURNAL: SOTSIOLOGICHESKIE ISSLEDOVANIYA, 1993, N10, P74-80
ISSN: 0132-1625
LANGUAGE: RUSSIAN   DOCUMENT TYPE: ARTICLE

1/3/19
DIALOG(R)File   7:Social SciSearch(R)
(c) 1997 Inst for Sci Info. All rts. reserv.

02530534   GENUINE ARTICLE#: LV938   NO. REFERENCES: 2
TITLE: A REPLY TO THE BELBIN TEAM-ROLE SELF-PERCEPTION
INVENTORY
AUTHOR(S): BELBIN RM
CORPORATE SOURCE: BELBIN ASSOCIATES,BURLEIGH BUSINESS CTR,52
BURLEIGH
   ST/CAMBRIDGE CB1 1DJ//ENGLAND/
JOURNAL: JOURNAL OF OCCUPATIONAL AND ORGANIZATIONAL
PSYCHOLOGY, 1993, V66,
   SEP (SEP), P259-260
ISSN: 0963-1798
LANGUAGE: ENGLISH   DOCUMENT TYPE: ARTICLE

1/3/20
DIALOG(R)File   7:Social SciSearch(R)
(c) 1997 Inst for Sci Info. All rts. reserv.

02443481   GENUINE ARTICLE#: KG532   NO. REFERENCES: 31
TITLE: UNDERSTANDING THE CEO CIO RELATIONSHIP
AUTHOR(S): FEENY DF; EDWARDS BR; SIMPSON KM
CORPORATE SOURCE: TEMPLETON COLL,OXFORD INST INFORMAT
MANAGEMENT/OXFORD OX1
   5NY//ENGLAND/
JOURNAL: MIS QUARTERLY, 1992, V16, N4 (DEC), P435-448
ISSN: 0276-7783
LANGUAGE: ENGLISH   DOCUMENT TYPE: ARTICLE (Abstract Available)

1/3/21
DIALOG(R)File   7:Social SciSearch(R)
(c) 1997 Inst for Sci Info. All rts. reserv.
02350569   GENUINE ARTICLE#: HP034   NO. REFERENCES: 70

Figure 2.8   cont'd

TITLE: RAPID RURAL APPRAISAL - A PARTICIPATORY PROBLEM
FORMULATION METHOD
    RELEVANT TO AUSTRALIAN AGRICULTURE
AUTHOR(S): ISON RL; AMPT PR
CORPORATE SOURCE: UNIV SYDNEY,SCH CROP SCI/SYDNEY/NSW
2006/AUSTRALIA/
JOURNAL: AGRICULTURAL SYSTEMS, 1992, V38, N4, P363-386
LANGUAGE: ENGLISH   DOCUMENT TYPE: ARTICLE (Abstract Available)

1/3/22
DIALOG(R)File   7:Social SciSearch(R)
(c) 1997 Inst for Sci Info. All rts. reserv.

02278531   GENUINE ARTICLE#: GF525   NO. REFERENCES: 54
TITLE: IVORY TOWER TO CONCRETE JUNGLE - THE DIFFICULT
TRANSITION FROM THE
    ACADEMY TO THE WORKPLACE AS LEARNING ENVIRONMENTS
AUTHOR(S): CANDY PC; CREBERT RG
CORPORATE SOURCE: QUEENSLAND UNIV TECHNOL,ACAD STAFF DEV
UNIT,GARDENS POINT
    CAMPUS/BRISBANE/QLD/AUSTRALIA/
JOURNAL: JOURNAL OF HIGHER EDUCATION, 1991, V62, N5, P570-592
LANGUAGE: ENGLISH   DOCUMENT TYPE: ARTICLE

1/3/23
DIALOG(R)File   7:Social SciSearch(R)
(c) 1997 Inst for Sci Info. All rts. reserv.

02278527   GENUINE ARTICLE#: GF525   NO. REFERENCES: 78
TITLE: THE THINKING TEAM - TOWARD A COGNITIVE MODEL OF
ADMINISTRATIVE
    TEAMWORK IN HIGHER-EDUCATION
AUTHOR(S): NEUMANN A
CORPORATE SOURCE: MICHIGAN STATE UNIV,EDUC ADM/E
LANSING//MI/48824
JOURNAL: JOURNAL OF HIGHER EDUCATION, 1991, V62, N5, P485-513
LANGUAGE: ENGLISH   DOCUMENT TYPE: ARTICLE

1/3/24
DIALOG(R)File   7:Social SciSearch(R)
(c) 1997 Inst for Sci Info. All rts. reserv.

02183459   GENUINE ARTICLE#: EL684   NO. REFERENCES: 83
TITLE: ITALIAN ADAPTERS AND INNOVATORS - IS COGNITIVE-STYLE
UNDERLYING
    CULTURE
AUTHOR(S): PREVIDE GP
CORPORATE SOURCE: UNIV MILAN,FAC MED,IST PSICOL,VIA F SFORZA

Figure 2.8   cont'd

23/I-20122
    MILAN//ITALY/
JOURNAL: PERSONALITY AND INDIVIDUAL DIFFERENCES, 1991, V12, N1,
P1-10
LANGUAGE: ENGLISH   DOCUMENT TYPE: ARTICLE

 1/3/25
DIALOG(R)File   7:Social SciSearch(R)
(c) 1997 Inst for Sci Info. All rts. reserv.

02173205   GENUINE ARTICLE#: EG867   NO. REFERENCES: 21
TITLE: TRAINING PROFESSIONAL LEADERS - THE NEW SCHOOL
MANAGERS
AUTHOR(S): DENNISON WF; SHENTON K
CORPORATE SOURCE: UNIV NEWCASTLE UPON TYNE,SCH
EDUC/NEWCASTLE TYNE NE1
    7RU/TYNE & WEAR/ENGLAND/
JOURNAL: OXFORD REVIEW OF EDUCATION, 1990, V16, N3, P311-320
LANGUAGE: ENGLISH   DOCUMENT TYPE: ARTICLE

 1/3/26
DIALOG(R)File   7:Social SciSearch(R)
(c) 1997 Inst for Sci Info. All rts. reserv.

02157295   GENUINE ARTICLE#: DZ443   NO. REFERENCES: 3
TITLE: MANAGING PEOPLE AT WORK - MAKIN,PJ, COOPER,CL, COX,C
AUTHOR(S): DEVADER CL
CORPORATE SOURCE: LOYOLA COLL MARYLAND,SELLINGER SCH
BUSINESS &
    MANAGEMENT/BALTIMORE//MD/21210
JOURNAL: PERSONNEL PSYCHOLOGY, 1990, V43, N3, P678-681
LANGUAGE: ENGLISH   DOCUMENT TYPE: BOOK REVIEW

 1/3/27
DIALOG(R)File   7:Social SciSearch(R)
(c) 1997 Inst for Sci Info. All rts. reserv.

02118299   GENUINE ARTICLE#: DE521   NO. REFERENCES: 38
TITLE: TEAM BUILDING, INTERAGENCY TEAM DEVELOPMENT AND
SOCIAL-WORK-PRACTICE
AUTHOR(S): ILES P; AULUCK R
CORPORATE SOURCE: OPEN UNIV,OPEN BUSINESS SCH,SCH
MANAGEMENT,WALTON
    HALL/MILTON KEYNES MK7 6AY//ENGLAND/; COVENTRY LANCHESTER
    POLYTECH,SOCIAL WORK/COVENTRY CV1 5FB/W
MIDLANDS/ENGLAND/; COVENTRY
    SOCIAL SERV DEPT/COVENTRY//ENGLAND/
JOURNAL: BRITISH JOURNAL OF SOCIAL WORK, 1990, V20, N2, P151-164
LANGUAGE: ENGLISH   DOCUMENT TYPE: ARTICLE

Figure 2.8   cont'd

1/3/28
DIALOG(R)File   7:Social SciSearch(R)
(c) 1997 Inst for Sci Info. All rts. reserv.

02070140   GENUINE ARTICLE#: CF354   NO. REFERENCES: 152
TITLE: MANAGEMENT DEVELOPMENT - A LITERATURE-REVIEW AND
IMPLICATIONS FOR
   FUTURE-RESEARCH .1. CONCEPTUALISATIONS AND PRACTICES
AUTHOR(S): STOREY J
CORPORATE SOURCE: UNIV WARWICK/COVENTRY CV4 7AL/W
MIDLANDS/ENGLAND/
JOURNAL: PERSONNEL REVIEW, 1989, V18, N6, P3-19
LANGUAGE: ENGLISH   DOCUMENT TYPE: REVIEW

1/3/29
DIALOG(R)File   7:Social SciSearch(R)
(c) 1997 Inst for Sci Info. All rts. reserv.

02021896   GENUINE ARTICLE#: AK844   NO. REFERENCES: 53
TITLE: TOP MANAGEMENT TEAMS AND ORGANIZATIONAL RENEWAL
AUTHOR(S): HURST DK; RUSH JC; WHITE RE
CORPORATE SOURCE: FED IND METALS
GRP/TORONTO/ONTARIO/CANADA/; UNIV WESTERN
   ONTARIO,SCH BUSINESS ADM/LONDON N6A 3K7/ONTARIO/CANADA/
JOURNAL: STRATEGIC MANAGEMENT JOURNAL, 1989, V10, NSI, P87-105
LANGUAGE: ENGLISH   DOCUMENT TYPE: ARTICLE

1/3/30
DIALOG(R)File   7:Social SciSearch(R)
(c) 1997 Inst for Sci Info. All rts. reserv.

02004317   GENUINE ARTICLE#: AA387   NO. REFERENCES: 26
TITLE: HIGHER-EDUCATION, PERSONAL QUALITIES AND EMPLOYMENT -
TEAMWORK
AUTHOR(S): BRADSHAW D
CORPORATE SOURCE: DONCASTER METROPOLITAN INST HIGHER
EDUC/DONCASTER DN1
   3EX/S YORKSHIRE/ENGLAND/
JOURNAL: OXFORD REVIEW OF EDUCATION, 1989, V15, N1, P55-71
LANGUAGE: ENGLISH   DOCUMENT TYPE: ARTICLE

1/3/31
DIALOG(R)File   7:Social SciSearch(R)
(c) 1997 Inst for Sci Info. All rts. reserv.

01953617   GENUINE ARTICLE#: R8354   NO. REFERENCES: 41
TITLE: GROUP INTELLIGENCE - WHY SOME GROUPS ARE BETTER THAN
OTHERS

Figure 2.8   cont'd

AUTHOR(S): WILLIAMS WM; STERNBERG RJ
CORPORATE SOURCE: YALE UNIV,DEPT PSYCHOL,BOX 11A,YALE STN/NEW
     HAVEN//CT/06520
JOURNAL: INTELLIGENCE, 1988, V12, N4, P351-377
LANGUAGE: ENGLISH   DOCUMENT TYPE: ARTICLE

 1/3/32
DIALOG(R)File   7:Social SciSearch(R)
(c) 1997 Inst for Sci Info. All rts. reserv.

01938022   GENUINE ARTICLE#: R0917   NO. REFERENCES: 10
TITLE: DEPUTY HEADSHIP RECONSIDERED - THE CONSOLIDATION OF SENIOR
     MANAGEMENT TEAMS
AUTHOR(S): GOULD W; DENNISON WF
CORPORATE SOURCE: HIRST HIGH SCH/ASHINGTON/NORTHD/ENGLAND/;
UNIV NEWCASTLE
     UPON TYNE,SCH EDUC/NEWCASTLE TYNE NE1 7RU/TYNE & WEAR/ENGLAND/
JOURNAL: EDUCATIONAL REVIEW, 1988, V40, N3, P277-288
LANGUAGE: ENGLISH   DOCUMENT TYPE: ARTICLE

 1/3/33
DIALOG(R)File   7:Social SciSearch(R)
(c) 1997 Inst for Sci Info. All rts. reserv.

01895873   GENUINE ARTICLE#: P2871   NO. REFERENCES: 8
TITLE: THE RESEARCH PROCESS AND RESEARCH TEAMS
AUTHOR(S): ALSOP K
CORPORATE SOURCE: BRUNEL UNIV,BRUNEL MANAGEMENT PROGRAM/UXBRIDGE UB8
     3PH/MIDDX/ENGLAND/
JOURNAL: R & D MANAGEMENT, 1988, V18, N3, P273-277
LANGUAGE: ENGLISH   DOCUMENT TYPE: NOTE

 1/3/34
DIALOG(R)File   7:Social SciSearch(R)
(c) 1997 Inst for Sci Info. All rts. reserv.

01872663   GENUINE ARTICLE#: N2224   NO. REFERENCES: 30
TITLE: MANAGING THE EXECUTIVE PROCESS
AUTHOR(S): MANGHAM I
CORPORATE SOURCE: UNIV BATH,SCH MANAGEMENT,CLAVERTON DOWN/BATH BA2
     7AY/AVON/ENGLAND/
JOURNAL: OMEGA-INTERNATIONAL JOURNAL OF MANAGEMENT SCIENCE, 1988, V16, N2

Figure 2.8   cont'd

, P95-105
LANGUAGE: ENGLISH   DOCUMENT TYPE: ARTICLE

1/3/35
DIALOG(R)File   7:Social SciSearch(R)
(c) 1997 Inst for Sci Info. All rts. reserv.

01837908   GENUINE ARTICLE#: L7219   NO. REFERENCES: 27
TITLE: INNOVATION CAN BE TAUGHT
AUTHOR(S): BUIJS JA
CORPORATE SOURCE: DELFT UNIV TECHNOL,FAC IND DESIGN ENGN,POB
5018/2600 GA
    DELFT//NETHERLANDS/; TNO,INNOVAT CONSULTING
GRP/DELFT//NETHERLANDS/
JOURNAL: RESEARCH POLICY, 1987, V16, N6, P303-314
LANGUAGE: ENGLISH   DOCUMENT TYPE: ARTICLE

1/3/36
DIALOG(R)File   7:Social SciSearch(R)
(c) 1997 Inst for Sci Info. All rts. reserv.

01736073   GENUINE ARTICLE#: G8138   NO. REFERENCES: 17
TITLE: MODELS FOR DEVELOPING MANAGERS
AUTHOR(S): SUTTON DC
CORPORATE SOURCE: SYST SIX,POB 67/WARRINGTON//ENGLAND/
JOURNAL: R & D MANAGEMENT, 1987, V17, N2, P127-136
LANGUAGE: ENGLISH   DOCUMENT TYPE: ARTICLE

1/3/37
DIALOG(R)File   7:Social SciSearch(R)
(c) 1997 Inst for Sci Info. All rts. reserv.

01568539   GENUINE ARTICLE#: A2406   NO. REFERENCES: 66
TITLE: WHAT DO MANAGERS DO - A CRITICAL-REVIEW OF THE EVIDENCE
AUTHOR(S): HALES CP
CORPORATE SOURCE: UNIV SURREY,DEPT MANAGEMENT STUDIES
TOURISM & HOTEL
    IND/GUILDFORD GU2 5XH/SURREY/ENGLAND/
JOURNAL: JOURNAL OF MANAGEMENT STUDIES, 1986, V23, N1, P88-115
LANGUAGE: ENGLISH   DOCUMENT TYPE: REVIEW, BIBLIOGRAPHY

1/3/38
DIALOG(R)File   7:Social SciSearch(R)
(c) 1997 Inst for Sci Info. All rts. reserv.

01423997   GENUINE ARTICLE#: TY770   NO. REFERENCES: 19
TITLE: AN ESSAY IN FUTUROLOGY - GROUPS, NETWORKS AND

Figure 2.8   cont'd

COMPLEXITY IN THE OPEN
   SOCIETY
AUTHOR(S): ROBB AC
CORPORATE SOURCE: MULTIPROBE
LTD/BOLLINGTON/CHESHIRE/ENGLAND/
JOURNAL: IEE PROCEEDINGS-A, 1985, V132, N1, P67-73
LANGUAGE: ENGLISH   DOCUMENT TYPE: ARTICLE

 1/3/39
DIALOG(R)File   7:Social SciSearch(R)
(c) 1997 Inst for Sci Info. All rts. reserv.

01348877   GENUINE ARTICLE#: ST961   NO. REFERENCES: 60
TITLE: BASIC MOTIVATION AND DECISION STYLE IN ORGANIZATION
MANAGEMENT
AUTHOR(S): GREIG ID
CORPORATE SOURCE: INT WOOL SECRETARIAT,CARLTON
GARDENS/LONDON SW1Y
   5AE//ENGLAND/
JOURNAL: OMEGA-INTERNATIONAL JOURNAL OF MANAGEMENT
SCIENCE, 1984, V12, N1
, P31-41
LANGUAGE: ENGLISH   DOCUMENT TYPE: ARTICLE

 1/3/40
DIALOG(R)File   7:Social SciSearch(R)
(c) 1997 Inst for Sci Info. All rts. reserv.

01276095   GENUINE ARTICLE#: RM832   NO. REFERENCES: 1
TITLE: MANAGEMENT TEAMS - WHY THEY SUCCEED OR FAIL - BELBIN,RM
AUTHOR(S): KNEPP GE
CORPORATE SOURCE: MEM HOSP REDDING/REDDING//CA/96001
JOURNAL: HOSPITAL & HEALTH SERVICES ADMINISTRATION, 1983, V28,
N4, P109-110
LANGUAGE: ENGLISH   DOCUMENT TYPE: BOOK REVIEW

 1/3/41
DIALOG(R)File   7:Social SciSearch(R)
(c) 1997 Inst for Sci Info. All rts. reserv.

01259045   GENUINE ARTICLE#: RE921   NO. REFERENCES: 32
TITLE: ANALYZING DECISION BEHAVIOR - LEARNING-MODELS AND
LEARNING STYLES AS
   DIAGNOSTIC AIDS
AUTHOR(S): JERVIS P
CORPORATE SOURCE: OXFORD CTR MANAGEMENT
STUDIES/OXFORD//ENGLAND/
JOURNAL: PERSONNEL REVIEW, 1983, V12, N2, P26-38
LANGUAGE: ENGLISH   DOCUMENT TYPE: ARTICLE

Figure 2.8   cont'd

1/3/42
DIALOG(R)File   7:Social SciSearch(R)

01208066   GENUINE ARTICLE#: QL205   NO. REFERENCES: 1
TITLE: MANAGEMENT TEAMS - WHY THEY SUCCEED OR FAIL - BELBIN,RM
AUTHOR(S): ALSOP K
JOURNAL: JOURNAL OF GENERAL MANAGEMENT, 1983, V8, N3, P102-104
LANGUAGE: ENGLISH   DOCUMENT TYPE: BOOK REVIEW

1/3/43
DIALOG(R)File   7:Social SciSearch(R)

01137162   GENUINE ARTICLE#: PH100   NO. REFERENCES: 1
TITLE: MANAGEMENT TEAMS - WHY THEY SUCCEED OR FAIL - BELBIN,RM
AUTHOR(S): FOGEL DS
CORPORATE SOURCE: LOUISIANA LAND & EXPLORAT CO,STAFFING &
   DEV/NEWORLEANS//LA/00000
JOURNAL: PERSONNEL PSYCHOLOGY, 1982, V35, N3, P738-740
LANGUAGE: ENGLISH   DOCUMENT TYPE: BOOK REVIEW

1/3/44
DIALOG(R)File   7:Social SciSearch(R)

01124358   GENUINE ARTICLE#: PA490   NO. REFERENCES: 1
TITLE: MANAGEMENT TEAMS - WHY THEY SUCCEED OR FAIL - BELBIN,RM
AUTHOR(S): DILL DD
JOURNAL: R & D MANAGEMENT, 1982, V12, N3, P147-148
LANGUAGE: ENGLISH   DOCUMENT TYPE: BOOK REVIEW

1/3/45
DIALOG(R)File   7:Social SciSearch(R)

00988322   GENUINE ARTICLE#: LV997   NO. REFERENCES: 20
TITLE: THE DEVELOPMENT OF CREATIVE ENGINEERS
AUTHOR(S): LIFE EA; WILD R
CORPORATE SOURCE: ADM STAFF COLL/HENLEY ON THAMES//ENGLAND/;
BRUNEL
   UNIV/UXBRIDGE UB8 3PH/MIDDLESEX/ENGLAND/
JOURNAL: OXFORD REVIEW OF EDUCATION, 1981, V7, N1, P3-9
LANGUAGE: ENGLISH   DOCUMENT TYPE: ARTICLE
?

Figure 2.8   concluded

of citation) cover applications of these ideas in a variety of contexts and subject areas.

To find information on topics not well described by indexing terminologies

Some kinds of search are intrinsically difficult to carry out using a conventional subject indexing approach. These include:

- very new topics, whose terminology has not become established, nor introduced into thesauri and similar tools, nor recognized by database producers' indexing policies
- interdisciplinary or multidisciplinary topics where the terminology used may depend on the background and viewpoint of the author
- searches involving 'general' concepts, whose nature is difficult to fix with specific terminology
- searches for material presented from a specific viewpoint, or with a particular 'slant', which may not necessarily be reflected in the terminology used.

Citation searching, because of its independence of terminology, is capable of consistently finding relevant material in these 'difficult' areas. It is not, of course, a general panacea. If the subject area is very new, there may not have been time for the publication process to generate a citation network. In multidisciplinary areas, authors may tend to cite only publications from their own discipline or school of thought.

With these provisos, citation searching should always be considered as a potentially useful resource for searches of this sort. The rapidly updated ISI databases are well suited for searching new and fast developing topics.

Garfield (1983) gives an example of the use of the SCIENCE CITATION INDEX to track the then rapidly developing topic of the use of Kerr4 geometry to describe black holes. At the time, the terminology of this very new and highly specific topic was not reflected in any indexing systems, while title terms would not be precise enough. Citation searching was able to provide a precise set of relevant documents.

Examples of the use of citation databases to overcome problems of variant nomenclatures and notations have been given by Synge (1990) for natural product chemistry and by Garfield (1985) for chemical reactions.

Other access points specific to citation databases, such as research fronts and journal category codes, can be used in conjunction with citation searching to restrict retrieval to material of a particular kind, or with a particular slant. One application of this would be to identify individuals or organizations publishing work from a particular perspective, perhaps as part of a search for possible collaborators.

To find information comprising only a small part of a publication

Sometimes information which is not itself the main subject of a publication may be of particular interest to a searcher. Examples include:

- techniques, methods, apparatus and so on used
- data and property values
- comparisons and analogies.

Because all of these comprise only a minor part of a publication, they are unlikely to be mentioned in the title or abstract, or included in the indexing of secondary services. One possible solution is the use of some form of 'data tagging', whereby the secondary service has a policy of always indexing certain topics or concepts, even when they take a minor role in the overall document; for example, some biomedical services do this for toxicity and adverse effects. Often, however, a reference citation will be made by the documents' authors to material relating to the minor topic, making it accessible to citation searching.

An example is shown in Figure 2.9. Citations to a well-known book on the statistical technique of cluster analysis are identified; there are 52. To make the example clearer, those which have terms with the stem CLUST or CLASSIF in the title or abstract, and which could readily be found by subject index searching, are removed. The remaining 23 cover a very wide subject spectrum; few give any indication that clustering is a feature of their content.

```
File 434:Scisearch(R) Cited Ref Sci  1974-1997/Oct W4
       (c) 1997 Inst for Sci Info

     Set Items  Description
     ----  -------  --------------
?e cr=everitt bs, 1974


Ref   Items  Index-term
E1       1   CR=EVERITT BS, 1972, V20, P143, BRIT J PSYCHIAT
E2       1   CR=EVERITT BS, 1973, V24, P37, STATISTICIAN
E3       0  *CR=EVERITT BS, 1974
E4       1   CR=EVERITT BS, 1974, ANAL CONTINGENCY TAB
E5      42   CR=EVERITT BS, 1974, CLUSTER ANAL
E6      10   CR=EVERITT BS, 1974, CLUSTER ANALYSIS
E7       2   CR=EVERITT BS, 1975, ANAL CONTINGENCY TAB
E8       3   CR=EVERITT BS, 1975, V126, P237, BR J PSYCHI
E9      18   CR=EVERITT BS, 1975, V126, P237, BRIT J PSYCHIAT
E10      4   CR=EVERITT BS, 1975, V24, P37, STATISTICIAN
E11      3   CR=EVERITT BS, 1976, ANAL CONTINGENCY TAB
E12      1   CR=EVERITT BS, 1976, P63, EXPLORING DATA STRUC
```

Figure 2.9   **Information comprising a small part of a publication**

```
        Enter P or PAGE for more
?s e5,e6

        42   CR=EVERITT BS, 1974, CLUSTER ANAL
        10   CR=EVERITT BS, 1974, CLUSTER ANALYSIS
   S1   52   E5,E6
?s cluster? or classif?

        169514   CLUSTER?
        108890   CLASSIF?
   S2   273230   CLUSTER? OR CLASSIF?
?c 1 not 2

            52   1
        273230   2
   S3        23   1 NOT 2
?t3/3/1-23


 3/3/1
DIALOG(R)File 434:Scisearch(R) Cited Ref Sci
(c) 1997 Inst for Sci Info. All rts. reserv.

09429596   Genuine Article#: U2184   No. References: 34
Title: CLINICAL VALIDITY
Author(s): KENDELL RE
Corporate Source: UNIV EDINBURGH,ROYAL EDINBURGH HOSP,DEPT
    PSYCHIAT/EDINBURGH EH10 5HF//SCOTLAND/
Journal: PSYCHOLOGICAL MEDICINE, 1989, V19, N1, P45-55
Language: ENGLISH   Document Type: ARTICLE


 3/3/2
DIALOG(R)File 434:Scisearch(R) Cited Ref Sci
(c) 1997 Inst for Sci Info. All rts. reserv.

09354110   Genuine Article#: T5423   No. References: 23
Title: FAST POWER-SYSTEM VOLTAGE PREDICTION USING KNOWLEDGE-
BASED APPROACH
    AND ONLINE BOX DATA CREATION
Author(s): CHANG CS
Corporate Source: HONG KONG POLYTECHN,DEPT ELECTR
ENGN/KOWLOON//HONG KONG/
Journal: IEE PROCEEDINGS-C GENERATION TRANSMISSION AND
DISTRIBUTION, 1989
, V136, N2, P87-99
Language: ENGLISH   Document Type: ARTICLE


 3/3/3
DIALOG(R)File 434:Scisearch(R) Cited Ref Sci
```

Figure 2.9   cont'd

09341682   Genuine Article#: T5671   No. References: 66
Title: COMPOSITIONAL DATA-ANALYSIS IN ARCHAEOLOGY
Author(s): BISHOP RL; NEFF H
Corporate Source: SMITHSONIAN INST,CONSERVAT ANALYT
    LAB/WASHINGTON//DC/20560
Journal: ADVANCES IN CHEMISTRY SERIES, 1989, N220, P57-86
Language: ENGLISH   Document Type: REVIEW

 3/3/4
DIALOG(R)File 434:Scisearch(R) Cited Ref Sci

08949972   Genuine Article#: P5717   No. References: 34
Title: THE EFFECTS OF DRAINAGE ON GROUNDWATER QUALITY AND
PLANT-SPECIES
    DISTRIBUTION IN STREAM VALLEY MEADOWS
Author(s): GROOTJANS AP; VANDIGGELEN R; WASSEN MJ; WIERSINGA WA
Corporate Source: STATE UNIV GRONINGEN,CTR BIOL,DEPT PLANT
ECOL,POB 14/9750
    AA HAREN//NETHERLANDS/
Journal: VEGETATIO, 1988, V75, N1-2, P37-48
Language: ENGLISH   Document Type: ARTICLE

 3/3/5
DIALOG(R)File 434:Scisearch(R) Cited Ref Sci

08718585   Genuine Article#: M9199   No. References: 47
Title: HOME-RANGE BEHAVIOR AND SOCIAL-ORGANIZATION OF SCOTTISH
BLACKFACE
    SHEEP
Author(s): LAWRENCE AB; WOODGUSH DGM
Corporate Source: EDINBURGH SCH AGR,W MAINS RD/EDINBURGH EH9
    3JG/MIDLOTHIAN/SCOTLAND/
Journal: JOURNAL OF APPLIED ECOLOGY, 1988, V25, N1, P25-40
Language: ENGLISH   Document Type: ARTICLE

 3/3/6
DIALOG(R)File 434:Scisearch(R) Cited Ref Sci

08623052   Genuine Article#: M1664   No. References: 31
Title: RECOGNITION OF DITYLENCHUS AND OTHER NEMATODES BY
SPORES OF THE
    ENDO-PARASITIC FUNGUS VERTICILLIUM-BALANOIDES
Author(s): DURSCHNERPELZ VV; ATKINSON HJ

Figure 2.9   **cont'd**

Corporate Source: UNIV LEEDS,DEPT PURE & APPL BIOL/LEEDS LS2 9JT/W
    YORKSHIRE/ENGLAND/
Journal: JOURNAL OF INVERTEBRATE PATHOLOGY, 1988, V51, N2, P97-106
Language: ENGLISH   Document Type: ARTICLE

3/3/7
DIALOG(R)File 434:Scisearch(R) Cited Ref Sci
(c) 1997 Inst for Sci Info. All rts. reserv.

08494421   Genuine Article#: L2645   No. References: 24
Title: MULTISPECTRAL MAGNETIC-RESONANCE IMAGE-ANALYSIS
Author(s): VANNIER MW; BUTTERFIELD RL; RICKMAN DL; JORDAN DM;
MURPHY WA;
    BIONDETTI PR
Corporate Source: WASHINGTON UNIV,SCH MED,EDWARD MALLINCKRODT
INST
    RADIOL/ST LOUIS//MO/63110; NASA,SPECIAL PROJECTS DEV
OFF/KENNEDY SPACE
    CTR//FL/00000; NASA,EARTH RESOURCES LAB,NATL SPACE TECHNOL
LABS/NSTL
    STN//MS/00000; OSPED CIVILE/PADOVA//ITALY/; UNIV FLORIDA, INST
FOOD &
    AGR SCI,REMOTE SENSING& IMAGE PROC LAB/GAINESVILLE//FL/32611
Journal: CRC CRITICAL REVIEWS IN BIOMEDICAL ENGINEERING, 1987, V15,
N2, P
    117&
Language: ENGLISH   Document Type: REVIEW, BIBLIOGRAPHY

3/3/8
DIALOG(R)File 434:Scisearch(R) Cited Ref Sci
(c) 1997 Inst for Sci Info. All rts. reserv.

08381050   Genuine Article#: K3443   No. References: 19
Title: DIFFERENTIAL FAMILY FORMATION IN GREAT-BRITAIN
Author(s): MURPHY MJ
Corporate Source: UNIV LONDON LONDON SCH ECON & POLIT SCI,DEPT
POPULAT
    STUDIES,HOUGHTON ST/LONDON WC2A 2AE//ENGLAND/
Journal: JOURNAL OF BIOSOCIAL SCIENCE, 1987, V19, N4, P463-485
Language: ENGLISH   Document Type: ARTICLE

3/3/9
DIALOG(R)File 434:Scisearch(R) Cited Ref Sci
(c) 1997 Inst for Sci Info. All rts. reserv.

08066743   Genuine Article#: H1707   No. References: 35
Title: THE STRUCTURE OF DEPRESSIVE SYMPTOMS IN THE ELDERLY
Author(s): GOOD WR; VLACHONIKOLIS I; GRIFFITHS P; GRIFFITHS RA

Figure 2.9   **cont'd**

Corporate Source: RADCLIFFE INFIRM,GERIATR MED/OXFORD OX2
6HE//ENGLAND/;
    UNIV OXFORD,DEPT BIOMATH/OXFORD//ENGLAND/; UNIV OXFORD,CTR
    COMP/OXFORD//ENGLAND/
Journal: BRITISH JOURNAL OF PSYCHIATRY, 1987, V150, APR, P463-470
Language: ENGLISH   Document Type: ARTICLE

 3/3/10
DIALOG(R)File 434:Scisearch(R) Cited Ref Sci
(c) 1997 Inst for Sci Info. All rts. reserv.

07976395   Genuine Article#: G4913   No. References: 19
Title: UNIDIMENSIONAL SCALING WITH EFFICIENT RANKING METHODS
Author(s): CHIGNELL MH; PATTY BW
Corporate Source: UNIV SO CALIF,DEPT IND & SYST ENGN,OHE 400,MC-
1452,UNIV
   PK/LOS ANGELES//CA/90089
Journal: PSYCHOLOGICAL BULLETIN, 1987, V101, N2, P304-311
Language: ENGLISH   Document Type: ARTICLE

 3/3/11
DIALOG(R)File 434:Scisearch(R) Cited Ref Sci
(c) 1997 Inst for Sci Info. All rts. reserv.

07397873   Genuine Article#: D0390   No. References: 20
Title: GENETIC-VARIATION IN THE SHAPE OF THE MOUSE MANDIBLE AND
ITS
   RELATIONSHIP TO GLUCOCORTICOID-INDUCED CLEFT-PALATE
ANALYZED BY USING
   RECOMBINANT INBRED LINES
Author(s): LOVELL DP; ERICKSON RP
Corporate Source: BRITISH IND BIOL RES ASSOC,WOODMANSTERNE
RD/CARSHALTON
   SM5 4DS/SURREY/ENGLAND/; UNIV MICHIGAN,SCH MED,DEPT HUMAN
GENET/ANN
   ARBOR//MI/48109
Journal: GENETICS, 1986, V113, N3, P755-764
Language: ENGLISH   Document Type: ARTICLE

 3/3/12
DIALOG(R)File 434:Scisearch(R) Cited Ref Sci
(c) 1997 Inst for Sci Info. All rts. reserv.

04922645   Genuine Article#: PZ910   No. References: 12
Title: EFFECTS OF POLLUTION ON THE BENTHOS OF THE FIRTH OF FORTH
Author(s): READ PA; ANDERSON KJ; MATTHEWS JE; WATSON PG; HALLIDAY
MC;
   SHIELLS GM

Figure 2.9   cont'd

Corporate Source: NAPIER COLL,DEPT BIOL SCI/EDINBURGH//SCOTLAND/
Journal: MARINE POLLUTION BULLETIN, 1983, V14, N1, P12-16
Language: ENGLISH   Document Type: ARTICLE

3/3/13
DIALOG(R)File 434:Scisearch(R) Cited Ref Sci
(c) 1997 Inst for Sci Info. All rts. reserv.

04706562   Genuine Article#: PH125   No. References: 52
Title: EFFECTS OF SECONDARY PLANT-COMPOUNDS ON THE BODY-
WEIGHT AND THE
    WEIGHT OF CERTAIN ORGANS OF LABORATORY MICE
Author(s): BERGERON JM; JODOIN L
Corporate Source: UNIV SHERBROOKE,FAC SCI,DEPT BIOL/SHERBROOKE J1K
    2R1/QUEBEC/CANADA/
Journal: CANADIAN JOURNAL OF ZOOLOGY-JOURNAL CANADIEN DE
ZOOLOGIE, 1982, V
    60, N8, P1855-1866
Language: FRENCH   Document Type: ARTICLE

3/3/14
DIALOG(R)File 434:Scisearch(R) Cited Ref Sci
(c) 1997 Inst for Sci Info. All rts. reserv.

04703232   Genuine Article#: PH277   No. References: 27
Title: A SIMULATION STUDY OF MOSS FLORAS USING JACCARDS
COEFFICIENT OF
    SIMILARITY
Author(s): RICE J; BELLAND RJ
Corporate Source: MEM UNIV NEWFOUNDLAND,DEPT BIOL/ST JOHNS A1B
    2X8/NEWFOUNDLAND/CANADA/
Journal: JOURNAL OF BIOGEOGRAPHY, 1982, V9, N5, P411-419
Language: ENGLISH   Document Type: ARTICLE

3/3/15
DIALOG(R)File 434:Scisearch(R) Cited Ref Sci
(c) 1997 Inst for Sci Info. All rts. reserv.

04679435   Genuine Article#: PF182   No. References: 3
Title: DETERMINATION OF WEIGHTING FACTORS FOR THE SENSORY
EVALUATION OF
    FOOD
Author(s): MOLNAR P; ORSI F
Corporate Source: CTR FOOD CONTROL & ANAL/BUDAPEST//HUNGARY/;
TECH UNIV
    BUDAPEST,DEPT BIOCHEM & FOOD TECHNOL/H-1521
BUDAPEST//HUNGARY/
Journal: NAHRUNG-FOOD, 1982, V26, N7-8, P661-667
Language: ENGLISH   Document Type: ARTICLE

Figure 2.9   cont'd

3/3/16
DIALOG(R)File 434:Scisearch(R) Cited Ref Sci
(c) 1997 Inst for Sci Info. All rts. reserv.

04583301   Genuine Article#: NW934   No. References: 17
Title: ALGORITHMIC COMPLEXITY - 3 NP-HARD PROBLEMS IN COMPUTATIONAL
    STATISTICS
Author(s): WELCH WJ
Corporate Source: UNIV LONDON IMPERIAL COLL SCI & TECHNOL,DEPT MATH/LONDON
    SW7 2BZ//ENGLAND/
Journal: JOURNAL OF STATISTICAL COMPUTATION AND SIMULATION, 1982, V15, N1
, P17-25
Language: ENGLISH   Document Type: ARTICLE

3/3/17
DIALOG(R)File 434:Scisearch(R) Cited Ref Sci
(c) 1997 Inst for Sci Info. All rts. reserv.

04523863   Genuine Article#: NS209   No. References: 25
Title: GENETIC-HETEROGENEITY AND POPULATION-STRUCTURE IN NORTHWEST INDIA
Author(s): PAPIHA SS; MUKHERJEE BN; CHAHAL SMS; MALHOTRA KC; ROBERTS DF
Corporate Source: UNIV NEWCASTLE UPON TYNE,DEPT HUMAN GENET/NEWCASTLE TYNE
    NE2 4AA//ENGLAND/; INDIAN STAT INST,ANTHROPOMETR & HUMAN GENET
    UNIT/CALCUTTA 700035/W BENGAL/INDIA/
Journal: ANNALS OF HUMAN BIOLOGY, 1982, V9, N3, P235-251
Language: ENGLISH   Document Type: ARTICLE

3/3/18
DIALOG(R)File 434:Scisearch(R) Cited Ref Sci
(c) 1997 Inst for Sci Info. All rts. reserv.

04292338   Genuine Article#: MY413   No. References: 39
Title: FROM INTENSIVELY AGRICULTURAL PRACTICES TO HAY-MAKING WITHOUT
    FERTILIZATION - EFFECTS ON MOIST GRASSLAND COMMUNITIES
Author(s): VANDUUREN L; BAKKER JP; FRESCO LFM
Corporate Source: UNIV GRONINGEN,CTR BIOL,DEPT PLANT ECOL/9750
    AAHAREN//NETHERLANDS/
Journal: VEGETATIO, 1981, V46-7, NOV, P241-258
Language: ENGLISH   Document Type: ARTICLE

Figure 2.9   **cont'd**

3/3/19
DIALOG(R)File 434:Scisearch(R) Cited Ref Sci
(c) 1997 Inst for Sci Info. All rts. reserv.

04189843   Genuine Article#: MQ936   No. References: 210
Title: NUMERICAL PHENETICS - ITS USES IN BOTANICAL SYSTEMATICS
Author(s): DUNCAN T; BAUM BR
Corporate Source: UNIV CALIF BERKELEY,DEPT BIOL/BERKELEY//CA/94720;
AGR
   CANADA,INST BIOSYST RES/OTTAWA K1A 0C6/ONTARIO/CANADA/
Journal: ANNUAL REVIEW OF ECOLOGY AND SYSTEMATICS, 1981, V12, P387-
404
Language: ENGLISH   Document Type: REVIEW, BIBLIOGRAPHY

3/3/20
DIALOG(R)File 434:Scisearch(R) Cited Ref Sci
(c) 1997 Inst for Sci Info. All rts. reserv.

03833122   Genuine Article#: LK091   No. References: 17
Title: A COMPUTATIONAL PROCEDURE FOR THE ANALYSIS OF ELECTRON
IMAGES OF
   NUCLEIC-ACID MOLECULES
Author(s): BREEPOEL HLP; BLANKSMA HJ; VANDERHOOG G;
VANHARTINGSVELDT EAA;
   MELLEMA JE
Corporate Source: STATE UNIV LEIDEN,DEPT
BIOCHEM/LEIDEN//NETHERLANDS/
Journal: ULTRAMICROSCOPY, 1981, V6, N1, P19-28
Language: ENGLISH   Document Type: ARTICLE

3/3/21
DIALOG(R)File 434:Scisearch(R) Cited Ref Sci
(c) 1997 Inst for Sci Info. All rts. reserv.

03441185   Genuine Article#: KB947   No. References: 168
Title: PROGRESS REPORT ON PATTERN-RECOGNITION
Author(s): VERHAGEN CJDM; DUIN RPW; GROEN FCA; JOOSTEN JC;
VERBEEK PW
Corporate Source: DELFT UNIV TECHNOL,DEPT APPL PHYS,PATTERN
RECOGNIT
   GRP/NL-2628 CJ DELFT//NETHERLANDS/
Journal: REPORTS ON PROGRESS IN PHYSICS, 1980, V43, N6, P785&
Language: ENGLISH   Document Type: REVIEW, BIBLIOGRAPHY

3/3/22
DIALOG(R)File 434:Scisearch(R) Cited Ref Sci
(c) 1997 Inst for Sci Info. All rts. reserv.

Figure 2.9   **cont'd**

```
01509579   Genuine Article#: DF492   No. References: 24
Title: TOWARD A MULTIVARIATE THEORY OF PERSONALITY STYLES -
MEASUREMENT AND
    RELIABILITY
Author(s): MILLER IW; MAGARO PA
Corporate Source: UNIV MAINE,DEPT PSYCHOL/PORTLAND//ME/04103
Journal: JOURNAL OF CLINICAL PSYCHOLOGY, 1977, V33, N2, P460-466
Language: ENGLISH   Document Type: ARTICLE


 3/3/23
DIALOG(R)File 434:Scisearch(R) Cited Ref Sci
(c) 1997 Inst for Sci Info. All rts. reserv.

00514154   Genuine Article#: V7561   No. References: 11
Title: MULTIVARIATE-ANALYSIS - NEED FOR DATA, AND OTHER
PROBLEMS
Author(s): EVERITT BS
Corporate Source: INST PSYCHIAT LONDON,BIOMETRICS UNITS,DE CRESPNY
    PK/LONDON SE5 8AF//ENGLAND/
Journal: BRITISH JOURNAL OF PSYCHIATRY, 1975, V126, MAR, P237-240
Language: ENGLISH   Document Type: ARTICLE
?
```

Figure 2.9   concluded

To identify reviews

Reviews, surveys, overviews and such like are often particularly valuable publications to the researcher or teacher, and may often be required in a search. By definition, such documents will usually have extensive bibliographies, and should be readily found by citation searching.

While the simple approach of carrying out a subject search and adding terms to reflect the Review concept may be effective, the ISI citation databases provide two useful additional access points. The document type includes a category for Review / Bibliography, although there will always be room for dispute as to what should go into it; examples can be found with the term 'review' in the title which are not so categorized. The number of cited references may also be searched, although this will fail with highly selective reviews citing only a small number of references, and equally with publications having extensive bibliographies which are not reviews; nevertheless, it may be argued that these may serve the searcher's purposes just as well.

An example is shown in Figure 2.10. A citation search on the original paper describing the anti-schistosomal drug oxamniquine, authored by H.C. Richards and published in *Nature* in 1969, gives 24 references. Seven of these have over 50 references and seem likely candidates to be reviews; four have the Review categorization, but the other three do not, although they seem similar in nature.

A second example, shown in Figure 2.11, illustrates how co-citation searching

```
File 434:Scisearch(R) Cited Ref Sci  1974-1997/Oct W4
    (c) 1997 Inst for Sci Info

    Set  Items  Description
    ---  -----  -----------
?e cr=richards hc, 1969


Ref  Items  Index-term
E1     7   CR=RICHARDS HC, 1963, V199, P354, NATURE
E2     1   CR=RICHARDS HC, 1964, BIOSYNTHESIS STEROID
E3     0  *CR=RICHARDS HC, 1969
E4    23   CR=RICHARDS HC, 1969, V222, P581, NATURE
E5     1   CR=RICHARDS HC, 1969, V222, P581, NATURE LONDON
E6     2   CR=RICHARDS HC, 1972, V63, P44, J EDUCATIONAL PSY
E7     2   CR=RICHARDS HC, 1980, V2, P333, J CLIN NEUROPSYCH
E8     1   CR=RICHARDS HC, 1982, V1, P257, CHRON DRUG DISCOV
E9     1   CR=RICHARDS HC, 1982, V1, P257, CHRONICLES DRUG D
E10    1   CR=RICHARDS HC, 1985, CH14 MED CHEM ROLE ORGANI
E11    1   CR=RICHARDS HC, 1985, P1001, CHEM BRITAIN NOV
E12    3   CR=RICHARDS HC, 1985, P271, MED CHEM ROLE ORGANI

        Enter P or PAGE for more
?s e4,e5

        23   CR=RICHARDS HC, 1969, V222, P581, NATURE
         1   CR=RICHARDS HC, 1969, V222, P581, NATURE LONDON
    S1  24   E4,E5
?s nr=50:500

    S2  728771   NR=50:500
?c 1 and 2

            24  1
        728771  2
    S3       7  1 AND 2
?t3/3/1-7


 3/3/1
DIALOG(R)File 434:Scisearch(R) Cited Ref Sci
(c) 1997 Inst for Sci Info. All rts. reserv.

14343504   Genuine Article#: TF009   No. References: 321
Title: ANTISCHISTOSOMAL DRUGS - PAST, PRESENT ... AND FUTURE
Author(s): CIOLI D; PICAMATTOCCIA L; ARCHER S
Corporate Source: INST CELL BIOL,43 VIALE MARX/I-00137 ROME//ITALY/;
    RENSSELAER POLYTECH INST/TROY//NY/12180
Journal: PHARMACOLOGY & THERAPEUTICS, 1995, V68, N1, P35-85
ISSN: 0163-7258
```

Figure 2.10   **Searching for reviews (a)**

Language: ENGLISH   Document Type: REVIEW   (Abstract Available)

3/3/2
DIALOG(R)File 434:Scisearch(R) Cited Ref Sci
(c) 1997 Inst for Sci Info. All rts. reserv.

13720116   Genuine Article#: BC45L   No. References: 91
Title: RELATIONSHIPS BETWEEN CHEMOTHERAPY AND IMMUNITY IN
SCHISTOSOMIASIS
Author(s): BRINDLEY PJ
Corporate Source: BANCROFT CTR,QUEENSLAND INST MED RES,MOLEC
PARASITOL
    UNIT,300 HERSTON RD/BRISBANE/QLD 4029/AUSTRALIA/; BANCROFT
    CTR,QUEENSLAND INST MED RES,TROP HLTH PROGRAM/BRISBANE/QLD
    4029/AUSTRALIA/
Journal: ADVANCES IN PARASITOLOGY, 1994, V34, P133-161
ISSN: 0065-308X
Language: ENGLISH   Document Type: REVIEW

3/3/3
DIALOG(R)File 434:Scisearch(R) Cited Ref Sci
(c) 1997 Inst for Sci Info. All rts. reserv.

12939230   Genuine Article#: NC019   No. References: 79
Title: DRUG-RESISTANCE TO SCHISTOSOMICIDES AND OTHER
ANTHELMINTICS OF
    MEDICAL SIGNIFICANCE
Author(s): BRINDLEY PJ
Corporate Source: QUEENSLAND INST MED RES,BANCROFT CTR,TROP HLTH
    PROGRAM,300 HERSTON RD/BRISBANE/QLD 4029/AUSTRALIA/
Journal: ACTA TROPICA, 1994, V56, N2-3 (MAR), P213-231
ISSN: 0001-706X
Language: ENGLISH   Document Type: ARTICLE   (Abstract Available)

3/3/4
DIALOG(R)File 434:Scisearch(R) Cited Ref Sci
(c) 1997 Inst for Sci Info. All rts. reserv.

11147795   Genuine Article#: GK909   No. References: 126
Title: SCHISTOSOMIASIS DRUG-THERAPY AND TREATMENT
CONSIDERATIONS
Author(s): SHEKHAR KC
Corporate Source: UNIV MALAYA,FAC MED,DEPT PARASITOL,JALAN
    LEMBAHPANTAI/KUALA LUMPUR 59100//MALAYSIA/
Journal: DRUGS, 1991, V42, N3, P379-405
Language: ENGLISH   Document Type: ARTICLE   (Abstract Available)

Figure 2.10   cont'd

```
 3/3/5
DIALOG(R)File 434:Scisearch(R) Cited Ref Sci
(c) 1997 Inst for Sci Info. All rts. reserv.

06399576   Genuine Article#: AFL78   No. References: 107
Title: THE CHEMOTHERAPY OF SCHISTOSOMIASIS
Author(s): ARCHER S
Corporate Source: RENSSELAER POLYTECH INST,DEPT CHEM,COGSWELL
   LAB/TROY//NY/12180
Journal: ANNUAL REVIEW OF PHARMACOLOGY AND TOXICOLOGY, 1985,
V25, P485-508
Language: ENGLISH   Document Type: REVIEW, BIBLIOGRAPHY


 3/3/6
DIALOG(R)File 434:Scisearch(R) Cited Ref Sci
(c) 1997 Inst for Sci Info. All rts. reserv.

03569381   Genuine Article#: KN455   No. References: 126
Title: DRUGS FOR TROPICAL DISEASES IN THE 3RD-WORLD
Author(s): WAGNER WH
Corporate Source: HOECHST AG,DEPT CHEMOTHERAPY/D-6230 FRANKFURT
80//FED REP
   GER/
Journal: INTERDISCIPLINARY SCIENCE REVIEWS, 1980, V5, N3, P186-203
Language: ENGLISH   Document Type: REVIEW, BIBLIOGRAPHY


 3/3/7
DIALOG(R)File 434:Scisearch(R) Cited Ref Sci
(c) 1997 Inst for Sci Info. All rts. reserv.

01121599   Genuine Article#: BY813   No. References: 57
Title: HISTORY OF CHEMOTHERAPY OF BILHARZIASIS .2. APPROACHES TO
   CHEMOTHERAPY
Journal: EAST AFRICAN MEDICAL JOURNAL, 1976, V53, N5, P300-307
Language: ENGLISH   Document Type: ARTICLE
```

Figure 2.10   concluded

```
File   7:Social SciSearch(R)  1972-1997/Nov W1
       (c) 1997 Inst for Sci Info

    Set  Items  Description
    ----  -------  --------------
?s cr-=wilson td,?

    S1    664  CR=WILSON TD,?
```

Figure 2.11   Searching for reviews (b)

?s cr=cronin b,?

   S2   484   CR=CRONIN B,?
?s cr=oppenheim c,?

   S3   216   CR=OPPENHEIM C,?
?c 1 and 2 and 3

      664 1
      484 2
      216 3
   S4   3 1 AND 2 AND 3
?t4/3/1-3

4/3/1
DIALOG(R)File 7:Social SciSearch(R)
(c) 1997 Inst for Sci Info. All rts. reserv.

02677264 GENUINE ARTICLE#: PP078 NO. REFERENCES: 102
TITLE: AN OPTIMAL FORAGING APPROACH TO INFORMATION-SEEKING
AND USE
AUTHOR(S): SANDSTROM PE
CORPORATE SOURCE: INDIANA UNIV,SCH LIB & INFORMAT
SCI/BLOOMINGTON//IN/47405
JOURNAL: LIBRARY QUARTERLY, 1994, V64, N4 (OCT), P414-449
ISSN: 0024-2519
LANGUAGE: ENGLISH DOCUMENT TYPE: REVIEW (Abstract Available)

4/3/2
DIALOG(R)File 7:Social SciSearch(R)
(c) 1997 Inst for Sci Info. All rts. reserv.

02594376 GENUINE ARTICLE#: NA048 NO. REFERENCES: 70
TITLE: DO CITATIONS MATTER
AUTHOR(S): BAIRD LM; OPPENHEIM C
CORPORATE SOURCE: UNIV STRATHCLYDE,DEPT INFORMAT SCI,26
RICHMOND ST/GLASGOW
  G1 1XH//SCOTLAND/
JOURNAL: JOURNAL OF INFORMATION SCIENCE, 1994, V20, N1, P2-15
ISSN: 0165-5515
LANGUAGE: ENGLISH DOCUMENT TYPE: ARTICLE (Abstract Available)

4/3/3
DIALOG(R)File 7:Social SciSearch(R)
(c) 1997 Inst for Sci Info. All rts. reserv.

01250718 GENUINE ARTICLE#: RC863 NO. REFERENCES: 183
TITLE: EDUCATION FOR LIBRARIANSHIP AND INFORMATION-SCIENCE - A

Figure 2.11   cont'd

RETROSPECT
   AND A REVALUATION
AUTHOR(S): MCGARRY K
CORPORATE SOURCE: POLYTECH N LONDON,SCH LIBRARIANSHIP &
   INFORMAT STUDIES/LONDON N7 8DB//ENGLAND/
JOURNAL: JOURNAL OF DOCUMENTATION, 1983, V39, N2, P95-122
LANGUAGE: ENGLISH   DOCUMENT TYPE: REVIEW, BIBLIOGRAPHY

Figure 2.11   concluded

may be used to identify reviews. T.D. Wilson, B. Cronin and C. Oppenheim are all well-known and widely cited authors, each writing on a variety of topics connected with information management. A search for documents citing at least one item with each of these three as first author gives three publications, on different topics of interest to the three named individuals: information users, citation analysis and education for information management. All three appear to be, in effect, reviews, although only two are categorized as such.

For current awareness

Online citation databases, because of their timeliness in processing the primary literature and their frequent updating, are particularly useful for current awareness. The most convenient means is to store a search profile with the host system, to be run each time that the database is updated.

The inclusion of citation searching in current awareness profiles, as well as, or even instead of, subject descriptors and author names, can prove very effective. Many users of current awareness services find it relatively easy to give a list of documents central to their interests – not least their own publications – so that any document citing any of them is likely to be of interest. Profiles of this sort may often be easier to construct, and more successful in operation, than profiles of subject terms. The vagaries of citation retrieval, owing to the inconsistencies of authors' citation practices, may be a positive advantage for current awareness, with unexpected, perhaps peripheral, material, which may be expected to spark off ideas in the recipients. The lack of comprehensive recall to be expected from citation searching (at least without iteration) is not likely to be important for this purpose, when overload from the volume of potentially useful material is a real problem for many users.

For verification of bibliographic references

At first sight, this may seem a peculiar application for a citation database, since reference checking is most commonly carried out by a search on author name or title word, if the identity of the author is in doubt. However, the great breadth of material included within a citation database, both in terms of documents included and of time period, makes this approach a useful one. It should be remembered that it is not necessary for the document being checked to have been published during the time period covered by the database, merely that it has been cited during that period. The method is particularly useful for checking older, or more obscure, material, which may be less likely to be included in a 'conventional' database. It is particularly valuable if one wishes to check the identity of a document that one knows to be 'influential', and thus probably highly cited.

An example is given in Figure 2.12; the search is to find the reference to an article by Vannevar Bush, published around 1945, which had considerable influence on the development of the concepts of information retrieval and the Internet in particular. A citation search shows two highly cited publications from 1945. Printing out the titles of the citing documents shows that those citing the former Bush publication are concerned with science policy; those citing the second deal with hypertext, the Internet, and similar issues. This second publication is therefore the one required, and its full reference, an article in *Atlantic Monthly*, is provided.

```
File   7:Social SciSearch(R)  1972-1997/Nov W1
       (c) 1997 Inst for Sci Info

       Set  Items  Description
       ----  -------  --------------
?e cr=bush v, 1945


Ref   Items  Index-term
E1       1   CR=BUSH V, 1944, MEMORANDUM C 1208
E2       1   CR=BUSH V, 1944, SAL POINTS FUT 0930
E3       0  *CR=BUSH V, 1945
E4       2   CR=BUSH V, 1945, ATLANTIC MONTHLY
E5       2   CR=BUSH V, 1945, ATLANTIC MONTHLY AUG
E6      10   CR=BUSH V, 1945, ATLANTIC MONTHLY JUL
E7       1   CR=BUSH V, 1945, ATLANTIC MONTHLY JUN
E8       1   CR=BUSH V, 1945, COMMUNICATION 0607
E9       1   CR=BUSH V, 1945, ENDLESS FRONTIER
E10      2   CR=BUSH V, 1945, ENDLESS FRONTIER REP
E11      1   CR=BUSH V, 1945, NSF6040 NAT SCI F
E12      1   CR=BUSH V, 1945, PERSPECTIVES COMPUTE

       Enter P or PAGE for more
?p


Ref   Items  Index-term
E13      1   CR=BUSH V, 1945, POLITICS SCIENCE
```

Figure 2.12   Reference verification

E14	1	CR=BUSH V, 1945, P1, SCI ENDLESS FRONTIER
E15	1	CR=BUSH V, 1945, P101, ATLANTIC MONTHLY
E16	42	CR=BUSH V, 1945, P101, ATLANTIC MONTHLY JUL
E17	2	CR=BUSH V, 1945, P106, ATLANTIC MONTHLY JUL
E18	1	CR=BUSH V, 1945, P107, ATLANTIC MONTHLY JUL
E19	1	CR=BUSH V, 1945, P12, SCI ENDLESS FRONTIER
E20	1	CR=BUSH V, 1945, P123, SCI ENDLESS FRONTIER
E21	2	CR=BUSH V, 1945, P13, SCI ENDLESS FRONTIER
E22	1	CR=BUSH V, 1945, P147, SCI ENDLESS FRONTIER
E23	3	CR=BUSH V, 1945, P176, ATLANTIC MONTHLY
E24	1	CR=BUSH V, 1945, P178, SCI ENDLESS FRONTIER

Enter P or PAGE for more

?p

Ref	Items	Index-term
E25	1	CR=BUSH V, 1945, P19, ENDLESS FRONTIER
E26	1	CR=BUSH V, 1945, P25, SCI ENDLESS FRONTIER
E27	1	CR=BUSH V, 1945, P3, SCI ENDLESS FRONTIER
E28	1	CR=BUSH V, 1945, P34, SCIENCE ENDLESS FRON
E29	1	CR=BUSH V, 1945, P5, SCI ENDLESS FRON JUL
E30	1	CR=BUSH V, 1945, P5, SCI ENDLESS FRONTIER
E31	1	CR=BUSH V, 1945, P7, SCI ENDLESS FRONTIER
E32	1	CR=BUSH V, 1945, P76, ATLANTIC MONTHLY JUL
E33	1	CR=BUSH V, 1945, P80, SCI ENDLESS FRONTIER
E34	1	CR=BUSH V, 1945, P83, SCI ENDLESS FRONTIER
E35	1	CR=BUSH V, 1945, P85, MEMEX HYPERTEXT VANN
E36	1	CR=BUSH V, 1945, P86, SCI ENDLESS FRONTIER

Enter P or PAGE for more

?p

Ref	Items	Index-term
E37	1	CR=BUSH V, 1945, REPORT PRESIDENT
E38	1	CR=BUSH V, 1945, SCI ENDLESS FRON JUL
E39	1	CR=BUSH V, 1945, SCI ENDLESS FRONTIE
E40	96	CR=BUSH V, 1945, SCI ENDLESS FRONTIER
E41	6	CR=BUSH V, 1945, SCIENCE ENDLESS FRON
E42	1	CR=BUSH V, 1945, V1, P101, ATLANTIC MONTHLY
E43	1	CR=BUSH V, 1945, V175, P101, ATLANTIC MONTHLY
E44	1	CR=BUSH V, 1945, V176, P10, ATLANTIC MONTHLY
E45	2	CR=BUSH V, 1945, V176, P101, ATLANTIC MONTHL 0700
E46	164	CR=BUSH V, 1945, V176, P101, ATLANTIC MONTHLY
E47	2	CR=BUSH V, 1945, V176, P101, ATLANTIC MONTHLY JUL
E48	1	CR=BUSH V, 1945, V176, P102, ATLANTIC

Enter P or PAGE for more

?p

Figure 2.12   cont'd

```
Ref   Items  Index-term
E49      1  CR=BUSH V, 1945, V176, P102, ATLANTIC MONTHLY
E50      1  CR=BUSH V, 1945, V176, P105, ATLANTIC MONTHLY
?s e40

    S1      96  CR="BUSH V, 1945, SCI ENDLESS FRONTIER"
?s e46

    S2     164  CR="BUSH V, 1945, V176, P101, ATLANTIC MONTHLY"
?t1/6/1-10
```

1/6/1
03102020   GENUINE ARTICLE#: YA387   NUMBER OF REFERENCES: 24
TITLE: A state-federal partnership in support of science and technology -
   Response (ABSTRACT AVAILABLE)

1/6/2
03094956   GENUINE ARTICLE#: XX574   NUMBER OF REFERENCES: 94
TITLE: The Cold War, RAND, and the generation of knowledge, 1946-1962

1/6/3
03090791   GENUINE ARTICLE#: XV536   NUMBER OF REFERENCES: 74
TITLE: The science-society contract in historical transformation: with
   special reference to "epistemic drift" (ABSTRACT AVAILABLE)

1/6/4
03065906   GENUINE ARTICLE#: XJ075   NUMBER OF REFERENCES: 65
TITLE: The virtues of mundane science

1/6/5
03041519   GENUINE ARTICLE#: WY096   NUMBER OF REFERENCES: 60
TITLE: Is there endogenous long-run growth? Evidence from the United States
   and the United Kingdom (ABSTRACT AVAILABLE)

1/6/6
03006086   GENUINE ARTICLE#: WG782   NUMBER OF REFERENCES: 67
TITLE: Bibliometrics, citation analysis and co-citation analysis: A review
   of literature .2. (ABSTRACT AVAILABLE)

1/6/7
02997543   GENUINE ARTICLE#: WD529   NUMBER OF REFERENCES: 46
TITLE: Education: Moving from chemistry to chemical engineering and beyond

Figure 2.12   **cont'd**

```
1/6/8
02972249   GENUINE ARTICLE#: VT054   NUMBER OF REFERENCES: 50
TITLE: NATIONAL POLICIES FOR TECHNICAL CHANGE - WHERE ARE THE
INCREASING
    RETURNS TO ECONOMIC RESEARCH  (Abstract Available)


1/6/9
02960849   GENUINE ARTICLE#: VM581   NUMBER OF REFERENCES: 25
TITLE: CONFLICTS-OF-INTEREST AND COMMITMENT IN ACADEMIC
SCIENCE IN THE
    UNITED-STATES


1/6/10
02958329   GENUINE ARTICLE#: VL593   NUMBER OF REFERENCES: 68
TITLE: THE GENERATION OF TECHNOLOGY AND THE ROLE OF ACADEMIC
RESEARCH  (
    Abstract Available)
?t1/6/1-10


1/6/1
03102020   GENUINE ARTICLE#: YA387   NUMBER OF REFERENCES: 24
TITLE: A state-federal partnership in support of science and technology -
    Response  (ABSTRACT AVAILABLE)


1/6/2
03094956   GENUINE ARTICLE#: XX574   NUMBER OF REFERENCES: 94
TITLE: The Cold War, RAND, and the generation of knowledge, 1946-1962


1/6/3
03090791   GENUINE ARTICLE#: XV536   NUMBER OF REFERENCES: 74
TITLE: The science-society contract in historical transformation: with
    special reference to "epistemic drift"  (ABSTRACT AVAILABLE)


1/6/4
03065906   GENUINE ARTICLE#: XJ075   NUMBER OF REFERENCES: 65
TITLE: The virtues of mundane science


1/6/5
03041519   GENUINE ARTICLE#: WY096   NUMBER OF REFERENCES: 60
TITLE: Is there endogenous long-run growth? Evidence from the United States
    and the United Kingdom  (ABSTRACT AVAILABLE)


1/6/6
03006086   GENUINE ARTICLE#: WG782   NUMBER OF REFERENCES: 67
```

Figure 2.12   cont'd

TITLE: Bibliometrics, citation analysis and co-citation analysis: A review
   of literature .2. (ABSTRACT AVAILABLE)

   1/6/7
   02997543   GENUINE ARTICLE#: WD529   NUMBER OF REFERENCES: 46
   TITLE: Education: Moving from chemistry to chemical engineering and beyond

   1/6/8
   02972249   GENUINE ARTICLE#: VT054   NUMBER OF REFERENCES: 50
   TITLE: NATIONAL POLICIES FOR TECHNICAL CHANGE - WHERE ARE THE
   INCREASING
      RETURNS TO ECONOMIC RESEARCH (Abstract Available)

   1/6/9
   02960849   GENUINE ARTICLE#: VM581   NUMBER OF REFERENCES: 25
   TITLE: CONFLICTS-OF-INTEREST AND COMMITMENT IN ACADEMIC
   SCIENCE IN THE
      UNITED-STATES

   1/6/10
   02958329   GENUINE ARTICLE#: VL593   NUMBER OF REFERENCES: 68
   TITLE: THE GENERATION OF TECHNOLOGY AND THE ROLE OF ACADEMIC
   RESEARCH (Abstract Available)
   ?t2/6/1-10

   2/6/1
   03102075   GENUINE ARTICLE#: YA500   NUMBER OF REFERENCES: 139
   TITLE: Human-computer interaction - Whence and whither? (ABSTRACT
      AVAILABLE)

   2/6/2
   03079975   GENUINE ARTICLE#: XQ101   NUMBER OF REFERENCES: 25
   TITLE: Virtual geography (ABSTRACT AVAILABLE)

   2/6/3
   03064259   GENUINE ARTICLE#: XH508   NUMBER OF REFERENCES: 39
   TITLE: Experience with developing multimedia courseware for the World Wide
      Web: The need for better tools and clear pedagogy (ABSTRACT AVAILABLE)

   2/6/4
   03064256   GENUINE ARTICLE#: XH508   NUMBER OF REFERENCES: 16
   TITLE: How people revisit web pages: Empirical findings and implications
      for the design of history systems (ABSTRACT AVAILABLE)

Figure 2.12   cont'd

```
2/6/5
03064254   GENUINE ARTICLE#: XH508   NUMBER OF REFERENCES: 128
TITLE: Fourth generation hypermedia: Some missing links for the World Wide
   Web  (ABSTRACT AVAILABLE)


2/6/6
03060622   GENUINE ARTICLE#: XF638   NUMBER OF REFERENCES: 3
TITLE: HAL's legacy; 2001's computer as dream and reality - Stork,DG


2/6/7
03054435   GENUINE ARTICLE#: XD318   NUMBER OF REFERENCES: 26
TITLE: The nature of prediction and the information future: Arthur C.
   Clarke's Odyssey vision  (ABSTRACT AVAILABLE)


2/6/8
03047014   GENUINE ARTICLE#: WZ982   NUMBER OF REFERENCES: 11
TITLE: The future of libraries revisited


2/6/9
03018118   GENUINE ARTICLE#: WN057   NUMBER OF REFERENCES: 58
TITLE: From laboratories to collaboratories: A new organizational form for
   scientific collaboration  (ABSTRACT AVAILABLE)


2/6/10
03007027   GENUINE ARTICLE#: WH163   NUMBER OF REFERENCES: 68
TITLE: The role of academic librarians in the era of information technology
(ABSTRACT AVAILABLE)
?
```

Figure 2.12   concluded

Citation searching and the Internet

The Internet is significant for citation searching in two ways.

First, it allows convenient access to citation databases, which is sometimes preferable to other network options in terms of response time and cost. Citation databases may also be searchable via a 'Web-like' front end, rather than a command-line or menu system. However, these improvements do not alter the nature of the database or the searching techniques and applications described above.

Second, and of greater significance, is the emergence of a close analogy to the citation process, and hence of citation searching, on the World Wide Web. The analogy is based on the similar role played by the citation, in linking published documents, and the hyperlink, in linking Web pages. Examining the links presented on a Web page is then the equivalent of consulting the references at the end of a published paper. Looking for citing documents is analagous to finding which Web sites have links to one of interest. This is now becoming possible, using several of the generally available Web search engines. On the ALTAVISTA engine, for example, this is done by means of the 'link' operator: thus 'link:*.city.ac.uk' will find all Web pages in the engine's index which have a link to any page at the site city.ac.uk – that of City University, London. Of course, no search engine indexes all pages on the Web, but then neither does any bibliographic database index all conventional publications. INFOSEEK and HOTBOT offer similar facilities.

The Web is a very different environment to a bibliographic database. Its dynamic nature means that links may be made and broken in a way unthinkable in the 'frozen' environment of bibliographic citations. What is found is a snapshot of a current situation, liable to unpredictable change, rather than a network incrementally increasing in complexity. Almind and Ingwersen (1997) have carried out an initial comparison of the Web with a bibliographic database from this perspective.

More research has been done on the application of 'citation-like' techniques to the Internet, using the hypertext links between Web sites as analogues of reference citation. Snyder and Rosenbaum (1999) review these applications, giving a rather critical view of the use of commercial search engines for the analysis of Web 'citations'. Their studies support the validity of using Web links as an equivalent of citations in mapping intellectual linkages, but they point out many limitations, inconsistencies and instabilities in using the current generation of search engines for this purpose. Various projects are under way, aiming at providing more reliable measures for Web linkages, for both analysis and searching. Most of these are as yet only research tools, an example being the Clever Project (Members of the Clever Project, 1999). One which is publicly available is the GOOGLE search engine, which identifies pages which are pointed to ('cited') by numerous others; these are presumed to be of high impact, and hence significance. The search engine ranks resources of this sort highly in the output from a conventional search, on the presumption that these are important resources which the searcher will want to see first. (The equivalent process with literature files – that of identifying from the output of any search those documents which are heavily cited – cannot be done automatically in literature search systems as yet.)

Smith (1999) has built upon Ingwersen's idea of the 'Web impact factor', as an analogy to the various impact factors used in conventional citation analysis, considering several forms of such measures. He concludes that they can be useful in assessing the impact of large organizations, such as research institutes, but have severe limitations in calculating the impact of both large domains, such as countries, or small domains, such as electronic journals.

Little is available in the way of experience to guide us in understanding how useful the Internet equivalent of citation searching will be. As it is based on the same principles that have been so effective in the bibliographic domain, it would be surprising if it were to have no, or little, value.

The significance of citation searching

This chapter has illustrated the range of searches for which a citation database can be a valuable tool. In some cases, citation searching is clearly the best tool available – for following up comments on a particular publication, for example. In others, citation searching is a valuable complement to other forms of information access. Several authors have emphasized the complementary nature of citation searching, pointing out its value as an alternative and support to 'conventional' subject retrieval (see, for example, Pao and Worthen, 1989; McCain, 1989; Brown, 1998). Citation searching should be an integral part of the 'toolkit' of all searchers, to be used as appropriate with other searching options. If more use were made of this valuable technique, the result would be a generally higher level of information provision.

Although the influence of the Internet, with its hypertext links, has heightened awareness of citation linkages, citation searching as a means of literature access remains a relatively little known alternative to conventional subject searching. The value of combining citation searching with other forms of retrieval in obtaining optimal results has been described for the topic of communicating risks to patients in primary health care (Matthews *et al.*, 1999), which the writers regard as a 'diffuse' area, of the kind noted above and therefore as suitable for citation searching.

The future development of the Internet, and the way in which analogous processes of citation searching may be used, is likely to form a topic of particular interest – perhaps even a new field of study – based on current ideas of 'infometrics'.

References

Almind, T. C. and Ingwersen, P. (1997), 'Informetric Analyses on the World Wide Web: Methodological Approaches to "Webometrics"', *Journal of Documentation*, **53** (4), pp. 404–426.

Atkins, A. (1999), 'The ISI Web of Science', *D-Lib Magazine*, **5**(9). Available at <URL http://www.dlib.org/dlib/september99/atkins/09atkins.html>.

Baird, L.M. and Oppenheim, C. (1994), 'Do Citations Matter?', *Journal of Information Science*, **20** (1), pp. 2–15.

Bawden, D. (1984), 'Computer-based Online Information Retrieval for Statistical Literature', *Journal of the Royal Statistical Society*, Series A 147, pp. 78–86.

Brown, C.M. (1998), 'Complementary Use of the SciSearch Database for improved Biomedical Information Searching', *Bulletin of the Medical Libraries Association*, **86** (1), pp. 63–67.

Cano, V. (1989), 'Citation Behaviour: Classification, Utility and Location', *Journal of the American Society for Information Science*, 40 (4), pp. 284–290.

Cawkell, T. (1998), 'Checking Research Progress on "Image Retrieval by Shape Matching" using the Web of Science', *Aslib Proceedings*, **50** (2), pp. 27–31.

Cronin, B. (1984), *The Citation Process*, London: Taylor Graham.

Garfield, E. (1983), *Citation Indexing; Its Theory and Application in Science, Technology and Humanities* (2nd edn), Philadelphia: ISI Press.

Garfield, E. (1985), 'History of Citation Indexes for Chemistry: A Brief Review', *Journal of Chemical Information and Computer Sciences*, **30** (1), pp. 170–174.

Garfield, E. (1989), 'Citation Behaviour – Aid or Hindrance?', *Current Contents*, May (editorial).

Knapp, S.D. (1984), 'Cocitation Searching: Some Useful Strategies', *Online*, **8** (4), pp. 43–48.

Lindsey, D. (1989), 'Using Citation Counts as a Measure of Quality in Science – Measuring What's Measurable Rather than What's Valid', *Scientometrics*, **15** (3–4), pp. 189–203.

Liu, M.X. (1993), 'The Complexities of Citation Practice – A Review of Citation Studies', *Journal of Documentation*, **49** (4), pp. 370–408.

McCain, K.W. (1989), 'Descriptor and Citation Retrieval in the Medical Behavioural Sciences Literature', *Journal of the American Society for Information Science*, **40** (4), pp. 110–114.

Matthews, E.J. *et al.* (1999), 'Efficient Literature Searching in Diffuse Topics', *Health Libraries Review*, **16**(2), pp. 112–120.

Members of the Clever Project (1999), 'Hypersearching the Web', *Scientific American*, June, pp. 44–52.

Oppenheim, C. and Renn, S. P. (1978), 'Highly Cited Old Papers and the Reason why they Continue to be Cited', *Journal of the American Society for Information Science*, **29** (5), pp. 226–231.

Pao, M.L. and Worthen, D.B. (1989), 'Retrieval Effectiveness by Semantic and Citation Searching', *Journal of the American Society for Information Science*, **40** (4), pp. 226–235.

Rosenberg, V. (1998), 'An Assessment of ISI's New Web of Science', *Information Today*, **15** (3), pp. 21, 61.

Sen, S.K. (1990), 'A Theoretical Glance at Citation Process', *International Forum on Information and Documentation*, **15** (1), pp. 3–7.

Smith, A.G. (1999), 'A Tale of Two Web Spaces: Comparing Sites Using Web Impact Factors', *Journal of Documentation*, **55**(5), pp. 577–592.

Snyder, H. and Rosenbaum, H. (1999), 'Can Search Engines be used for Web-link Analysis? A Critical View', *Journal of Documentation*, **55**(4), pp. 375–384.

Sweetland, J.H. (1989), 'Errors in Bibliographic Citations – A Continuing Problem', *Library Quarterly*, **59** (4), pp. 291–304.

Synge, R.L.M. (1990), '25 years of Science Citation Index – Some Experiences', *Journal of Chemical Information and Computer Sciences*, 30 (1), pp. 33–35.

Weinstock, M. (1971), 'Citation Indexes', *Encyclopedia of Library and Information Science*, Vol. 5, New York: Marcel Dekker, pp. 16–40.

White, H.D. (1981), 'Cocited Author Retrieval Online: An Experiment with the Social Indicators Literature', *Journal of the American Society for Information Science*, **32** (1), pp. 16–21.

White, H.D. and McCain, K.W. (1989), 'Bibliometrics', *Annual Review of Information Science and Technology*, **24**, pp. 119–186.

Wiley, D.L. (1998), 'Cited References in the Web: A Review of ISI's Web of Science', *Searcher*, **6** (1), pp. 32–39.

Chapter 3

Social and behavioural sciences
Mark Watson

Introduction

This chapter in the last edition of the *Manual* provided a table that identified virtually every significant online social science database – some 80 titles available through 22 hosts. Written in 1992, it made only passing reference to CD-ROMs, gave only a paragraph or two on full-text databases and naturally made no mention of the Internet. The last six years have seen the map of the online world change dramatically. Those changes are discussed in detail in the introduction to this volume, and feature in other chapters. The online searcher supporting most organizations with information needs in social and behavioural sciences could previously rest assured that, with subscriptions to two or three online hosts and printed abstracting/indexing services, coverage was as comprehensive as realistically could be expected. That has become a much more difficult task.

Databases are available in a confusing combination of online, CD-ROM and Web versions. With the costs of CD-ROM production falling, many new database providers are now in the marketplace. The full texts of articles are available either as added-value benefits to databases, directly from publishers or from intermediary services such as UnCover.

The differences between publisher and host are blurring, with publishers offering e-mail table-of-contents services, some journals appearing in a combination of both paper and electronic versions, and others in solely electronic versions.

The Internet is now being promoted as offering free access to the world's knowledge, with search engines describing themselves as offering access to the Internet as a 'virtual library'. The previous editions of this *Manual* were based around the concept of the online searcher as expert with access to databases which were too complicated for end users to master. The current scenario, however, is that of end-user access and no need for such intermediaries: the threat of disintermediation hangs over the head of the online searcher.

Against this background, librarians are being told that referring to themselves as information scientists or information managers is now no longer sufficient; they must become cybrarians, knowledge engineers, knowledge choreographers or chief knowledge officers, and must help in harnessing the 'corporate wisdom' through knowledge management programmes.

To help librarians burst from the dusty cocoon of traditional librarianship, there have been programmes such as the UK Higher Education Joint Information Systems Committee (JISC) eLib 'Netskills' and an Oxford/Anglia Health Authority initiative entitled 'The Librarians of the 21st Century'. In the United States a consortium of West coast universities developed a programme entitled 'How to Build a Digital Librarian' – suggesting a combination perhaps of Mary Shelley and Philip K. Dick!

The impact that these developments have had on the online searcher in the social and behavioural sciences forms a recurrent theme through this chapter. It looks in detail at a number of broad social science databases in a variety of formats (online, CD-ROM and Internet-accessible), and the online hosts and CD-ROM publishers through which they are available, drawing out the differences between each format.

To cover the whole of the social and behavioural sciences would take a book in itself, and consequently this chapter has to be selective. In order to address issues that impact on the strategy online searchers must take, regardless of the exact focus of their subject interest, it takes a vertical slice through one area of the social and behaviour sciences – social welfare. The increasing range and type of online resources are covered in some detail, with suggestions as to how such resources need to be approached by the online searcher.

The chapter will also hopefully benefit from being written by someone who is both an online searcher and a database producer, enabling different perspectives to be brought to bear on the subject.

Background

In the early to mid-1980s online searching was a relatively straightforward process. The online searcher, nearly always a librarian, would maintain subscriptions to a small number of online hosts. The pay-as-you-go model, with a modest annual subscription and further charges for online searching and printing, offered cost-effective access to a wide range of databases which could not possibly have been collected in printed format. The online searcher would have a shelf or two of manuals, thesauri, search tips, database descriptions, and log-on and password details. Library users who could not satisfy their information needs through the printed indexing and abstracting services to which the library subscribed, or through the various current contents or citation indexes on the shelves, and for whom the card catalogue or OPAC (online public access catalogue) yielded little or no success, approached the online searcher to discuss their information needs.

The online searcher would consider which online database(s) would be most likely to provide the information being sought, based on a sound knowledge of the content of key databases, and would consult the appropriate manuals and thesauri to prepare a search strategy. Subject terms from the thesauri, synonyms, broader and narrow terms and further search strategies (to be used should the initial search prove too broad or narrow) would be written down in advance – indeed, online hosts often supplied special stationery for this very purpose.

This model of the librarian as the online expert, with shelves of arcane reference tomes, may well seem a bizarre scenario for the younger generation of librarians for whom the principal sources of information are the World Wide Web and CD-ROM databases, and for whom retrieval of information through manual systems such as card catalogues and optical co-incidence cards may only have been taught in a History of Librarianship module in their qualifying studies.

The Internet's lack of speed is a frequently cited irritation to many – for whom delays of more than a couple of seconds are felt to be insufferable. Much has changed since the days when online searching was carried out using 2400 bps modems. At those speeds the time taken to print out lengthy lists of retrieved documents was such that, in many cases, it made economic sense for the search results to be printed offline at the online host and mailed to the online searcher. Eagerly awaiting an envelope from DataStar in Switzerland is such a dim and distant memory for those online searchers with ten or more years' experience.

Whilst the situation has changed dramatically in terms of the range of resources available, there is still a need to be familiar, as far as possible, with the range of options that are open to the online searcher. Choosing services to which to subscribe, based on a thorough understanding of user needs and the range of services available, is half the battle. Without that information and range of resources to hand, the online searcher will not be able to carry out a fully comprehensive search.

Until recently, the online searcher had a relatively straightforward task of choosing between several online hosts. As a rule, low-cost annual subscriptions enabled all but the most financially challenged organization to subscribe to a number of hosts such as DataStar, DIALOG and BRS. Whilst these hosts tended to have a specific focus in terms of scientific or humanities content, this was not sufficiently marked for there to be a single choice for the social science field.

The online searcher now has a much more complex task. The minimum monthly charge introduced by DIALOG in 1998 meant that a relatively inexpensive annual subscription to that host for the occasional search on one or two databases became an unviable option. The cost of annual licences of CD-ROM subscriptions can also be problematic: large academic libraries may find network licences to a number of CD-ROM titles prove cost-effective in servicing thousands of students and academics over a number of sites. For the solo online searcher in a smaller organization that, of course, is not an option, and difficult choices may have to be made in terms of which online hosts, which CD-ROMs and which Web-based services offer the best balance of coverage, content and cost.

Major bibliographic databases in the social and behavioural sciences

The mainstay for the online search will usually be the major bibliographic databases of long standing, which typically will contain several hundred thousand records and have a relatively comprehensive coverage of academic journals across a wide breadth of topics and countries. It is these benefits that make such resources so cost-effective. The availability of a number of such databases through online vendors continues to enable relatively low-cost searching of high-quality databases.

For the online searcher supporting large numbers of staff and students across several disciplines in an academic setting, a single source can often meet the needs of the majority of situations and will often take precedence over OPACs in offering subject access to local collections. For the online searcher supporting a small number of research staff in a relatively small organization, such databases offer access to a range of resources that will be obtainable through inter-library loan or electronically.

SOCIOLOGICAL ABSTRACTS

In the social and behavioural sciences major databases such as SOCIOLOGICAL ABSTRACTS, APPLIED SOCIAL SCIENCES INDEX AND ABSTRACTS, ERIC and PsycINFO are databases of high profile and long standing. Each is available in a variety of CD-ROM and online database options. The searcher will need to be aware of the coverage of each database in order to decide which database to search in specific instances, and also because of the potential for the content of a particular database to differ between the various incarnations of that database – due either to differences between formats or between the online hosts.

SOCIOLOGICAL ABSTRACTS has been one of the principal online databases in the social and behavioural sciences. Sociological Abstracts Inc. have been the driving force behind the development of this database for many years, but it is now owned by Cambridge Scientific Abstracts <URL http://www.csa.com>. The main SOCIOLOGICAL ABSTRACTS database is available online through hosts such as DIALOG and SilverPlatter, in addition to now being available as CSA SOCIOLOGICAL ABSTRACTS through the CSA Internet Database Service. SOCIOLOGICAL ABSTRACTS coverage dates from 1963, with records added after 1974 containing abstracts. The database is currently drawn from an international selection of over 2 500 journals and other serials publications.

The DataStar Web version of SOCIOLOGICAL ABSTRACTS offers both easy and advanced search screens. The easy search screen provides three search boxes in which search terms can be entered. Each box can be linked to a particular field of the database (author, title, descriptor and so on). By entering terms in each of

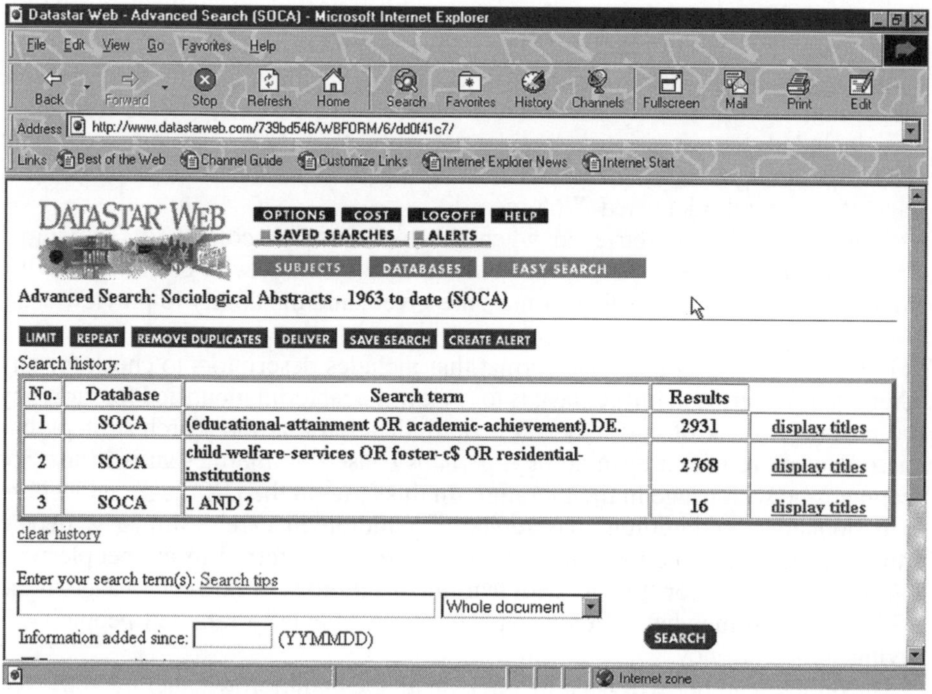

Figure 3.1   SOCIOLOGICAL ABSTRACTS on DataStar Web

the boxes, Boolean AND searches can be executed. The advanced search differs in that there is only one search box, but the search history is displayed, and the 'sets' can be combined to make up more sophisticated searches than would be possible through the easy search screen.

Figure 3.1 shows how a variety of descriptors have been combined to identify material on a topic 'the educational achievement of children in care' on DataStar Web. A key initial element in any search is to identify descriptors that best match the subject being searched. In this example two descriptors are identified as appropriate for the first part of the topic – 'educational-attainment' and 'academic-achievement'. The difference between the two descriptors may be quite apparent to those in the education field, perhaps less so for others. When browsing descriptors, it is always prudent to check beyond what may appear to be an initial match. Use of a thesaurus or descriptor listing, where available, is one means of doing this. Alternatively, viewing the first few results from a search carried out on initial descriptors in a format that includes descriptors for each record can be a useful means of double-checking for other descriptors that may help in the search. In the illustration the resultant number of hits for either of the two descriptors is 2931. For the second element of the search, in the absence of a catch-all keyword such as 'children in care', a variety of other terms have to be used: 'child-welfare-services', 'foster-care', 'foster-children', and 'residential-institutions'. In the illustration the use of a truncation symbol after 'foster-c$' will retrieve both 'foster-care' and 'foster-children'. The online searcher must be wary of using the truncator too often, particularly as a means of saving time. In this example 'residential-$' was initially used, but the search was distorted as the truncation thus included the descriptor 'residential-mobility'. This problem was only identified through viewing records in a format that included descriptors. This stage of the search identified 2768 records.

Sixteen records are retrieved when the two sets are combined. The initial display on DataStar Web is for titles only to be displayed, with each item having a tick box. A variety of display formats are given, and the ability to preview costs is a useful option.

In addition to using a display format that includes descriptors to check for any other potential terms, a further task is to review the material identified for currency and coverage. Lack of currency can be an indication that the search strategy has missed out more recent terminology, perhaps caused by the thesaurus in use not keeping pace with usage in the literature. In this case, in the UK the social welfare term 'looked after children' has replaced 'children in care'. Similarly, people previously labelled 'mentally handicapped' are now referred to as 'people with learning difficulties' or 'people with learning disabilities' – however, usage in the USA remains somewhat different with the term 'mentally retarded people' still having some currency.

The online searcher will need to assess, with the enquirer, whether the retrieved records seem to offer a satisfactory range of material. It would be possible to search ERIC for material from sources with an educational rather than a sociological focus, or to search more subject-specific focus databases on social work or child care.

SOCIOFILE

A variant of SOCIOLOGICAL ABSTRACTS is SOCIOFILE, which indexes and abstracts articles from 1800 journals published worldwide, with abstracts of journal articles published in *Sociological Abstracts* from 1974 to date and the enhanced bibliographic citations for relevant dissertations that have been added from 1986 to date, plus the SOCIAL PLANNING AND DEVELOPMENT ABSTRACTS (SOPODA) database, covering applied sociology, with detailed journal article abstracts from 1980 to date. The SOCIOFILE variant of SOCIOLOGICAL ABSTRACTS, with content dating from 1974, has to all intents and purposes ceased to exist since its coverage was brought into line with that of SOCIOLOGICAL ABSTRACTS. At the time of writing there are still references to be found to the SOCIOFILE variant, but only a very limited number of hosts now maintain this database.

APPLIED SOCIAL SCIENCES INDEX AND ABSTRACTS (ASSIA)

The APPLIED SOCIAL SCIENCES INDEX AND ABSTRACTS (ASSIA) database was launched in the mid-1980s as a monthly printed abstracting service, with annual cumulations. An online version became available on DataStar, and a CD-ROM edition was subsequently produced, currently published by Bowker-Saur. The coverage primarily dates from 1986 and between 14 to 20 000 abstracts have been added each year. ASSIA claims to be the only major service to offer the combination of psychology and sociology, as well as journals from the whole social sciences spectrum. ASSIA aims to 'provide a comprehensive reference database on modern society and its problems', and aspects of law, business, national politics, and, in particular, local government are included. The database has a strong emphasis on the applied aspects of social sciences, and their inclusion of 'grass roots practitioner journals' will enable access to a wider spread of sources than many other databases.

Approximately 680 worldwide English-based journals and newspapers representing 16 countries are routinely scanned, with about 80 per cent abstracted cover-to-cover and 20 per cent selectively. About 40 per cent of the coverage is on the UK, 45 per cent on North America and 15 per cent on the rest of the world.

The extent to which material is published in specific countries or continents is of importance when searching any large international database, and may be a deciding factor if a subscription choice between titles has to be made.

The search interface on the ASSIA CD-ROM is, in many ways, similar to a Web interface, offering selectable search boxes and drop-down lists. Each of the initially displayed search boxes has a droplist that enables the user to change the field to which that particular box refers. Fields that are not initially included are the abstract, ISSN (International Standard Serial Number) and CODEN (a six-letter unique code for journal titles).

The View Index button displays the index listing and the number of hits for the search box currently selected. In Figure 3.2 a search for material on 'day care for older people' is being carried out and the descriptor 'elderly people' has been entered in one box. It should be noted that the term 'older people' is also available as a descriptor, with a much smaller number of hits, and this will have to be combined with 'elderly people' as an OR search in this search box. The box below has been changed so that it also relates to the subject field, and the index for the subject field is being displayed. The availability of several terms to cover the concept of day care is identified, each of which will be needed to ensure a comprehensive search. Had a search been carried out simply on 'older people' and 'day care' only 20 references would have been found. By combining 'day care' and 'day centres' and 'day care centres' with 'elderly people' and 'older people' the total rises to 59. It should always be remembered that assigning subject key terms is not an automated task, and there is always bound to be some degree of inconsistency in assigning key terms to records on a database.

The ASSIA database is subject indexed through a thesaurus of more than 8000

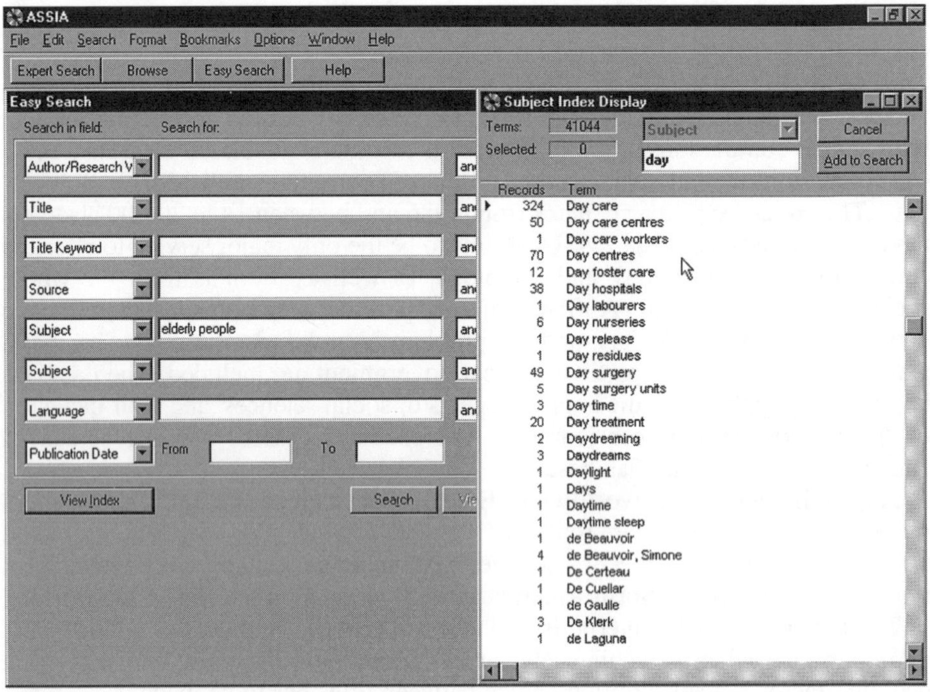

Figure 3.2   ASSIA CD-ROM

terms that can be interrogated. The view index option is used to choose a thesaurus term, which is then displayed, with related broader and narrower terms displayed. One or several terms in the thesaurus entry can be chosen and a search carried out in this way.

The expert mode offers a form of command line searching within a Windows environment, with field names helpfully displayed alongside the command line box, and the facility to combine sets. The facility to bring up the index for a particular field remains.

INTERNATIONAL BIBLIOGRAPHY OF THE SOCIAL SCIENCES (IBSS)

The INTERNATIONAL BIBLIOGRAPHY OF THE SOCIAL SCIENCES (IBSS) is an interesting relatively new major database, made available as part of a changing online landscape for the academic sector in recent years. IBSS is made available through BIDS, the Bath Information and Database Service. BIDS is supported by the Joint Information Systems Committee (JISC), which is funded by the Scottish Higher Education Funding Council, the Higher Education Funding Council for England, the Higher Education Funding Council for Wales and the

Department of Education, Northern Ireland. The JISC mission is: 'To stimulate and enable the cost effective exploitation of information systems and to provide a high quality national network infrastructure for the UK higher education and research councils communities'. BIDS is one of the many responses to this mission, and is attempting to secure access to resources on behalf of the whole of the UK academic sector.

Launched in 1991, BIDS claims a world first – a national service providing widespread network access to commercially supplied bibliographic databases, free at the point of delivery. Subscriptions to BIDS databases are free to those UK institutions funded by the Higher Education Funding Councils.

IBSS coverage dates from 1951 onwards, providing access to over 1.5 million records from nearly half a century of social science research. Current data are taken from over 2400 selected international social science journals and around 7000 books per annum. The database is updated weekly.

Bibliographic details are given of articles and reviews from journals, and chapters from some books. Abstracts are available for up to 5 per cent of the journals covered, starting from the first issues of 1997. Over 30 per cent of the original material is in languages other than English. A subject key term list is available on the Web, some 330 kb long. The list is not a structured thesaurus, as in the ASSIA database, but simply a controlled vocabulary. The lengthy listing could benefit from being broken up into smaller letter-by-letter sections.

Enhanced and basic service options are given initially. The enhanced option then offers further easy/advanced search screens. The IBSS search interface is greatly improved in terms of accessibility now that it is in Web format. The search screen offers search boxes for a combination title/keyword/abstract search, author name, journal title and book details. The online searcher should note that the default setting on the search screen is for the year range to be pre-set to the 1995–to date option, which the searcher must remember may need changing.

Available options enable the searcher to move between easy and advanced search screens, load previous sets, and save or retrieve sets. The facility to e-mail results to someone else could be of great benefit to the searcher, removing a final stage in the process of delivering results to an enquirer. For those with Java-enabled browsers, Help pulls up a screen overlay. Figure 3.3 shows the initial results from an author search for material written by E. Matilda Goldberg. IBSS covers material back to 1951 and this can be a major advantage when undertaking occasional searches for older material.

One of the major drawbacks of IBSS is the absence of abstracts, which can be a problem when no appropriate keyword can be found. In a database with such broad coverage, the keywords are necessarily not going to be as detailed as in more specific databases, and whilst the IBSS keywords are broad in scope they are not particularly deep in detail.

The aforementioned broad coverage social science databases can be supplemented by similarly comprehensive databases that have a slightly narrower focus – such as ERIC and PSYCINFO, which cover education and psychology respectively.

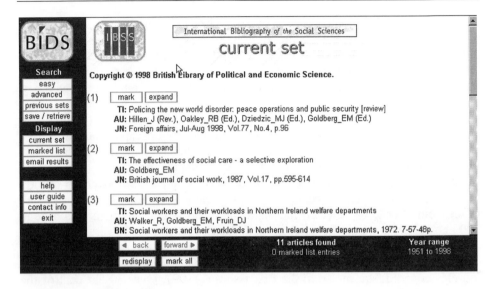

Figure 3.3   IBSS on BIDS

Whilst broad-scope bibliographic databases with large collections are the mainstay of the online searcher, as storage capacity and the speed at which data can be transmitted has increased the ability to deliver full text has produced new options. Indeed, full text offers a threat to the traditional bibliographic database as users become accustomed to obtaining direct access to primary material rather than simply to abstracts.

H.W. Wilson's SOCIAL SCIENCES ABSTRACTS FULL TEXT database uses WilsonDisc for Windows software, a modified version of SilverPlatter's WinSpirs software, previous editions having used proprietary DOS software. The online and CD-ROM sector has pressed ahead with Windows and Web access in recent years, regardless of the extent to which the online searcher is 'still' using DOS. Interestingly, in late 1998 DIALOG introduced character-based access through its Web services – 1970s retro-chic for the Digital Age. The move to using WinSpirs may be a major selling-point for the online searcher – rather than having to learn yet another database search engine, the familiarity of the software will allow concentration on the content of the database, rather than the search interface. Windows software in general has the benefit of a more standard approach to software, whereas DOS-enabled programmers tend to utilize a wide range of key combinations, function keys and so forth. However, there will be others who continue to sing the praises of DOS for its flexibility, speed of response, ability to run on low-specification PCs and so forth. Certainly it is the case that a PC running a DOS package can be booted up and the database searched in the time the latest Windows PCs take to get to their desktop.

SOCIAL SCIENCES ABSTRACTS FULL TEXT

The fairly new SOCIAL SCIENCES ABSTRACTS FULL TEXT database indexes articles from 415 journals with 115 in full text. The abstracts start from January 1994, with full text, where available, starting from January 1995.

The online guide lists the journals, with those available in full text marked accordingly. One benefit is an easily browsable list of journals, showing the range of the titles covered and enabling online searchers to identify any gaps – provided that they have the subject knowledge to make that assessment. For example, the database has abstracts and full text for the journal *International Social Work*, which is published by Sage. It abstracts, but does not have full text for, the journal *Social Work*, published by the National Association of Social Workers in Washington DC. The database does not, however, index the *British Journal of Social Work*, published by Oxford University Press on behalf of the British Association for Social Workers. For someone approaching this database looking for material relating to social work in the UK but without knowledge of the subject, there is a potential for failing to spot a significant gap in the journal literature coverage of the database.

One area that has never been clear is the gap between appearance in the print publication and appearance on the database. Some journal titles have full text available with the most recent record on the database. Others have a gap before full text appears, with the most recent records containing abstracts only. This is the most common practice throughout the database industry, as it allays publishers' fears over lost subscriptions to their print titles. Consequently, the records retrieved and displayed in the default date order with most recent first, will often be abstracts only, with items further down the retrieved list having the full text available. An option to toggle between a short display and a full display with the full text enables the user to navigate the list of references easily without being encumbered by lengthy full text. The option to search for full text only is similarly quite straightforward.

The full-text print/download options which are limited to ASCII on the CD-ROM are expanded to include HTML and Adobe Acrobat .PDF files in the Web version (see Figure 3.4).

One of the key questions for the online searcher will be the extent to which the full-text content will be of benefit compared to comparable databases that simply provide abstracts (for example, ASSIA, SOCIOLOGICAL ABSTRACTS). The exact nature of the full text is also of importance. The SOCIAL SCIENCE ABSTRACTS database contains 120 000 records, 26 000 of which are available in full text. However, it should be noted that one quarter (30 000) of the 120 000 records are book reviews, and 7000 of the 26 000 full-text records are book reviews.

The extent to which the full-text content of the database is of importance to the online searcher will, of course, depend on a wide range of issues. For the online searcher in the UK a large number of primarily North American full-text resources might offer access to information that would be otherwise difficult, or expensive and time-consuming, to obtain through inter-library loan. For students the facility

```
 Netscape - [WilsonWeb: Search]                                    _ 8 X
 File  Edit  View  Go  Bookmarks  Options  Directory  Window  Help
 ┌────┐ ┌────┐ ┌────┐  ┌────┐ ┌────┐ ┌────┐ ┌────┐ ┌────┐  ┌────┐
 │ ⇦o │ │ o⇨ │ │ 🏠 │  │ ⟲  │ │ 🖼 │ │ ≋  │ │ 🖨 │ │ 🔍 │  │ ●  │
 │Back│ │Fwd │ │Home│  │Reld│ │Imgs│ │Open│ │Prnt│ │Find│  │Stop│
 └────┘ └────┘ └────┘  └────┘ └────┘ └────┘ └────┘ └────┘  └────┘
 Location: http://wilsonweb3.hwwilson.com/cgi-bin/webspirs.cgi         ▼    ┌──┐
 ┌──────────┬───────────┬───────────┬───────────┬────────────┬─────────┐ │ N│
 │What's New!│What's Cool!│ Handbook │ Net Search │Net Directory│Software│ └──┘
 └──────────┴───────────┴───────────┴───────────┴────────────┴─────────┘
```

☐ **Entry 1 of 3 in Social Sciences Abst FT 1/83-1/98** <u>FULL TEXT, HTML VERSION</u> or <u>FULL TEXT, PDF VERSION</u>

TITLE
   Polish social services to families of children with disabilities: practice in an emerging setting
PERSONAL AUTHOR
   Gammon,-Elizabeth-Ann; Dziegielewska,-Jolanta
SOURCE
   International-Social-Work.v. 40 Oct. '97 p. 393-406.
DESCRIPTORS
   Handicapped-children-Services-for; Handicapped-children-Family-relationships;
   Social-work-Poland; Family-services-Poland .

```
 ┌──┐ Document: Done                                                    ✉?
 ┌─────────┬──────────────┬───────────┬──────────────┬──────────┬───────────┬──────────┐
 │ Start   │ VirusGuard...│ Turnpike C│  Netscap...  │ SnagIt/32│ Acrobat Re│     15:05 │
 └─────────┴──────────────┴───────────┴──────────────┴──────────┴───────────┴──────────┘
```

Figure 3.4   SOCIAL SCIENCES ABSTRACTS FULL TEXT Web interface

to search a database that will allow them to print out the full text of many items, will doubtless be an advantage. A note of caution must, of course, be offered with regard to the search habits of many users: coming across the full text of an article which appears to meet their needs (and, cynics would suggest, enables a certain amount of cribbing) will doubtless be of considerable importance to them, and the fact that there may be more relevant – but less easily accessible – material elsewhere in the library may not occur to them.

Of much smaller scope, but potentially useful for the online searcher with a need to have access to official UK government publications, is HEALTH-CD which contains over 2500 full-text documents published by the UK Department of Health since 1990, totalling over 80 000 SGML pages.

Social welfare databases

The databases covered so far in this chapter have been broad in scope, and may be familiar to the online searcher with little knowledge of the social sciences field. As has been discussed, they are useful due to the very breadth of their coverage, the sheer volume of records they contain and the international scope of their collection.

However, when a particularly in-depth search of a particular subject area is necessary, the online searcher will have to consider more subject-specific databases. The initial obstacle that the searcher will face is that these databases will typically be less available than other databases – perhaps only available on CD-ROM and not available through the major online hosts.

One of the earliest databases online in the field of social welfare was DHSS-DATA, the database of the library of the UK Department of Health and Social Security. The printed forerunner, *Social Services Abstracts*, a monthly abstracting service, was launched in 1977 with annual indexes. The database became available online in the early 1980s through DataStar.

The database utilizes a hefty thesaurus, DHSS-DATA, which covers the whole of health and personal social services, reflecting the content of the database. It should be noted however, that the social welfare content was reduced following the cessation of production of *Social Services Abstracts*. The Department of Health Library database, along with databases from the Nuffield Institute for Health and the Kings Fund Centre, are now available through SilverPlatter as the HMIC health management database, with over 265 000 abstracts.

The National Association of Social Workers in Washington DC made their SOCIAL WORK ABSTRACTS+ database available online through BRS in the mid-1980s. Covering primarily US journals, the database is now available through SilverPlatter on CD-ROM. The database mainly covers the journal literature.

The American Association of Retired Persons' AGELINE database contains 50 000 abstracts, primarily from 1978 onwards, although with selected coverage of the years 1966 to 1977. Over 300 journal titles are abstracted in its international coverage of English-language material. In addition, ageing-related dissertations from UMI's DISSERTATION ABSTRACTS and descriptions of videos are included. Subject keywords are assigned using AARP's *Thesaurus of Aging Technology*, and the database is available through a variety of hosts, including SilverPlatter, Ovid and HealthGate.

More recently, following the purchase of SOCIOLOGICAL ABSTRACTS by Cambridge Scientific Abstracts, a 'new' social welfare database has become available. The subfile of SOCIOLOGICAL ABSTRACTS, previously entitled SOPODA (Social Planning and Development Abstracts), has recently been retitled SOCIAL SERVICES ABSTRACTS and is made available through the CSA Internet Database Service.

At the time of writing these changes are only slowly filtering their way through the online world, with some confusion apparent: for example, SilverPlatter hosts 'Sociological Abstracts (previously SOCIOFILE)'.

A feature of the CSA-hosted SOCIAL SERVICES ABSTRACTS is its 'Recent References' service which provides a daily-updated supplemental database of references from over 100 core journals. This database is automatically searched at the same time as the main CSA databases.

As part of its refocusing, CSA has also developed a linked database of Web sites in this field, in addition to promoting a 'best practice' initiative within social work practice in the USA. These 'added value' resources, allied to traditional bibliographic resources which online hosts and database providers have had as their mainstay, are one indication of how the online scenario is changing in response to the challenge of the Internet.

The National Center for Child Abuse and Neglect's CHILD ABUSE & NEGLECT database is accessible free of charge through the National Information Services Corporation (NISC) both on CD-ROM (to non-profit organizations) and on the Web at <URL http://www.nisc.com>. CHILD ABUSE & NEGLECT coverage begins in 1965 and its scope is international. The Web interface offers BiblioLine Lite and BiblioLine Professional. Lite enables searching by free text and author, with the facility to view index terms and to paste them to the search screen – a simple process. The display output lists 20 records at a time with basic bibliographic details, although this number can be changed. Each item has an icon to view in full, and a tick box to mark for later printing. The free access has limited marking functions, which do not include a 'mark all' option. The searcher wishing to mark a large number of records will need to do a lot of clicking on tick boxes! The professional search screen gives further options, including the option to view the subject thesaurus and to limit by source. In this way it is possible, for example, to search for anything on satanic or ritual abuse in particular journals. For the searcher requiring UK material, a search on 'satan*' or 'ritual*' and 'british journal of social work' or 'child abuse review', quickly retrieves useful references from two major UK sources. The NISC Web site also provides links to 68 National Center for Child Abuse and Neglect Information full-text documents, a US state statutes collection, bibliographies and reference to 14 'user manuals' covering child abuse issues. These user manuals are available on the CD-ROM version, and some are available, along with the other resources, on the NCCAN Web site <URL http://www.calib.com/nccanch>.

In addition to being aware of the range of online and CD-ROM resources available in a particular field, the online searcher should also identify databases which are not available electronically. For example the major UK database of child abuse literature can be found at the NSPCC Library in London, but is not, at the time of writing, available online or on CD-ROM.

Another NISC title is the FAMILY STUDIES DATABASE, which provides over 180 000 abstracts from 1970 onwards on family welfare.

In 1989, a consortium of voluntary sector libraries (its Community Development Foundation, its Volunteer Centre and the Barnardos National Youth Agency) merged their databases and made them available online as VOLNET through the University of North London – an innovative move for the voluntary sector. The HEADFAST search interface was also innovative, although not without its idiosyncrasies, utilizing the numeric keypad to provide a windows-type interface, with pull-down lists of index terms. The VOLNET database became available on CD-ROM in 1994, and underwent a major refocusing in 1998, emerging as COMMUNITY MATTERS, with less of a focus on its bibliographic content.

The VOLNET CD-ROM was followed in quick succession by three other similar databases, developed by the libraries of three major social welfare organizations,

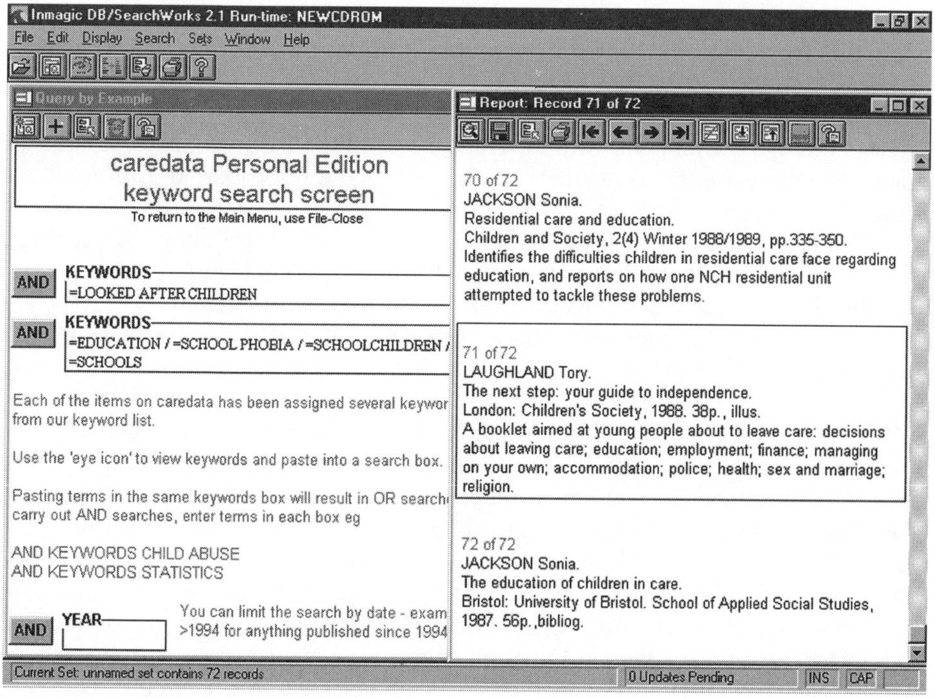

Figure 3.5   CAREDATA database search on educational attainment of children in care

and published using the *HeadFast* search engine originally utilized by VOLNET. The National Institute for Social Work's CAREDATA database contains 40 000 abstracts to the social welfare literature, with the majority of material being UK in origin and dating from the mid-1980s. The content is evenly balanced between monograph and journal article literature. Some 900 records are available in full, from a small number of journal titles which are not major academic titles from recognized publishers, but rather journals which are well known within the field (for example, *Elders*, *Practice*, *Social Work in Europe*, *New Technology in the Human Services*, and *Research Policy and Planning*). The CAREDATA database is now available on the Web, utilizing DBWebPublisher software and on CD-ROM, utilizing DBSearchWorks from Inmagic Inc. This offers another example of the shifting tectonic plates: a small non-profit organization can now publish on CD-ROM and on the Web data that formerly was the prerogative of specialized online vendors.

In Figure 3.5 the topic 'educational attainment of children in care' identifies 72 records through the use of the keywords 'looked after children' and 'education' or 'schools' or 'schoolchildren' or 'school phobia'. The final three records are displayed. The penultimate record refers to a Children's Society booklet, and the final record to a report published by a university-based research unit that appears to be particularly relevant. Both of these would be unlikely to appear on the larger bibliographic databases that concentrate on periodical literature. It should also be noted that the other article is from the journal *Children and Society*, which appears in full text on the CHILDDATA database.

CHILDDATA is published by Oxmill, the publishing arm of Head Software International, in conjunction with the National Children's Bureau, and contains the library database of the Bureau, with the full text of its journal *Children and Society*.

A limited-content Web trial version of the Centre for Policy on Ageing's AGEINFO database is available through its Web site <URL http://www.cpa.org. uk>, and it publishes the CD-ROM itself, using HeadFast software.

The extent to which these databases compare with other databases will be of importance to the online searcher who may have to choose to which to subscribe. For example, the CAREDATA database is of similar size to the SilverPlatter SOCIAL WORK ABSTRACTS+ database, and has a primarily UK coverage, as opposed to the primarily US coverage of SOCIAL WORK ABSTRACTS+. The CAREDATA database covers monographs as well as journal literature, whilst the SOCIAL WORK ABSTRACTS+ database covers a greater timespan. Additionally, the CAREDATA database has the full text of some journal articles, whilst the SOCIAL WORK ABSTRACTS+ database contains a register of licensed social workers in the USA. The CAREDATA database is available on both CD-ROM and the Web but utilizes slightly less well-known search software than the SOCIAL WORK ABSTRACTS+ database, which is available as part of the SilverPlatter Electronic Reference Library.

AUSTRALIAN FAMILY RESOURCES ON CD-ROM, published by the Australian Institute of Family Studies (AIFS) in association with RMIT Publishing, offers an interesting insight into the more confusing online landscape. A first edition published in 1994 covered documents published between 1990 and 1993. The second edition covered documents published to 1997. There are two main databases – the AUSTRALIAN FAMILY RESOURCES DATABASE and the NATIONAL CHILD ABUSE CLEARING HOUSE database.

The AUSTRALIAN FAMILY RESOURCES DATABASE includes 1346 citations and abstracts extracted from the AUSTRALIAN FAMILY & SOCIETY ABSTRACTS (FAMILY) database, linked to full-text image files (Adobe Acrobat .PDF files).

The documents are predominantly articles from a selection of key Australian journals which address social issues, policy and services of importance to families and individuals, including the *Australian Journal of Social Issues*, *Australian Journal on Ageing*, *Australian Journal of Marriage and Family*, *Family Matters* and the *Journal of Family Studies*. Other publications included are research and discussion papers, policy submissions and fact sheets.

The abstracts are initially presented in a Web-type browser, on a single, long (very long!) page. It is possible to scroll manually through the page, although a thesaurus is available which makes it possible to select and use terms to search the database. In addition to the thesaurus, a search template enables simple searches by author, title and year of publication.

Once a search has been carried out the number of hits is shown and the first record is displayed with the search terms highlighted. Rather than displaying the record on a separate page the first hit is displayed within the initial scrollable long page. Other hits are accessed by navigation through the page using Back/Next buttons. Each record gives bibliographic information and the abstract as well as a clickable link to view the full text. This link loads up the supplied Adobe Acrobat reader and the document in question. One problem with a majority of records on the database is that the images, having been scanned from originals, are not as crisp as they could be. Further problems are caused by the fact that many were in triple-column, magazine-style layout, which requires the user to scroll up, down and across the page a number of times.

The second database, the NATIONAL CHILD PROTECTION CLEARING HOUSE, contains a dozen Issues and Discussion Papers, covering topics such as 'Child abuse and neglect: incidence and prevention', 'Intergenerational transmission of maltreatment' and 'Child maltreatment and substance', typically several pages in length and widely referenced. Several shorter items taken from the *Clearing House Newsletter* and three miscellaneous articles complete the collection of CLEARING HOUSE publications. The CLEARING HOUSE database presents information relating to over 600 child abuse and neglect prevention programmes in Australia. A final resource on the database is an Adobe Acrobat version of a monograph, *Australian Family Profiles: Social and Demographic Patterns*, which, unlike the other documents on the disc, has been generated from within Adobe Acrobat software rather than from a scanned original.

The AIFS Web site is a major resource, offering access to the AIFS library database (LOIS), and the NATIONAL CHILD ABUSE CLEARING HOUSE database which appears on this CD-ROM. The Web site also contains a weekly abstracting service. The LOIS database contains over 20 000 abstracts and is freely accessible, although the search software does have limitations in terms of search options. Searching for the phrase 'united kingdom' will retrieve some 263 records. Viewing the first record, the searcher should notice that the LC (Library of Congress) headings used to classify items include Great Britain. Searching for 'Great Britain' retrieves 941 records. Combining these two searches as previous sets retrieves some 1100 records. 'Child abuse prevention' finds 4348, and combining these with the 1100 finds 308 records.

Journals on CD-ROM and online

The distinct roles of publisher and database host have become blurred in recent years. Publishers are increasingly e-mailing contents lists of their titles direct to potential customers. As mentioned earlier, full text can be made available through intermediary agencies such as UnCover, or through other proprietary systems such as Catchword. Examples of this in the UK social welfare field include the journal *Disability & Society* from Carfax, made available through the Catchword Web site.

An example of a CD-ROM from a journal publisher is FAMILY PROCESS ON CD-ROM which offers the full text of the first 36 volumes (1962–1997) of this key American journal on family therapy. Whether this type of resource is technically a database is a point of some debate. The database utilizes DynaText software, an SGML tool, which is geared primarily to presenting the full text of monographs in electronic format. The help text refers to 'books', which can cause some confusion as the contents of this particular CD-ROM are journal articles. The screen offers a 'table of contents' in one narrow column, which lists initially the 36 volumes included on the disc, with a larger portion of screen displaying the text appropriate to the selected item in the table of contents. It is fairly similar to the Web approach of using a left-column frame as a navigational tool. Each volume has a clickable box with + or –, which enables the 'tree' to be expanded or compressed as required. In this way, the contents of one particular issue of one volume can be viewed in the lefthand column and individual articles then chosen.

Double-clicking on an item in this column changes the display in the main box on screen to the item selected. SGML enables the text of articles to be displayed in high resolution with bold, italics and colour used helpfully. Tables are included as thumbnails, which are clickable, and opened as large TIFF files. The articles include references – in many cases, quite comprehensive lists. The search function is relatively simple, allowing searches for words and phrases with the use of wild cards. Once a search term or phrase has been entered, the number of hits in each particular volume is given, and Previous/Next buttons are used to move throughout the list of hits.

Databases such as the FAMILY PROCESS CD-ROM could be a potentially useful resource whether a library subscribes to the journal or not.

The absence of a controlled search vocabulary requires some attention to be paid by the online searcher. For example, a search for the phrase 'Milan Approach' (a key methodology in family therapy) identifies 97 references, the earliest being to Volume 22 in 1983. However a search for the word 'Milan' identifies references to work being carried out in Milan by Palazzoli as early as 1974 – some ten years before the 'Milan Approach' developed by Palazzoli became a regularly used term in the literature.

The American Psychological Association has developed a range of Online Members Services, based around a range of Web-based information tools which are aimed to 'assist APA Members with their professional endeavours'. In addition to over 100 years of journal article references from PSYCINFO, at the time of writing, a full-text APA Journals database is under development at <URL http://members.apa.org>.

These developments have taken place alongside the newest APA database – HISTORIC PSYCINFO, with over 250 000 citations, most with abstracts, from 1887 to 1996. Inter-library loan librarians in the psychology field should brace themselves for an increase in requests for some very old material indeed!

Citation indexes

In addition to the standard bibliographic databases that form the bulk of this chapter, the existence of an online citation index in the form of SOCIAL SCISEARCH is a major boon for a more academic approach to searching for material. The academic as an 'expert searcher' has been identified – someone for whom following a citation trail from a key article is a preferred methodology to that of a straightforward literature search. A single author or even a single article is often the starting-point for a citation search, with the questions 'who subsequently cited this article' or 'who else cited the material this author has cited' (see also Chapter 2 in this volume).

In the absence of descriptors, the use of abstracts will be the only way in which a subject approach can be made to SOCIAL SCISEARCH and, consequently, SOCIAL SCISEARCH, used in conjunction with a subject-searchable database, is likely to be most useful to online searchers approaching areas with which they are less familiar. A subject search in a database with thesaurus control and/or a Rank function to identify authors who have written several articles on a subject in question could be a useful lead-in to SOCIAL SCISEARCH.

The online SOCIAL SCISEARCH, available through DataStar Web, is a multidisciplinary index to the international journal literature of the social sciences, corresponding to the *Social Sciences Citation Index* (*SSCI*) in print and on CD-ROM, and to the journal coverage of *Current Contents/Social and Behavioral Sciences*. The database indexes all significant items (articles, book reviews, corrections, discussions, editorials, biographical items, letters, meetings and so on) from over 1400 social sciences journals published worldwide, together with selective coverage of approximately 1000 additional journals in the biomedical, natural and physical sciences areas. The coverage is from 1972 to date and the database is updated weekly. The coverage of over 1400 journals will go some way to assuring the online searcher that a search will be comprehensive in terms of the mainstream academic journal literature from 1972. Of course, the database does not cover monograph material or the more practice-oriented journal literature.

The DataStar Web interface for SOCIAL SCISEARCH offers the online searcher an easy-to-use screen with three search boxes. Boolean AND searches are carried out by entering search terms in different boxes, with each box having a drop-down list which enables the search term to be applied to either the whole document or specific elements – title, source, author, author affiliation or cited references. Options which can be included with the search are: limit searches to records added since a specific date, and restrict to documents with abstracts or to specific editions of current content editions (social and behavioural sciences, physical chemical and earth sciences, life sciences, engineering computing and technology, clinical medicine, and agriculture biology and environmental sciences).

The use of a question mark after a search term produces an index listing, which helps ensure that the search criteria are entered correctly. This is doubly helpful as the number of citations to a specific item are listed, enabling the online searcher to browse several cited items by a particular item and to find those that have been cited most.

Truncation can be used to search for citations to several articles written by the same author, provided that the author's name is not too common or that the author has not written too many articles, in which case an error message is thrown up. For example, using the truncation symbol to carry out a citation search for anything written by Everett M. Rogers, a key author in the field of the management of innovation since the late 1950s, using 'ROGERGS-E-M$', throws up an error message:

> Too many terms in truncation. Last term searched: ROGERS-E-M-1995-V22-P664

This is a tribute to the extent to which Everett M. Rogers' work is cited: even the awesome data processing power of The Dialog Corporation cannot handle this task!

Figure 3.6 shows results from a search for citations to:

> **GOLDBERG E.** Matilda, CONNELLY Naomi. The effectiveness of social care for the elderly: an overview of recent and current evaluative research. London: Heinemann/Policy Studies Institute 1982

which finds 39 records, including two published in 1998, some 16 years after the publication of the original.

DATASTAR WEB   OPTIONS   COST   LOGOFF   HELP
                      ▪ SAVED SEARCHES   ▪ ALERTS
                      SUBJECTS   DATABASES   SEARCH PAGE

Select titles and scroll down to Display choices box at the bottom of the page, or click the link above a title to display directly.

DELIVER ORDER

Documents 1 to 39 of 39 from your search GOLDBERG-E-M-1982$.CR.:

☐ Select All
☐ 1 display full format
'98 (SSCI) Are there differences in standard of care for the elderly? A comparative study of assistance decisions in Stockholm.

☐ 2 display full format
'98 (SSCI) Daycare for elderly people in Sweden: a national survey.

☐ 3 display full format
'97 (SSCI) A postmodern approach to structured dependency theory.

☐ 4 display full format
'96 (SSCI) TRANSFERRING TO AN INSTITUTION - AN ANALYSIS OF FACTORS BEHIND THE

Figure 3.6   SOCIAL SCISEARCH citation search

An interesting development in the use of citations has been made by the *British Medical Journal*. The Web version of the *BMJ* now contains the full text of all articles from each weekly issue with an increasing variety of options for readers, one of which is to register their e-mail address in order to receive details of any articles which subsequently cite an article in which they are interested. Citation searching has been very much left to the online searcher – principally, the expert online searcher – and has primarily been preferred by researchers to track literature on particular topics. Initiatives such as the e-*BMJ* might possibly bring citation searching into more popular usage.

Statistical databases

Less use may be made of statistical databases in the social and behavioural sciences than in other subject areas. It has been suggested that social workers, for instance, have achieved only a basic level of numeracy, consistent with Piaget's 'one, two, a few, many' stages of development.

SOCIAL TRENDS 1970–1995, published on CD-ROM by the Central Statistical Office (now the Office of National Statistics), provides the full text of the first 25 years' issues of the annually published volume.

One of the key resources for social science data sets for many years has been the UK Economic and Social Research Council's Data Archive, and the ESRC DATA ARCHIVE is now online at <URL http://dawww.essex.ac.uk>. The DATA ARCHIVE is a specialist national resource containing the largest collection of accessible computer-readable data in the social sciences and humanities in the UK. There are several ways to search the Archive's data holdings. Bibliographic Information Retrieval Online (BIRON) is the Data Archive's primary search engine, with searches performed on catalogue records (study descriptions) and keywords describing the studies in the Archive's collection. It is also possible to browse a title list of the major data sets held by the Archive which include, among other items, large government data series such as the Family Expenditure Survey and the Labour Force Survey. The Integrated Data Catalogue links to other European and worldwide data archive catalogues. The HUMANITIES AND SOCIAL SCIENCE ELECTRONIC THESAURUS (HASSET) is a thesaurus of terms used for indexing data sets in the Archive.

Other online data include BRITISH ELECTION STUDIES, 1963–1992, which contains files from the national General Election Surveys conducted in Great Britain between 1963 and 1992. The data can be downloaded as SPSS files (a statistical package, originally Statistical Package for the Social Sciences but now Statistical Product and Service Solutions). The GREAT BRITAIN HISTORICAL DATABASE is a large database of geographically located nineteenth- and twentieth-century aggregate statistics for Great Britain.

Access to overseas statistics is being enabled through NETWORKED SOCIAL SCIENCE TOOLS AND RESOURCES (NESSTAR), supported by ESRC with the Danish Data Archives and Norwegian Social Science Data Services. The proposed NESSTAR system will include an enhanced version of the INTEGRATED DATA CATALOGUE which will enable users to search for relevant data across several countries in one action, allowing searching of study descriptions of identified data sets. A text search system will enable searches by individual field names or variable names within data sets, including the ability to search for similar themes across data sets. A data browsing and visualization system will enable users to conduct simple data analysis online, and an authentication system will facilitate access to more sensitive data sets.

R·CADE <URL http://www-rcade.dur.ac.uk> provides efficient access to key statistical data about Europe, with official statistics available from the European Union Statistical Office (Eurostat), United Nations Educational, Scientific and Cultural Organization (Unesco), the International Labour Organization (ILO) and the United Nations Industrial Development Organization (UNIDO).

In order to keep track of resources of this type on the Internet the DIRECTORY OF OPEN ACCESS STATISTICAL INFORMATION SITES <URL http://www.plym.ac.uk/oasis/index.html> OASIS database contains information about sites on the World Wide Web which contain secondary statistical data, most of which are free of charge.

Internet subject gateways as databases

The use of Internet gateways as routes into social and behavioural science databases has increased with the dramatic growth of the Internet. In the UK the academic sector has taken significant steps in developing the potential of the Internet to support learning, particularly through the Joint Information Systems Council Electronic Libraries Programme (eLib).

The SOCIAL SCIENCE INTERNET GATEWAY (SOSIG) <URL http://www.sosig.ac.uk> is an online catalogue of thousands of high-quality Internet resources, both UK and worldwide, relevant to social science education and research. SOSIG is part of a Resource Discovery Network <URL http://www.rdn.ac.uk> that links several such gateways across the academic sector in the UK. Each catalogued resource has been selected and described by a librarian or subject specialist, and the user has the option to search or browse the catalogue.

Searching for the term 'database' with a worldwide coverage finds more than 300 references. Unfortunately the software is unable to display this many. Limiting the search to UK Web sites identifies almost 100 of them. The list covers some large databases such as IBSS, but neglects to mention others. Smaller Web-based databases, which may be of interest to the social science enquirer and which might otherwise be difficult to locate, include the STATEWATCH DATABASE <URL http://www.statewatch.org.uk> which aims to monitor the state and civil liberties in the European Union and which covers:

- policing and Europe
- security and intelligence agencies

- the Schengen Agreement
- prisons, immigration and asylum
- racism and fascism
- Northern Ireland
- civil liberties
- the law and the European courts
- The Council of Justice
- home affairs ministers and issues in the European Union.

The database contains over 23 000 entries including: features; books; pamphlets; reports; EU resolutions and agreements; debates in the UK Houses of Commons and Lords and the European Parliament; reports on cases in the European courts; and the Institute of Race Relations' European Race Audit. As with any Web-based resource, the nature of the material that is freely accessible needs to be monitored. This free access database is an archive of Statewatch's work, and the contents of the regular subscriber bulletin, published six times per year, are not entered into the database until six months after publication.

A further database that is identified is the Counselling in Primary Care Trust's Web site COUNSEL.LITDATABASE <URL http://www.cpct.co.uk> – a relatively small database, but tightly focused and free of charge.

One of the leading US resources is the SCOUT REPORT FOR SOCIAL SCIENCES <URL http://scout.cs.wisc.edu/scout/report/socsci/index.html>, the target audience of which is the faculty, students, staff and librarians in the social sciences. Each bi-weekly issue offers a selective collection of Internet resources covering topics in the fields that have been chosen by librarians and content specialists in the given area of study. The REPORT is divided into two parts – site annotation and current awareness – although there may be some overlap between the two.

Site annotations are organized in thematic areas of research, learning resources and professional and general interest. Selected current awareness resources are provided in the areas of publication resources (books, journals, technical reports and other reports), conference and meeting announcements and calls for papers, grant announcements and updated data sets, among others. These current awareness resources are not meant to be exhaustive, but rather a sample of what is currently available. There is a link from the current awareness and data sections to a current awareness metapage which provides current resources for: Full Text Papers and Articles, Tables of Contents for New Journals, Government Papers, Publishers, Think Tank Policy Papers, Data/Statistics, Conferences, Employment/ Funding. THE SCOUT REPORT FOR SOCIAL SCIENCES is also provided via e-mail.

The SOCIAL POLICY VIRTUAL LIBRARY <URL http://www.bath.ac.uk/ ~hsstp/world3.htm>, is part of the WWW Virtual Library. The term 'virtual library' is attractive and snappy, but somewhat misleading and the somewhat more prosaic term 'distributed subject catalogue' is also used less prominently, but more accurately.

Research databases

In the UK the Economic and Social Research Council's (ESRC) REGARD <URL http://www. regard.ac.uk> Web database contains details of research projects which have been granted awards by the ESRC as well as publications and other research activities which are products of those awards. One particularly interesting aspect of REGARD is that research award holders are able to modify their entries online. A search on 'child abuse' identifies some 71 records, with researcher(s) and project title displayed, ten per page, with a tick box against each record. Selecting items takes you to a full display such as the one shown in Figure 3.7. The award record number is a clickable link, taking you to the research award from which this output (a monograph) derives. The researcher name is also a link to other research and research outputs by that researcher.

Another major research funder in the social welfare sector, the Joseph Rowntree Foundation, offers several hundred of its research findings searchable through its Web site <URL http://www.jrf.org.uk>, available both onscreen as HTML and as .PDF files for downloading. When displayed as HTML the reader can carry out preformatted searches to identify other research findings on the same topic.

The NHS NATIONAL RESEARCH REGISTER is available through the UK Department of Health Web site <URL http://www.doh.gov.uk> and includes amongst its records a number of social welfare research projects, although the use of MeSH subject headings makes retrieval of non-medical material problematic.

A recent initiative following the September 1998 White Paper, *Information for Health*, in the United Kingdom was the establishment of a NATIONAL ELECTRONIC LIBRARY FOR HEALTH <URL http://www.nelh.nhs.uk>, which includes 'virtual branch libraries' on topics that include Learning Disabilities. There has also been a similar development in social welfare: the ELECTRONIC LIBRARY FOR SOCIAL CARE <URL http://www.elsc.org.uk>. Both these initiatives aim to promote access to key databases and research findings in their respective subject areas.

Record type :	Book
Click for award record :	R000232018
Title :	Child sexual abuse: a review of literature and educational materials / Mayes, G M: Author
Click for other products/awards :	*Mayes, G.M.*
Place: name, date :	Edinburgh : Scottish Academic Press, 1992
Pages :	227pp ISBN : 0707307066

Figure 3.7   ESRC REGARD record

Conclusion

The online searcher has a much wider range of databases in the field of the social and behavioural sciences from which to choose than was the case even five years ago. However, the proliferation of CD-ROM databases has meant that, for many online searchers, choices will have to be made regarding subscriptions. Decisions will also have to be made with respect to electronic document delivery services and subscriptions to Web sites of publishers which are making their content available online either themselves or through other commercial document delivery services.

Having made these decisions, based firmly on content, scope and currency related to user needs and continuously monitoring the range of databases to which access is available, the online searcher must become completely familiar with each database in order to work with the enquirer to attempt to identify relevant materials.

In addition to working according to this traditional model, the online searcher must also seek to be proactive, working with enquirers (or would-be enquirers) to identify electronic table of contents services, e-mail current awareness services and Web sites which can provide a steady trickle of information to the user's desktop.

It is also important for online searchers to ensure that their organization is not seduced by Web gateways/portals and intranet solutions, push–pull, intelligent agents and the like. A focus predominantly on IT solutions to meeting the needs of individuals will invariably end in tears! The expertise and skills of the online searcher will remain crucial to the cost-effective retrieval of useful information to support an organization's goals.

Chapter 4

Humanities

Vince Graziano

Introduction

A comprehensive definition of the humanities is elusive. Some describe the humanities as a branch of knowledge dealing with human beings and culture. Others prefer to view the humanities as sharing a common analytical or critical methodology. Still others group them by specialized subjects or academic disciplines, though without any consensus on which disciplines. For the purposes of this chapter, the humanities are defined as the visual and performing arts, philosophy, religion, history, and literature and language. While there are many cogent arguments to place history and language within the social sciences, the information needs and research habits of scholars and students in history and language parallel those of students and scholars in other humanities disciplines. Furthermore, in the field of library technology, bibliographic databases in history and language are usually associated with other humanities databases: the HUMANITIES INDEX has a much greater coverage of journals in the discipline of history than the SOCIAL SCIENCES INDEX, and the MLA INTER-NATIONAL BIBLIOGRAPHY is described as an index for both language and literature.

At the outset of online searching, commercial vendors clearly concentrated on offering databases in the sciences and engineering. Some would even argue that online databases were created for, and by, scientists. During the 1980s commercial online vendors increased the number of offerings in the humanities, although these were usually grouped with the social sciences. Alongside this development was the appearance and proliferation of databases in CD-ROM format. In the latter part of the 1990s database producers and commercial online vendors migrated toward fee-based access on the Internet or, more precisely, the World Wide Web, with its hypertext and hypermedia capabilities. This is a new development that promises to change the very nature of online searching. For the humanities, Internet access to bibliographic databases is growing. It should be pointed out, however, that some humanities databases (for example, the MLA INTERNATIONAL

BIBLIOGRAPHY, ATLA RELIGION INDEX and MUSIC LITERATURE INTERNATIONAL [RILM]) are no longer available through the traditional commercial online vendors. Although it is not entirely correct to state that these vendors have abandoned humanities databases, there seems to be a trend toward a return to the roots of online searching, as traditional vendors concentrate on offering science and business databases. For these and other reasons (such as availability), this chapter will focus on humanities databases in CD-ROM format, supplemented by the Web version on DIALOG.

Overview and history

Financial and market considerations are often cited as possible reasons for the slow development and availability of humanities databases. Commercial online vendors and database producers targeted a market of scientists and engineers during the 1960s and 1970s. As larger amounts of information became increasingly accessible to remote users during the 1970s, and as demand increased, the market was enlarged to include the fields of business, law and health. Targeting these groups was advantageous for database search service suppliers, as these disciplines are well represented and well funded within a broad spectrum of organizations, including universities, research institutes and corporations. By contrast, humanities scholars are usually limited to academia and their share of the total research funding is relatively small in comparison to that of scholars in the sciences, engineering, business, law and health services. As the latter constitute a much larger market and offer a greater potential for revenue, it is not surprising that they are the main target groups for commercial online vendors and database producers.

The designers of online databases also responded to the needs of the scientific and engineering communities. Matching natural language terms with Boolean operators might be considered more suitable for disciplines that typically use a fairly precise vocabulary. Many argue that the vocabulary of the humanities is not precise and that titles of scholarly works in the humanities often use figurative language which poses challenges to online database designers. Some also argue that information in the humanities is often multidimensional, highly interpretive and sometimes ambiguous or vague, benefiting more from the flexibility of the newer hypertext and hypermedia systems than the traditional Boolean systems.

Nevertheless, the number of humanities databases, including those in CD-ROM format, continues to grow. Although there may be no consensus on how to define the humanities, there is an increasing amount of literature that describes the information-seeking behaviour of students and scholars in the humanities. Naturally, there are many topics and subtopics within the humanities that are highly divergent and require diverse strategies for effective information retrieval. Yet there are also many similarities among the various humanities disciplines that justify a discussion of shared information-seeking patterns. One such similarity, reflecting the multidisciplinary nature of humanities information-seeking, is a frequent requirement to search in more than one database to retrieve relevant information on a single topic. It should be noted, however, that each discipline in the humanities does have its own requirements regarding information retrieval, and each database design attempts to match these specific requirements. Before examining the various bibliographic databases that serve the humanities, it is necessary to describe the nature of humanities research.

The nature of humanities research

An understanding of the information needs and the information-seeking behaviour of students and scholars in the humanities is a precursor to successful online or CD-ROM searching and the implementation of an effective database training programme. This section concentrates on the common elements that constitute this information-seeking behaviour.

The humanities scholar

The literature of library and information science, written during the 1970s and 1980s and dealing with electronic resources in the humanities, is replete with discussions of how humanities scholars are more likely than other groups to dislike or resist the computer. Humanists were described as slow in adopting electronic resources in comparison to scientists and engineers. However, it is perhaps more accurate to argue that the electronic information industry was slow to respond to the needs of humanists or, to be more precise, electronic secondary access services in the humanities, such as bibliographic databases, were slow to develop in comparison to the sciences, engineering, business, law, health and the social sciences. The authors of this literature generally agree that the academic community in the humanities adopted some computer applications before others. They acknowledge that humanists in various academic disciplines endorsed word-processing software, online public access catalogues, electronic mail and machine-based humanities projects before they did online searching. The reason for the low demand for online searching in the humanities lies not so much in resistance to or dislike of computers, but in the nature of humanities research and in the design and availability of online and CD-ROM databases.

Basic research in the humanities is conducted by using primary and secondary resources. Humanities scholars rely heavily on primary sources that vary widely in content, format and date of creation. These primary sources are found in several types of repositories including archives, museums and some libraries, often requiring travel to examine unique items, manuscripts or documents. It should also be noted that sometimes the medium is as important, or even more important, than the content; the original representations of specific documents or items contribute to the scholar's interpretation of events, texts or works of art. Interpretation is central to humanities scholarship. This is partly why the humanist scholar usually works alone. Research methods in the humanities are individualistic and multiple authorship, unlike in many other fields, is not common. Most humanities students and scholars, while working alone, discover additional sources of information through browsing or serendipity, which is not practical or economical online. Delegation of responsibility for searching is problematic as it usually precludes the scholar's ability to browse. On the other hand, online searching in humanities databases, as offered by the traditional online vendors, is often complex and demands the use of intermediaries. A conflict exists between the scholar's need to work alone and the need to use proficient intermediaries for online searching, and this may be another reason for the low demand and use of online databases in the humanities. The appearance and proliferation of humanities databases aimed at the end user, such as those in CD-ROM format, have partially redressed this problem.

Information needs

Scientific research is usually evolutionary, as scientists test new theories and discover new facts, generally replacing prior knowledge. Discoveries and results of experiments are published mainly in journals and conference proceedings. Information needs in business fields concentrate mostly on current data, such as financial facts, mergers, acquisitions or marketing, and are also mainly reported in the serial literature. Social scientists use a variety of research methods. Instruments such as surveys and questionnaires provide them with the evidence that forms the basis of their research, the results of which are also published largely in journals. By contrast, the monograph is normally the preferred type of publication for humanities scholars, although journal articles are sometimes equally important. Research in the humanities is based on the observation of primary sources created by the subjects of the research. This research is characterized by subjective interaction with the sources, often involving philosophical and aesthetic judgement. Research does not generally invalidate prior knowledge; information is cumulative and does not replace past endeavours. There is a greater need for retrospective materials, and scholars use sources in a wide range of formats. However, this is not to diminish the utility of secondary sources such as monographs, journal articles and other documents which are integral parts of the humanist's extensive reading list. In some ways the library, as a repository of secondary sources, is the humanities scholar's laboratory. Most of the secondary sources do not depreciate in value. Citation studies reveal that humanities scholars cite secondary sources that pre-date their research, on average, by 20 to 30 years, or even longer, depending on the research topic (Watson-Boone, 1994, p. 213).

Online search services and CD-ROM databases do not respond effectively to these information needs. First, only a few databases offer retrospective coverage as long as 30 or more years. The electronic version of PHILOSOPHER'S INDEX, which begins coverage in 1940, is an exception. The retrospective coverage of CD-ROM databases extends no further back than the starting dates of the CD-ROMs themselves, although this is beginning to change as several database producers are publishing backfiles. The Modern Language Association (MLA), for example, recently released a retrospective version of its MLA INTERNATIONAL BIBLIOGRAPHY with coverage from 1963 to 1980, H.W. Wilson has released a retrospective disc for ART INDEX, and ABC-CLIO has extended coverage for AMERICA: HISTORY AND LIFE, ARTBIBLIO-GRAPHIES MODERN and HISTORICAL ABSTRACTS. Second, most electronic indexing services in the humanities are based on the science model in the sense that they emphasize periodical articles. Humanities scholars do not use journal articles to the same extent as scholars in the sciences, engineering, business and the social sciences. Electronic indexing services usually do not cover the primary sources that are central to humanities scholarship. Coverage of monographs is limited, although some databases feature analytical indexing for the individual contents of monographic collections of essays. Humanities scholars find information in a variety of formats, and they require several bibliographic sources to create reading lists. Depending on the research topic, identifying journal articles sometimes occupies a minor role within the research process. In this sense, electronic indexing services in the humanities could only respond to a fraction of the information needs of humanities scholars.

Information-seeking practices

Information-seeking practices in the humanities differ from those in other fields in many respects: there is a greater need to retrieve different kinds of information; names and time periods are especially important; and the vocabulary of the humanities poses special problems for effective subject access.

Names

Much research in the humanities is concerned with personal names, place names and names of events. Searching electronic databases for names is often straightforward. Names of people as well as literary, musical or artistic works are often unique and therefore easily indexed and retrieved, but nevertheless name searches can be complicated by several factors. The challenges of searching for names in electronic resources are certainly not limited to the humanities, but the central role of names in humanities research magnifies the problems. Variations in spelling and standardization, especially with foreign-language names and the transliterated versions of such names, can cause difficulties. Transliterating proper names from Russian, Chinese and other languages is complicated by variant or former spellings such as Mao Tse Tung, Mao Tsetung and Mao Zedong or Koran,

Quran and Qu'ran. Some family names are common and need first names to differentiate them, often further complicated by use of initials or variant versions of first names. Some family names are also commonly found as subject terms such as White, Wood or More. Personal names with titles such as Sir or Dame, or religious titles, are difficult and often complicated by inherited titles such as Duke of Somerset or Prince of Wales, which require distinction with dates of birth and death. Pseudonyms, literary names or nicknames cause problems, especially since many bibliographic databases in the humanities do not have adequate name authority files. Many of these databases do not include cross-references and some databases do not include personal names in the Descriptor field.

Place names present special problems, in addition to variant spellings. Most database producers index place names, although indexing practices lack consistency across disciplines and databases. Place names change over time and important place names, such as cities (St Petersburg, Petrograd, Leningrad and, again, St Petersburg) and countries (Ceylon, Sri Lanka), often enter new eras in their histories with new names. Borders of countries or empires change as new countries emerge and others shrink or vanish (Czechoslovakia, Czech Republic, Slovakia). Some places are identified by more than one name such as Great Britain or the United Kingdom and its various components. Names of states or provinces are not always accompanied by the name of their larger political entity. Some databases use proper place names such as 'United States', while others use the adjectival form such as 'American'. Finally, some terms are quite vague such as 'Western', 'Eastern', or 'non-Western'.

Names of historical events are also problematic, especially when events occur in many places and are discussed in publications from several countries. An example is the Second World War which is also known as World War Two or World War II or World War 1939–1945 in Western literature and the Great Patriotic War in Russian literature. Some historical events are described in vague terms with ambivalent starting or ending dates, often depending on geographical specification. Examples of these are the Inquisition, Renaissance or Industrial Revolution. The latter is especially problematic as it can refer to a specific event or an ongoing phenomenon.

Time

Research in the humanities is concerned with the whole timespan of human achievement, but students and scholars usually focus on an era, an age or an event. Retrieving relevant information on chronological periods is often difficult and usually frustrating. Some chronological periods are known by more than one name such as the Middle Ages, the Dark Ages or the Medieval period, which is further complicated by variant spellings such as 'mediaeval'. Materials about the nineteenth century, for example, may be retrieved by using numbers or words such as nineteenth, 19th, 1800–1899, by specific dates or ranges of dates, or by commonly used descriptions such as 'Victorian'. Certain chronological periods such as ages, and even centuries, are open to interpretation. The beginning and end of a century may not be expressed in 'chronological' years, but rather by a crucial event. Many historians, for example, consider the 'nineteenth century' to have ended with the death of Queen Victoria (1901), while others believe that it ended with the outbreak of the First World War (1914). Some descriptions of time periods, such as 'modern', are especially frustrating. This adjective is used to describe something 'progressive' or 'fashionable'. It also describes a chronological period, which is frequently vague and open to interpretation. It has different meanings for different people and the chronological period to which it refers differs across disciplines. Historians generally agree that 'modern history' begins between 1450 and 1500, while the 'modern art movement' refers to a specific type of art and architecture that began in Europe in the middle of the nineteenth century. The *Philosopher's Index* uses the term 'modern' for the seventeenth and eighteenth centuries. Some database producers have attempted to index time periods, but indexing is inconsistent and errors in searching are common. It should also be noted that many secondary sources in the humanities have titles that include dates. This practice is both helpful and discouraging, depending on the topic and the dates used.

The use of various calendars over the centuries has resulted in significant errors with specific historical dates. When the Gregorian calendar was adopted in 1582 by the Catholic Church, ten days were skipped in October to correct the miscalculations of the Julian year. Most Catholic states adopted the Gregorian calendar by 1587, while the Germanies embraced the changes by 1700, Great Britain and its colonies by 1752, Japan by 1873 and Russia by 1918. By 1918 the discrepancy between the Old Style (Julian) calendar and the New Style (Gregorian) calendar was 13 days, which changed the name of an important historical event. The Russian October Revolution (also known as the November Revolution) of 1917 occurred on 25 October (Old Style) and 5 November (New Style). While most of the world has adopted the Gregorian calendar, the Muslim calendar continues to be used in most Arab countries, and the Hindu and Jewish calendars are normally used for religious purposes. The Chinese have adopted several calendars throughout their history, including the traditional Chinese calendar, the Hindu calendar (618–907), the Muslim calendar (1206–1368) and the Gregorian calendar (from 1912).

Subject access and the vocabulary of the humanities

The authors of the literature on subject access in the humanities generally describe the vocabulary as imprecise and ambiguous. Most authors agree that this imprecision renders subject access very difficult. However, evidence from two studies indicates that some of the vocabulary used by humanists is not as imprecise as had been characterized. Stephen Wiberley, in a series of articles beginning in 1983, argues that singular proper terms constitute a precise vocabulary and that subject access in the humanities is more straightforward than had been assumed. Data from the Getty End-User Online Searching Project, as reported by Marcia Bates (1996), confirm Wiberley's findings. Singular proper terms include names of unique entities such as proper names or names of creative works. Searches for such items are relatively easy but, as we have seen, problems in name searching do arise frequently and are complicated by several factors. Wiberley acknowledges and confirms that subject access in the humanities is often difficult because the vocabulary used by humanists, other than singular proper terms, is imprecise.

Many humanities databases provide only bibliographic information, and when they include abstracts, they are usually brief which essentially limits searching to words in the Title and Subject fields. Titles are especially noted for their metaphorical or figurative vocabulary. It is not readily apparent that the book *American Studies* by Mark Merlis is a novel or that the book *The Mirror and the Lamp* by M.H. Abrams is about romantic theories of poetry. Natural language in the humanities features some terms that have a range of meanings and others that are difficult to define. The term 'magic' is an example of this. The humanities are concerned with creativity, symbolism, analysis and expression – concepts that use a wide variety of words to define them. Controlled vocabulary or subject headings in humanities databases are based on their print counterparts, which usually adopted a classified arrangement. Not unlike natural language, subject headings, other than singular proper terms, are equally ambiguous and lack the detail and specificity often requested by humanists. Narrow concepts are not usually indexed, and indexing is not exhaustive since not all of the concepts contained in a document are indexed. Some database producers have attempted to modify the electronic versions of indexes to suit the requirements of humanists, but such modifications are not always reliable. Since interpretation is central to the humanities, students and scholars are sometimes concerned with the perspective employed by the author of a secondary source. Included among these approaches are Marxist, feminist, conservative or liberal points of view. Some databases allow for retrieval of such items, but indexing is inconsistent.

Databases

Bibliographic databases such as indexes and abstracts are core features of traditional online searching and are, of course, still popular. Yet many other types of databases are becoming increasingly available in electronic format. These include statistical, financial, full-text and image databases, as well as reference databases with biographical, directory, encyclopedic, dictionary and geographical information. Many of these databases are available in CD-ROM format and, following a recent trend, are expanding on to the World Wide Web, usually through fee-based subscription. Some of these databases are general reference tools and others are multidisciplinary, which render them useful for scholars in many fields. For the humanities, the major databases are still the bibliographic ones, but there are many projects that convert older texts into electronic format and others that provide digitized images, both of which are potentially helpful for humanities scholars. In addition, bibliographic databases in other fields contain useful information on the humanities. This section will describe some general reference databases and some online sources that have humanities information.

Reference databases

Producers of reference materials have entered a new era of publishing in developing electronic versions of their products. Common reference tools such as encyclopedias, dictionaries and directories are being produced on CD-ROM and on the Internet. Most of the major general encyclopedias are available in CD-ROM format, usually within a multimedia environment. ENCYCLOPAEDIA BRITANNICA is freely available on the Internet at <URL http://www.britannica. com>. One of the principal publishers of ready reference sources, Gale, created an Internet resource called GALENET, which includes the electronic versions of its well-known directories such as the ENCYCLOPEDIA OF ASSOCIATIONS, the GALE DIRECTORY OF DATABASES, the RESEARCH CENTERS DIRECTORY and the GALE DIRECTORY OF PUBLICATIONS AND BROADCAST MEDIA. Available via subscription, the Gale directories are searchable by main entry and by keyword, allowing more complete searching than is available in printed format. Gale's *Encyclopedia of Associations* and its *Research Centers and Services Directory* are also searchable online via DIALOG, allowing for comprehensive field searching including abstract, descriptor and director or officer name.

Several types of dictionary are available in electronic format. Sooner or later, most researchers will need to consult an unabridged or desk dictionary to find the definition, spelling or pronunciation of specific words. One of the classic desk dictionaries is *Merriam-Webster's Collegiate Dictionary, Tenth Edition*, now freely available on the Internet as the WWWEBSTER DICTIONARY <URL http://www.m-w.com/netdict.htm>. This online dictionary includes the main listing of words from its printed counterpart, a thesaurus, abbreviations, foreign words and phrases and biographical and geographical names. Searching is limited to the main entry by either word or phrase, and word searches retrieve all main entries that contain the word; for example, a search for the word 'music' retrieved 17 records (see Figure 4.1). Each record includes the definition as well as pronunciation, function and etymology. Hypertext links to cross-references are useful enhancements, such as the link to the definition of 'euphony' in the sample record shown in Figure 4.2.

Many dictionaries are searchable on the Internet. YAHOO! <URL http://dir. yahoo.com/Reference/Dictionaries/> provides access to several Web sites including two that contain numerous links to English, dual-language and multilingual dictionaries: the Language Dictionaries and Translators page <URL http://rivendel.com/~ric/resources/dictionary.html> and the Dictionaries page <URL http://math-www.upb.de/dictionaries/Dictionaries_noframes.html>. The

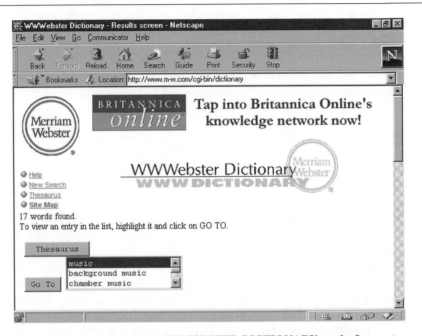

Figure 4.1   Sample search in the WWWEBSTER DICTIONARY on the Internet
Screen shot by permission of Merriam-Webster Inc., publishers of Merriam-Webster Online <URL http://www.m-w.com>.

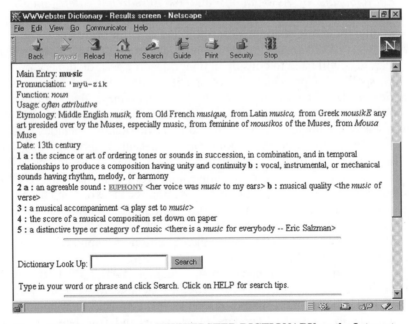

Figure 4.2   Sample record in the WWWEBSTER DICTIONARY on the Internet
Screen shot by permission of Merriam-Webster Inc., publishers of Merriam-Webster Online <URL http://www.m-w.com>.

WEB OF ON-LINE DICTIONARIES site <URL http://www.facstaff.bucknell. edu/rbeard/diction.html> contains an extensive list of language, dual-language and special dictionaries, including artificial languages. Other dictionaries and thesauri available on the Internet include several from the ARTFL Project (Project for American and French Research on the Treasury of the French Language), a cooperative project of the Institut National de la Langue Française of the Centre National de la Recherche Scientifique and the Divisions of the Humanities and Social Sciences of the University of Chicago. These are as follows:

- ARTFL Project: *Webster's Revised Unabridged Dictionary*, 1913 edition
  <URL http://humanities.uchicago.edu/forms_unrest/webster.form.html>
- ARTFL Project: *Roget's Thesaurus*, 1911 edition
  <URL http://humanities.uchicago.edu/forms_unrest/ROGET.html>
- ARTF Project: *Dictionnaires d'autrefois* which includes *Trésor de la langue française* (1606) and the *Dictionnaire de l'Académie Française*, 1st (1694), 5th (1798) and 6th (1835) editions
  <URL http://www.lib.uchicago.edu/efts/ ARTFL/projects/dicos/> (Figure 4.3)
- ARTFL Project: *French–English Dictionary*
  <URL http://humanities.uchicago.edu/forms_unrest/FR-ENG.html>.

As humanities scholars are concerned with the whole timespan of human achievement and since many primary sources consist of textual or written materials, historical or etymological dictionaries are helpful in understanding how words were used in specific eras. The *Oxford English Dictionary* (Second Edition) (*OED*) is the most authoritative source for etymology and the changing definitions of words in the English language. Available in electronic format for several platforms, the *OED* is a scholarly compilation that includes more than half a million words and traces the histories of words and meanings in use since 1150. The OXFORD ENGLISH DICTIONARY ON COMPACT DISC allows searching by keyword and four fields: text, etymology, definition and quotation. Records include pronunciation, parts of speech, etymology and variant forms, the latter usually preceded by numbers indicating the centuries in which a particular form was used (see Figure 4.4). Normally arranged in chronological order, quotations are searchable by date, author, title and text, thereby permitting extensive searches that are not possible in the printed version. Most quotations include the author and the title of the work from which a quotation is taken. Some frequently quoted authors are identified by surname only and some famous authors and titles are abbreviated and must be searched by the abbreviation, as in the case of quotations by Shakespeare (see Figure 4.5).

Searching for quotations in electronic format has the great advantage of full keyword access, allowing for a more comprehensive retrieval of quotations. The QUOTATIONS DATABASE on DIALOG is based on the third edition of the *Oxford Dictionary of Quotations* (1979), a resource with a primarily literary orientation. Although the DIALOG Blue Sheet promised that 'other quotations sources' would be added to the database, there is no indication of a plan to include the fourth edition of the *Oxford Dictionary of Quotations* (1992). The

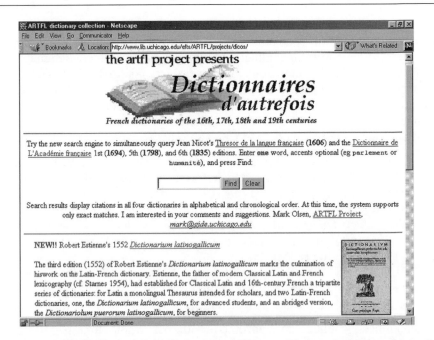

Figure 4.3   ARTFL Project at the University of Chicago: *Dictionnaires d'autrefois* **on the Internet**

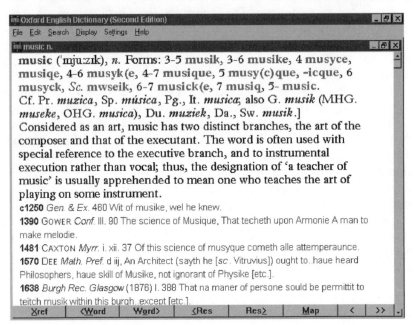

Figure 4.4   Sample record from the OXFORD ENGLISH DICTIONARY ON COMPACT DISC, 2nd edition, 1992
Reproduced by permission of Oxford University Press

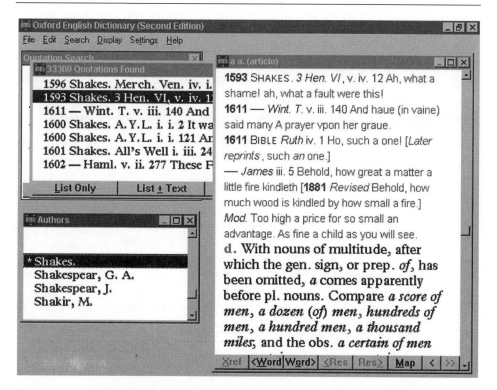

Figure 4.5   **Searching for quotations in the OXFORD ENGLISH DICTIONARY ON COMPACT DISC, 2nd edition, 1992**
Reproduced by permission of Oxford University Press

QUOTATIONS DATABASE contains more than 14 000 quotations from approximately 650 poets, novelists, playwrights, public figures and politicians. Each record includes the text of the quotation along with the author's name, birth and death dates, and the source of the quotation, all of which are searchable fields (see Figure 4.6). All words are searchable although users should remember that DIALOG stop words (for example, A, I, FOR), logical operators (AND, OR, NOT) and reserved words (FILES, FROM, STEPS, etc) must be enclosed within quotation marks. Another source of quotations is the acknowledged standard in the field of quotation books, Bartlett's *Familiar Quotations*, first compiled by John Bartlett in 1855 and now in its seventeenth edition (June 2000). The ninth edition (1901) of Bartlett's *Familiar Quotations* is searchable on the Internet <URL http://www.bartleby.com/99/index.html>, courtesy of Bartleby.com. The database is searchable by keyword and features an alphabetical list of authors, as well as a chronological index of primary authors. The Boolean OR is represented by a comma and the Boolean AND is replaced with a semi-colon. Curly brackets are used to combine Boolean expressions (nesting) and full truncation is automatic but sometimes problematic since a search for the word 'love' will retrieve 'glove', 'love' and 'lovely'.

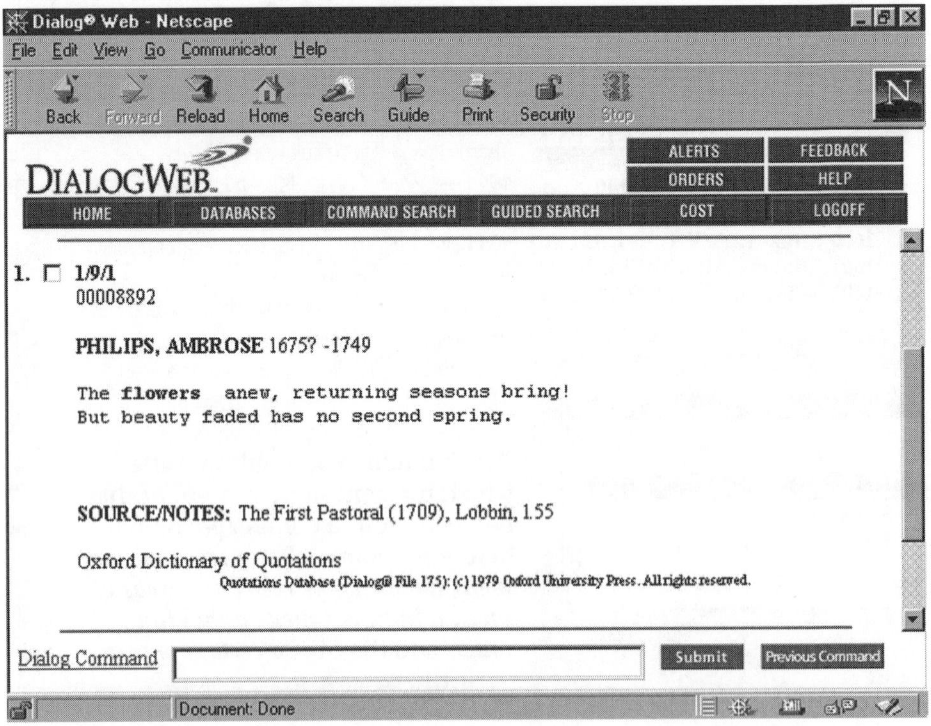

Figure 4.6   **Sample record from the QUOTATIONS DATABASE on DIALOG**

Humanities information in other fields

A review of the literature on online searching in the humanities clearly indicates that humanists are concerned with a wide variety of topics. Many studies show that humanities scholars, especially historians, identify secondary sources through the bibliographies of recent monographs and journal articles on their topics. Searches in databases outside their fields may retrieve citations that they would normally not identify through such bibliographies. These searches allow humanities scholars to identify two types of information. First, humanists occasionally require materials in other fields to elucidate, clarify or support their research. For example, the historian might be interested in the manufacturing or engineering processes of inventions to gain a greater understanding of industrialization. This type of information can be found in tertiary sources such as encyclopedias and dictionaries or in secondary literature identified through searches in databases outside the humanities. Second, databases in other fields contain ample information on the humanities. Databases in fields as diverse as agriculture, engineering, education, management, medicine and economics contain information of interest to humanities scholars such as cultural life, creative

```
 Dialog® Web - Netscape                                          _ □ ×
File  Edit  View  Go  Communicator  Help

                                              ALERTS      FEEDBACK
DIALOGWEB.                                    ORDERS        HELP
   HOME        DATABASES    COMMAND SEARCH  GUIDED SEARCH    COST       LOGOFF

                              Dialog Response

       Ref    Items  Type  RT   Index-term
       R1      1663         12  *HUMANITIES  (January 1969)
       R2       485    F     1   HUMANITIES DATA PROCESSING
       R3       352    F     1   MUSEUMS
       R4      8337    T    28   COMPUTER APPLICATIONS  (January 1969)
       R5     29796    N     4   ART  (January 1971)
       R6     41469    N     9   HISTORY  (January 1969)
       R7      2539    N     9   LANGUAGE TRANSLATION  (January 1977)
       R8     10816    N     9   LINGUISTICS  (January 1977)
       R9     62027    N     4   LITERATURE  (January 1973)
       R10     6965    N     4   MUSIC  (January 1971)
       R11     1109    R     4   ARCHAEOLOGY  (January 1973)
       R12     1966    R     5   PHILOSOPHICAL ASPECTS  (January 1969)
       R13    12694    R    13   CC=C7820 Humanities computing



Dialog Command  [                                          ]  Submit   Previous Command

        Document: Done
```

Figure 4.7   Humanities information in other fields: INSPEC on DIALOG

arts, folklore, the history of medicine and other topics. The following examples from INSPEC and MEDLINE are intended solely to illustrate humanities information found in non-humanities databases.

Using DIALOG's **Expand** command, the search on 'humanities' in INSPEC on Dialog Web reveals an abundance of information in this field (see Figure 4.7). A search combining the descriptor 'literature' with 'Beowulf' retrieved eight items, an example of which is found in Figure 4.8.

Produced by the National Library of Medicine, the MEDLINE database is available through several providers, including the National Library of Medicine <URL http://www.ncbi.nlm.nih.gov/entrez/query.fcgi?db=PubMed>. A search on 'medicine in art' as a MeSH (Medical Subject Heading) Major Topic retrieved 1012 items (see Figure 4.9). When combined with another MeSH Major Topic 'neoplasms', the search retrieved 28 documents (see Figure 4.10), four of which are displayed in Figure 4.11.

LEXIS-NEXIS

With its strong reputation as a leading provider of full-text resources in law, business and current affairs, LEXIS-NEXIS appears to be, at first glance, an

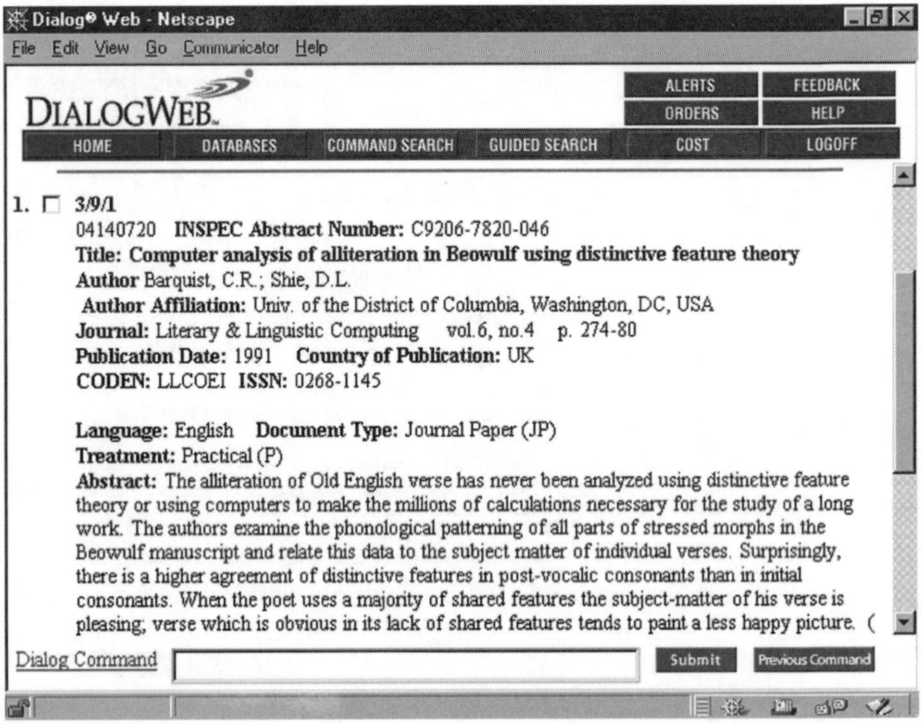

Figure 4.8   **Humanities information in other fields: INSPEC on DIALOG**

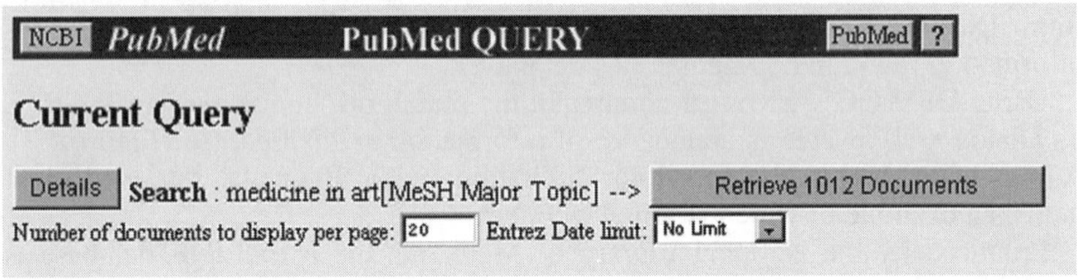

Figure 4.9   **Humanities information in other fields: MEDLINE on the Internet – medicine in art search**

unlikely source of humanities information. In fact, LEXIS-NEXIS delivers a wide variety of humanities literature, especially within the 'news' libraries. Simultaneous access to a great number of international newspapers and the ability to furnish current material, with daily updates, are among its advantages. Along with reviews of books in every discipline, newspapers offer analysis, criticism and feature stories on topics in literature, fine arts, performing arts and other humanities disciplines. Figure 4.12 shows a search in the 'current news' file (last two years) of the 'news' library, which retrieved several documents relating to the

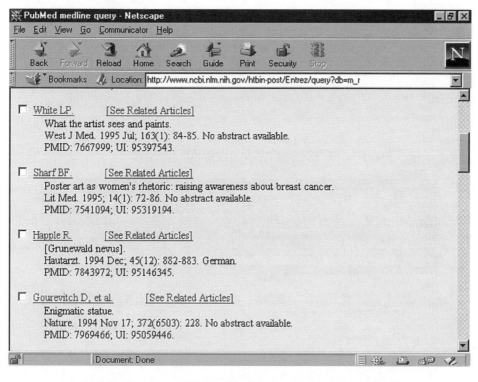

**Figure 4.10   Humanities information in other fields: MEDLINE on the Internet –
medicine in art and neoplasms search**

**Figure 4.11   Humanities information in other fields: MEDLINE on the Internet –
examples of documents retrieved by medicine in art and neoplasms search**

performance of a specific opera (see Figure 4.13). LEXIS-NEXIS facilitates
access to full-text resources that would otherwise either be unavailable or would
be slow or difficult to obtain. These include smaller local newspapers and those
from other countries or continents that would not normally be found in the
collections of nearby libraries. Such materials offer different perspectives or
interpretation of a given topic, including local opinions. Newspapers are often

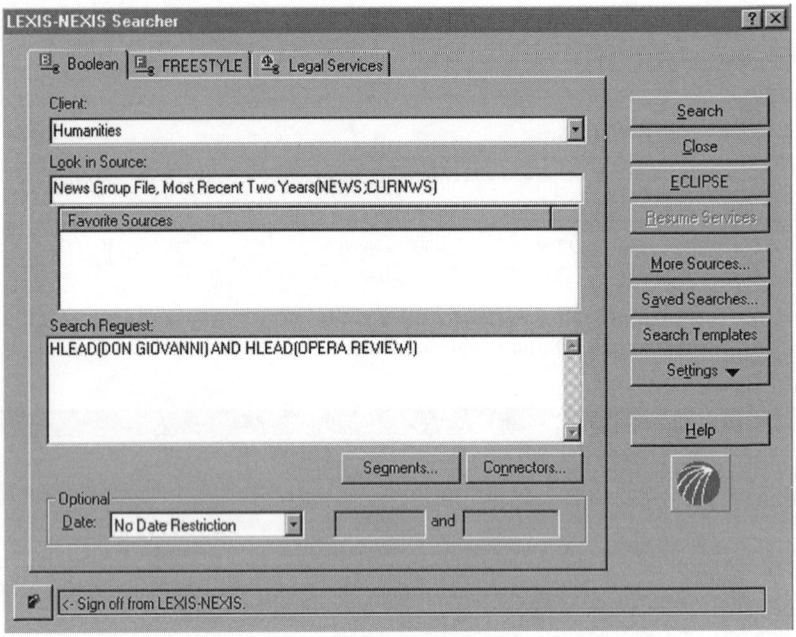

Figure 4.12   LEXIS-NEXIS *Don Giovanni* search
Reprinted with permission of LEXIS-NEXIS Group

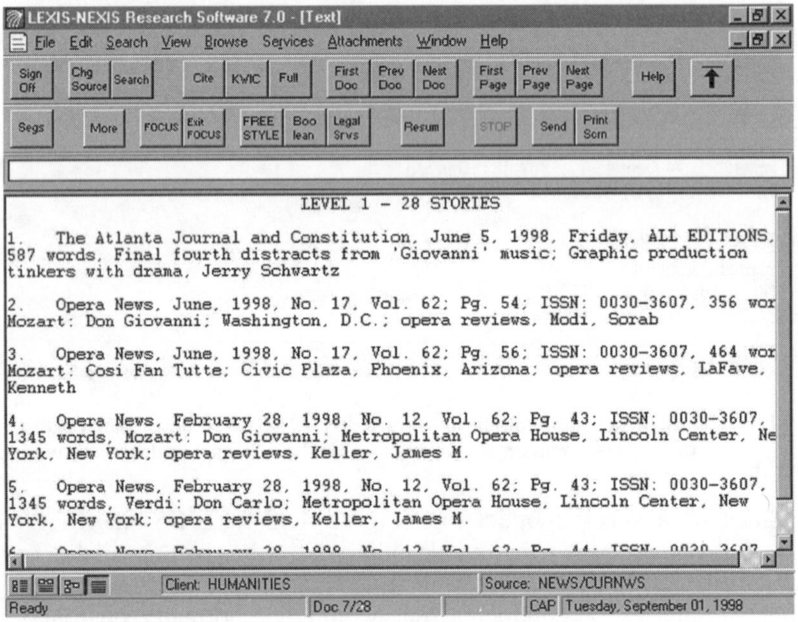

Figure 4.13   LEXIS-NEXIS *Don Giovanni* retrieved documents
Reprinted with permission of LEXIS-NEXIS Group

considered primary sources, especially for historical topics. Unfortunately, LEXIS-NEXIS does not provide the retrospective coverage often demanded by humanities scholars, but some major newspapers, such as the *Washington Post*, are covered since 1977.

Full-text and image databases on the Internet

Primary sources are often the objects of study in the humanities, and these are frequently creative works. They include written works such as manuscripts and letters, and published works such as those written by poets or philosophers. In many ways, writings of all kinds form the basis of research in the humanities. Primary sources in the visual and performing arts, in addition to written material, often include works of art or musical scores. Some of these are available in electronic format. Several commercial database producers have developed electronic products that contain the full text of literary, philosophical or religious materials, while others have developed databases that contain reproductions of paintings or drawings. Chadwyck-Healey, for example, is the leading producer of digitized texts of the traditional literary canon with CD-ROM products and Web-based databases, the latter based on recognition of the IP (Internet Protocol) address of subscribers. Commonly known as e-texts, many of these electronic texts and image resources are freely accessible on the World Wide Web. It cannot be over-emphasized that the original format of the creative works often contributes to their interpretation. Nevertheless, the Internet provides full-text and image resources that hitherto have not been freely available in electronic format.

One of the earliest digitized texts projects, PROJECT GUTENBERG, began in 1971 and is now accessible on the Web at <URL http://www.promo.net/pg/>. Project Gutenberg's goal is to provide electronic access to 10 000 texts in the public domain, generally defined in the USA as 50 years after the death of an author. Most of these texts target a general audience, but the Project also plans to provide access to authoritative editions of Shakespeare and other classics by 2001. Works can be browsed by author and title (Figure 4.14) and searched by author, title, language and subject at several FTP (File Transfer Protocol) sites (Figure 4.15). Subjects are quite broad and usually consist of one word such as 'fiction', 'adolescence' or 'mathematics'.

The ON-LINE BOOKS PAGE, hosted by the University of Pennsylvania <URL http://digital.library.upenn.edu/books/> provides links to more than 10 000 full-text works in English. The site can be searched by author, title, subject and serials (Figure 4.16). The author/title search has options for exact words or exact start of root words, a type of automatic truncation (Figure 4.17). The subject search allows for browsing by broad Library of Congress classification categories.

Other full-text Web sites include ATHENA <URL http://un2sg1.unige.ch/athena/html/athome.html> which features links to more than 3500 texts and documents in English and French, organized alphabetically by author, covering philosophy, literature, history, science and the arts. THE ENGLISH SERVER

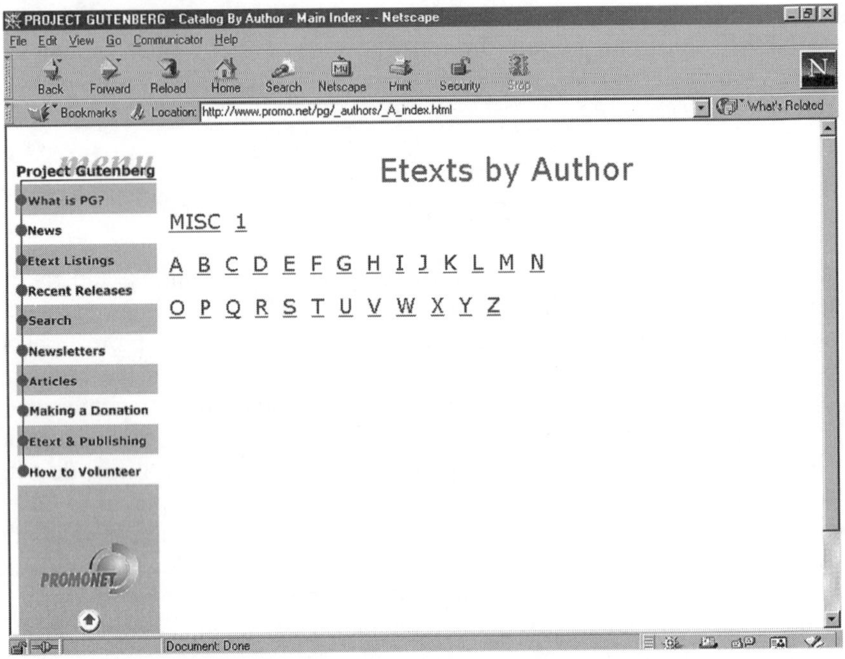

Figure 4.14   PROJECT GUTENBERG listings by author

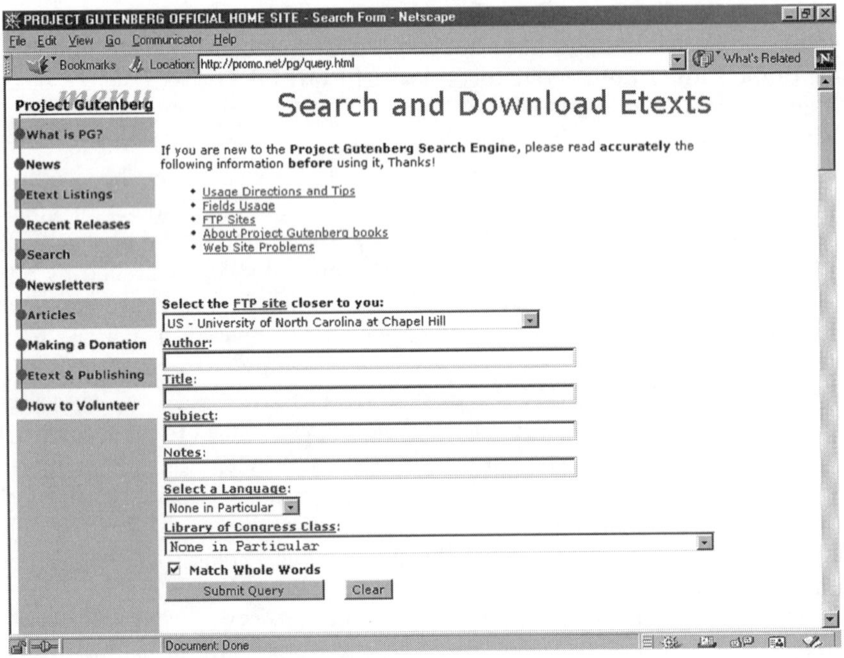

Figure 4.15   PROJECT GUTENBERG search form

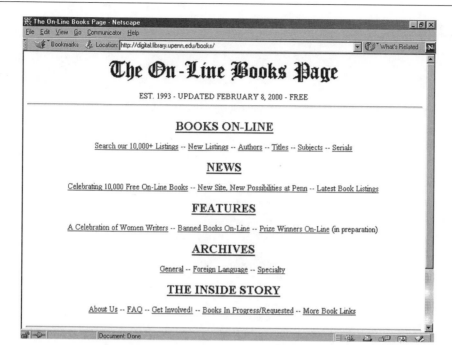

Figure 4.16   **The University of Pennsylvania's ON-LINE BOOKS PAGE**

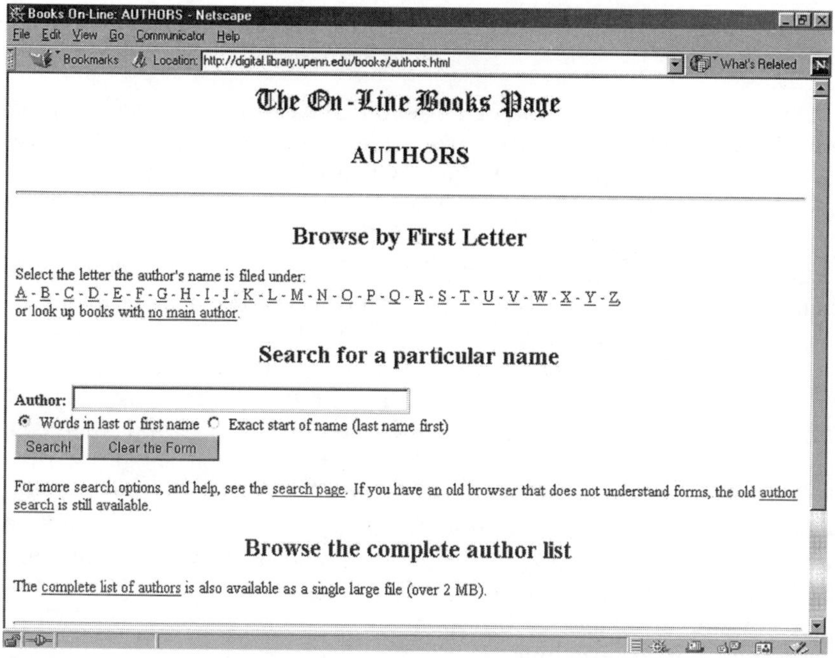

Figure 4.17   **The University of Pennsylvania's ON-LINE BOOKS PAGE search form**

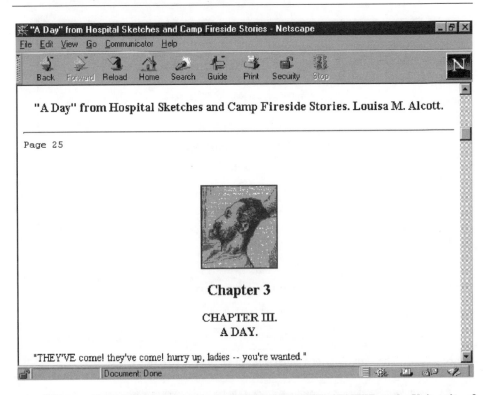

Figure 4.18   **Sample record from the ELECTRONIC TEXT CENTER at the University of Virginia**

<URL http://eserver.org> at Carnegie Mellon University is a cooperative project that provides subject browsing and keyword searching for more than 27 000 works in the humanities. The HUMANITIES TEXT INITIATIVE <URL http://www.hti. umich.edu> at the University of Michigan contains a collection of fiction and poetry texts including the American Verse Project, the Michigan Early Modern English Materials and the Middle English Collection. More than 400 Greek and Roman texts (in English translation) are searchable by title and/or author and by keyword on the INTERNET CLASSICS ARCHIVE <URL http://classics.mit. edu>. The ELECTRONIC TEXT CENTER at the University of Virginia <URL http://etext.lib.virginia.edu/> is an exemplary site for academic use. It identifies the print source, reproduces the title page and plates and other illustrations, notes changes made to the text, and retains original pagination (Figure 4.18). The CHRISTIAN CLASSICS ETHEREAL LIBRARY (CCEL) server at Wheaton College in Illinois <URL http://ccel.wheaton.edu/> houses more than 200 books, with a goal to expand coverage to 1000 titles, and represents several Christian denominations and traditions, including the works of canonical writers in English studies. Texts are available for downloading in several formats, and CCEL also provides full keyword searching.

Some of the major institutional Web sites with full-text resources include:

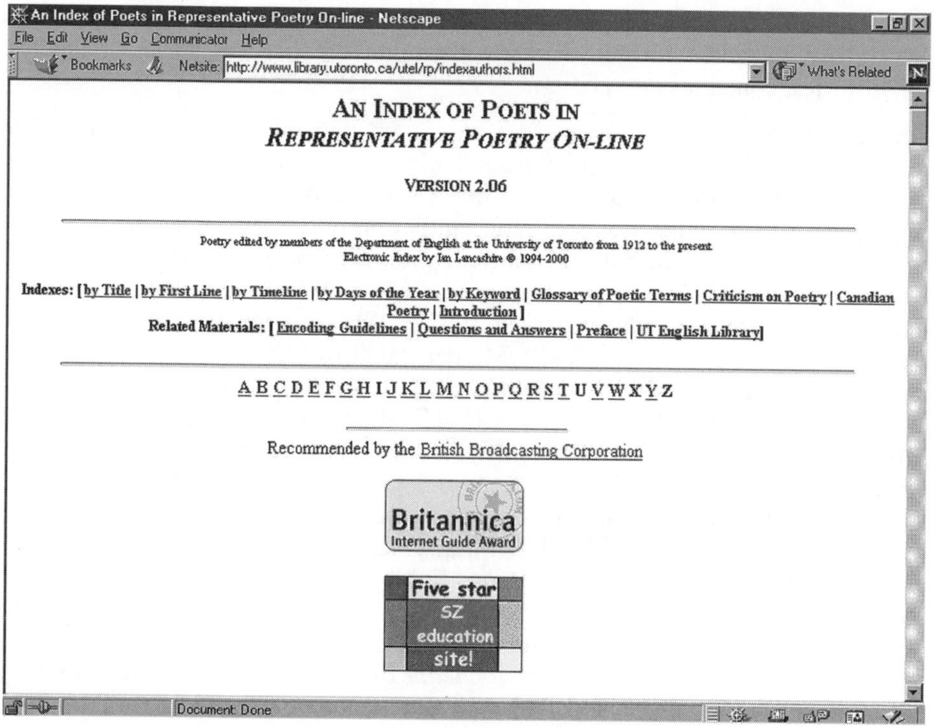

Figure 4.19   An Index of Poets in Representative Poetry at the University of Toronto

- BARTLEBY'S GREAT BOOKS ONLINE
  <URL http://www.bartleby.com>
  Provides access to literature and reference materials based on availability of authoritative editions.

- the UNIVERSITY OF TORONTO ENGLISH LIBRARY
  <URL http://www.library.utoronto.ca/www/utel/index.html>
  Electronic editions of works of poetry, drama and prose commonly studied by the English Department. Its Representative Poetry <URL http://library. utoronto.ca/www/utel/rp/indexauthors.html>
  Provides the full text of selected poems by 227 poets, including anonymous works and poetry criticism, spanning several centuries. Edited by the members of the Department, it may be browsed by poet, title, first line and timeline, and the full text can be searched by keyword (Figure 4.19).

- Western Michigan University English Department
  <URL http://www.wmich.edu/english/tchg/lit/pms/index.html>
  Lists poems organized alphabetically by author, some with study questions or commentary.

- Massachusetts Institute of Technology – *Complete Works of Shakespeare*
  <URL http://tech-two.mit.edu/Shakespeare/works.html>

Searchable by keyword. Search options include all works or single works, as well as searches for all works within one of four categories: tragedies, histories, comedies and poetry.

Unlike full-text databases, image databases, whether on CD-ROM or the Web, require state-of-the-art equipment, including a high-quality colour monitor, preferably with 16 million colours and extra Random Access Memory (RAM) and disk space. Although technology is constantly improving, image databases cannot match the high resolution of photographs. Nevertheless, image databases containing works of art are proliferating on CD-ROM and the Web. One of the leading commercial producers of art CD-ROMs is EMME, a French/Italian company that manufactures CD-ROMs dedicated to historical periods of art or individual artists. The Internet also boasts many sites with 'virtual exhibits' and 'virtual galleries'. The EINET GALAXY HUMANITIES COLLECTION <URL http://www.einet.net/galaxy/Humanities.html> lists resources organized by category, including arts, classics, literature, philosophy and religion. The Arts section provides links to numerous image resources on the Web. An example is the WEBMUSEUM NETWORK <URL http://metalab.unc.edu/wm/> that features exhibitions such as the Famous Paintings Exhibition. It includes an artist index, a theme index and a glossary. The artist index is arranged alphabetically by names (some with cross-references) and each entry includes a short biography, sometimes extracted from the *Encyclopaedia Britannica*, followed by thumbnail descriptions of the works and their physical features (see Figure 4.20). Each thumbnail description can be enlarged.

Containing more than images and full text, the AMERICAN MEMORY PROJECT is a multimedia resource compiled by the Library of Congress National Digital Library Program. The aim of this programme is to digitize documents from the Library's vast collections pertaining to American history and culture and to make them freely accessible on the World Wide Web. These include historical documents, motion pictures, manuscripts, photographs, prints, maps and sound recordings, many of which are already accessible via the Project's Web site <URL http://memory.loc.gov/ammem/amhome.html>. The Project features a Collection Finder which is organized by broad topic (see Figure 4.21). Searches may be limited by format, including photographs and prints, text documents, motion pictures, sound recordings and maps.

Catalogues on the Internet

The migration of databases to the World Wide Web includes library public access catalogues, now known as Webpacs. Taking full advantage of Web technology, many libraries are listed in the directory *Library Web-based OPACS* <URL http://www.lights.com.webcats>, which provides access to library catalogues and features a geographical index, a library-type index and a vendor index.

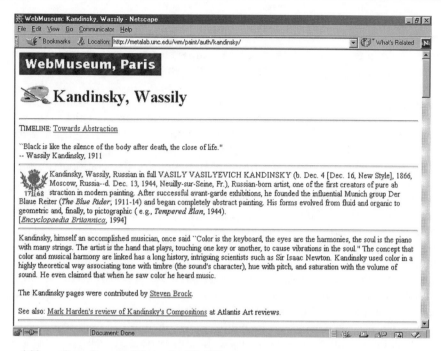

Figure 4.20   Sample record from the WEBMUSEUM

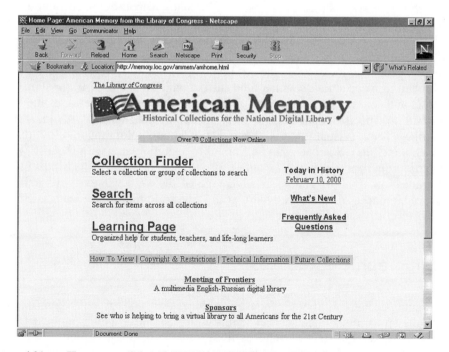

Figure 4.21   Homepage of the AMERICAN MEMORY PROJECT

Smithsonian Institution Research Information System (SIRIS)

Some catalogues on the Internet provide references to specialized collections of primary sources. One such catalogue is SIRIS, which contains large inventories of archival materials of interest to humanities scholars. In addition to Web access <URL http://www.siris.si.edu/>, SIRIS is available via modem, Telnet and TN3270. A valuable research tool, SIRIS contains six distinct catalogues, including the Smithsonian Institution library catalogue, Art Inventories, Archives and Manuscripts, Research/Bibliographies, the Juley Photographic Collection and the Smithsonian Chronology Catalog. Maintained by the National Museum of American Art, the Art Inventories database contains more than 335 000 records of American paintings and sculpture, with location information. The Archives and Manuscripts Catalog contains more than 145 000 records of items in varying media in the collections of the Archives Center of the National Museum of American History, the Archives of American Art, the Archives of American Gardens, the Eliot Elisofon Photographic Archives, the Human Studies Film Archives and the National Anthropological Archives. The Archives Center of the National Museum of American History stores hundreds of collections of manuscripts relating to American history, including social and cultural history and the histories of advertising and technology. A valuable research resource for art historians, the Archives of American Art houses papers of artists, art dealers and art historians, as well as records of museums, art galleries and art organizations.

Each of the six distinct catalogues is searchable separately (see Figure 4.22). The Web version of SIRIS allows searching by author (creator or artist), title, subject and keyword, which includes a drop-down menu with further choices such as 'cultural background' and 'genre and forms' in the Archives and Manuscripts Catalog, and 'state location' in the Art Inventories Catalog. Keyword searches can be limited to specific fields with a field suffix qualifier, such as .su. for subject, .ti. for title and so on. The format field suffixes are particularly useful, as they limit searches to specific document types. These include u.fmt. (mixed archival materials), f.fmt. (visual materials such as films and photographs), b.fmt. (books) and s.fmt.(serials). Searches can be limited to specific dates with the .dt1. suffix. Searches with root words are automatically truncated, and the (?) is also used as the truncation symbol. The great advantage of the Web version is its ability to retrieve similar items through hypertext links in important fields, such as creators or subjects, as shown in Figure 4.23.

Bibliographic databases

The remainder of this chapter focuses on the major bibliographic databases that serve the humanities. Each section begins with basic information on the database, followed by sample records and a discussion of database structure, indexing patterns, special features and problem areas. Information is gathered from printed

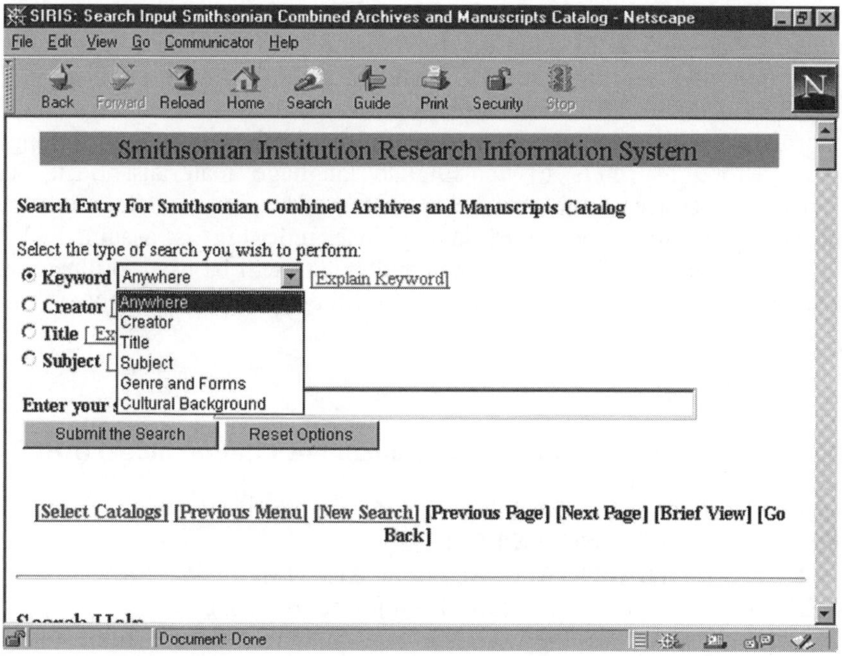

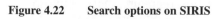

Figure 4.22 Search options on SIRIS

WebPAC: Long View Anywhere = papers and u.fmt. - Netscape

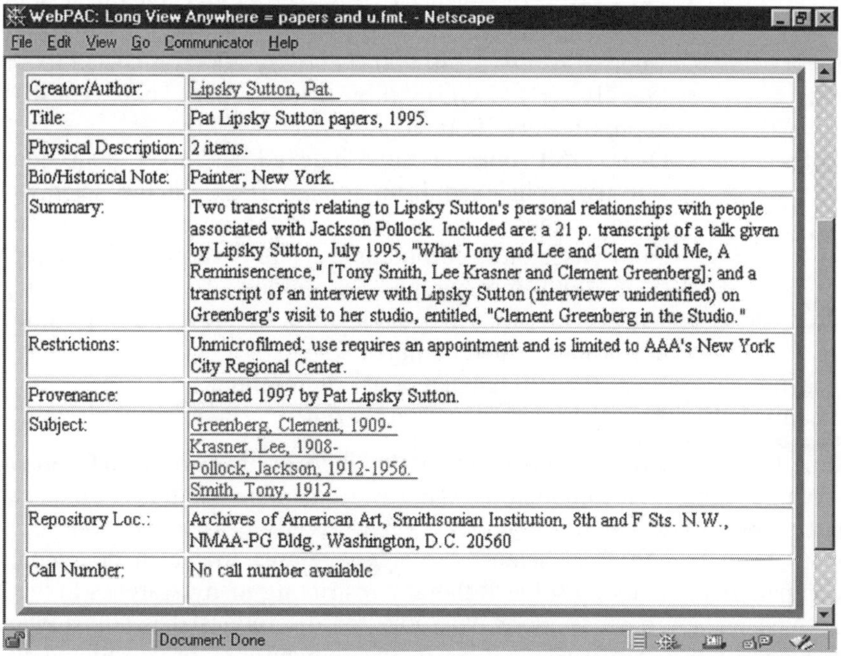

Creator/Author:	Lipsky Sutton, Pat.
Title:	Pat Lipsky Sutton papers, 1995.
Physical Description:	2 items.
Bio/Historical Note:	Painter; New York.
Summary:	Two transcripts relating to Lipsky Sutton's personal relationships with people associated with Jackson Pollock. Included are: a 21 p. transcript of a talk given by Lipsky Sutton, July 1995, "What Tony and Lee and Clem Told Me, A Reminisencence," [Tony Smith, Lee Krasner and Clement Greenberg]; and a transcript of an interview with Lipsky Sutton (interviewer unidentified) on Greenberg's visit to her studio, entitled, "Clement Greenberg in the Studio."
Restrictions:	Unmicrofilmed; use requires an appointment and is limited to AAA's New York City Regional Center.
Provenance:	Donated 1997 by Pat Lipsky Sutton.
Subject:	Greenberg, Clement, 1909- Krasner, Lee, 1908- Pollock, Jackson, 1912-1956. Smith, Tony, 1912-
Repository Loc.:	Archives of American Art, Smithsonian Institution, 8th and F Sts. N.W., NMAA-PG Bldg., Washington, D.C. 20560
Call Number:	No call number available

Document: Done

Figure 4.23 Sample record from the Archives and Manuscripts Catalog on SIRIS

user aids, Web sites, online or CD-ROM guides, and from the *Gale Directory of Databases*. The goal is to describe the database and to present searching tips without supplying a critical review. Standard fields such as publication year, source citation, author affiliation, accession and standard book and serial numbers will normally not be discussed. Since most of the databases are English language in origin, 'foreign' refers to non-English language materials. Basic search techniques and concepts will not be discussed. Knowledge of the concepts of recall and precision, and word and phrase indexing is assumed. Where appropriate, examples of search screens and results will be used to illustrate and enhance the discussion. Databases are organized by general subject area.

Multidisciplinary

ARTS & HUMANITIES SEARCH (Arts & Humanities Citation Index) (AHCI)

Producer:	Institute for Scientific Information (ISI).
Online:	DIALOG, OCLC, DataStar.
Internet:	DIALOGWeb, Web of Science (ISI).
CD-ROM:	Institute for Scientific Information (ISI).
Coverage:	Archaeology, architecture, classics, dance, film, fine arts, history, language and linguistics, literature, music, philosophy, poetry, radio, religion, television and theatre.
Start date:	1975 (Web of Science); 1980 (DIALOG, OCLC, DataStar); 1990 (CD-ROM).
Size:	Approximately 2 340 000 (February 2000 on DIALOG).
Update:	Weekly (DIALOG); three times per year (CD-ROM); approximately 2000 records added weekly.
Materials:	Over 1150 journals fully indexed and over 5000 journals selectively indexed from related fields in the sciences and social sciences. Citations include journal articles, letters, editorials, notes, chronologies, bibliographies, filmographies, books and monographs, conference proceedings, creative works (including musical scores), and reviews of print media, performances and exhibits.
Languages:	More than 30 languages are represented.
Print equivalent:	*Arts & Humanities Citation Index.*

Although the specifics of searching citation indexes are covered in Chapter 2 of this volume, some of the content of AHCI warrants discussion here since certain elements are unique to this database. First, AHCI is modelled on its older counterpart in the physical sciences, which attempts to match documents by citation patterns and not by subject, thereby restricting many searches to the Title field. Such an approach is more workable for disciplines that tend towards a precise vocabulary. Since some titles in the humanities are considered vague, AHCI indexers provide enhanced titles for such documents to add clarity and

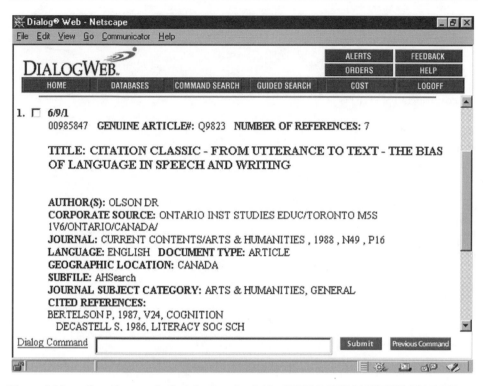

Figure 4.24 **Sample record of a 'citation classic' in ARTS & HUMANITIES SEARCH on DIALOG**

access points. Exclusive to AHCI, these title enhancements are normally enclosed within parentheses. For heavily cited source documents, the phrase 'citation classic' is added to the Title field, usually preceding the document title, allowing searchers to identify these documents and to trace the works that cite them (see Figure 4.24). Except for creative works, foreign titles are translated into English and are not accompanied by the original title.

Citation patterns in the humanities differ from those in the sciences or social sciences. Some works are not formally cited by authors in the humanities, assuming perhaps a shared or implied common knowledge with the reader. Acknowledging these citation patterns, AHCI provides general implicit citations, which are added to the Cited Reference (CR) field. General implicit citations are based on an implied reference that AHCI indexers identify and then provide, using both author and title, sometimes followed by the phrase 'cited indirectly'. Two other types of implicit citations are added to the Cited Reference field, allowing for extra access points. Defined as reproductions of works of art appearing in journals, illustrations are marked as such in the CR field and receive added entries for the artist and the work. Bars of music that appear in journal articles are also identified by AHCI indexers, who add references to the composer and the work, followed by the term 'music example' (see Figure 4.25). The (W)

01896216 GENUINE ARTICLE#: VH917 NUMBER OF REFERENCES: 18

TITLE: DUO AND DIALOG -- A STRUCTURAL AND STYLISTIC

PROBLEM IN CHAMBER-MUSIC

AUTHOR(S): EPPSTEIN H

JOURNAL: MUSIKFORSCHUNG , 1996 , V49 , N3 (JUL-SEP) , P252-275

ISSN: 0027-4801

LANGUAGE: GERMAN DOCUMENT TYPE: ARTICLE

SUBFILE: AHSearch; CC ARTS--Current Contents, Arts & Humanities

JOURNAL SUBJECT CATEGORY: MUSIC

CITED REFERENCES:

ABERT H, 1956, V2, WA MOZART

  ADORNO TW, EINLEITUNG MUSIKSOZI

  APEL W, 1969, HARVARD DICT MUSIC

  BACH JS, SONATA N1 BWV 1014, MUSIC EXAMPLE

  BEETHOVEN LV, SONATA G MAJOR VIOLI, MUSIC EXAMPLE

  BEETHOVEN LV, SONATA N2 C MINOR, MUSIC EXAMPLE

  BRAHMS J, SONATA CELLO E MINOR, MUSIC EXAMPLE

  DAHLAHUS C, 1973, V134, P561, NZFM

  ENGLANDER R, 1956, DRESDNER INSTRUMENTA

  EPPSTEIN H, 1966, STUDIEN JS BACHS SON

  EPPSTEIN H, 1972, V54, SVENSK TIDSKRIFT MUS

  FISCHER W, 1926, P21, MOZART JB

  MOZART WA, SONATA A MAJOR VIOLI, MUSIC EXAMPLE

  MOZART WA, SONATA B MAJOR KV378, MUSIC EXAMPLE

  MOZART WA, SONATA C MAJOR KV296, MUSIC EXAMPLE

  MOZART WA, SONATA E MINOR KV304, MUSIC EXAMPLE

  MOZART WA, SONATA E SHARP MAJOR, MUSIC EXAMPLE

  NEWMAN WS, 1959, SONATA BAROQUE ERA S

Figure 4.25   Sample record from ARTS & HUMANITIES SEARCH on DIALOG

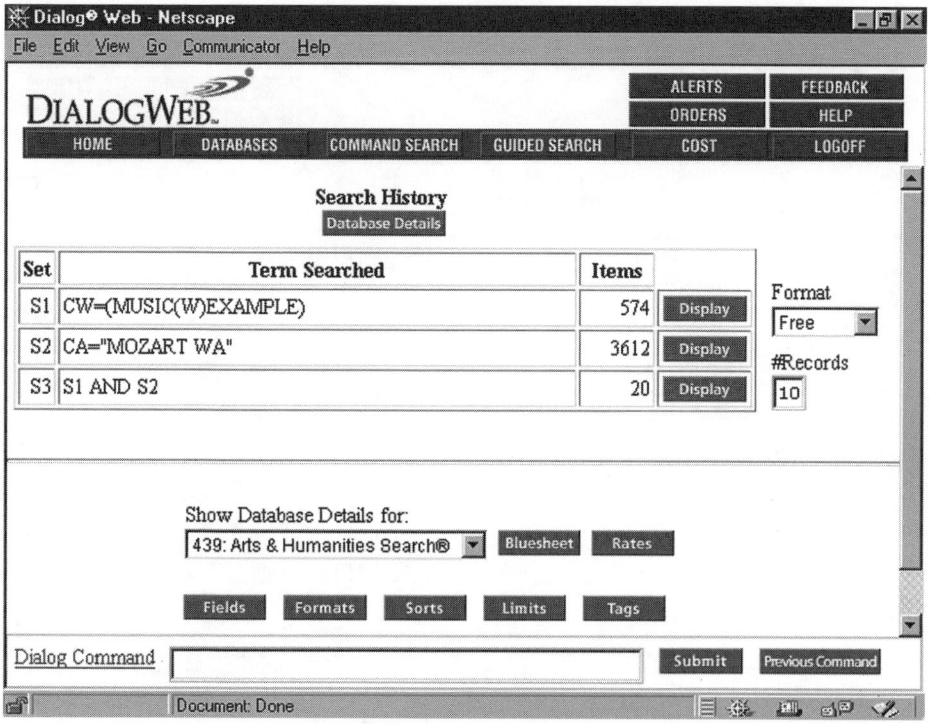

Figure 4.26 **Searching for implicit citations in ARTS & HUMANITIES SEARCH on DIALOG**

operator is effective for retrieving implicit citations (see Figure 4.26). The Cited Reference (CR) field is divided into three subfields: the Cited Work (CW) field for titles, the Cited Author (CA) field, and the Cited Year (CY) field. Additionally, each journal is assigned up to four journal subject categories, enabling broad subject searches in the SC field. Figure 4.27 shows a search for documents that cited *The English Patient*. The search is limited to both film or literary journals. Alternatively, the Cited Author (CA) field can be used to limit the search to cited references to *The English Patient* as a film, cited under the director Minghella, and as a novel, cited under the author Ondaatje.

All authors are indexed in the Author (AU) field, while only the first cited author is indexed in the CA field, which includes composers and film-makers. Names are entered without punctuation, including apostrophes, and without spaces between initials, such as 'Mozart WA', which usually dictates the use of the **Expand** command. For some authors, the online authority file will indicate the 'preferred' form, but this is not consistently used. Searches can be limited to specific languages, including English, or they can be limited to 'eng' or 'noneng'. Searches can also be limited to records that contain cited references (/CR) or those that do not (/NOCR). Other limit commands include journal article (/**ART**) and non-article (/**NART**), and for records since 1989, reviews or bibliographies

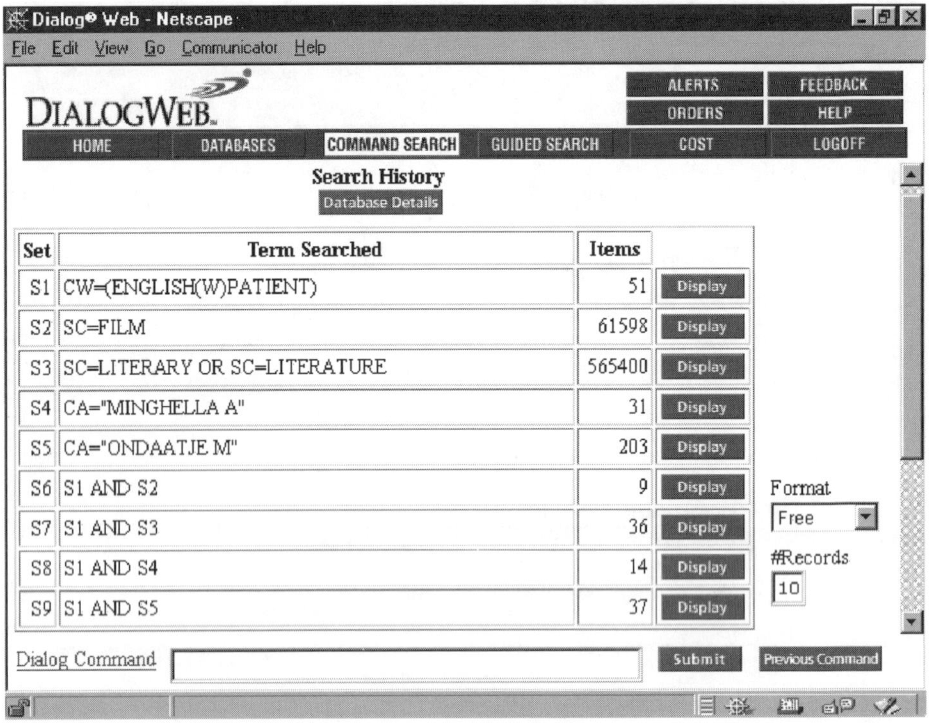

Figure 4.27   **Finding cited references for *The English Patient* as a film or literary work in ARTS & HUMANITIES SEARCH on DIALOG**

(/REV) or those that are not (/NREV). The number of references can be searched in the NR field, using numeric and range operators.

Art and interdisciplinary

ART INDEX (and ART ABSTRACTS) (AI)

Producer: H.W. Wilson.
Online: WilsonLine, OCLC.
Internet: WilsonWeb, OCLC, SilverPlatter.
CD-ROM: WilsonDisc, SilverPlatter, Ovid.
Scope: Art and architecture, including advertising art, archaeology, city planning, computer applications and graphics, crafts, film, folk art, graphic arts, industrial and interior design, museology, painting, performance art, photography, pottery, sculpture, television, textiles and video.
Start date: Indexing coverage from September 1984. Abstracting coverage

from Spring 1994. Full-text coverage from January 1997. ART INDEX RETROSPECTIVE covers 1929–84.

Size: Approximately 444 000 records in ART INDEX (February 2000).

Update: Semi-weekly, WilsonLine; monthly, WilsonDisc, SilverPlatter, Ovid; approximately 2600 records added monthly.

Materials: Includes indexing of articles, book reviews, film reviews, interviews, and reproductions of works of art in approximately 377 periodicals and museum bulletins.

Languages: Mainly English, as well as Danish, Dutch, French, German, Greek (Ancient and Modern), Italian, Japanese, Norwegian, Spanish and Swedish.

Print equivalent: *Art Index.*

HUMANITIES ABSTRACTS (and HUMANITIES INDEX) (HUA)

Producer: H.W. Wilson.
Online: WilsonLine, OCLC.
Internet: WilsonWeb, OCLC, SilverPlatter.
CD-ROM: WilsonDisc, SilverPlatter, Ovid.
Scope: Art, archaeology, classics, dance, drama, film, folklore, history, journalism, communications, language, literature, music, performing arts, philosophy, photography, and religion and theology.
Start date: Indexing coverage from February 1984. Abstracting coverage from March 1994. Full-text coverage from January 1995.
Size: Approximately 465 000 records (February 2000).
Update: Semi-weekly, WilsonLine; monthly, WilsonDisc, SilverPlatter, Ovid; approximately 3000 records added monthly.
Materials: Indexes articles and book reviews from approximately 400 periodicals.
Languages: English.
Print equivalent: *Humanities Index.*

ART INDEX (AI) and HUMANITIES ABSTRACTS (HUA) will be discussed together for several reasons. They both use the same software (CD-ROM, online and Internet versions) and are produced by the same company. Fields are essentially identical in both databases. They are both general periodical indexes, with AI covering the vast field of the visual arts and some coverage of the performing arts, and HUA covering the even more extensive field of the general humanities. Each is especially useful to an undergraduate audience; comprehensive searches, especially for graduate-level audiences and higher, should be supplemented with searches in databases that feature greater depth of coverage. Both databases follow the same indexing principles that characterize

```
#2
    AUTHOR:  Ressort, Claudie; Martin, Elisabeth
     TITLE:  Une récente acquisition du Louvre: un panneau dominicain de
             Juan de Borgoña
    SOURCE:  La Revue du Louvre et des Musées de France (ISSN:0035-2608) p
             66-77 December '96
  CONTAINS:  bibliographical footnotes; illustration(s) (pt color)

SUBJECTS COVERED:
Painting, Spanish/15th century
Crucifixion in art
Panel paintings/Conservation and restoration
Borgoña, Juan de:fl. 1495-1533
    il: Saint Jean l'Evangéliste; Le retable de l'Epiphanie; La Pietà; Le
    mariage de la Vierge; il(col): La Vierge, saint Jean, deux saintes
    femmes et saint Dominique de Guzman (4); La Madeleine, saint Pierre
```

Figure 4.28   Sample record from ART INDEX

```
#12
    AUTHOR:  Harris, Simon
     TITLE:  The Byzantine office of the genuflexion (with appendix)
    SOURCE:  Music and Letters (ISSN:0027-4224) v 77  p 333-47 August '96

SUBJECTS COVERED:
Vespers (Music)
Music/Manuscripts
Antiphons
Chants (Byzantine)

ABSTRACT: A discussion of the Byzantine Office of the Genuflexion.  The
writer explains that this service is significant because it is not a
normal vespers, being dominated by three prayers of obscure and ancient
origin for which there is no normal provision in any of the forms of
vespers used by today's Orthodox Church.  The solution, he observes, seems
```

Figure 4.29   Sample record from HUMANITIES ABSTRACTS

most Wilson indexes and abstracts. Periodicals are indexed by professional librarians and some subject specialists who assign subject headings from the literature itself, reference works, other Wilson indexes, and especially Library of Congress Subject Headings. Wilson databases use their own name authority file to verify all corporate names, personal names and uniform titles used as subjects. Indexers assign between one and four subject terms for AI (see Figure 4.28) and one and six controlled subject terms per record for HUA (see Figure 4.29), although some records may feature more. Subject headings are not assigned to book and other reviews. Wilson indexes and abstracts also provide title enhancements for ambiguous titles and titles of exhibitions, reviews, anthologies and interviews. Records in AI include titles of illustrations for up to ten works of art per article. Foreign titles are not translated. Usually written by subject

```
Command language disc search (Wilsonline) EXPAND MODE

REF    ENTS    #RTS    RELATION    SUBJECT
---    ----    ----    --------    -------

  0     112      6                 VIDEO ART
  1      52      4     BT          ART AND MOTION PICTURES
  2     104    244     BT          ART, TWENTIETH CENTURY
  3       1      3     NT          CAMERA ARTS
  4       2      2     NT          NEW YORK VIDEO FESTIVAL
  5      18      2     RT          TELEVISION AND ART
  6       *      1     USED FOR    TV ART
```

Figure 4.30   Sample thesaurus entry in ART INDEX

specialists and occasionally by the document authors, abstracts, when available, are generally between 50 to 150 words in length. Book review records also include abstracts. HUMANITIES ABSTRACTS FULL TEXT features the full text of almost 100 journals with coverage beginning in 1994. H.W. Wilson has also published ART INDEX RETROSPECTIVE, covering 1929–84 and bringing the electronic version in line with the full print equivalent. The following discussion is based on the WilsonDisc versions of AI and HUA.

Five types of subject access points are available in AI and HUA: subject heading (SH), descriptor strings (DS), corporate name subject (CS), personal name subject (PS), and uniform title subject (UT), all of which feature single-word and phrase indexing. Individual words from all five access points, plus title, are included in the basic index (BI), which uses single-word indexing. Words from abstracts are not included in the basic index. Subject headings are terms used by Wilson indexes and abstracts as controlled vocabulary, while descriptor strings are descriptive phrases of one or more terms that include a subject heading as part of the string or, in other words, they are main headings with subdivisions. Generally, searches with the SH qualifier increase recall and searches with the DS qualifier increase precision. The SH qualifier retrieves all subject headings including those that are part of descriptor strings. Both AI and HUA feature electronic thesauri, which are searchable with the **Expand** (**E**) command in the command-language disc search (Wilsonline mode). The thesaurus includes broader, related and narrower terms of subject headings, as well as 'use' and 'used for' references for subject headings, personal names, corporate names and uniform titles (see Figure 4.30). The **Neighbor** (**NBR** or **N**) command displays an alphabetical list of terms above or below a specified word or phrase and shows term qualifiers. The **Get** (or **G**) command, followed by the line number of the term, is particularly useful for searches on descriptor strings, since the latter can be laborious to type.

The **Neighbor** command is especially useful for verifying the spelling or existence of terms, which in turn helps to formulate an effective search statement.

```
WILSON HUMANITIES ABSTRACTS              Data Coverage: 2/84 thru 01/30/97

──────────────────────────────────────────── PCNAME: 3ORIENTRH      ─
Command language disc search (Wilsonline) NEIGHBOR MODE



    NUMBER    ENTRIES      TERM
      1.           1    (DS)  WORLD WAR, 1914-1918/TURKEY
      2.          20    (DS)  WORLD WAR, 1914-1918/UNITED STATES
      3.           3    (DS)  WORLD WAR, 1914-1918/VETERANS
      4.           3    (DS)  WORLD WAR, 1914-1918/WAR WORK
      5.          14    (DS)  WORLD WAR, 1914-1918/WOMEN
      6.        1026    (SH)  WORLD WAR, 1939-1945
      7.           3    (DS)  WORLD WAR, 1939-1945
      8.           5    (DS)  WORLD WAR, 1939-1945/AERIAL OPERATIONS
      9.           5    (DS)  WORLD WAR, 1939-1945/AERIAL OPERATIONS/AMERICAN
     10.           8    (DS)  WORLD WAR, 1939-1945/AERIAL OPERATIONS/BRITISH
     11.           1    (DS)  WORLD WAR, 1939-1945/AERIAL OPERATIONS/FRENCH
     12.           1    (DS)  WORLD WAR, 1939-1945/AERIAL OPERATIONS/SOVIET
     13.           4    (DS)  WORLD WAR, 1939-1945/AMERICAN PROPAGANDA
UP, DOWN OR GET N OR EXPAND a 'DS'                                      ─
```

Figure 4.31   Using the Neighbor command in HUMANITIES ABSTRACTS

```
 SEARCH           Command language disc search (Wilsonline)        NUMBER of
  SET  |                      COMMAND                             | ENTRIES

 :─────────────────────────── HUA ───────────────────────────────:
   ─   | WORLD WAR AND 1939-1945 AND (FRANCE OR FRENCH)           |    0
       |                       WORLD WAR....      0 Entries       |
       |                       1939-1945....   1278 Entries       |
       |                          FRANCE....   5447 Entries       |
       |                          FRENCH....   5906 Entries       |
   1   | WORLD WAR: AND 1939-1945 AND (FRANCE OR FRENCH)          |   120
       |                       WORLD WAR:....   1408 Entries       |
       |                       1939-1945....   1278 Entries       |
       |                          FRANCE....   5447 Entries       |
       |                          FRENCH....   5906 Entries       |
```

Figure 4.32   Truncating descriptors in HUMANITIES ABSTRACTS

For example, the search for 'NBR world war' in HUA retrieves a long list of phrases, some of which are individual subject headings and most of which are full descriptor strings. Figure 4.31 shows that some descriptor strings use geographic subdivisions and others use ethnic or national qualifiers. This example also shows that HUA uses Library of Congress Subject Headings to differentiate between the two World Wars. Figure 4.32 displays two examples of search statements that would retrieve documents about France and the Second World War. The first search statement failed to retrieve any documents, while the second search statement yielded 120 items. Terminal unlimited truncation (':', '?', '$'), rather than the single-character truncation symbol ('#'), is especially useful to retrieve all

```
Command language disc search (Wilsonline) NEIGHBOR MODE
─────────────────────────────────────────────────────────────────────

    NUMBER     ENTRIES         TERM
      1.             1     (BI)  MICHELANGELESQUE
      2.             1     (PS)  MICHELANGELO
      3.           198     (TI)  MICHELANGELO
      4.           621     (BI)  MICHELANGELO
      5.             4     (AU)  MICHELANGELO BUONARROTI
      6.           239     (PS)  MICHELANGELO BUONARROTI
      7.            27     (DS)  MICHELANGELO BUONARROTI/REPRODUCTIONS
      8.             1     (DS)  MICHELANGELO BUONARROTI/REPRODUCTIONS/ATTRIBUTED
                                 WORKS
      9.             7     (DS)  MICHELANGELO BUONARROTI/REPRODUCTIONS/INFLUENCE
     10.             1     (DS)  MICHELANGELO/REPRODUCTIONS
     11.            66     (TI)  MICHELANGELO'S
     12.            66     (BI)  MICHELANGELO'S

 UP, DOWN OR GET N OR EXPAND a 'DS'
```

Figure 4.33   Reproductions in ART INDEX

subject headings and descriptor strings that begin with a phrase, such as 'world war'. Alternatively, the search statement '1939–1945 and (france or french)' retrieves 133 records. This search retrieves all items classified under the headings 'World War, 1939–1945' and 'Jewish Holocaust, 1939–1945', thereby increasing recall without imposing harsh false drops.

Artists and art historians, both students and scholars, frequently require visual information; this is a major characteristic of their information-seeking behaviour. Fortunately, AI allows a searcher to find reproductions or illustrations of works of art. Using Michelangelo as an example, Figure 4.33 shows the results for the search 'NBR michelangelo' in AI. This search displays terms from several indexes, including the basic index, descriptor strings and personal name subject. Line six of this search displays the personal name subject (PS), Michelangelo Buonarroti, which is the name authority entry for Michelangelo. Using the **Get** command to retrieve descriptor strings generated by the **Neighbor** command retrieves only the descriptor string represented by the specific line number. This example displays four descriptor strings with the subdivision 'reproductions'. A search for only one of these descriptor strings does not retrieve the other three. The record type qualifier (RT) allows the searcher to limit the query to specific record types by using the proper three-letter codes (see Figures 4.34 and 4.35). ART INDEX assigns the subdivision 'reproductions' to the artist personal name subject entry for all art reproductions that are not accompanied by text. Each reproduction receives a title entry for the name of the artistic work, and AI enhances the title, if necessary. Reproductions are searchable by using the record type code, rep (as 'rep (RT)'), combined with either an artist personal name, subject or a title.

The physical descriptor qualifier (PD) is used to find illustrative or graphic material that accompanies an article (see Figure 4.36). Illustrations of up to ten works of art that accompany articles in AI are listed by title in a note following the

CODE	RECORD TYPE
art	article
brv	book review
frv	form review
rep	art reproduction

Figure 4.34   Record types in ART INDEX

CODE	RECORD TYPE
art	article
blk	blanket reference
brv	book review
frv	form review
lit	literature

Figure 4.35   Record types in HUMANITIES ABSTRACTS

CODE	PHYSICAL DESCRIPTION	CODE	PHYSICAL DESCRIPTION
bibl	bibliography	il	illustration(s)
bibl f	bibliographical footnote	map(s)	map(s)
col	color	plan(s)	plan(s)
cov(s)	cover(s)	por(s)	portraits
diag(s)	diagram(s)	tab(s)	tables

Figure 4.36   Physical descriptor codes used in ART INDEX

artist personal name subject entry (see Figure 4.28). High-recall searches for illustrations or art reproductions need to be limited to both record type and physical description qualifiers. In the example shown in Figure 4.37 the two searches retrieve mutually exclusive records. Also, in an art reproduction record, the medium of the work of art is searchable as a basic index term, by using the abbreviations listed in Figure 4.38.

Another important search qualifier in AI and HUA is article contents (CT), a five-letter code that describes the contents of a document. The contents code for an exhibition (exhib) is especially useful in AI. Some of the more important article contents codes in HUA represent creative works, such as short stories (shsto),

```
 SEARCH     |        Command language disc search (Wilsonline)        |  NUMBER of
   SET      |                         COMMAND                         |   ENTRIES

 :─────────────────────────────── ART ─────────────────────────────────:
    1       | (PS) MICHELANGELO BUONARROTI                            |     239
    2       | 1 AND IL(PD)                                            |     173
                                   (ss # 1) ....      239 Entries
                                   (PD) IL....     167860 Entries
    3       | 1 AND REP(RT)                                           |      35
                                   (ss # 1) ....      239 Entries
                                   (RT) REP....      89046 Entries
    4       | 2 OR 3                                                  |     208
                                   (ss # 2) ....      173 Entries
                                   (ss # 3) ....       35 Entries
```

Figure 4.37   **Illustrations and art reproductions in ART INDEX**

ABBREVIATION	MEDIUM
drwg	drawings
engr	engraving(s)
etch	etching(s)
litho	lithograph(s)
paint	painting(s)
photo	photograph
sculp	sculpture

Figure 4.38   **Searching by medium in ART INDEX**

plays (drama), fiction (fictn) and poems (poems), as well as reviews of creative works such as opera reviews (oprar), dance reviews (dancr), television programme reviews (telpr) and motion picture reviews (mpicr) (see Figures 4.39 and 4.40).

Other search qualifiers in AI and HUA include language (LA), author (AU), review of a performing arts work (WK), year of publication of a periodical (YR) and year of publication of a book being reviewed (YP). However, Wilson databases do not provide search qualifiers for time periods – an important characteristic of information-seeking behaviour in the humanities. Time periods are searchable by the name of an era such as 'renaissance', by subject heading subdivision such as '19th century', by subject heading qualifiers such as 1939–1945, or even by specific dates and date ranges such as 1990–1999. The latter type of keyword search retrieves documents in which dates appear anywhere in the record. These include dates in titles of journal articles, dates of birth and death of personal name subjects, and date of composition of a creative work. Both terminal unlimited truncation and single-character truncation can be used to find specific dates or date ranges, especially if high recall is desirable.

```
┌─────────────────────────────────────────────────────────────────────────────┐
│   SEARCH            Command language disc search (Wilsonline)    NUMBER of     │
│   SET │                         COMMAND                        │ ENTRIES      │
│                                                                                │
│  :─────────────────────────── HUA ───────────────────────────────────────:   │
│    1  │ (AU) MOURE, ERIN AND POEMS(CT)                                  11     │
│       │                  (AU) MOURE, ERIN....     12 Entries                  │
│       │                  (CT) POEMS....       31809 Entries │                 │
│       │                                                                        │
└─────────────────────────────────────────────────────────────────────────────┘
```

Figure 4.39   Using the CT qualifier to identify creative works in HUMANITIES ABSTRACTS

```
┌─────────────────────────────────────────────────────────────────────────────┐
│  #1                                                                            │
│    Literature                                                                  │
│       AUTHOR:  Mouré, Erin:1955-                                               │
│        TITLE:  Oars                                                            │
│       SOURCE:  Canadian Literature  (ISSN:0008-4360) no133  p 76-7 Summer '92  │
│                                                                                │
│    SUBJECTS COVERED:                                                           │
│    Poems/English language                                                      │
│                                                                                │
└─────────────────────────────────────────────────────────────────────────────┘
```

Figure 4.40   Record from CT qualifier search in HUMANITIES ABSTRACTS

Art

BIBLIOGRAPHY OF THE HISTORY OF ART (BHA)

Producer: Getty Information Institute and the Institut de l'Information Scientifique et Technique (INIST), a division of the French Centre National de la Recherche Scientifique (CNRS). BHA is the successor to the International Repertory of the Literature of Art (RILA) (1975–1989) and Répertoire d'Art et d'Archéologie (RAA) (1910–1989).

Online: DIALOG, file 190 (BHA), file 191 (RILA); Research Libraries Group; Questel-Orbit.

Internet: DIALOGWeb (BHA and RILA), Francis.

CD-ROM: Getty Information Institute and INIST/CNRS.

Scope: Western art and art reflecting the Western tradition in Asia, Africa and Australia from antiquity (fourth century) to the present, including sculpture, architecture, painting, drawing, prints, decorative arts, manuscripts and illumination, books and illustration, photography, industrial design, landscape architecture, conceptual art and new media, iconography, exhibitions, art theory and criticism, artists, movements, schools, museums and galleries.

Start date: 1991 (BHA), 1975 (RILA on DIALOG).

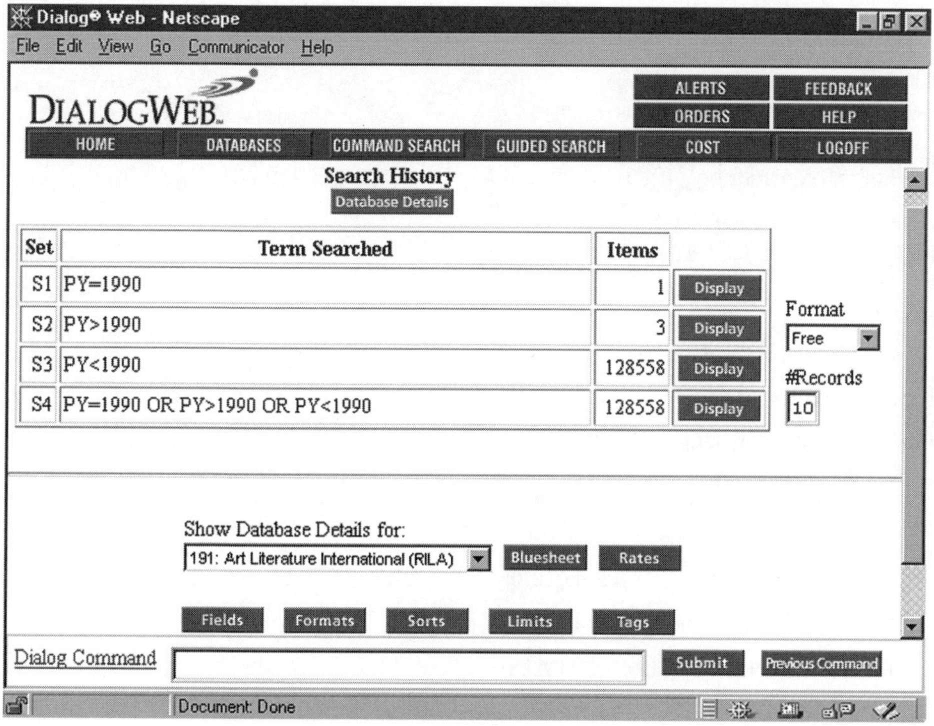

Figure 4.41   Publication years in RILA on DIALOG

Size:	Approximately 185 000 records (BHA) (February 2000); 154 027 (RILA) (January 1993).
Update:	Quarterly (online); annual (CD-ROM); approximately 24 000 records added per year.
Materials:	Monographs, collected essays, dissertations, exhibition and art dealers' catalogues, *Festschriften*, conference proceedings and approximately 2500 periodicals.
Languages:	Approximately 45 languages are represented; CD-ROM interface functions in either French or English.
Print equivalent:	*Bibliography of the History of Art/Bibliographie d'Histoire de l'Art.*

The *Gale Directory of Databases* (March 1998) indicates that RILA is a closed file, but the DIALOG Blue Sheet (August 1998) and some other sources of information regarding BHA and RILA indicate that RILA (Art Literature International on DIALOG) continues to be updated. The results of the DIALOG search displayed in Figure 4.41, however, show the contrary. It seems safe to conclude that coverage in RILA ends in 1989, and that BHA continues RILA. The following discussion is based on the DIALOG version of BHA.

10142574   BHA No.:6 23056 (1996)

Whitefriars glass

WATSON, Oliver

Burlington magazine ; 1996, v. 138, no. 1119, June p. 418-419 2 ill.

PUBLICATION YEAR:1996

ISSN: 0007-6287

ABSTRACT:

Reviews a book and exhibition catalogue on the London glassworks and its wares

1834-1980.

COUNTRY CODE: GBR

LANGUAGE: English

DESCRIPTORS:

Whitefriars Glass Works, London (GBR); Glass factories; Great Britain; 1800-2000;

1834-1980; Glass (objects); Exhibitions

IDENTIFIERS (TIME PERIOD AND STYLES):

1800; 1900 1800-2000; 1834-1980

SECTION HEADING(S): 1800-1945; Decorative arts ; Ceramics and glass

REVIEWS:

1.Whitefriars glass : James Powell & Sons of London

EVANS, Wendy; ROSS, Catherine; WERNER, Alex

Museum of London : Dist. by Art Books International , 1996

Review of a monograph /Compte-rendu d'une monographie

English /Anglais , 416 p. ill. (some col.)

2. Whitefriars glass : the art of James Powell & Sons

JACKSON, Lesley, ed.

Shepton Beauchamp : R. Dennis , 1996

Review of an exhibition catalogue /Compte-rendu d'un catalogue d'exposition

Manchester (GBR), Manchester City Art Galleries, to 30 June 1996 London (GBR),

Museum of London, 30 July 1996-26 Jan 1997

English /Anglais , 160 p. ill. (some col.)

Figure 4.42   Sample record from BHA on DIALOG

Although quite similar, the DIALOG versions of BHA and RILA do differ in several respects. Records in BHA include attachments of up to ten reviews, while reviews and source records in RILA are distinct entries. The review display in BHA (see Figure 4.42) includes document type, author, title, place of publication, publisher, publication year, journal title and so on, but abstracts are not present and only the title of the reviews is searchable. Most records include abstracts, which are variable in length, although many are rather short. Descriptors are based on six authority files for personal names, geographic names, corporate names, named works of art, conferences and topical subjects. Most names are cited in the original language. Countries and continents, topical subjects, saints' names, and ancient, biblical, mythological and literary names are cited in English (and French in the print, CD-ROM and Francis versions). All authors, including editors, translators, compilers and corporate authors, appear in the author index. Searches can be restricted by language using the Language (LA) field, or limited to 'eng' or 'noneng'.

Exhibition catalogues and reviews of exhibitions are usually indexed in the Exhibition (EX) and Exhibition Year fields (EY). These include city name, abbreviated country name and the institutional name (and postal state code for the USA and abbreviated province name for Canada). Figure 4.43 shows the difficulty of searching on the complex exhibition entries in both the Descriptor and Exhibition fields. This search also demonstrates that an exhaustive search for exhibitions should include the Descriptor field, which features the subdivision 'exhibitions'. This search retrieved five additional records by adding the Descriptor field to the search, an example of which is shown in Figure 4.44. Note the use of the original French language for the institutional name in the Descriptor field.

The identifier (ID) and section heading (SH) fields, both of which are word- and phrase-indexed, contain valuable information that complements the Descriptor field. The identifier field holds information about time periods including historical century, historical period and style. The historical century is represented numerically as, for example, 1800 for the nineteenth century. Historical periods are represented by several date ranges, and style is depicted with words such as medieval or renaissance. Not all records have style identifiers. Section headings correspond to the classification schedule of the printed version of the BHA. Although the primary function of the classification schedule is to arrange the records in the printed version, it is a useful access point in the online product. The BHA classification schedule is a hierarchical schema consisting of three tiers. The first tier consists of six broad headings: General works; General history of art; 300–1400; 1400–1800; 1800–1945; 1945–2000. The latter four ranges of dates represent major stylistic divisions, which are, respectively, medieval, renaissance and baroque, modern (nineteenth and twentieth centuries), and contemporary (post-Second World War). These six headings are divided into two further levels which are customized for each major stylistic division. Figure 4.45 displays the two levels of subdivisions for the general heading 1945–2000.

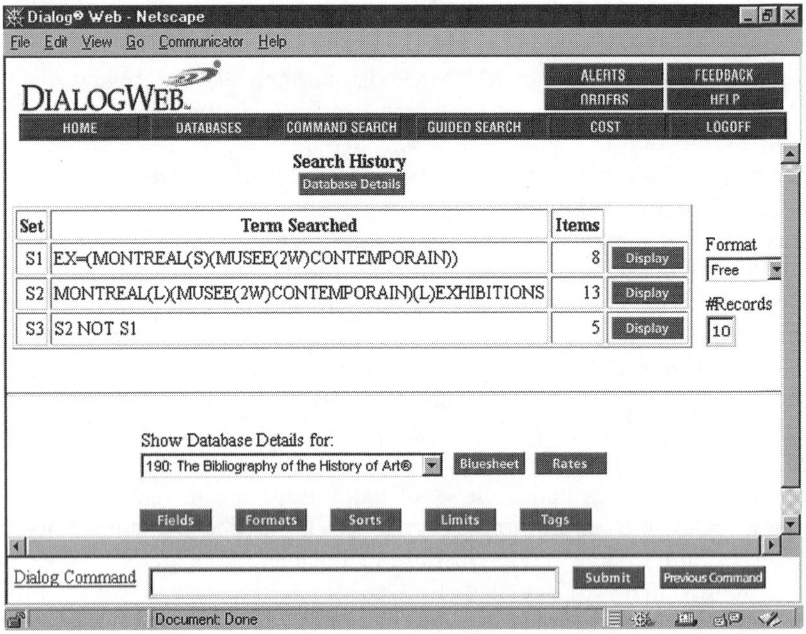

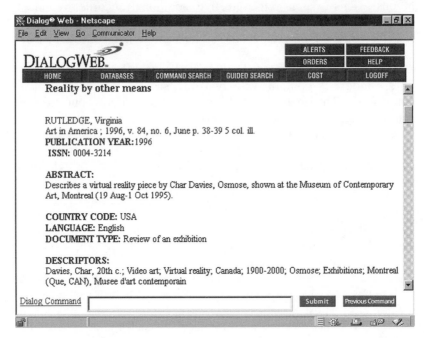

Figure 4.43   Searching for exhibitions in the Exhibition and Descriptor fields in BHA on DIALOG

Figure 4.44   Partial exhibition record retrieved by searching the Descriptor field in BHA on DIALOG

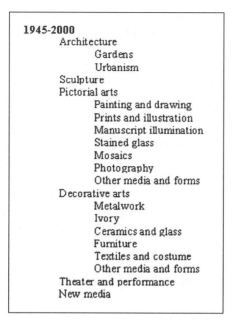

Figure 4.45   Example of the classification schedule in BHA

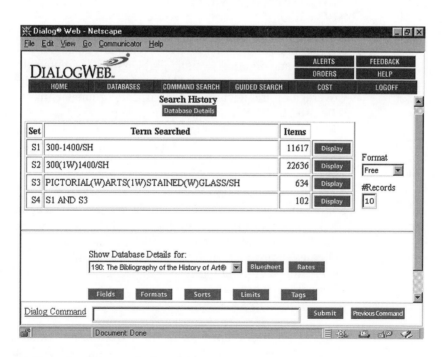

Figure 4.46   Searching section headings in BHA on DIALOG

Both the Identifier and Section Heading fields contain time period information. The Identifier field is especially useful to limit searches by historical century, such as 1800/ID, and the Section Heading field is more effective to narrow searches to specific major stylistic divisions. The (W) operator is useful for searching elements in a specific section heading, followed by the /SH search suffix. Figure 4.46 displays a section heading search using the (W) operator, and Figure 4.47 shows a record retrieved by this search. Although searches for date ranges that include hyphens are successful, they are not recommended as many date ranges exhibit data entry variations, such as spaces between a date and the hyphen. It should also be noted that records classified under the section heading 1945–2000 have an open entry (1945–) in the current DialogWeb version of BHA, which necessitates a search with the statement 1945-/SH (with the hyphen) or the search statement 1945/SH not 1800/SH, either of which retrieves the same number of records and eliminates documents classified under the section heading 1800–1945.

ARTBIBLIOGRAPHIES MODERN (ABM)

Producer:	ABC-CLIO.
Online:	DIALOG.
Internet:	DIALOGWeb, ABC-CLIO.
CD-ROM:	ABC-CLIO.
Scope:	All aspects of twentieth-century art and design, including fine arts, ceramics, computer and electronic art, costume, folk art, furniture and interior design, glass, graffiti, graphic design, iconography, needlecraft, posters, prints, textiles, and video art. Coverage of architecture and all aspects of nineteenth-century art ceased in 1988. Photography is covered since its invention. ABM also covers twentieth-century artists and movements whose output precedes 1900 (such as Impressionism) and all subjects that represent the roots of twentieth-century art.
Start date:	1974.
Size:	Approximately 267 000 records (February 2000).
Update:	Semi-annually; approximately 12 000 records added annually.
Materials:	Monographs, essays, dissertations, exhibition catalogues, and articles from approximately 500 journals and museum bulletins, supplemented by selected articles from over 2000 historical and cultural journals.
Languages:	Data not available.
Print equivalent:	*ARTBibliograhies Modern.*

Figure 4.48 shows a sample record from the Web-based version of ARTBIBLIOGRAPHIES MODERN. The following discussion is based on the CD-ROM version with a few relevant examples from the DIALOG and Web-

10139033   BHA No.:6 19515 (1996)

RAGUIN, Virginia C.

Speculum ; 1996, v. 71, no. 2, Apr p. 480-482

PUBLICATION YEAR:1996

SERIES: (Corpus vitrearum Medii aevi, Deutschland)

ISSN: 0038-7134

ABSTRACT:

Richter's book focuses on 14th c. stained glass in the city of Muhlhausen. Becksmann and

Korn concentrate on the stained glass of monasteries for noblewomen in the area of northern

Saxony ca.1300-1530, also treating the Luneburg Rathaus.

COUNTRY CODE: USA

LANGUAGE: English

DESCRIPTORS:

Stained glass; Germany; Corpus Vitrearum Medii Aevi; Catalogues; 1300-1600; 1300-1530;

Luneburg (DEU); Region; Convents; Luneburg (DEU), Rathaus; Muhlhausen (Thuringen,

DEU); Medieval; Women; Nuns; 1300-1400

IDENTIFIERS (TIME PERIOD AND STYLES):

1300; 1400; 1500 1300-1400; 1300-1530; 1300-1600 Medieval

SECTION HEADING(S): 300-1400 ; Pictorial arts ; Stained glass

REVIEWS:

1.Die mittelalterlichen Glasmalereien in Muhlhausen / Thuringen

RICHTER, Christa

Berlin : Akademie , 1993

Review of a monograph /Compte-rendu d'une monographie

German /Allemand , li, 151 p. ill. (some col.)

2. Die mittelalterlichen Glasmalereien in Luneburg und den Heideklostern

BECKSMANN, Rudiger; KORN, Ulf-Dietrich; HERZ, Fritz, contrib.

Berlin : Deutscher Verlag fur Kunstwissenschaft , 1992

Review of a monograph /Compte-rendu d'une monographie

German /Allemand , liv, 295 p. ill. (some col.)

Figure 4.47   Record retrieved by searching section headings in BHA on DIALOG

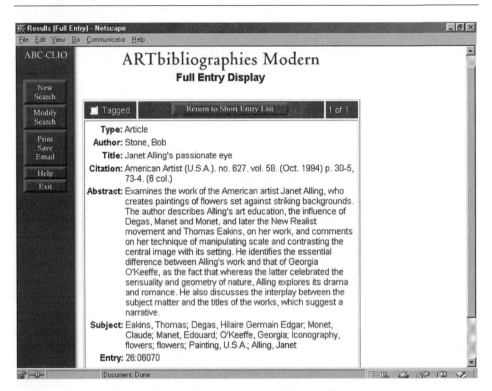

Figure 4.48   Sample record from ARTBIBLIOGRAPHIES MODERN (Web-based version)

based versions. Abstracts, which range in length from a few lines of text to over ten lines, are included with most records, except for some older exhibition reviews. Figure 4.49 displays the searchable fields on the initial screen of the CD-ROM version of ABM. The Subject field in the CD-ROM version is the equivalent of the basic index in the DIALOG version, which includes words from abstracts, titles and descriptors. The Keyword field in the Web-based version retrieves text from the Abstract, Title, Subject/Artist, Gallery, Publisher/University and Author fields. The DIALOG version allows searches to be limited to the Abstract field with the /AB search suffix, but the CD-ROM and Web-based versions do not have a separate index for this. The Title field includes all document titles in the original language, with English translations for foreign titles. All personal authors and editors are included in the author index. Truncation is suggested for author searches, especially for pre-1988 records, which featured only the initials of first names. Alternatively, the browse function (F2) in the CD-ROM version or the expand function in the DIALOG version can be used to search for author names, although such searches may retrieve many unwanted records. Language is not a searchable field in all versions of ABM, but DIALOG allows searches to be limited to 'eng' or 'noneng'.

The Document Type field in the CD-ROM version contains five entries: article, book, catalog (exhibition catalogues), dissertation and essay (catalogues or

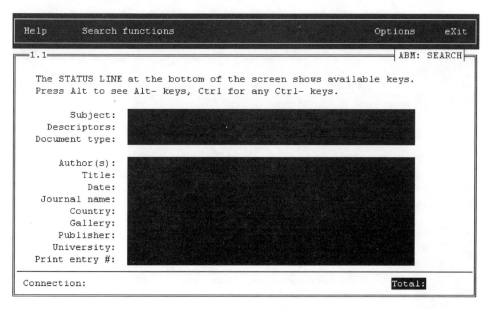

Figure 4.49   General search screen and searchable fields in ARTBIBLIOGRAPHIES MODERN on disc

books); and the Web-based version adds a sixth type – exhibition review. Essay entries do not include full bibliographic information, as publishing information (place, publisher, and date) is missing (see Figure 4.50). This applies to all versions. However, the full bibliographic record is viewable through a title search that retrieves the book or catalogue in which the essay appears. Searches for essays cannot be limited by date, since this field contains only the publication year for articles and monographs, exhibition year for catalogues, and authorship year for dissertations. The Country, Publisher and University fields are linked to the Document Type field. Not used to find place names as subjects, the Country field (eliminated in the Web-based version), indexed only by initials, contains the country of publication (or name of international organization as publisher) for a journal. Similarly, the Publisher field applies only to monograph entries, while the University field retrieves only dissertations.

The Descriptor field contains both subject descriptors and the names of artists, artists' groups, collectors and critics. The equivalent to the Descriptor field in the Web-based version is the Subject/Artist field, which is more appropriately named. Most records include several descriptors, sometimes as many as ten or more – a great advantage for searchers. The records of exhibition catalogues feature as many as ten or more artists' names as descriptors, which greatly enhances searches for lesser-known artists. Using British spelling conventions, subject descriptors are assigned from a list of approximately 200 classification headings, some of which have topical subdivisions. These are derived from four categories of subheadings. The first consists of the subheading 'general', the second includes miscellaneous subheadings such as 'criticism' and 'theory', the third refers to the

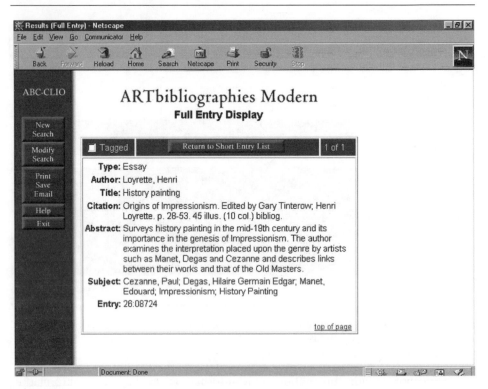

Figure 4.50   Essay entry in ARTBIBLIOGRAPHIES MODERN (Web-based version)

century and the fourth subheading holds country names. Note that the country subheading for the USA is U.S.A. (see Figure 4.48), the country subheading for the UK is British Isles, and the country subheading for Ireland is Eire. A few of the major subject headings receive special topical subdivisions, such as 'Iconography', which features numerous subdivisions; a partial list is shown in Figure 4.51. None of the versions of ABM feature an online thesaurus, but the list of classification headings in the printed version of ABM can be consulted to identify related terms, such as 'crosses' or 'crucifixes'.

The gallery index in ABM contains the names of the exhibiting galleries or museums. A great majority of searches in this index retrieve exhibition catalogues, but some journal articles and monographs are retrieved if they include catalogues. Although all gallery names are indexed, only four venues of a travelling exhibit are displayed in the citation, while the others are normally mentioned in the abstract. Figure 4.52 shows an example of an exhibition catalogue record with four venues listed, one of which is the Musée des Beaux Arts in Montreal, Canada. Previously on DIALOG, the gallery index of ABM generally took the form of city/state or province/country/gallery name, but the country name was omitted for major cities. Currently, the gallery index cannot be searched by place name in all versions of ABM (unless the place name is part of the gallery name), but the place name is included in the citation (see Figure 4.52). The name of the gallery is

Browsing "Descriptors": 37475 / 92250

1	ICONOGRAPHY, CHESS
1	ICONOGRAPHY, CHESSMEN
52	ICONOGRAPHY, CHILDHOOD
217	ICONOGRAPHY, CHILDREN
3	ICONOGRAPHY, CHIMNEYS
15	ICONOGRAPHY, CHRISTIANITY
8	ICONOGRAPHY, CHRISTMAS
2	ICONOGRAPHY, CHURCH
1	ICONOGRAPHY, CHURCH FURNISHINGS
49	ICONOGRAPHY, CHURCHES
1	ICONOGRAPHY, CIGARETTE LIGHTERS
1	ICONOGRAPHY, CIGARETTE PACKETS
9	ICONOGRAPHY, CIGARETTES
1	ICONOGRAPHY, CIGARS
1	ICONOGRAPHY, CINEMAS

Figure 4.51   **Partial list of subheadings for 'Iconography' in ARTBIBLIOGRAPHIES MODERN on disc**

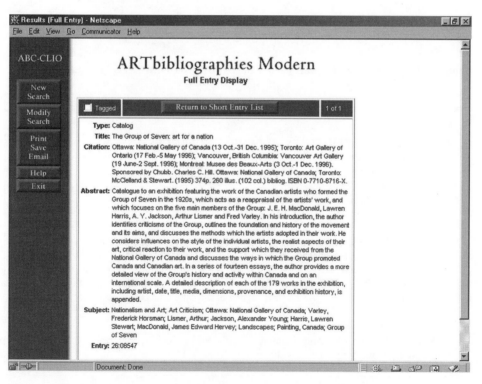

Figure 4.52   **Sample record of an exhibition catalogue in ARTBIBLIOGRAPHIES MODERN (Web-based version)**

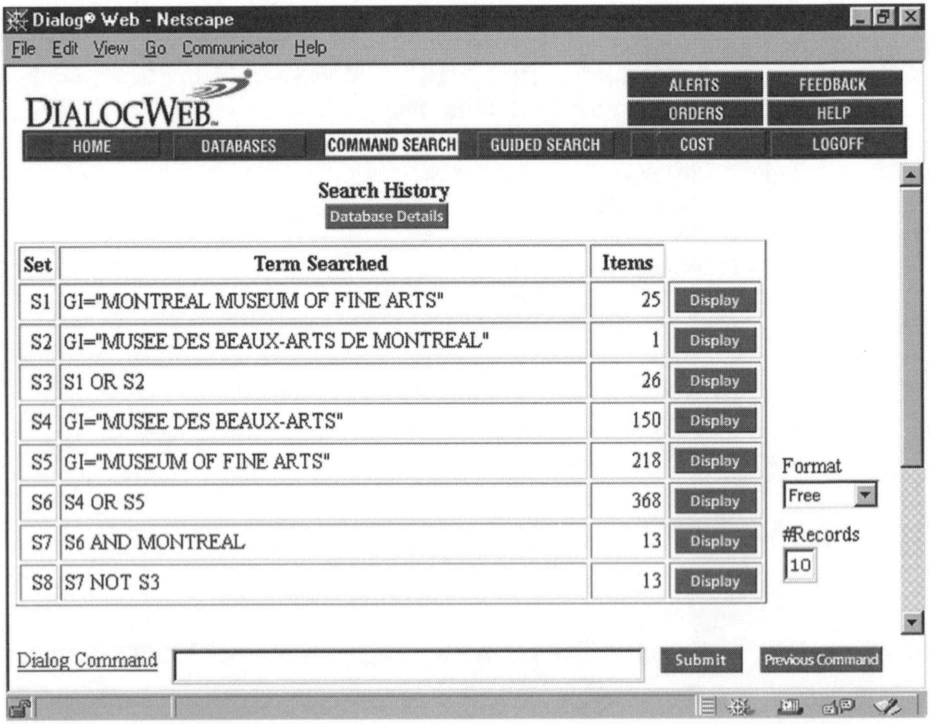

Figure 4.53   Searching the gallery index in ARTBIBLIOGRAPHIES MODERN on DIALOG

00255572 27-01278
ALEX COLVILLE: PEINTURES, ESTAMPES ET PROCESSUS CREATIFS, 1983-1994
Alex Colville: paintings, prints and creative processes, 1983-94
Fry, Philip; Theberge, Pierre
Montreal: Musee des Beaux-Arts (30 Sept. 1994-15 Jan. 1995). Philip Fry; preface by Pierre Theberge. 184p. 392 illus. (62 col.) biog. bibliog. ISBN 2-891921-85-2. Also in English
DOCUMENT TYPE: Catalog
Catalogue to an exhibition of recent paintings, prints and sketches by the Canadian artist Alex Colville. The author analyses 22 paintings, 10 silk-screen prints, and the preliminary drawings for these works. He also explores two older works by Colville in the collection of the Musee des Beaux-Arts in Montreal . An English version of the catalogue is also available.
NOTES: Available from Artexte's Distribution Service.
GALLERY NAME: Musee des Beaux-Arts
DESCRIPTORS: Colville, Alex; Painting, Canada; Prints, Canada; Montreal : Musee des Beaux-Arts; serigraphy; preparatory drawings

---

Figure 4.54   Name variations in the gallery index on ARTBIBLIOGRAPHIES MODERN on DIALOG

normally listed in the original or local language. The Musée des Beaux Arts in Montreal is also known in English as the Montreal Museum of Fine Arts, which appears to be the preferred entry in ABM. Yet Figure 4.52 displays the gallery name in French. Using the **Expand** command in ABM on DialogWeb, the gallery 'Montreal Museum of Fine Arts' retrieves 25 records, while the gallery 'Musée des Beaux Arts de Montréal' retrieves one item. Figure 4.53 shows a search using several versions of the gallery name in the gallery index. This search reveals some of the inconsistencies within the gallery index, as the search with the city name included in the gallery name failed to retrieve several relevant records, an example of which is shown in Figure 4.54.

History

AMERICA: HISTORY AND LIFE (AHL)

Producer:	ABC-CLIO.
Online:	DIALOG, CompuServe.
Internet:	DIALOGWeb, ABC-CLIO.
CD-ROM:	ABC-CLIO.
Scope:	Covers the history of the USA and Canada, including American studies, bibliography, cultural history, economic history, ethnic studies, family history, folklore, historiography and methodology, history of ideas, history of science, technology and medicine, international relations, libraries and archives, local history, military history, oral history, politics and government, popular culture, prehistory, religious history, teaching of history, urban affairs and women's studies.
Start date:	1954.
Size:	Approximately 425 000 records (February 2000).
Update:	Quarterly (DIALOG); three times a year (CD-ROM); monthly (Web version); approximately 16 000 records added annually.
Materials:	Monographs, dissertations and articles from approximately 2100 international journals. Also indexes book, film and video reviews from approximately 140 scholarly journals. Film and video reviews are covered from 1989.
Languages:	Approximately 40 languages are represented.
Print equivalent:	*America: History and Life*.

HISTORICAL ABSTRACTS (HA)

Producer:	ABC-CLIO.
Online:	DIALOG, CompuServe.
Internet:	DIALOGWeb, ABC-CLIO.

CD-ROM: ABC-CLIO.
Scope: Covers the history of the world (except Canada and the USA) from 1450 to the present, including area studies, bibliography, cultural history, diplomatic history, economic history, historiography and methodology, history of science, technology, and medicine, intellectual history, international relations, libraries and archives, military history, philosophy of history, political history, social history, social sciences with historical perspectives and teaching of history.
Start date: 1954 (DIALOG); 1960 (ABC-CLIO).
Size: Approximately 557 000 records from 1954 onwards (February 2000).
Update: Six times a year (DIALOG); three times a year (CD-ROM); monthly (Web version); approximately 22 000 records added annually.
Materials: Articles from approximately 2100 journals; monographs and dissertations since 1980; book reviews from 13 major journals.
Languages: Approximately 50 languages are represented.
Print equivalent: *Historical Abstracts – Part A: Modern History Abstracts, 1450–1914; Historical Abstracts – Part B: Twentieth Century Abstracts, 1914 to the present.*

Similar in content but different in detail, the CD-ROM versions of AMERICA: HISTORY AND LIFE and HISTORICAL ABSTRACTS are produced by the same company and use the same Dataware software as ARTBIBLIOGRAPHIES MODERN. Discussion of AHL and HA is based on the CD-ROM versions with a few examples extracted from the DIALOG and Web-based versions. Over the years, many indexes and abstracts, whether printed or electronic, have incorporated changes to their classification systems, record structures, chronological coverage and many other areas. Both AHL and HA have sustained several enhancements, and these are not limited to the starting date of the specific modification. In 1972 AHL published a retrospective print product (based on records indexed in *Historical Abstracts*) that extended chronological coverage to include the period from 1954 to 1963. In 1997 ABC-CLIO extended the starting dates of its CD-ROM versions of AHL to 1964 and HA to 1973. Now, the Web-based versions and the Expanded Editions of the CD-ROMs include the entire AHL database (from 1954); and the starting date for HA is 1960. Even the DIALOG versions of both databases have expanded retrospective coverage to 1954. The retrospective files themselves are not static, as these have exhibited changes. Records entered before 1975 in HA or 1974 in AHL did not have descriptors (DE), historical starting dates (HS) and historical ending dates (HE). The Historical Period (HP) field was introduced in both databases in 1979. Figures 4.55 and 4.57 show sample 'old' records, while Figures 4.56 and 4.58 display records from the same year of publication (1964) that include the modifications introduced in the 1970s. Most records sampled in the DIALOG versions of both

109597   001-00604
THE FARMER, THE ARMY AND THE DRAFT.
Blum, Albert A
Agric. Hist. 1964 38(1): 34-42.
ABSTRACT: In spite of America's unsatisfactory experience with group deferment from selective service in World War I, numerous attempts were made early in World War II to obtain industry-wide deferments. The army opposed successfully all such demands except the one for West Coast aircraft workers. The American farmer, as a result, came close to receiving group deferment. The special deferment for farmers was achieved through political pressure on federal officials by members of the farm bloc rather than by mandatory legislation. The pressure on federal officials was reflected in instructions to local boards. (W. D. Rasmussen)

Figure 4.55   Sample 'old' record in AMERICA: HISTORY AND LIFE on DIALOG

676422   21A-01340
THE CONTEMPORARY SIGNIFICANCE OF THE DOCTRINE OF JUST WAR.
Miller, Lynn H
World Pol. 1964 16(2): 254-286.
DOCUMENT TYPE: ARTICLE
ABSTRACT: Assesses the historical doctrine of Just War (bellum justum), the present international system (that eclipsed the balance-of-power system), and the technological advances in weaponry to determine the viability and relevance of such a doctrine for international law and politics, 1940's-60's.
DESCRIPTORS: 1940's-1960's ; Just War ; International law ; Politics
HISTORICAL PERIOD: 1940D 1950D 1960D 1900H
HISTORICAL PERIOD (Starting): 1940's
HISTORICAL PERIOD (Ending): 1960's

Figure 4.56   Sample record with 'new' fields in AMERICA: HISTORY AND LIFE on DIALOG

databases were 'new' records, including those with publishing dates before 1975. The 'old' records in both databases seem to have been corrected, as both 'old' records (Figures 4.55 and 4.57) include Subject, Language and Period fields in the Web version of both databases.

Abstracts or annotations are included for almost all articles or essays, but they are not usually attached to records of books, reviews and dissertations. Records considered 'central' to the field of history feature abstracts that range between 75 and 100 words, while records of articles indexed from 'peripheral' journals or those that pertain to 'sub-areas' of history are given short entries, unless these

274338   019-00129
**Hungarian-Slovak relations and the Slovak nationality movement in
Hungary after the Vienna Award (1938-41)**
MAGYAR-SZLOVAK VISZONY ES SZLOVAK NEMZETISEGI MOZGALOM
MAGYARORSZAGON A BECSI DONTES UTAN (1938-1941)
Tilkovszky, Lorant
Szazadok (Hungary) 1964 98(3): 383-418.
ABSTRACT: Analyzes the policy of the Hungarian government relating to the Slovak
minority and the attitude of the Slovak government toward the Hungarian minority living in
Slovakia. Discusses primarily the activities of Pal Teleki, Prime Minister of Hungary, and
Vojtech Tuka, Prime Minister of Slovakia. Difficulties in establishing a Slovak national party
Hungary are discussed in detail, especially the actions of Emanuel Bohm, and Ludovit
Obtulovic, who were among leaders of the Slovak minority in Hungary. Based chiefly on
archival documents. (F. S. Wagner)

Figure 4.57   Sample 'old' record in HISTORICAL ABSTRACTS on DIALOG

1129775   30B-04514
THE BATTLE OF THE GHETTO BENCHES.
Rabinowicz, H
Jewish Q. Rev. 1964 55(2): 151-159.
DOCUMENT TYPE: ARTICLE
ABSTRACT: Educational discrimination against Jews in Poland took the form of admissions
quotas and attempts to force segregated seating, or Ghetto benches, within university
classrooms, 1932-39.
DESCRIPTORS: 1932-1939 ; Discrimination ; Education ; Jews ; Poland
HISTORICAL PERIOD: 1930D 1900H
HISTORICAL PERIOD (Starting): 1932
HISTORICAL PERIOD (Ending): 1939

**Figure 4.58   Sample record with 'new' fields in HISTORICAL ABSTRACTS on
                  DIALOG**

titles are clear enough not to warrant any abstracts at all. Unlike
ARTBIBLIOGRAPHIES MODERN, AHL and HA provide two levels of search
screens, the first of which shows the general searchable fields (see Figure 4.59),
and the second expands some of the fields for more precise searching (see Figures
4.60 and 4.61). The Subject field is the equivalent of the basic index on DIALOG,
which includes words from the Title, Abstract and Descriptor fields. Up to three
authors are indexed for each record. The Author/Editor field includes all
document authors, except book/media reviewers (AHL), translation/series editors
(HA) and abstractors (AHL and HA), who are only searchable by using the
enhanced specific fields screen. As evident in the sample records, the names of
abstractors, unlike author names, are not inverted and only last names and initials
are used. Titles are entered in the original language or transliterated form with

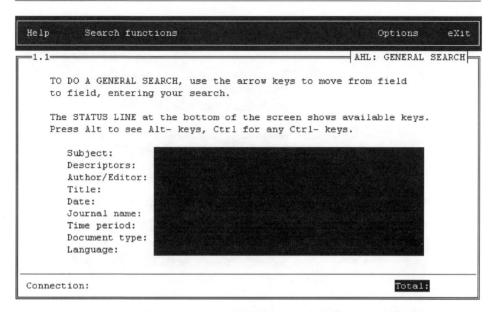

Figure 4.59   General search screen on AMERICA: HISTORY AND LIFE on disc

```
  Help      Search functions                          Options    eXit
╔1.1══════════════════════════════════════════╡AHL: SPECIFIC FIELDS╞═
║
║     SPECIFIC FIELDS lets you search for words in individual fields in
║     the database, as well as in combined general fields like SUBJECT.
║     TO DO A SPECIFIC FIELDS SEARCH, use the arrow keys, PAGEDOWN, and
║     PAGEUP to move from field to field, entering your search.
║
║     The STATUS LINE at the bottom of the screen shows available keys.
║
║
║        Subject:
║          Descriptors:
║
║        Author/Editor:
║          Article/Diss. author:
║          Book/Media author:
║          Review author:
║          Abstracter:
║
╟ Connection:                                            Total:
```

Figure 4.60   Specific fields screen on AMERICA: HISTORY AND LIFE on disc (a)

English translations. The Title field searches all titles, and the specific fields screen in HA allows searches to be limited to book title and series title, while AHL adds the specific field book/media title which retrieves citations to reviews. Searches can be limited to individual languages, but records created before 1980

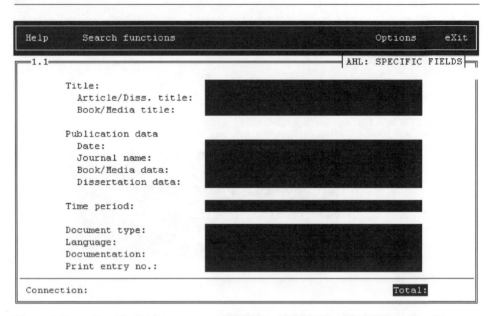

Figure 4.61   Specific fields screen on AMERICA: HISTORY AND LIFE on disc (b)

did not usually carry a Language field although many of these records have had the Language field added retrospectively. Document types in HA include article, book, collection, dissertation and journal. This field in AHL also includes book and media reviews, but searches cannot be limited to books. The four-digit date field corresponds to the year of publication of all documents. In addition to logical operators, searches for dates can use symbols ('>', '<', '>=', '<=') to find several dates, or two periods (or 'TO') to find ranges of publication dates, such as 1990..1995. This does not apply to the Web-based versions. Rather, truncation can be used in the Publication Date field to retrieve, for example, all records published in the 1960s, entered as '196*'.

Descriptors include natural-language terms, subject headings, and authority-controlled proper names. An average of four or five descriptors is assigned to each record, including book reviews, but some documents may contain more. In the DIALOG versions of AHL and HA, proximity operators should be used to search for descriptors indexed with punctuation, such as commas or hyphens, which include all inverted personal names. Subdivisions are entered as parenthetical qualifiers, many of which are place names (see Figure 4.62). When using the browse function (F2) in the CD-ROM version, spaces and parentheses must be entered to retrieve a list of these descriptors. Parentheses are unimportant in terms of searching the Subject field in the Web-based versions. Rather, searches can be enclosed within quotation marks to search for exact phrases, such as 'french revolution alsace'. Without the quotation marks, the search uses the default operator AND which increases recall.

Searching for events in HA and AHL is often problematic since descriptors do not reflect all the various names associated with specific events, and some major

```
========================================= Browsing "Descriptors": 40536 / 125770|
        1 | FRENCH PURCHASING MISSION.
    2,356 | FRENCH REVOLUTION.
        1 | FRENCH REVOLUTION. (LIMOUSIN).
        1 | FRENCH REVOLUTION (AIRE-SUR-LA-LYS).
        1 | FRENCH REVOLUTION (AIRVAULT, PARTHENAY).
        1 | FRENCH REVOLUTION (AIX-EN-PROVENCE).
        1 | FRENCH REVOLUTION (ALES).
        3 | FRENCH REVOLUTION (ALSACE).
        1 | FRENCH REVOLUTION (ALSACE, LORRAINE).
        2 | FRENCH REVOLUTION (ANJOU).
        1 | FRENCH REVOLUTION (ANJOU, MAINE).
       43 | FRENCH REVOLUTION (ANTECEDENTS).
        2 | FRENCH REVOLUTION (ANTECEDENTS; REVIEW ARTICLE).
        1 | FRENCH REVOLUTION (ARDENNES).
        3 | FRENCH REVOLUTION (ARLES).
```

Figure 4.62   Parenthetical descriptor subdivisions in HISTORICAL ABSTRACTS on disc

```
==1.1.1========================================== HA: FULL ENTRY: 1 of 1 |
    Press RIGHT ARROW for the next entry, LEFT ARROW for the previous entry.

    Document type:      Article                              Date:  1990
    Descriptors:        Radicals and Radicalism. England. Civil war. Revolu
                        tion.
    Author:             Wootton, David.
    Title:              FROM REBELLION TO REVOLUTION: THE CRISIS OF THE
                        WINTER OF 1642/3 AND THE ORIGINS OF CIVIL WAR
                        RADICALISM.
    Journal citation:   English Historical Review [Great Britain] 1990 105
                        (416): 654-669.
    Abstract:           The revisionists who put forth the account of
                        widespread consensus about constitutional
                        principles and traditions changing to adversary
                        politics in 1646 would be better served to look at
                        the crisis of the winter of 1642-43 to find the
                        transition from rebellion to revolution. The
                        origins of this radicalism were found neither in
                        Christian sectarianism nor in aspirations of the
```

Figure 4.63   General descriptors in HISTORICAL ABSTRACTS on disc

events are not indexed by name. Searching for events by descriptor is effective, if descriptors exist, as in the case of the French Revolution (see Figure 4.62). However, there is no descriptor for the English Revolution of the 1640s, which is also known as the English Civil War, depending on each historian's interpretation of the event, all of which culminated with the Glorious Revolution of 1688. Records that outline these events are usually assigned the descriptors, 'revolution' or 'civil war' or both (see Figure 4.63). Figure 4.64 shows a complex search that

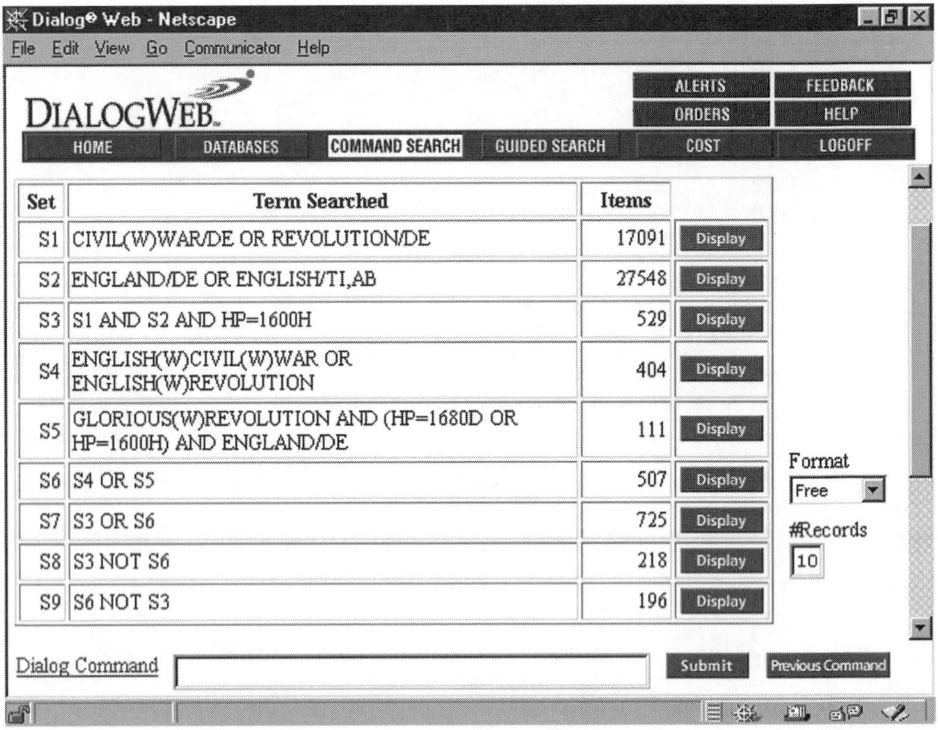

Figure 4.64   Using controlled vocabulary and free text in HISTORICAL ABSTRACTS on DIALOG

applies both free text and controlled vocabulary in HA on DIALOG, a search that is not possible on the CD-ROM version since the Dataware software does not accommodate the creation of sets. The search that used mainly controlled vocabulary (set 3) did not retrieve the record shown in Figure 4.65, while the (largely) free-text search (set 6) did not retrieve the record displayed in Figure 4.66. Combining controlled vocabulary and free text is recommended for searches that require high recall.

Similarly, the general descriptor 'depressions' is usually assigned to documents dealing with economic depressions, including the Great Depression of 1929, which does not have its own descriptor in AHL. The free-text search for 'great depression' retrieves many records that are not assigned the descriptor 'depressions'. A possible reason for this is that only major descriptors are assigned to each record; descriptors that are considered 'minor' or 'secondary' do not seem to be included. Records retrieved in the search displayed in Figure 4.67 represent those documents that are assigned more specific descriptors, such as 'New Deal', or those records whose major topic is, for example, theatre or art. The policy of assigning general descriptors to specific events is problematic for retrieval since such descriptors must be limited to geographic locations, or time periods, or both.

```
1515016   48A-6302
THE BRIDGE OF BOATS AT GLOUCESTER 1642-44.
Evans, D S
Journal of the Society for Army Historical Research (Great Britain) 1993 71(288): 232-242.
DOCUMENT TYPE: ARTICLE
ABSTRACT: Describes how the train of pontoon bridges mounted on carts attached to the
earl of Essex's army in 1642 found its way to Gloucester and was put to good use by the city
corporation throughout the Civil War.
DESCRIPTORS: England -(Gloucester) ; Bridges -(pontoon) ; Military Engineering ; Civil
War ; 1642-1644
HISTORICAL PERIOD: 1640D 1600H
HISTORICAL PERIOD (Starting): 1642
HISTORICAL PERIOD (Ending): 1644
```

Figure 4.65   Record retrieved with controlled vocabulary in HISTORICAL ABSTRACTS on DIALOG

```
1515184   48A-6470
"CONFORMISTS" AND "CHURCH TRIMMERS": THE
LITURGICAL LEGACY OF RESTORATION ANGLICANISM.
Ramsbottom, John D
Anglican and Episcopal History 1995 69(i.e., 64*)(1): 17-36.
DOCUMENT TYPE: ARTICLE
ABSTRACT: Following the restoration of the Stuart monarchy in 1660, Nonconformity in
the Anglican Church provoked a movement among the hierarchy demanding greater
adherence to the traditional sacramental program and the liturgy. These "true sons" of the
church were gaining ground, with increasingly less tolerance for deviancy allowed by the
bishops, when in 1688 James II was overthrown and replaced by William and Mary. The
Glorious Revolution meant that the Anglican Church would continue to follow a "moderate"
approach, much to the chagrin of the declining "sacramentalist" party. (R. W. Howard )
DESCRIPTORS: England ; Conservatism ; Nonconformism ; Church of England ; Liturgy ;
1660-1700
HISTORICAL PERIOD: 1660D 1670D 1680D 1690D 1600H
HISTORICAL PERIOD (Starting): 1660
HISTORICAL PERIOD (Ending): 1700
```

Figure 4.66   Record retrieved with free text in HISTORICAL ABSTRACTS on DIALOG

Place names are entered in the Descriptor field according to the political name at the time of indexing, a particular problem with African countries and the former USSR. Variations occur even for countries with fixed names, such as Great Britain, which is favoured over the term United Kingdom in HA. Descriptor entries in HA also include all of the smaller units within Great Britain. Without a classification approach, place names should be searched with the generic name and its alternatives, as well as the smaller units. In HA counties, cities, towns and even smaller geographical subdivisions are normally listed in parentheses,

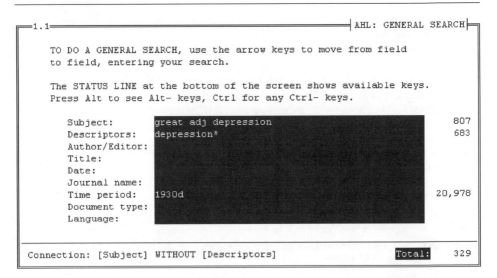

Figure 4.67   **Free text versus controlled vocabulary in AMERICA: HISTORY AND LIFE on disc**

following the country name, as in France (Paris). In AHL place names are entered with the state or province as the main heading, followed by the smaller units (cities and districts) in parentheses, such as California (San Francisco; Chinatown). New York City, which is entered without the state name, includes several subdivisions. In AHL 'Canada' is used as a main heading, but is not usually included as a descriptor in records that have provinces as main headings. The descriptors 'Canada' and 'USA' or 'North America' are assigned to records that refer to both Canada and the USA. If a document refers to the USA and other countries, only the other countries are usually used as descriptors, since 'United States' is not a main heading in AHL.

Date searching is often an essential component of historical research, and both AHL and HA index time periods, but not without difficulties. The Historical Starting Date (HS), the Historical Ending Date (HE) and the Historical Period (HP) fields were introduced in the DIALOG versions of the two databases in the mid-1970s, but they proved to be problematic since they did not permit enough flexibility for time period searches. The solution adopted in 1979 was to standardize the HP field to its present form, which consists of centuries (for example, 1800H) and decades (for example, 1960D). Not available in the CD-ROM versions, the HS and HE fields contain specific dates, but these fields should be used sparingly since they eliminate many relevant records. Figure 4.68 shows two searches that are mutually exclusive. The alternatives are to use the HP field (Time Period field in the CD-ROM version) to retrieve records pertaining to the time period as a decade, or to use a descriptor that represents the time period. The Time Period field indexes up to six centuries and up to six decades for any record. Although the record itself displays specific dates or even phrases such as '19th c.', the Time Period field should not be searched in this fashion. Inevitably, searches

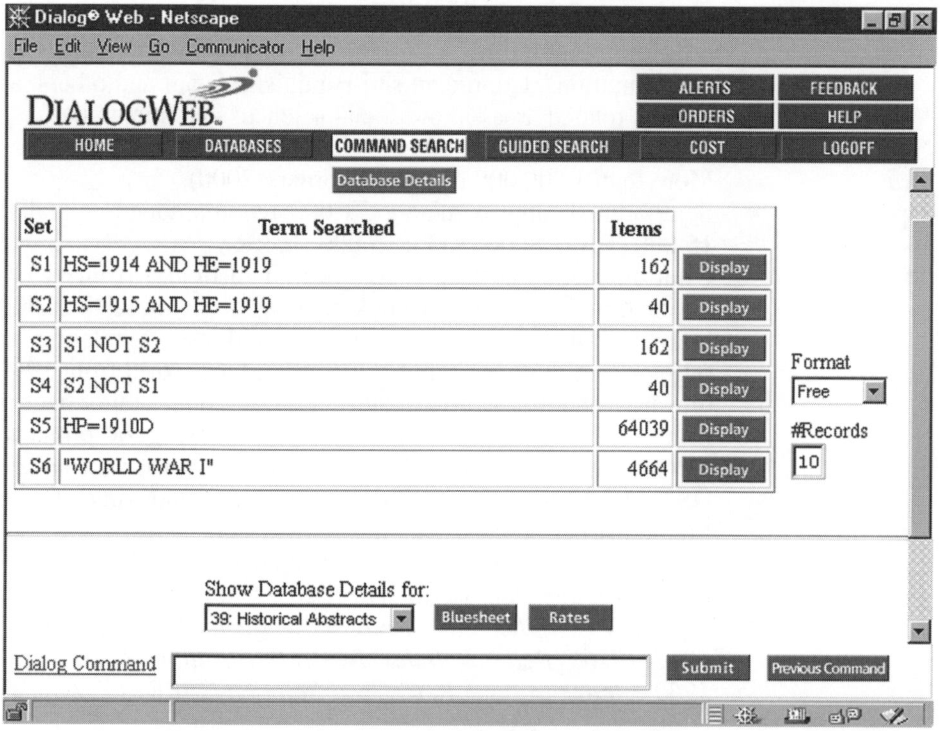

2

Figure 4.68   Searching time periods in HISTORICAL ABSTRACTS on DIALOG

that use too many time periods may retrieve some irrelevant records, while searches that focus too narrowly on time periods may miss some pertinent documents.

On a final note, the Documentation field, available on the specific fields screen on the CD-ROM versions of HA and AHL, contains additional information for many documents. This field can be searched for records that include charts, graphs, maps, figures, tables, photographs, illustrations, letters, notes, references and bibliographies. Since this field uses abbreviations, truncation is required.

Religion and theology

ATLA RELIGION DATABASE (RDB)

Producer:	American Theological Library Association (ATLA).
Online:	Not available.
CD-ROM:	ATLA (Dataware software); SilverPlatter.
Internet:	SilverPlatter, OCLC, Ovid, EBSCO.
Coverage:	Religion and theology, church history, biblical studies, liturgy, mythology, cults and sects, ethics, philosophy, history of

religions, sociology and psychology of religion, and world religions including Buddhism, Christianity and its denominations, Confucianism, Hinduism, Islam and others, as well as related areas in the social sciences and humanities.

Start date:	1949.
Size:	More than 1 000 000 records (February 2000).
Update:	Semi-annual; approximately 38 000 records added annually: 15 000 (RIO), 8000 (RIT), 15 000 (IBRR).
Materials:	Citations and abstracts to journal articles from 1380 international journals, to book reviews from more than 500 journals, and to conference papers and essays relating to religion and religious scholarship around the world from 1949 onwards and for approximately 13 000 multi-author works from 1960 onwards. It also includes indexing of projects, reports and theses from Doctor of Ministry programs in the USA and Canada from 1981 onwards, and indexing of five Methodist periodicals spanning 1818–1985.
Languages:	More than 20 languages are represented.
Print equivalent:	*Religion Index One: Periodicals (RIO) 1977–* *(continues Index to Religious Periodical Literature 1949–1976); Religion Index Two: Multi-Author Works (RIT) 1960–; Index to Book Reviews in Religion (IBRR) 1949–.*

The ATLA RELIGION DATABASE on CD-ROM is available in several subsets, and the complete database adds coverage of *Research in Ministry* from 1981 and *Methodist Reviews Index* from 1818 to 1985. Containing approximately 1 000 000 records, RDB is available from the American Theological Library Association with the original Dataware software and, as of July 1998, from SilverPlatter, which offers the complete database and a rolling ten-year subset. A sample record from the CD-ROM version is shown in Figure 4.69. The following discussion is based on one of the subsets using the Dataware software. Similar but

```
    Year: 1993     Type: Article        Language: English

  Author: DeSilva, David A
   Title: Recasting the moment of decision: 2 Corinthians 6:14-7:1 in its
          literary context [pericope is integral to letter]
 Journal: Andrews University Seminary Studies 31:3-16 Spr 1993

   Subject Headings: BIBLE (NT)--CORINTHIANS II--CRITICISM, LITERARY
                     BIBLE (NT)--CORINTHIANS II 1-7

 Scriptures: 2 Cor 6:14-7:1
 Journals: Andrews University Seminary Studies   ISSN: 0003-2980
```

Figure 4.69   **Sample record from ATLA RELIGION DATABASE on CD-ROM**

not identical to the other databases that use the Dataware software, RDB features three levels of screens: the default standard search, the name search and the thesaurus search. Abstracts are not included, except for journals indexed from 1975 through 1985. Tables of contents are added for multi-author books, defined as collections of works with more than three authors. Chinese and Japanese titles are translated into English, and other non-Roman titles are usually transliterated, but may be translated into English. Indexers enhance non-descriptive titles. Most searches can be limited by language, including English, except book reviews, which are not identified in this way. The Record Type field includes article, book, essay and review. Records of essays in books do not have the full citation for the book, but they include book/essay link numbers that are searchable in their own field. Such searches are necessary to retrieve full citations of multi-author books, including tables of contents, which lead to the individual records for the other essays in the book. Personal names are indexed in two fields: the Author/Editor field and the Person as Subject field. All authors, editors, translators and reviewers are indexed in the Author/Editor field. Reviewers also receive their own field on the name-search-format screen, which adds specified fields for corporate names. Surnames must be entered with a comma, followed by the first name or initial (with or without truncation). Since the software interprets a comma as a Boolean OR, it is advisable to enclose the name within quotation marks. A search for a name without quotation marks requires the use of the truncation symbol (*) to replace the comma; otherwise no records will be retrieved.

Over the years author entries have exhibited many variations. The browse function (F2) is useful for finding names, and their variations, which also applies to the Person as Subject field. Personal and corporate names as subjects are derived from the Library of Congress Name Authority file or from appropriate encyclopedias, including *Encyclopaedia Britannica*, the *Encyclopedia of Religion*, *Encyclopedia Judaica* and the *New Catholic Encyclopedia*. Normally, dates are included for personal subjects, but variations, changes, additions or errors occur. Figure 4.70 shows two variants on 'Dathenus, Petrus' and three on Charles Darwin as personal subjects, each of which retrieves different records. The latter must be entered as 'darwin, charles*' to include all three variations. The Personal Subject field indexes all people as subjects, including biblical figures, but excluding mythical, fictional or literary characters, which are indexed in the Subject Heading field. Occasionally biblical figures appear in literature, and these receive separate entries in the Subject Heading field (see Figure 4.71).

Subject headings and personal subjects are listed in the *Religion Indexes Thesaurus*, the sixth printed edition of which was published in 1994. Comprising over 14 000 subject headings and approximately 4500 personal names, the *Thesaurus* resembles the Library of Congress Subject Headings, modified and enhanced to suit subject areas related to religion. Book reviews do not have subject headings, and books receive up to seven headings which describe the book as a whole or several of the essays within it. Subject headings consist of main headings and subdivisions, also resembling Library of Congress standard subdivisions, which may include titles of people and historical dates (see Figure

```
┌───────────────────────────────────────────────────────────────────────┐
│          ╣Browsing "Person as Subject": 8137 / 39629╠                   │
│     1  │ DARTLEY, A C                                          .         │
│     1  │ DARTMOUTH, WILLIAM LEGGE, 2D EARL, 1731-1801                    │
│   134  │ DARWIN, CHARLES                                                 │
│     2  │ DARWIN, CHARLES, 1809-1882                                      │
│     4  │ DARWIN, CHARLES, 1809-1892                                      │
│     1  │ DAS, GHASI, B 1756                                             │
│     2  │ DASBACH, GEORG FRIEDRICH, 1846-1907                            │
│     1  │ DASIUS, SAINT, D 303                                           │
│     1  │ DASSETTO, FELICE                                              │
│     2  │ DASTA TAKLA WALD, 1901-1985                                   │
│     3  │ DATHENUS, PETRUS, 1531-1588                                   │
│     1  │ DATHENUS, PETRUS, 16TH CENT                                   │
│     1  │ DATINI, FRANCESCO, 1335-1410                                  │
│     1  │ DAUB, KARL, 1765-1836                                         │
│     1  │ DAUBANTON, FRANCOIS E, 1853-1920                             │
│     6  │ DAUBE, DAVID                                                   │
└───────────────────────────────────────────────────────────────────────┘
```

Figure 4.70   Person as Subject field in ATLA RELIGION DATABASE on CD-ROM

```
┌───────────────────────────────────────────────────────────────────────┐
│ ═1.1═                                              ╣Standard Search╠     │
│              [F2]  Browse Index       [ Esc ]  Clear Line               │
│  [F1] Help   [F3]  Display Results    [ALT-C]  Clear Screen             │
│              [Enter] Execute Search   [ALT-R]  Search Format            │
│ ═══════════════════════════════════════════════════════════════════════│
│              Keyword:                                                    │
│                Title:                                                    │
│         Author/Editor:                                                   │
│   Person as Subject: "MOSES (BIBLICAL LEADER)"                 243       │
│       Subject Heading: "MOSES (BIBLICAL LEADER) IN LITERATURE"  26       │
│         Scripture Ref:                                                   │
│         Journal Title:                                                   │
│      Journal Citation:                                                   │
│            Publisher:                                                    │
│             Language:                                                    │
│          Record Type:                       Year:                        │
│                 ISSN:                        ISBN:                        │
│     Book/Essay Link #:                       LC #:                       │
│ ─────────────────────────────────────────────────────────────────────── │
│ Connection: ALL OR [Person as Subject] OR [Subject Heading]  Total:  269 │
└───────────────────────────────────────────────────────────────────────┘
```

Figure 4.71   Biblical figures in ATLA RELIGION DATABASE on CD-ROM

4.72). Geographic designations, whether subdivision or main heading, use the country name and its adjectival form, and even standard abbreviations. Bible subject headings include distinctions for the Old (OT) and New Testaments (NT), chapter name, book and chapter numbers (if applicable), followed by standard

```
UNITED STATES--CHURCH HISTORY
UNITED STATES--CHURCH HISTORY--1600-1699
UNITED STATES--CHURCH HISTORY--1600-1775
UNITED STATES--CHURCH HISTORY--1700-
UNITED STATES--CHURCH HISTORY--1700-1799
UNITED STATES--CHURCH HISTORY--1700-1850
UNITED STATES--CHURCH HISTORY--1775-1783  (REVOLUTION)
UNITED STATES--CHURCH HISTORY--1800-
UNITED STATES--CHURCH HISTORY--1800-1899
UNITED STATES--CHURCH HISTORY--1850-
UNITED STATES--CHURCH HISTORY--1865-
UNITED STATES--CHURCH HISTORY--1900-
UNITED STATES--CHURCH HISTORY--1920-
UNITED STATES--CHURCH HISTORY--1930-
UNITED STATES--CHURCH HISTORY--1940-
```

Figure 4.72   **Dates as subject subdivisions in ATLA RELIGION DATABASE on CD-ROM**

```
     [Enter]    Full Display          [ALT-Q]  Print Record
 [Space Bar]    Extended List         [ALT-P]  Printing Menu
    [ Esc ]     Search Screen         [ALT-E]  Export to disk

     BIBLE (OT)--EXODUS--CHAPTERS 1-18
     BIBLE (OT)--EXODUS--CHAPTERS 19-40
     BIBLE (OT)--EXODUS--COMMENTARIES
     BIBLE (OT)--EXODUS--CRITICISM, FORM
     BIBLE (OT)--EXODUS--CRITICISM, INTERPRETATION
     BIBLE (OT)--EXODUS--CRITICISM, INTERPRETATION--HISTORY
     BIBLE (OT)--EXODUS--CRITICISM, LITERARY
     BIBLE (OT)--EXODUS--CRITICISM, REDACTION
     BIBLE (OT)--EXODUS--CRITICISM, SOURCE
     BIBLE (OT)--EXODUS--CRITICISM, TEXTUAL
     BIBLE (OT)--EXODUS--THEOLOGY
     BIBLE (OT)--EZEKIEL
     BIBLE (OT)--EZEKIEL 1-24
     BIBLE (OT)--EZEKIEL 1-24--COMMENTARIES
     BIBLE (OT)--EZEKIEL 1-24--CRITICISM, INTERPRETATION
```

Figure 4.73   **Criticism of the books of the Bible in ATLA RELIGION DATABASE on CD-ROM**

subdivisions, all of which contribute to complexity of entry. Searches for biblical descriptors in the Subject Heading field must be enclosed in quotation marks and, when they contain book and chapter numbers, the two hyphens must be used as well. Once again, the browse function (F2) is particularly useful to retrieve biblical subject headings. The electronic *Thesaurus*, though buried in another search screen, is also useful. Figure 4.73 displays a list of biblical subject headings

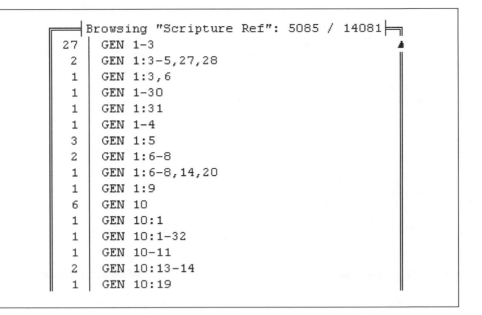

```
┤Browsing "Scripture Ref":  5085 /  14081├┐
27 │  GEN  1-3                             ▲
 2 │  GEN  1:3-5,27,28
 1 │  GEN  1:3,6
 1 │  GEN  1-30
 1 │  GEN  1:31
 1 │  GEN  1-4
 3 │  GEN  1:5
 2 │  GEN  1:6-8
 1 │  GEN  1:6-8,14,20
 1 │  GEN  1:9
 6 │  GEN  10
 1 │  GEN  10:1
 1 │  GEN  10:1-32
 1 │  GEN  10-11
 2 │  GEN  10:13-14
 1 │  GEN  10:19
```

Figure 4.74   Scripture Reference field in ATLA RELIGION DATABASE on CD-ROM

that include several variations of the standard subdivision 'criticism', which may be entered after the book name or after the chapter numbers. Keyword searches, which should also include the abbreviations OT or NT, are recommended for comprehensive retrieval of criticism and interpretation of books of the Bible.

Biblical references can also be searched through the Scripture Reference field, which differs from the biblical Subject Heading field in several respects. First, the Scripture Reference field was introduced in 1986 and was not applied retrospectively. Second, each book of the Bible is represented by an abbreviation in the Scripture Reference field, which is indexed digit by digit and not in standard numerical order (see Figure 4.74). Third, biblical subject headings use Roman numerals, entered after the book name, to indicate a specific biblical book, while the Scripture Reference field uses Arabic numerals, entered before the abbreviation, as evident in the sample record displayed in Figure 4.69. The same record in the SilverPlatter version (on WebSPIRS) displays the Scripture field as such: 'Corinthians, -2nd-c6-v14-c7-v1'. Finally, the main purpose of the Scripture Reference field is to find citations to documents that discuss specific chapters and verses within the books of the Bible. Some short chapters such as Obadiah in the Old Testament and Philemon and Jude in the New Testament do not have chapter divisions and are not indexed in the Scripture Reference field. Instead, these short books are assigned biblical subject headings, which are usually reserved for documents that deal with an entire book of the Bible. Some biblical subject headings include chapter numbers, but they normally do not include references to verses, which are found in the Scripture Reference field. Sermons are not usually assigned a scripture reference citation, except for sermons by biblical scholars that deal with passages in a scholarly manner.

Literature and language

MLA INTERNATIONAL BIBLIOGRAPHY (MLAIB)

Producer:	Modern Language Association of America.
Online:	OCLC, Ovid.
Internet:	OCLC, Ovid, SilverPlatter.
CD-ROM:	SilverPlatter.
Scope:	International literature, languages, linguistics, and folklore; English, American, European, Asian, African, and Latin American literature and folklore; theoretical, descriptive, comparative and historical linguistics.
Start date:	1963.
Size:	Approximately 1 365 000 records (February 2000).
Update:	Ten times per year (OCLC, Ovid); quarterly (SilverPlatter); over 45 000 records added annually.

```
TI: Authorial Audiences in Shakespeare's A Midsummer Night's Dream
AU: Gertz,-Sunhee-Kim
SO: Semiotica:-Journal-of-the-International-Association-for-Semiotic-Studies-
    Revue-de, Hawthorne, NY (Semiotica). 1995, 106:1-2, 153-70
IS: 0037-1998
LA: English
PT: journal-article
PY: 1995
DE: English-literature; 1500-1599; Shakespeare,-William; A
    Midsummer-Night's-Dream; comedy-; language-; rhetoric-; relationship to
    audience-; as writer-; treatment of transformation-; semiotic-approach
SN: 96-1-1431
UD: 9607
AN: 96091656
```

Figure 4.75   Sample literature record from MLA INTERNATIONAL BIBLIOGRAPHY (a)

```
TI: The Amerind Personal Pronouns
AU: Nichols,-Johanna; Peterson,-David-A.
SO: Language:-Journal-of-the-Linguistic-Society-of-America, Washington, DC (
    Language). 1996 June, 72:2, 336-71
IS: 0023-8260
LA: English
PT: journal-article
PY: 1996
DE: Native-American-languages; morphology-; nasal-consonants; in
    personal-pronoun; statistical-approach; diachronic-approach; areal-approach
SN: 96-3-10576
UD: 9606
AN: 96014401
```

Figure 4.76   Sample language record from MLA INTERNATIONAL BIBLIOGRAPHY (b)

Materials: Monographs, essay collections, dissertations, bibliographies, and articles from approximately 3000 journals.
Languages: Almost 60 languages are represented.
Print equivalent: *MLA International Bibliography of Books and Articles on the Modern Languages and Literatures.*

In 1994 The Modern Language Association moved its MLA INTER-NATIONAL BIBLIOGRAPHY (MLAIB) on CD-ROM from WilsonDisc to SilverPlatter, and it is generally acknowledged that the CD-ROM version is much more popular than the FirstSearch version on OCLC. The following discussion is based on the SilverPlatter version using the WinSpirs software. Two important enhancements accompanied the migration to SilverPlatter: the inclusion of the *MLA Bibliography Thesaurus*, and the publication of the 1963–1980 backfile, now subsumed within the 1963–1990 backfile. The current indexing and classification system was introduced in 1981 and records created before 1981 have less depth of indexing than recent ones. However, some information has been added retrospectively to the backfile. The languages of documents, for example, were not specified before 1981, but they have been added to many records. This enhancement is based on the language of the document title or the preferred language of the source (cited journal or series) and may thus include inaccuracies. Another major difference in pre-1981 records involves the descriptors. Before 1981 only the last names of the subject authors were included as descriptors, but most of the pre-1981 records have been expanded to include the full name of the subject author. Titles of literary works as subjects are still not included in the Descriptor field for pre-1981 records, except for records about Chaucer and Shakespeare. To retrieve records about *Great Expectations* by Charles Dickens, for example, the title of the literary work would have to be found in the Title field or Note field of the source document (see Figure 4.77) since MLAIB does not include abstracts. A natural language search for 'great expectations' would not retrieve all relevant records since, as shown in Figure 4.78, some records include the names of major characters in *Great Expectations*, though not the title of the literary work.

```
TI: Implied Author, Extradiegetic Narrator and Public Reader: Gerard Genette's
    Narratological Model and the Reading Version of Great Expectations
AU: Bronzwaer,-W.
SO: Neophilologus, Amsterdam-C, Netherlands 1978, 62, 1-18
IS: 0028-2677
LA: English
PT: journal-article
PY: 1978
DE: French-literature; 1900-1999; Genette,-Gerard; literary-theory;
    English-literature; 1800-1899; Dickens,-Charles
SN: 79-1-721
UD: 7901
AN: 79100721
```

Figure 4.77   Sample pre-1981 record from MLA INTERNATIONAL BIBLIOGRAPHY

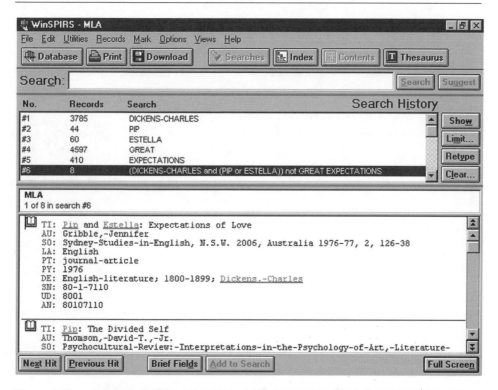

Figure 4.78   Sample pre-1981 record from MLA INTERNATIONAL BIBLIOGRAPHY showing character names but not title of work

Never published in print format, the MLAIB thesaurus is based on the printed version of the *MLA International Bibliography*, but the printed index in each volume does not necessarily include all thesaurus terms. As acknowledged by the Modern Language Association, the thesaurus uses 'loosely-controlled' vocabulary. Indexers do not rely solely on these terms and they sometimes use vocabulary found in the document being indexed. This allows for the incorporation of new terminology into the Descriptor field, but sometimes increases the need to search by natural language. Indexing terms are constantly re-evaluated as new terms are added and others modified. In an attempt to make terms consistent, these changes are applied to the backfile as well as to new records. The thesaurus on the SilverPlatter version of MLAIB is fully searchable and allows the searcher to display related, narrower and broader terms. Electronic access to the MLA thesaurus has greatly enhanced searching capabilities. Figure 4.79 shows the terms linked to the descriptor 'allegory': related, broader and narrower terms. The SilverPlatter software allows the searcher to 'explode' any thesaurus term. Rather than laboriously combining many narrower terms with the OR operator, the Explode feature instructs the software to search and retrieve records that include all the narrower terms of the selected descriptor. For example,

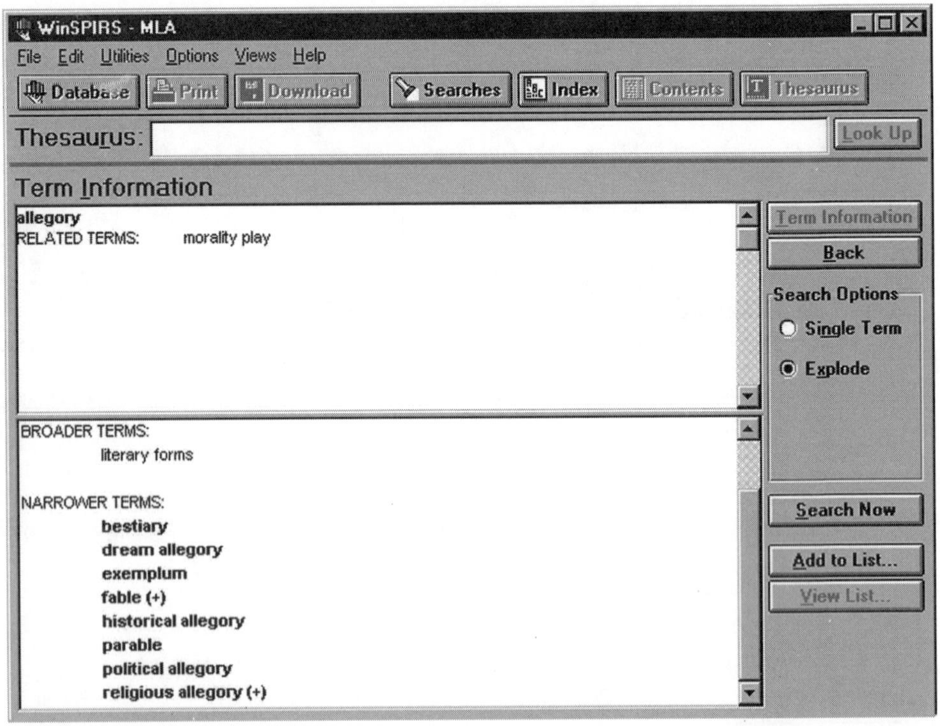

Figure 4.79   Example of thesaurus entry in MLA INTERNATIONAL BIBLIOGRAPHY

combining a search for 'allegor* in de' with 'chaucer-geoffrey' retrieves 36 records, while a search that combines 'explode allegory' with 'chaucer-geoffrey' retrieves 49 documents (see Figure 4.80). The Explode feature is particularly useful for searching place names that are subsets of larger place names. For example, the search statement 'explode spanish-american-literature' will retrieve all documents pertaining to the literature of 21 different regions and countries including Central America, the Caribbean and South America, but excluding Brazilian literature, and French and English Caribbean literature.

MLAIB features two types of descriptors that describe the content of a document – namely, classifying descriptors and subject descriptors, both of which are searchable through the Descriptor field. Based on the printed version of MLAIB which employs a classified arrangement, classifying descriptors are very broad categories that describe the class within which items are grouped. For documents concerning literature, these include national literatures such as 'English literature' and time periods, usually represented by the years of the century such as 1500–1599 (see Figure 4.75). For documents concerning languages, linguistics or folklore, broad linguistic or folklore categories are used, such as Native American languages (see Figure 4.76). Subject descriptors apply to the specific subject of a document. These include the title of the literary work, genre, the subject author and all the topical descriptors that relate to the document.

```
WinSPIRS - MLA                                                      [_][□][X]
File  Edit  Utilities  Records  Mark  Options  Views  Help

[≜ Database] [≜ Print] [≜ Download]   [Searches] [Index] [Contents] [T Thesaurus]

Search:[                                                    ] [Search] [Suggest]

No.      Records     Search                              Search History
#1       2840        explode "ALLEGORY"                              [▲]  [Show]
#2       2760        ALLEGOR*                                             
#3       4993        CHAUCER-GEOFFREY                                     [Limit...]
#4       36          (ALLEGOR* in DE) and CHAUCER-GEOFFREY               
#5       49          #1 and #3                                           [Retype]
#6       13          #5 not #4                                      [▼]  [Clear...]

MLA
1 of 13 in search #6

 TI: Chaucer's Clerk's Tale: A Disrupted Exemplum                       [▲]
 AU: Moon,-Hi-Kyung
 SO: The Journal-of-English-Language-and-Literature, Seoul, Korea (JELL). 1994
     Winter, 40:4, 643-55
 IS: 1016-2283
 LA: English
 PT: journal-article
 PY: 1994
 DE: English-literature; 1100-1499-Middle-English-period; Chaucer,-Geoffrey; The
     Canterbury-Tales; The Clerk's-Tale; poetry-; as exemplum-; role of
     interruption-
 SN: 95-1-468
 UD: 9501                                                                [▼]
 AN: 95067814                                                            [▼]

[Next Hit] [Previous Hit]    [Brief Fields] [Add to Search]      [Full Screen]
```

Figure 4.80   The SilverPlatter Explode feature of the MLA thesaurus

Not all descriptors are listed in the thesaurus. Subject, authors and titles of literary works are not found in the thesaurus, but are indexed terms which are listed in the Index on the SilverPlatter version of MLAIB. This is important because there are no cross-references for names of literary authors and titles of literary works. The MLAIB database does not have its own name authority files, but it uses, wherever possible, the Library of Congress name authorities to establish descriptors for subject authors. This requires the searcher to be knowledgeable about name variations. MLAIB uses actual names instead of pseudonyms; for example, Samuel Clemens is used as a descriptor, not Mark Twain. It also requires searchers to be familiar with the Library of Congress transliteration standard for foreign-language personal names and the transliterated titles of literary works. A search for 'Tolstoy' would only retrieve items in which Tolstoy appears in the title, whereas a search for 'Tolstoi' (the Library of Congress transliteration) will retrieve documents with Tolstoi as the descriptor. The search for the subject work, *War and Peace* (also complicated by common nouns and a Boolean operator in the title) must employ the descriptor 'Voina i Mir' (the transliterated Russian title) to retrieve all relevant records, or at least those created after 1980.

In addition to classifying descriptors and subject descriptors, MLAIB features subfield descriptors in its indexing system. These descriptors are searchable through their three-letter codes, which do not appear in the record, unlike past

```
SLN   Specific Language
SLT   Specific Literature
FLK   Folklore
LIN   Linguistic Topic
GLT   General Literature Topic
MED   Performance Medium
LWK   Alternate Language of Literary Work
LOC   Place
TIM   Time Period
SAU   Subject Author
SWK   Work
WTR   English Language Title of a Foreign Language Work
GRP   Group
GEN   Genre
LFE   Literary Feature
LTC   Literary Technique
LTH   Literary Theme/Motif
LPR   Process
SCP   Scholarly Theory/Discipline/Type
SAP   Scholarly Approach
SDV   Scholarly Tool/Device
SCH   Scholar
```

Figure 4.81   Subfield descriptor codes in MLA INTERNATIONAL BIBLIOGRAPHY

practice (see Figure 4.81). The Modern Language Association cautions against the overuse of descriptor subfields, preferring to recommend such searches only when single index terms can be used in more than one way. The genre subfield is an excellent example. MLAIB assigns to each record about a specific novel a 'novel' descriptor but, to search for records that discuss the novel as a genre, it is necessary to limit the search to the genre subfield. In the SilverPlatter version of MLAIB the search statement would be 'novel in gen'. It should be noted that searching subfield descriptors in the pre-1981 records produces mixed results. The search for 'novel in gen' retrieved only 27 records here, while the search for 'poetry in gen' retrieved 18 505 items.

Subfield descriptors are intended to increase precision, but some of the subfield descriptors are more useful than others. The specific literature subfield (slt) differentiates between records that are about a specific national literature and those that merely mention a specific literature. For example, a search for 'american-literature' retrieved 120 290 records, while the search for 'american-literature in slt' resulted in 120 126 items, a net difference of 164 records. The usefulness of this distinction is limited. Some of the more important subfield descriptors are performance medium (med), literary theme/motif (lth), scholarly approach (sap), scholarly theory/discipline/type (scp) and time period (tim).

Each of these subfield descriptors increases precision, but sometimes some relevant records are missed through such searches. Consider a search for

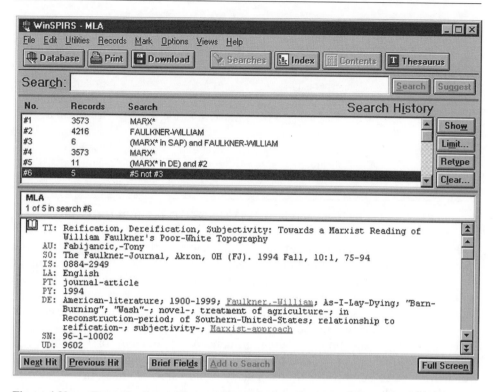

Figure 4.82   **Example of searching subfield descriptors in MLA INTERNATIONAL BIBLIOGRAPHY**

documents about William Faulkner that adopt a Marxist perspective. The search for 'faulkner-william' combined with the descriptor 'marxist-literary-theory-and-criticism' retrieves only one document. The search for 'faulkner-william and marx* in sap' retrieves six records, while the search for 'faulkner-william' combined with 'marx* in de' retrieves 11 items. One of the five net records is a false drop, since it retrieves an item about Leo Marx, but another is a very relevant record, displayed in Figure 4.82. To alleviate this problem, limiting the search to 'marx* in sap' or 'marx* in scp' retrieves eight records, including the one missed in the previous search statement, thereby slightly increasing recall and not sacrificing precision.

Two important subfield descriptors are no longer available: influence (lif) and source (lso). The (lif) subfield code was used to limit searches to influence studies in which the subject is influencing the author, while the (lso) subfield code was used to retrieve items in which the author is doing the influencing. Without these subfield descriptors, searchers must be more creative in order to retrieve records dealing with influence studies. Normally, a natural-language search for influence will retrieve items in which the word is found anywhere in the record, but the direction of the influence cannot be established. Even with the loss of the influence subfield codes, the MLAIB attempts to distinguish between the subjects

against	(date)	influence of	study example
and	discusses	influence on	theories of
application in	during	into	to
application of	especially	of	to and from
applied to	for	on	treatment in
as	for (audience)	relationship to	treatment of
at	from	role in	use in
between	in	role of	use of
by	includes	sources in	with
compared to			

Figure 4.83   List of role indicators in MLA INTERNATIONAL BIBLIOGRAPHY

and objects of influence by inserting role indicators in the Descriptor field. Role indicators define the relationship between a descriptor and the document or between two descriptors within the same document (see Figure 4.83). Role indicators are searchable but they often include stop words. Fortunately, two role indicators can be used to establish the direction of the influence. The role indicators, 'influence in' and 'influence of', are assigned to descriptors indicating that someone or something is being influenced by someone or something. A search for 'influence* in de', combined with an author's name, will increase recall but will produce some false drops. The role indicator, 'sources in', is used to indicate the influencing role of someone. However, a search for 'sources in de' combined with a literary author will result in many false drops. To increase precision, it is necessary to use the phrase-searching feature of the SilverPlatter software. Using James Joyce as an example, a search for 'joyce-james and sources in de' retrieves 447 records, many of which are false drops. The search for '"sources in joyce-james"' within quotations limits the search to records in which Joyce is doing the influencing. Note that the word 'influence' does not appear in the record displayed in Figure 4.84. Other useful role indicators are treatment, relationship, application and role. Role indicators are not included in the pre-1981 records.

Finally, the Note field in MLAIB merits special attention since it contains valuable information about a document. Fully searchable, it holds descriptive data about the record, such as illustrations and photographs, and whether the record contains filmographies or bibliographies, and even translation information. The text in the Note field is usually abbreviated, which normally calls for truncated searches, but not all of the searches should be truncated. The search for 'filmog* in nt' retrieves 15 records, while the same search without truncation retrieves only four items; many of these do not include the subject descriptor 'filmography'. On the other hand, the search for 'illus* in nt' retrieves 10 857 records, 47 of which are false drops that include the word 'illustrated' in the title of a work cited in the Note field. The search for the abbreviated 'illus' without the truncation increases precision. The same is true for the search for translations with its abbreviation,

```
WinSPIRS - MLA                                                    _  🗗  ✕
File  Edit  Utilities  Records  Mark  Options  Views  Help
  🖳 Database    🖨 Print    🖫 Download      Searches   🔠 Index   📋 Contents   🔢 Thesaurus

Search: [                                                    ]   Search   Suggest

 No.      Records    Search                              Search History
 #2       29509      SOURCES                                               ▲   Show
 #3       447        JOYCE-JAMES and (SOURCES in DE)                           Limit...
 #4       29509      SOURCES
 #5       555510     "IN"                                                      Retype
 #6       5868       JOYCE-JAMES
 #7       90         "SOURCES IN JOYCE-JAMES"                             ▼    Clear...

 MLA
 37 of 90 in search #7

 📖 TI: The Impact of James Joyce on William Carlos Williams: An Uneasy Ambivalence
    AU: Cumpiano,-Marion-W.
    SO: William-Carlos-Williams-Review, Austin, TX (WCWR). 1989 Spring, 15:1, 48-58
    IS: 0196-6286
    LA: English
    PT: journal-article
    PY: 1989
    DE: American-literature; 1900-1999; Williams,-William-Carlos; fiction-; and
        poetry-; sources in Joyce,-James
    SN: 89-1-10243
    UD: 8901
    AN: 89060657

 Next Hit   Previous Hit      Brief Fields   Add to Search              Full Screen
```

Figure 4.84   Example of the use of role indicators in MLA INTERNATIONAL BIBLIOGRAPHY

'tr', which should not be truncated. On the other hand, a search for photographs by using the abbreviation 'photo' with truncation will yield better results.

LINGUISTICS AND LANGUAGE BEHAVIOR ABSTRACTS (LLBA)

Producer:	Sociological Abstracts.
Online:	DIALOG, CompuServe.
Internet:	DIALOGWeb, SilverPlatter, Cambridge Scientific Abstracts.
CD-ROM:	SilverPlatter.
Scope:	Linguistics and language behaviour, including psycho-linguistics, applied linguistics, phonology, syntax, semantics, morphology, anthropological linguistics, sociolinguistics, communications, child language acquisition, computational and mathematical linguistics, language therapy, artificial intelligence, bilingualism, philosophy of language, and theory and history of linguistics.
Start date:	1973.
Size:	Approximately 255 000 records (February 2000).

Update:	Semi-annually (CD-ROM); five times per year (DIALOG); approximately 12 000 records added annually.
Materials:	Monographs, book reviews, dissertations, conference proceedings, technical papers and articles selected from approximately 2000 journals published worldwide.
Languages:	More than 40 languages are represented.
Print equivalent:	*Linguistics and Language Behavior Abstracts*.

Since 1992 the LINGUISTICS AND LANGUAGE BEHAVIOR ABSTRACTS (LLBA) database has undergone two major changes, both of which involve descriptors. Starting in April 1992, all documents have been indexed using the *Thesaurus of Linguistic Indexing Terms*, replacing the AUTHORITY file that had been used to assign descriptors since 1973. Beginning with records added in 1996,

```
TI: Significant Predictors of the Use of Whole Language in Elementary
Schools
AU: Mahony,-Joseph; Archwamety,-Teara
IN: U Nebraska, Kearney 68849
JN: Reading-Improvement; 1996, 33, 2, summer, 103-110.
IS: 0034-0510
CO: RDIMAE
AVA: Document delivery from University Microfilms International (UMI).
DT: aja Abstract-of-Journal-Article
LA: English
CP: United-States
PY: 1996
AB: A study was conducted to assess attitudes of elementary school teachers
toward whole language & determine significant predictors of the use of whole
language on a statewide basis. Nebraska elementary school teachers (N = 637)
responded to a questionnaire assessing background, attitudes toward whole
language, & the use of whole language in the classroom. Background questions
included information on location of school, grade level taught, & training
in whole language instruction. The results from stepwise logistic regression
clearly indicated that comfort with the whole language approach, background
training in whole language, & belief that whole language should either
replace or be used in conjunction with basal instruction were the
significant predictors of teachers who are more likely to use whole language
in teaching reading. Attitudinal variables are believed to predict whole
language use better than demographic or background variables. 3 Tables, 11
References. Adapted from the source document. (Copyright 1996, Sociological
Abstracts, Inc., all rights reserved.)
DE: *Elementary-Education (21500); *Teacher-Attitudes (87840);
*Reading-Instruction (70950); *Whole-Language-Approach (96900)
DE: Nebraska- (56650)
IP: whole language method application predictors;
attitudinal/demographic/background factors; questionnaire; elementary school
teachers, Nebraska
SH: applied linguistics; reading instruction and remediation (4117)
CC: 4117; 4100
AN: 9611368
AV: UMI
```

Figure 4.85   Sample record from LINGUISTICS AND LANGUAGE BEHAVIOR ABSTRACTS

the Descriptor field has been divided into two fields, which allows searchers to distinguish between major and minor descriptors, abbreviated DEM and DES, respectively, in the SilverPlatter version of the database, on which the following discussion is based. These changes have not been applied retrospectively – an important consideration for search strategies involving comprehensive retrieval.

Many of the abstracts in LLBA are fairly lengthy, but dissertations, book reviews (since 1978) and association papers (since 1980) do not include abstracts. Foreign titles are accompanied by English translations, and non-Roman alphabets are transliterated. Languages are searchable in the Language (LA) field. The Document Language (DL) field indicates the language of the item being reviewed, such as films or books. All authors are indexed exactly as they appear in the source document; several variations of an author's name, with or without full first name, may need to be used for effective retrieval. The index function of the SilverPlatter software is useful to find variations of author names. Authors of reviewed books and other media are indexed in the Document Author (DA) field. The Publication Date (PD) field contains the date of publication of the document being reviewed, while the Publication Year field (PY) indicates the publication year of the document. A reviewer's assessment of a book or other media is found in the Review Evaluation (RE) field. The five designations are: very-favorable, favorable, neutral, unfavorable, and very-unfavorable. The Note field (NT) is used to provide translators' names or ordering information for a dissertation. It is also used to indicate that an article is a comment, reply or rejoinder. Document types may be searched by the three-letter code or the text equivalent, which include, among many, abstract of a journal article (aja), dissertation (dis), book abstract (bka), book chapter abstract (bca), book review (brv), film review (frv) and software review (swr).

An average of five descriptors is assigned to LLBA records from the thesaurus of approximately 1400 words. For records entered since 1996, the DEM field contains major descriptors and the DES field consists of minor descriptors, but these three-letter tags are not displayed in the record. Instead, both fields are identified with the DE tag, one before the other. In the sample record reproduced in Figure 4.85, the second descriptor is the DES field. As displayed in Figure 4.86,

```
No.     Records  Request

#1:        6841  BILINGUALISM
#2:        4885  BILINGUALISM in DE
#3:        6841  BILINGUALISM
#4:         175  BILINGUALISM in DEM
#5:        6841  BILINGUALISM
#6:        4710  BILINGUALISM in DES
#7:        4885  #4 or #6
```

Figure 4.86   **Searching Descriptor fields in LINGUISTICS AND LANGUAGE BEHAVIOR ABSTRACTS**

```
Genetics
  DC  27600
  HN  Added, 1992. Prior to 1992, see DC he5, Heredity
  UF  Heredity (1973-1991)
  RT  Biology
      Disorders
      Downs Syndrome
      Medicine
```

Figure 4.87   Sample entry in the *Thesaurus of Linguistic Indexing Terms*

```
No.      Records   Request

#1:          39    27600
#2:          39    27600 in DE
#3:          82    HE5
#4:          82    HE5 in DE
#5:          39    GENETICS-
#6:          82    HEREDITY-
#7:         121    #5 or #6
#8:         121    #2 or #4
```

Figure 4.88   Descriptor terms and codes in LINGUISTICS AND LANGUAGE
BEHAVIOR ABSTRACTS

searches limited to the DE field find all descriptors, whereas searches limited to the DES field retrieve all descriptors except the DEM field, indicating that the DEM field retrieves only those records that have been entered into the database since 1996. Note that a search limited to the DEM field may retrieve records that were published as early as 1992 but entered into the database in 1996 or later.

Published in printed format by Sociological Abstracts, the *Thesaurus of Linguistic Indexing Terms* assigns five-digit codes to each descriptor. All three Descriptor fields are searchable with either the text or the code numbers. Many of the descriptor terms from the AUTHORITY file (that had been used before 1992) have been incorporated into the *Thesaurus*, but all the previous alphanumeric codes have changed. Fortunately, the *Thesaurus* provides history notes (HN) that identify the former descriptor code, the former descriptor term if it has changed, and the years in which a term had been used. Figure 4.87 displays an example of a thesaurus entry. For maximum retrieval, it is necessary to search for both the old and new descriptor terms and codes (see Figure 4.88). Book and other media reviews do not have descriptors.

```
No.      Records   Request

#1:        180    GREAT-BRITAIN
#2:        134    ENGLAND-
#3:         48    SCOTLAND-
#4:         33    WALES-
#5:         21    NORTHERN-IRELAND
#6:        131    UNITED-KINGDOM
#7:        534    #1 or #2 or #3 or #4 or #5 or #6
```

Figure 4.89   Searching for place names in LINGUISTICS AND LANGUAGE BEHAVIOR ABSTRACTS

The *Thesaurus* includes personal names and geographic place names. Unlike the previous AUTHORITY file, descriptor personal names include first names and, whenever possible, dates of birth and death. Place name descriptors include country names, as well as the US states and the provinces of Canada which normally do not include the country name as an additional descriptor. Modifiers are added to some geographic places with the same name, such as Georgia (USA) and Georgia (Republic). The USA is entered as the United States of America, and both continents and their narrower terms, such as Southeast Asia or Far East, are used as descriptors. The *Thesaurus* scope note for Great Britain includes England, Scotland and Wales, while the scope note for the UK adds Northern Ireland – all of which are descriptor terms – in addition to the undefined 'British English'. Comprehensive searches for geographic place names require the use of the OR operator (see Figure 4.89).

Organized into 29 major subject areas and 80 sub-areas, the LLBA Classification Scheme serves to arrange the entries in the printed version, but may also be searched in the electronic version of the database (see Figure 4.90). The current Scheme was adopted in 1977 and older materials were reclassified. Each major subject area and subcategory is accompanied by a four-digit classification code – the CC field on the SilverPlatter version. The text part of the classification is searchable in the Subject Heading (SH) field. Searches for major subject areas, by either text or code, retrieve all the narrower headings subsumed under them (see Figure 4.91). In this example the term 'psycholinguistics' is both a major subject area and a subcategory. The classification code (4010) is useful to distinguish between such terms. Subject-heading searches are particularly effective in the absence of a suitable descriptor: 'Child language acquisition' is an example of a subject heading that does not have a corresponding descriptor. Another useful field for retrieving terms not found in the *Thesaurus* is the Index Phrase (IP) field, which is the equivalent of the Identifier (ID) field in the DIALOG version of LLBA. Index phrases are natural language terms that summarize the document, usually based on the abstract. Index phrases reflect several, or all, of the following five elements:

```
4000   PSYCHOLINGUISTICS
  4010   Psycholinguistics
  4011   Theories and Models
  4012   Language and Cognition
  4013   Syntactic Processing
  4014   Semantic Processing
  4015   Child Language Acquisition
  4016   Verbal Learning: Paired Associate, Serial Learning,
           Memory, Recognition
  4017   Psychoacoustics
  4018   Neurolinguistics
  4019   Phonological Processing
  4020   Morphological Processing
```

Figure 4.90   Partial listing from the LLBA Classification Scheme

```
No.     Records   Request

#1:      24433   PSYCHOLINGUISTICS
#2:      22179   PSYCHOLINGUISTICS in SH
#3:      22179   4000 in CC
#4:       1767   4010 in CC
#5:        882   4011 in CC
#6:       2216   4012 in CC
#7:        803   4013 in CC
#8:       1600   4014 in CC
#9:       6399   4015 in CC
#10:      5127   4016 in CC
#11:      1926   4017 in CC
#12:      1546   4018 in CC
#13:       331   4019 in CC
#14:        16   4020 in CC
#15:     22179   #4 or #5 or #6 or #7 or #8 or #9 or #10 or #11 or #12 or
                 #13 or #14
```

**Figure 4.91   Searching subject headings and classification codes in LINGUISTICS AND
LANGUAGE BEHAVIOR ABSTRACTS**

- main focus of the document
- secondary focus of the document
- methodology
- research population, geographic location
- additional information, such as type of study.

The IP field is useful for finding interviews, surveys or questionnaires. Since it
contains natural language, it is of particular assistance in finding new or emerging
terms.

Philosophy

PHILOSOPHER'S INDEX (PI)

Producer:	Philosopher's Information Center.
Internet:	SilverPlatter.
CD-ROM:	SilverPlatter.
Scope:	Aesthetics, epistemology, ethics, history of philosophy, logic, metaphysics, philosophical anthropology, social and political philosophy, and the philosophy of related disciplines including education, history, law, religion and science.
Start date:	1940.
Size:	Approximately 235 000 records (February 2000).
Update:	Quarterly; approximately 8000 records per year.
Materials:	Monographs including anthologies, bibliographies, biographies, and textbooks; articles selected from over 300 international and interdisciplinary journals.

WebSPIRS: Full Record Display - Netscape

From: The Philosopher's Index (1940-1999/09)   ⑦ 🖨Print 🖫Save ✉E-mail Close Window

A Critique of Rawls's Hermeneutics as Translation

TI: A Critique of Rawls's Hermeneutics as Translation
AU: Josefson,-Jim; Bach,-Jonathan
SO: Philosophy-and-Social-Criticism. 1997; 23(1), 99-124.
JN: Philosophy-and-Social-Criticism;
IS: 0191-4537
AB: This paper seeks to demonstrate that hermeneutics is a powerful conceptual tool for exploring the current trend towards theorizing justice as a conversation. Specifically we explore the work of John Rawls in order to describe the particular variety of hermeneutics at work in both political liberalism' and justice as fairness' and to critique this hermeneutics from the perspective of the ontological hermeneutics of Hans-Georg Gadamer. Using the critique of Quinean pragmatism found in Joseph Rouse's epistemology, we draw a parallel between the hermeneutics as translation' in Quine and Rawls's public reason. This parallel, we argue, helps us better understand the features and the limitations of political liberalism, especially when Rawls's hermeneutics is contrasted with the possibility of a theory of justice inspired by Gadamer.
DE: DEMOCRACY-; HERMENEUTICS-; SOCIAL-PHIL; TRANSLATION-
PS: GADAMER,-H; RAWLS,-J
LA: English
DT: Journal-Article
PY: 1997
UD: 311

Document: Done

Figure 4.92   **Sample record from PHILOSOPHER'S INDEX**

Languages: More than 20 languages are represented.
Print equivalent: *Philosopher's Index.*

Available online since 1967, and now exclusively on SilverPlatter, PHILOSOPHER'S INDEX (PI) is one of the few secondary-access services in the humanities with coverage dating back to 1940, at least for English-language journals and books. Indexing of non-English-language journals began in 1967 and coverage of books in other languages started in 1980. Although indexed in the printed version, book reviews are not included in the electronic version. Variable in length, abstracts are usually supplied by the authors of the documents, some of which are written in languages other than English. Titles are in the original language and, for non-Roman titles, the transliterated title is taken from the table of contents of the journal. Author names are entered as they appear in the source document, not verified in a name authority file. SilverPlatter's Index function is useful for identifying variations in author name entries, but careful attention should be given to names with spaces or apostrophes, which may be scattered in between other authors' names. Up to three authors are listed for each record. For documents with four or more authors, only the first author is listed, along with the designation 'and others'. Languages, including English, are searchable in the LA field. Journal titles are no longer abbreviated in the SilverPlatter version, unlike past practice.

Descriptors are selected from the *Philosopher's Index Thesaurus*, the second edition of which was published in 1992. A revised second edition was published in 1998. Scholarly books usually receive an average of between eight and ten descriptors, while an average of four or five descriptors are assigned to journal articles, translations of books, textbooks and other documents. Numbers of assigned descriptors vary widely depending on the content, nature and length of the document. Place name descriptors use the adjectival form of a country, continent or other geographically-related term, such as American, Asian, Eastern or Latin American. Since the Document Type field contains only three choices (contribution, journal article or monograph), form descriptors can be used to retrieve a 'bibliography', a 'biography' or a 'textbook'. Most subject descriptors comprise single words, and each document must be assigned one or more descriptors selected from either a major field of philosophy or a major historical period:

1. Major fields in PHILOSOPHER'S INDEX
    – Aesthetics
    – Axiology
    – Education (used for Philosophy of Education)
    – Epistemology
    – History (used for Philosophy of History)
    – Language (used for Philosophy of Language)
    – Logic (also used for Philosophy of Mathematics)
    – Metaphysics (includes Philosophy of Mind and Phenomenology)
    – Philosophical Anthropology

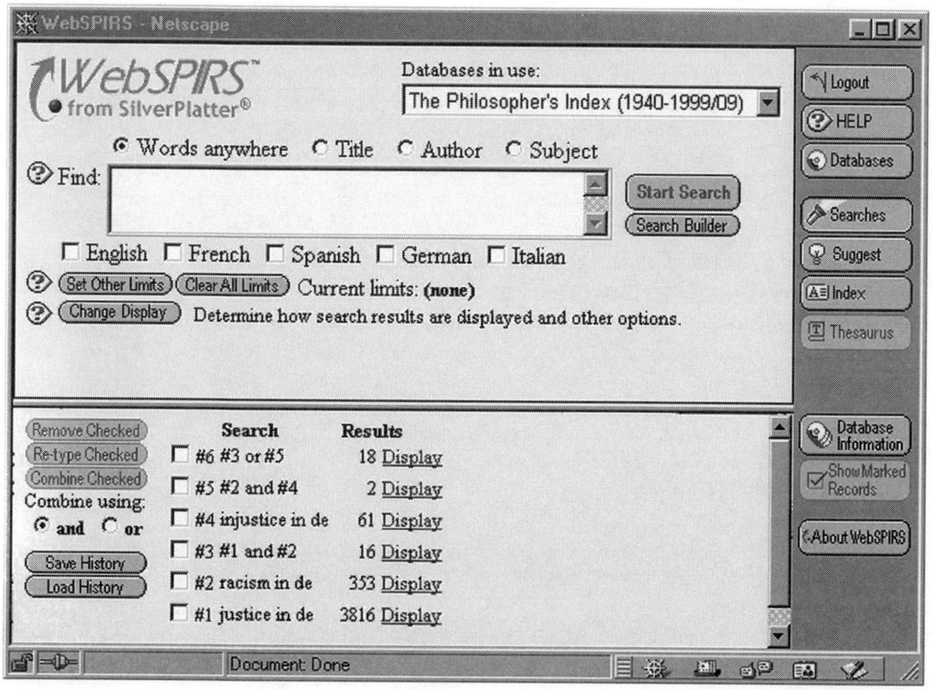

Figure 4.93   Positive and negative descriptor terms in PHILOSOPHER'S INDEX

- Philosophy
- Political Philosophy (includes Philosophy of Law)
- Religion (used for Philosophy of Religion)
- Science (used for Philosophy of Science)
- Social Philosophy
2. Major historical periods in PHILOSOPHER'S INDEX
   - Ancient
   - Medieval
   - Renaissance (used for the fifteenth and sixteenth centuries)
   - Modern (used for the seventeenth and eighteenth centuries)
   - Nineteenth
   - Twentieth

The positive form of a descriptor term is usually preferred to the negative form, but searching both forms is suggested for maximum retrieval (see Figure 4.93). Although abbreviations are not normally used in descriptors, the one common exception is 'phil' (see Figure 4.94).

Personal names are indexed in the Personal Name as Subject (PS) field. Famous philosophers are included as descriptors under their last name only. For all other philosophers, last names and initials are used. Personal name descriptors that are assigned to documents must meet the minimum requirements established by the

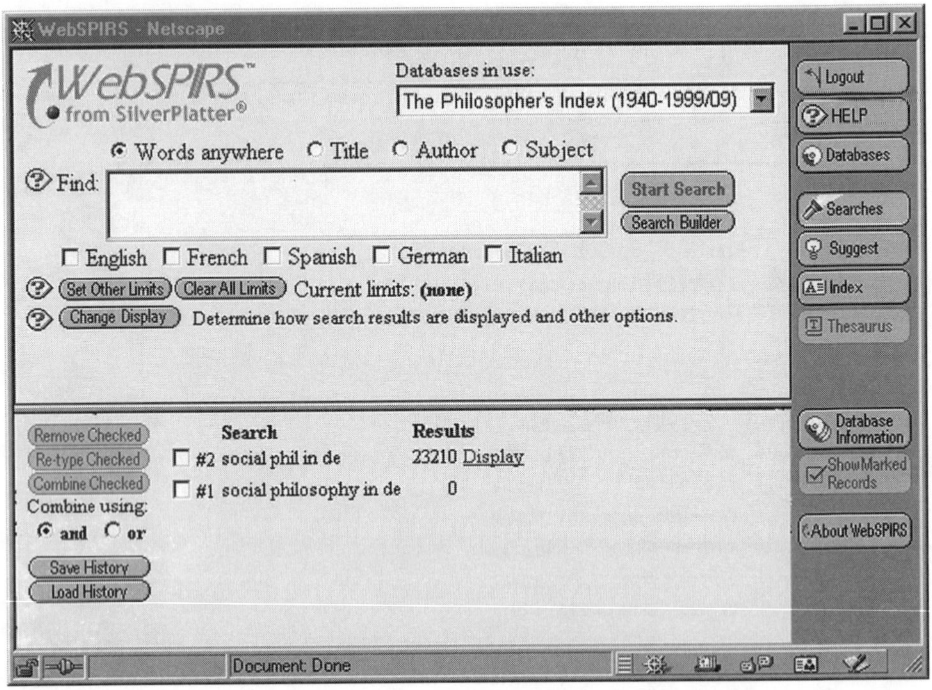

Figure 4.94   Abbreviations in descriptors in PHILOSOPHER'S INDEX

PI guidelines: named persons in journal articles must have a minimum of two pages written about them, and for books a minimum of ten pages must be devoted to a specific person.

Prospects

Whether constructed by intermediaries or end users, search strategies in the humanities are not easily designed. The expressed desire among humanities scholars to do their own database searching and the proliferation of databases targeted at end users indicate that the role of the intermediary is changing. Although some intermediaries continue to conduct searches in humanities databases, the task of the intermediary is increasingly to help end users with search strategies, either through formal bibliographic instruction or on an individual basis. In either situation, intermediaries require an understanding of information-seeking patterns in the humanities and knowledge of the structure and content of the databases. An effective search strategy may involve the use of standard reference tools to identify variant name forms and to find different ways of expressing time periods, movements, events or concepts, often striking a delicate balance between free-text and controlled vocabulary. Subject access in humanities databases is problematic. Even with electronic thesauri, indexing patterns are inconsistent and subject terms are often broad or vague and do not usually include narrower concepts or minor descriptors. Searches for subject terms, including geopolitical units and time periods, are frustrating not only owing to the various ways these are expressed from database to database, but also as a result of differences within the same database. Over the years, many humanities databases have undergone one or more adjustments, including changes in indexing practices, modification of classification systems, adoption of new thesauri, addition of new fields and transfer to other software or platforms. Many of these alterations are not applied retrospectively, contributing to the possible need for several search strategies to answer the same research question. Although such changes are not unique to the humanities, the demand for retrospective information underscores the need to be familiar with them. The challenge for all searchers – intermediaries and end users alike – is to be familiar with the structure, content and coverage of several humanities databases as well as any changes to them, and to apply this knowledge to formulate effective search strategies that match specific research queries.

Many developments in computer applications in the humanities are rendering electronic resources more attractive for humanities scholarship. Online public access catalogues are widely used since humanists tend to be more dependent on libraries than their colleagues in other disciplines. The growth and availability of indexes and abstracts on CD-ROM have increased the possibility of end-user searching, but the complexities of searching these databases, along with their limited scope and chronological coverage, dictated low usage among humanists. This is becoming less of an issue as time passes and as several database producers have begun or completed retrospective conversion projects, once considered unlikely.

The conversion of classic texts and other primary sources into electronic format and the digitization of images, sounds and other media open tremendous opportunities for humanities scholarship. Many full-text and multimedia resources are available on CD-ROM and, increasingly, on the World Wide Web. The veritable explosion of information on the World Wide Web includes the recent migration of indexes and abstracts from traditional online and CD-ROM formats to Web-based applications. The hypertext and hypermedia capabilities of the Web permit the creation of links to multimedia resources that enhance and amplify texts, meeting the visual and auditory information needs often expressed by students and researchers in the arts and humanities. Webpacs, for example, have the capability of displaying a record for an Internet document, such as an electronic journal, and establishing a hyperlink to that item. Web-based indexes and abstracts have the potential to link to the image or the full text of a document cited in a record, thereby facilitating the retrieval of related information without reliance on subject access and allowing searchers to browse. However, integration of electronic resources requires the continued development of front-end software, while overcoming fiscal restraints and copyright restrictions – all of which pose tremendous challenges for librarians and database designers.

Further reading

Bates, M.J. (1996), 'The Getty End-User Online Searching Project in the Humanities: Report No. 6: overview and conclusions', *College & Research Libraries*, **57**(6) pp. 514–523.

Bénard, C-L. and Bordeianu, S. (1995), 'Electronic Resources in the Humanities', *Reference Services Review*, **23** (2), pp. 41–50.

Saule, M.R. (1992), 'User Instruction Issues for Databases in the Humanities', *Library Trends*, 40 (4), pp. 596–613.

Spink, A. and Leatherbury, M. (1994), 'Name Authority Files and Humanities Database searching', *Online & CD-ROM Review*, **18** (3), pp. 143–147.

Stebelman, S. (1994), 'Vocabulary Control and the Humanities: A Case Study of the *MLA International Bibliography*', *Reference Librarian*, **47**, pp. 61–78.

Stone, S. (1982), 'Humanities Scholars: Information Needs and Uses', *Progress in Documentation*, 38 (4), pp. 292–313.

Watson-Boone, R. (1994), 'The Information Needs and Habits of Humanities Scholars', *RQ*, 34 (2), pp. 203–16.

Wiberley, S.E. (1983), 'Subject Access in the Humanities and the Precision of the Humanist's Vocabulary', *Library Quarterly*, 53 (4), pp. 420–430.

Wiberley, S.E. (1988), 'Names in Space and Time: The Indexing Vocabulary of the Humanities', *Library Quarterly*, **58** (1), pp. 1–28.

Wiberley, S.E. and Jones, W.G. (1994), 'Humanists Revisited: A Longitudinal Look at the Adoption of Information Technology', *College & Research Libraries*, **55** (6), pp. 499–509.

Chapter 5

Education resources

Lynne Lighthall and Linda Dunbar, with assistance from Brenda Smith

Introduction

This edition of the *Manual of Online Search Strategies* recognizes education as a discipline in its own right – separate from, but connected to, the other disciplines making up the social sciences. Education is a topic which is both wide-ranging and nebulous. In one sense, it is the act or process of imparting or acquiring general knowledge, developing the powers of reasoning and judgement, and generally preparing oneself or others intellectually for work and life. Education is the aggregation of the processes that help develop the potentialities of human beings to contribute positively to the society in which they live and to attain optimum individual development. In another sense, education is the science or art of teaching, where teaching implies imparting knowledge or skills, or giving systematic instruction, training or guidance.

Education is closely allied with, yet different from, training. It develops the general and special abilities of the mind; it is learning to *know*. Training is practical education, or instruction in carrying out specific functions – learning to *do* – usually under supervision, in some art, trade or profession, to develop functional skills and knowledge.[1]

This chapter deals with education in all these senses and at all levels from the preschool years through postgraduate studies into lifelong learning. It identifies useful resources for educational research or for other enquiries in education. It focuses on special search or bibliographic services that provide access to education-related information including, but not limited to, educational policy, educational administration, teacher education, curriculum, educational psychology, educational sociology, special education and teaching.

Most of the resources described in this chapter focus on education as a separate discipline. However, they will not necessarily always provide a full answer to a searcher with an education-related question. Even within one discipline such as education, the searcher must contend with different approaches to, and perspectives on, the topic as well as a great variety among the clients themselves.

This chapter also deals with CD-ROM and Internet educational resources for school-age young people. Coverage of these is necessarily selective and focuses on levels and/or broad categories with examples of individual resources.

There have been changes in the vendors and their services, as well as many new resources on the market, since the publication of the second edition of the *Manual*: this is the uncertain reality of online resources. However, the major databases – whether online or on CD-ROM – and their information coverage remain remarkably consistent, as do the strategies to search them effectively.

Factors affecting the search

Effective online searches for education information are realized when the searcher understands the nature of the subject area – its structure, organization, terminology and the various contexts in which it may be studied – as well as the nature of those who have an interest in education.

Three searches are discussed and illustrated (Figures 5.1–5.3) at the end of this chapter and are referred to throughout the text.

Terminology

Many subject areas have no generally accepted rule of nomenclature. Education is no exception. As for any evolving subject area, new concepts and new terms for them are constantly being introduced and may take a while to become established. In the meantime, different individuals and groups (even within the discipline) with their different perspectives and different needs may begin to use the terminology in different, and sometimes conflicting, ways. Those who compile resources may use the terminology in yet other ways. In addition, the inertia of large existing databases means that many terms that have been replaced by newer terms in current common usage remain entrenched. Although it is possible to update a term used as a descriptor or other controlled vocabulary access point, it is not possible to update terms used in the citations (or, in the case of full-text databases or Internet resources, the text of the documents) themselves. It is also true that even quite specific education topics can often be expressed in terms that will turn up in dozens, if not hundreds or thousands, of documents. For example, in late December 1999, ERIC listed approximately 14 000 references to the term 'learning disabilities'. Some documents, including those on the World Wide Web, may have whimsical, literary or allusive titles that give no indication of their subject content. And, as mentioned below (see also 'Geographic factors'), national and regional differences also come into play.

The experienced searcher will be aware of these problems of terminology and know how to overcome them. Not only will the searcher – particularly one who is incorporating keywords into a search strategy, or relying solely on keywords as for an Internet search – be aware of current terminology but also of how and if that terminology has changed over time (see also 'Time factors' below). A search on ERIC for current materials on 'Early Intervention', for example, will probably turn up all that is relevant. But if the client is interested in a more comprehensive retrospective search, the searcher will have to know what terms have been used to express the same concept in the past. More will be said about terminology later in this chapter in the section on 'Developing the search strategy'.

Context

Education involves human activity and, as such, may be approached from a variety of perspectives. English as a second language (ESL) education, for example, may be a topic of concern to practitioners interested in *how* best to teach those whose first language is other than English. They may require materials as practical as actual lesson plans or more theoretical material such as a synopsis of the latest research on techniques in ESL education. If the practitioner is new to the subject, he or she may require retrospective as well as current materials about what constitutes a successful ESL education programme, including the stage of intellectual development at which it is best introduced. An administrator may be interested in the most cost-effective ways of delivering ESL education and determining priorities for it in the overall curriculum. Other teachers in the school may wonder about the impact of ESL programmes on their classrooms and/or subject areas.

Despite the variety of perspectives, the experienced searcher should have no problems meeting these needs using essentially single-discipline resources focusing on education. Even so, the searcher will also realize when an overlap of subjects occurs and the request strays into other areas. The above request for ESL information provides a good example of 'cross-searching' from an education-specific resource to another discipline-based resource such as LINGUISTIC AND LANGUAGE BEHAVIOR ABSTRACTS. Educational psychology provides another example. A psychological approach is not uncommon in education and any resource in education that purports to be comprehensive will allow for this viewpoint as well as many others. On the other hand, a resource whose major focus is psychology rather than education may be the preferred one for a particular search. The searcher must be aware not only of the different approaches to education topics, but also when these different approaches call for using different (from education) resources. He or she must also be aware of the major resources in other disciplines that may include information on topics relevant to educationalists. Context is extremely important. The searcher must establish with the client at the outset what perspective is being brought to bear on the topic. This enables the searcher to choose the most appropriate resource(s) and take the most appropriate approach to the search. These are crucial first steps in developing an effective search strategy.

The clients

A wide variety of clients have an interest in education. They, in turn, have a wide variety of needs for information about education. This has important implications for the searcher who must consider what type(s) of information will best satisfy a particular need.

At one end of the spectrum are the *academics* or *scholars* – university and college faculty, graduate students and researchers. They usually require a comprehensive and retrospective search of resources with an international scope. They want to ensure that their review of the literature is all-inclusive and that they have all the appropriate background data before embarking on their own research projects. Also, they tend to be interested in detailed discussions of various (perhaps all) methodologies and want access to the results of all related existing research. No researcher wants to unwittingly replicate another's project! Academic clients are much more interested in the theoretical or analytical perspective than are practitioners, who tend to define their information needs from a more practical perspective.

Practitioners include most of those involved on a day-to-day basis with the education process. Teachers at all educational levels – including student teachers and teachers of teachers, trainers and trainers of trainers, counsellors, librarians (including teacher-librarians and school library media specialists), information technologists, school administrators and other policy-makers, and support staff – comprise this group. Their information needs tend to focus on practical application rather than on theory and principles. They are frequently looking for information about the most recent trends and issues in education and are less interested in a retrospective search. They are also often looking for more 'local' information or articles, surveys and so on that have a national (rather than international) perspective. Because education tends to come under the jurisdiction of a geographic entity, practitioners, for the most part, are little interested in applications that are not relevant to their situation. Being able to limit a search by geographic area or to exclude everything from outside one's own region is very useful. Using geographic delimiters is just one technique the searcher will employ to adjust the search strategy to the needs of the practitioner as different from those of the academic.

Although most school-based practitioners are not expected to engage in much theoretical research, they are expected to engage in action research to improve and inform their own practice and to advance the profession in this respect. In fact, most school accrediting bodies in North America require that teachers and other school-based personnel provide evidence that they have conducted action research in their schools. Anyone conducting such research needs detailed yet practical information about the methodology itself as well as articles, reports and other documentation that outline the results of projects carried out elsewhere.

Students, except graduate students and student teachers who are already accounted for under academics and practitioners respectively, constitute a third client group. This group includes young people enrolled in primary and secondary school (kindergarten to grade twelve in the United States – see page 219), undergraduate college and university students, apprentices and others engaged in vocational education and/or training, and adult learners of all kinds.

Parents, as individuals, as members of formal groups (for example, parent–teacher associations) and as members of informal groups, school board trustees, public officials and community leaders, as well as ordinary citizens are at the other end of the spectrum. Their interests and concerns are as varied as the group itself, but their need for current, concise information presented in language comprehensible to the layperson is relatively uniform across the group. They may want to know specifics such as what assistance or services are available to their school-age children in an isolated area, or where they can find reviews of materials that make up the collection in the neighbourhood school library or lists of recommended supplementary study materials for certain grades or subject areas. Alternatively, their interests and concerns may be more wide-ranging and less focused on the local situation. For example, they may want to know if there are national standards for teachers in certain subject fields and, if so, how the teachers are assessed for competence. Or they, like the practitioners, may want to know generally what are the latest trends in education. As with the other client groups, the searcher will adjust the search to find the most appropriate materials.

Geographic factors

As mentioned earlier, most education systems fall under the jurisdiction of the geographic entity (city, county council, state or province, country) in which they are located, although there are exceptions – international schools administered by boards with representatives from many nations, 'American' schools in other countries, 'independent' schools administered by their own boards and financed (wholly or in part) from private fees and the like. Exceptions aside, geographic factors are one of the most important considerations in developing effective strategies for searching for information about education. Databases in the field of education tend to be compiled on a national, rather than an international, basis. The searcher must take into account the geographical source and application of the information included in any resource. A client's request for information on research carried out to show the relationship between class size and student achievement in Australian schools would best be met by Australian sources and therefore a search in the AUSTRALIAN EDUCATION INDEX database. If insufficient or no such data existed for Australia, data for other countries may be useful. The searcher would need to verify the relevance of data from other locations to meet the client's needs before broadening the search to other resources. Separate searches of the BRITISH EDUCATION INDEX or CBCA FULLTEXT EDUCATION (formerly the CANADIAN EDUCATION INDEX) databases may yield parallel studies reported in British or Canadian sources. Until late 1999, these were conveniently accessible on the one INTERNATIONAL ERIC CD-ROM, where the same search could be conducted on each database without the necessity of rekeying the query. (Now the searcher would have to conduct the search in all three databases.) However, transferring a search from one database to another may not always provide the expected useful results because of problems of terminology (see Figure 5.1, pp. 286–90).

The searcher must also consider the geographical origin of the resource itself. Even ERIC, which claims international coverage of topics in education and is an excellent resource for a worldwide perspective on the subject, remains an American database and one of the best sources for American materials and information about education in the USA. A search for information with a truly international perspective, therefore, may require consulting several national databases to ensure that all relevant material is located. Ideally, the searcher would have simultaneous access to several such databases. Using DIALOG, for example, the searcher can access ERIC, BRITISH EDUCATION INDEX and WILSON EDUCATION ABSTRACTS and can transfer search strategies from one database to another. (However, as Figure 5.1 illustrates, the searcher should be aware of potential problems of terminology and be prepared to revise the search strategy as necessary when switching databases.)

Geography is also important because it influences terminology. Perhaps the most striking and familiar example of a transatlantic difference in terminology is 'public school'. In North America, a public school is one that is sponsored and operated by a governmental unit and supported from tax revenues and other public funds; in the UK a public school is a privately endowed and operated school – what North Americans would most likely call a 'private' secondary school or a 'prep' school. 'Integration' is another term with different meanings depending on geographic location. In the USA integration refers to the integration of minority students (for example, African Americans) into the public school system; in the UK integration refers to the assimilation of disabled and other special needs students into regular classrooms – a concept for which the term 'mainstreaming' would be more appropriate in the USA and for which 'inclusive education' is coming into use in some sectors.

In addition to the same term having variant meanings depending on geographic location, the same concept or topic can be expressed in different terms in different geographic areas. For example, the British use 'assessment' and 'examinations' whereas the ERIC descriptors are 'Evaluation' and 'Tests'. The AUSTRALIAN EDUCATION INDEX uses 'Teacher Librarians' (without a hyphen as a descriptor, but sometimes with a hyphen in titles and abstracts), the BRITISH EDUCATION INDEX and CBCA FULLTEXT EDUCATION use 'School Librarians', and ERIC uses 'Media Specialists' all to convey the same concept. In the search illustrated in Figure 5.1 (pp. 286–90) the list of authorized descriptors for the AUSTRALIAN EDUCATION INDEX includes 'Student Teacher Ratio' as a related term for 'Class Size'. The corresponding term in the CBCA FULLTEXT EDUCATION and the BRITISH EDUCATION INDEX is 'Teacher Student Ratio', formerly 'Teacher Pupil Ratio' in BEI.

Educational level presents another geographically-based problem of terminology. It was stated earlier that this chapter covers education at all levels from preschool to postgraduate. However, clearly defining what is meant by 'primary' or what constitutes 'secondary' education can be difficult and, to a degree, depends on one's geographic perspective. Even within one jurisdiction (local or national) the breakdown by levels of education may not be consistent and may have changed over time. Along this continuum the major traditional division is between K-12 (that is, kindergarten to grade 12) and post-secondary although what is commonly called post-secondary (sometimes with a hyphen, sometimes without) education in North America may be labelled higher or tertiary education elsewhere. There are other examples that serve to illustrate the variations that make each country's educational structure unique as well as highlight some basic similarities. This section summarizes the elementary and secondary structures and terminology used in the USA, Canada and the UK, based on the descriptors in the *Thesaurus of ERIC Descriptors*, the *Canadian Education Thesaurus* and the *British Education Thesaurus*. (See also 'Educational level' under 'Refining the search' later in this chapter.)

The United States

The ERIC descriptor, 'elementary education' (or 'elementary grades, 1966–1980') covers 'education provided in kindergarten or grade 1 through grade 6, 7, or 8', depending on the state. It comprises primary and intermediate education. The term 'primary education' (formerly 'primary grades') refers to 'education provided in kindergarten through grade 3', and 'intermediate grades' refers to the 'middle and/or upper elementary grades, but usually 4, 5, or 6'. Normally, students in the USA attend elementary schools between the ages 6 to 11. In some school districts, 10 to 13-year-olds attend middle schools with grades 4/5 to 6/7/8. The ERIC descriptor 'secondary education' (formerly 'secondary grades') covers 'education provided in grade 7, 8, or 9 through grade 12' – again, depending on the state. The USA does not have a uniform approach to secondary education. Some school districts provide secondary education in unified secondary schools that cover all the grades 7 to 12. Other districts provide secondary education in junior high schools (grades 7/8 to 9/10) and (formerly senior) high schools (grades 9/10 to 12). Still others have middle schools that lead to three- or four-year high schools. The searcher may also use more specific descriptors such as 'kindergarten', 'grade 1', 'grade 2' and the like, or broader descriptors such as 'elementary secondary education'.

'Streaming' or 'tracking' is a key feature of secondary education in the USA. Students are divided into three distinct curricular tracks: college preparatory, vocational or lower-level academic. Some school systems have abandoned this third stream. There is no official examination system to assess competency for high school graduation in the USA, but there are a variety of private examination companies that administer tests to aid colleges and universities in the selection of secondary school graduates for admission. However, not all post-secondary institutions rely on them to the same extent and some do not rely on them at all.

Canada

With respect to general levels of education, the Canadian system is similar to the American system. For instance, the definitions of elementary education and secondary education in the *Canadian Education Thesaurus* (*CET*) are identical to those in the ERIC *Thesaurus*. But *CET* recognizes fewer levels overall, defines some levels differently, and does not include specific descriptors for individual grades nor for ERIC's broader 'elementary secondary education'. Even though Canadian educationalists speak informally of, and frequently refer to, the 'primary grades' or simply 'primary' as a distinct level, *CET* does not recognize primary education as a separate component of elementary education. Also in contrast to ERIC, *CET* equates middle schools with junior high schools – the concept does not warrant a descriptor of its own. Furthermore, *CET* defines intermediate grades differently from the ERIC *Thesaurus* and in such a way that the term's meaning coincides with junior high schools – that is, schools with 'students under a grade organization system that separates out part, or all, of grades 7 through 9 as a distinct educational level'. Once again, this formal usage may not match the informal. Canadian educationalists frequently use 'intermediate' in the American sense to refer to intermediate divisions (grades 4 to 6) in elementary schools in some jurisdictions. Secondary education in the province of Quebec includes five years in grades 7 through 11, followed by two or three years at a *collège d'enseignement général et professionnel* (CEGEP). Secondary education in Ontario includes grade 13 for university preparation.

There are guidelines in each province that specify the number of course credits that students must complete for secondary school graduation. In addition, several provinces require students to take graduation examinations in certain subjects set by the Ministry of Education.

The United Kingdom

Levels of education in the British system differ significantly from those in North America. The *British Education Thesaurus* uses 'primary education' rather than 'elementary education' to refer to the first six years of compulsory education in the UK. There are no 'grades' in the North American sense. Levels are based on age. Pupils enter primary schools at five, the statutory school-starting age. Traditionally primary education comprises two levels and is provided in infant schools and junior schools. Some jurisdictions in England have three levels of schools – primary or 'first' schools, middle schools, and secondary schools. Middle schools may be classified as primary or secondary depending on the number of pupils over the age of 11. In the UK, secondary education is geared to pupils from age 12 or 13 to 16 (the earliest statutory school-leaving age) and older, and takes place in either grammar schools or comprehensive schools. Grammar schools are academic secondary schools that select pupils by ability. Comprehensive schools are non-selective; they accept pupils regardless of academic ability. Although a few grammar schools and single-sex schools still exist, education in the UK is increasingly becoming comprehensive and coeducational.

At 16, after a two-year programme, students in England, Wales and Northern Ireland take examinations for General Certificates of Secondary Education (GCSEs). Alternatively, after only one year of study, students can take examinations for Certificates of Prevocational Education (CPVEs). Students continuing their education after their GCSEs are said to be in the sixth form. From age 16 to 18 or 19, students prepare, in a secondary school or further education college, to take General Certificates of Education Advanced Level (GCE A-levels). Other secondary education opportunities for students aged 16 to 18 are available in urban areas in city technology colleges and city colleges for the technology of the arts. In Scotland, after four years of secondary education, pupils receive a profile of their abilities. The SCE Standard grades courses with three levels of examination – Foundation, General and Credit. A further year of study leads to the SCE Higher Grade examination, taken in four or five subjects. At 18, students may sit for the Certificate of Sixth Year Studies (CSYS).

Time factors

Currency may not be as much an issue with education as it is with some other disciplines, like the pure sciences. Even so, change, especially technological change, is such an important aspect of modern education that access to information about the latest developments and breakthroughs in thinking is crucial. Practitioners, in particular, often want the most current information. The searcher must know:

- what sources (for example, newspaper articles, press releases, news reports, and so on) are most likely to include this current information
- where such sources are indexed
- the indexing delay for each source
- the frequency of updating for a particular resource
- the overall coverage for each type of information.

Concerning the latter, journal articles, for example, may date from the resource's inception to the current month for a resource updated monthly. News reports, on the other hand, may date from only the current year or two, on the assumption that information first released in a brief news report will eventually make its way into a more detailed journal article or research report, or is of such an ephemeral nature that it is not worth keeping in the current database for very long (although it may be archived somewhere).

Searches for information about current trends, practices and applications in education tend to present few obstacles. However, searches for information with a 'historical' perspective can be problematic. The searcher must keep in mind that he majority of education databases index documents dating from the 1960s and (sometimes much) later. This has significant implications for an extensive and truly retrospective search, especially one where the client requires information from an earlier period. For example, detailed contemporary information about 'platooning' or the 'Gary plan' (introduced in 1908) is much more likely to be found in an older print resource than in an online database or CD-ROM. In fact ERIC includes only four references to the topic. In such cases the searcher must refer the client to print resources and/or consult with the client to determine whether historical studies more recently produced (and thus included in the electronic resources) are acceptable.

Time is also a factor in updating the resources. How often it is updated is only one important consideration in choosing and using a particular resource. The searcher must also consider how much of it is updated at any one time, how the updates are announced and acknowledged (the latter is particularly at issue with Internet resources), and how readily available or accessible is the updated material.

The importance of each of these factors – terminology, context, client, place and time – varies from search to search, but none can be ignored in the initial stages. Being aware of how these factors can influence any given search, the searcher is then in the best position to choose the most appropriate resource(s) and to develop an effective search strategy.

Steps in the search process

Choice of resource

Having conducted a detailed consultation with the client to determine needs as precisely as possible, the searcher must now decide what type of search will satisfy those needs. The first step is choice of resource.

Databases focusing on education, such as ERIC and INTERNATIONAL ERIC, attempt to be comprehensive and include information in a variety of formats – research reports, conference proceedings, journal articles, dissertations and so forth – and from a wide variety of sources, including government agencies. Even so, it is not possible for one database to be entirely inclusive; there will always be aspects of a discipline or types of information left out. For example, education students frequently are looking for policies and similar information from a government agency. Because such information is geographical in content, focus and/or publishing criteria, it is produced by national, state, provincial or county agencies and much more likely to be available in a government database or Web site than in a discipline-based resource. A search for an education-related document known to have been issued by the US Congress or any federal government agency will be most effective in GPO MONTHLY CATALOG or GPO PUBLICATIONS REFERENCE FILE. A good starting-point for a similar search for British information is the BRITISH OFFICIAL PUBLICATIONS (HMSO) database on BLAISE-LINE and BLAISE-WEB or THE STATIONERY OFFICE'S PUBLICATIONS DATABASE on CD-ROM and the Internet <URL http://www.ukop.co.uk>. Most states and provinces, and even many local authorities, have established Web sites to provide online access to their annual reports, curriculum guides and policy manuals. Other jurisdictions are covered in other databases or sites on the World Wide Web, as described elsewhere in this *Manual*.

Academics frequently and practitioners occasionally are looking for dissertations on education and/or related topics. A searcher may wish to limit a search specifically to theses, particularly if the client's focus is locating and verifying the contributions of other researchers before proceeding with his or her own research. Although ERIC, INTERNATIONAL ERIC and other discipline-based resources include some theses and dissertations, and the searcher can limit a search to theses, the citations rarely include the detailed and informative abstracts found in DISSERTATION ABSTRACTS (see below).

Likewise, clients are often looking for statistics related to education. A resource that focuses on statistical information, such as NewsBank, Inc.'s STATBANK (world statistics in all subject areas) may be a better source of more current and comprehensive data than an education database. Clients also need information from directories – for example, names and addresses of educational associations. General resources such as DIALOG's ENCYCLOPEDIA OF ASSOCIATIONS and Bowker's YEARBOOK OF INTERNATIONAL ORGANIZATIONS ON CD-ROM, and more specialized ones such as SilverPlatter's ASSOCIATIONS CANADA are worth remembering, as is the fact that much directory information is accessible via the Internet.

In addition, clients require education-related information that may best be located in an almanac, encyclopedia or yearbook whose contents are available as a full-text database and not reproduced in a discipline-based resource such as ERIC. Which one the searcher chooses to consult depends on the resources (either online or CD-ROM) available at the local institution or to which the local institution has access on the Internet. With no, or limited, access, it may be necessary to consult print resources. For now and the foreseeable future, effective searchers will remain as knowledgeable about print resources for education as about electronic resources. They will also remain aware of the more important resources in other disciplines (as mentioned below and described in other chapters in this *Manual*).

Searchers should also be aware that some resources do not necessarily index all the information included in an issue of a journal. Editorials and research summaries, for example, are not always accessible. In addition, there are occasions when an entire issue is not indexed because the indexing agency did not receive it, or it is indexed much later than expected because the indexing agency only received it later.

Access options

Education information is found in a number of online databases, often also available on CD-ROM, and increasingly via the Internet using specially adapted Web-based versions of the search and retrieval software. In addition, the number of education resources for professionals and students on the Internet is growing daily (see separate section on the Internet below). When alternatives exist, the searcher must weigh the advantages and disadvantages of each access option.

Online

Online access is through commercial services provided by various vendors or 'hosts'. Some vendors, such as the Dialog Corporation, host a number of databases, including ERIC and WILSON EDUCATION ABSTRACTS, from a variety of publishers. Others, such as Wilson, host only their own databases – in this case, the EDUCATION INDEX, WILSON EDUCATION ABSTRACTS and WILSON EDUCATION FULL TEXT. The choice of resource therefore frequently determines the choice of host or vendor.

Other major online hosts/vendors providing access to education databases are Ovid Technologies, Inc. (incorporating the former BRS Online services and CDP Technologies, Inc.) and OCLC Online Computer Library Center, Inc.

Online resources are good for current information and access to the widest possible range of databases. On the negative side, telecommunication links can be unreliable and slow, adding to the already considerable cost of accessing online databases. Online costs can include the 'membership' or subscription fee, online connect charges and printing or downloading charges.

Online access, although expensive, is also very powerful and sophisticated and provides access to the entire database at once. With large CD-ROM databases, such as ERIC, it may be necessary to scan several discs to complete a comprehensive search. Such a time-consuming search with its attendant frustrations may be less cost-effective than going online.

CD-ROM

Some CD-ROMs replicate their counterparts as online databases, some are available in the CD-ROM format only, and some include specially selected segments aimed at a particular audience. INTERNATIONAL ERIC, for example, is an amalgam of two separate databases, only one of which is also available as a single online database. AUSTROM is a CD-ROM compilation of 13 databases all of which deal with Australian topics, including education.

INTERNATIONAL ERIC and ERIC are available on CD-ROM from the Dialog Corporation. A large number of education and other databases of interest to educationalists is available on CD-ROM from SilverPlatter or through its Information Partners, including RMIT Publishing in Australia, Micromedia in

Canada, and InfoNordic in Sweden. Other major vendors of education databases on CD-ROM include The H.W. Wilson Company, whose WilsonDisc service complements WilsonWeb, and Ovid Technologies, Inc. whose Ovid CD-ROM service for stand-alone PCs or workstations complements Ovid Online.

CD-ROM technology offers the kind of sophisticated databases found online but with unlimited usage at a fixed price. Once a CD-ROM has been purchased or a subscription paid, there is no additional cost to access it. The more often the CD-ROM is consulted the more cost-effective it becomes in relation to an online database since there are fewer constraints on time spent searching and fewer technical failures. On the negative side, CD-ROMs are usually updated less frequently than the online databases, and CD-ROMs can be more expensive in the long run if they are not used frequently enough to justify the purchase or subscription price. In addition, some resources are simply not available in CD-ROM format, and some institutions do not have the necessary infrastructure to mount large numbers of CD-ROMs. Thus, CD-ROMs bring with them their own challenges in dealing with equipment and software, and terms and conditions of use, as well as search strategies (see the section on 'Developing the search strategy' later in this chapter).

Where currency of information, frequency of, and even continuous, updating are important, online databases and/or Internet resources are preferable to CD-ROMs which tend to be updated less frequently than their online counterparts. It makes little sense to purchase the CD-ROM GRANTS which is updated every two months if the institution already has a subscription to DIALOG providing online access to the GRANTS DATABASE which is updated monthly.

Site licence

Some resources, including ERIC, are available through site licences whereby an institution purchases a version of the database and mounts it on an in-house automated library system. With appropriate links, the database can be searched using the same commands as the OPAC and/or other locally mounted databases. Remote access to the database is often (but not always) restricted to authorized users. Site licensing arrangements have much the same advantages and disadvantages as in-house CD-ROMs, but with the additional concern that few databases are available this way.

Internet

The major vendors are making many education and other databases accessible via the Internet. Increasingly the Internet is serving as a gateway to various commercial databases previously only available through dial-up services or on CD-ROM. The Dialog Corporation's DialogWeb and DataStarWeb provide searchers with the extensive content, power, precision and full functionality of, respectively, DIALOG and DataStar online in the environment of the World Wide

Web. WilsonWeb is The H.W. Wilson Company's information retrieval system for the World Wide Web. Many SilverPlatter databases are available with an Internet subscription option; WebSpirs (SilverPlatter Information Retrieval System) offers searching of SilverPlatter databases from any forms-capable browser within an ERL (Electronic Reference Library) environment. The Ovid Web Gateway allows access to Ovid's databases (including ERIC and WILSON EDUCATION ABSTRACTS) via the Internet. FirstSearch provides Web-based access to OCLC's databases.

Enabling access via the Internet eliminates the need for a server on site; searchers can connect to the vendor's (or another institution's) server at a remote site on a fixed-fee or pay-as-you-go basis. This latter option may provide a less expensive alternative than an ongoing subscription for the searcher who requires only infrequent or irregular access to certain databases. Furthermore, this option is less expensive overall because there is no upfront capital investment in hardware and no ongoing maintenance costs. It also entails fewer administrative concerns. On the other hand, 'local' access allows for more control over customization and, often, faster response time.

Determining the best access option may also depend on the alternatives available for searching. Each vendor has developed its own search and retrieval software, such that the strategies employed to successfully search a database differ somewhat between versions. Searching the SilverPlatter version of ERIC, for example, differs from searching the Dialog OnDisc version, or the DIALOG online version, or the Web-based version of the database (see Figures 5.2a and 5.2b, pp. 293–30). In addition, most search software provides for different skill levels – novice, experienced, expert – to achieve good results. The professional searcher may not want to pursue the step-by-step method imposed by a menu-driven interface, especially when searching a familiar database. On the other hand, such an option may be welcome when the searcher first confronts an unfamiliar database.

Access, on the same host, to additional databases containing information of interest to educationalists is an important consideration. In addition, software that allows simultaneous multifile searching is usually preferable to software that requires the searcher to initiate a new search with each different database. On the other hand, the searcher must recognize when a search strategy will not necessarily transfer effectively to another database. Simultaneous multifile searching may not be as helpful or as important a feature for education searches as for other disciplines. Other features, such as the ability to create pre-log-on searches, to save searches and search strategies, to customize displays, and to receive output in various forms, also influence the searcher's choice of vendor and access option.

Depending on the particular search – the extent and nature of the topic, any geographic or time constraints, the client – the searcher will choose one or a combination of resources. All things considered, however, the searcher's choice of resource depends ultimately on availability and cost. The most useful resource for a particular search is useless if the searcher's institution does not have passwords to utilize an online database, does not subscribe to a CD-ROM, or has limited access to the World Wide Web. But access to the database is only part of the consideration with respect to availability. The other is access to the information itself. A list of citations, no matter how relevant to the client's query, will be more frustrating than useful if the documents are not readily available. Those resources that contain significant amounts of 'grey literature' are more likely than others to present problems with respect to availability of materials identified in a search. Does the resource provide access to the full text of the desired information? If so, this is a good solution to the availability problem, especially where relatively fast downloading of data is possible. If not, does the resource provide for document delivery? Is there an abstract and, if so, does it contain enough information to allow the searcher to make an informed decision about whether or not to initiate an order for document delivery? (An abstract can also help a scholar determine the merits of a given document for his or her targeted research, or even provide enough information to a teacher or student so that access to the full document is unnecessary.) More will be said about document delivery in the following section. In cases where the resource does not provide for some kind of access to the documents that it indexes, the searcher and client must depend on their own institution's stock and/or document delivery services.

There is no denying that the desired output can affect the search strategy. What the client expects as output must be determined in the early stages of consultation so that an appropriate resource can be chosen from the outset. In addition, the searcher must inform the client about what delays and/or costs, if any, to expect in obtaining the required documents.

The resources

Education, as a discipline in its own right, boasts a number and variety of online databases, CD-ROMs and World Wide Web sites from which the searcher may choose. In addition, there are many resources from other disciplines and some non-discipline-based resources that contain information useful to the educationalist.

Context, again, becomes an important concern. Education topics considered from a historical or psychological perspective, for instance, may be better treated in AMERICA: HISTORY AND LIFE or PsycInfo. Education in a particular geographic region may be better treated in a general national database – for example, INDEX NEW ZEALAND – than in a specific education resource.

The following discussion begins with the major resources in education, moves on to minor and more general resources, and concludes with specialized resources. Additional details about the principal education-specific databases can be found in 'Database details' at the end of this chapter.

Major resources

ERIC

Major resources are those whose primary focus is education in general. Of these the most important and most used is ERIC, the world's largest resource for education information. The ERIC system consists of 16 Clearinghouses, several Adjunct Clearinghouses, and additional support components. ERIC is produced by the Educational Resources Information Center (ERIC), sponsored by the US Department of Education, National Library of Education, Washington, DC, and prepared in machine-readable form since its inception in 1966.

ERIC abstracts and indexes over 980 000 documents and journal articles on education research and practice. It covers all types of print materials (published and unpublished) dealing with education and, since 1993, includes abstracts for books from the major commercial publishers. ERIC indexes some international material but is predominantly American. However, its wide coverage of education and related fields in published and unpublished materials makes it an essential source for many education searches.

The database corresponds to two printed indexes: *Current Index to Journals in Education*, dating from 1969 and covering published articles from over 900 journals; and *Resources in Education* which covers unpublished papers, conference proceedings, research reports, project reports and curriculum material from 1966 onwards. Journal indexing is cover-to-cover for the major education titles, selective for others.

ERIC covers the entire range of education literature from preschool to higher and adult education. It also covers such areas as: disabled and gifted students; tests, measurements, and evaluation; counselling; educational management; teacher education; and educational facilities. The database also includes the full text of ERIC Digest reports. These one- to two-page research syntheses, produced by the Clearinghouses and written specifically for teachers, administrators and other practitioners, provide brief overviews of current educational issues and include references to more detailed information. The ERIC Digests are available on the CD-ROM versions of ERIC, via the ERIC Web site and directly at the searchable US Department of Education site <URL http://www.ed.gov/databases/ERIC_Digests/index/>.

Access options
Six online vendors, including The Dialog Corporation, as well as five CD-ROM vendors, offer access to ERIC. Some institutions mount the ERIC database on their in-house computers. Searchers can also access ERIC via the Internet at many library OPACs. In addition, the ERIC system maintains a network of Internet sites, including AskERIC, an electronic question answering service and Virtual Library begun in 1992, all linked through one Web site <URL http://www.accesseric.org>. The 'Search ERIC Database' option at this site provides the searcher with four search engines to access the database.

Indexing vocabulary
ERIC indexers assign up to six major descriptors and as many minor descriptors as are necessary to identify a document's subject content, educational level, age level, type/form and so on from the *Thesaurus of ERIC Descriptors* (Phoenix, AR: Oryx Press, 1995). The *Thesaurus* is an integral part of the online and CD-ROM ERIC databases but not of the Web-based version.

Document delivery
The text of ERIC documents can be purchased in paper copy or microfiche from the ERIC Document Reproduction Service (EDRS) or from institutions subscribing to the ERIC microfiche service. The full text of the ERIC Digests reports is available on the Internet as noted above; the full text of other ERIC documents is available at the EDRS site <URL http://edrs.com/>. Downloading and printing these documents can take a long time, however, because they are scanned images of the documents and not text files.

The *Directory of ERIC Resource Collections 1996* (Washington: Dept. of Education, National Library of Education, Office of Educational Resources and Improvement) – formerly, the *Directory of ERIC Information Service Providers* – lists over 2400 organizations providing access to the ERIC database and related resources. It includes those that provide online and CD-ROM access to the database, those that maintain collections of the ERIC microfiche, and those that subscribe to, and collect, ERIC publications.

WILSON EDUCATION ABSTRACTS and EDUCATION INDEX

The second major education resource is the H.W. Wilson Company's suite of education databases: EDUCATION INDEX, WILSON EDUCATION ABSTRACTS and WILSON EDUCATION FULL TEXT. Together, these databases provide comprehensive abstracting and indexing of nearly 600 core international English-language periodicals and monographic series and, since 1995, English-language books related to education. The Wilson education databases are much less comprehensive, and more exclusively American, than ERIC.

Providing the same indexing and journal coverage as EDUCATION INDEX, WILSON EDUCATION ABSTRACTS offers, in addition, abstracts (50 to 150 words) describing the scope and content of the source materials. The WILSON EDUCATION FULL TEXT database contains the full text of more than 133 periodicals plus comprehensive indexing and abstracting for all the periodicals covered in EDUCATION INDEX. In its printed form, *Education Index* (first published in 1929) is the earliest indexing service in education, but its online history dates only from 1983. Abstracts were added in 1994 and full-text coverage in January 1996.

The Wilson education databases cover all levels of education – preschool, elementary, primary, secondary, higher and adult education. They cite: feature articles; regular columns; editorials; interviews; industry news; reports of meetings and conferences; current book, film and software reviews; critiques of theses; and education-related legal cases. Subject coverage includes administration, audiovisual education, competency-based education, computers, comparative education, critical thinking, curriculum, government funding, information technology, instructional media, language and linguistics, legal issues in education, literacy standards, multicultural education, psychology, special education, student counselling, teacher education, teacher–parent relations, teaching methods and vocational education.

Access options
The Wilson education databases are available through WilsonWeb and WilsonDisc. In addition, the databases are available on several other online systems and from several other CD-ROM vendors, and through Wilson's Information Partners – OCLC, Ovid Technologies and SilverPlatter. Some institutions purchase the Wilson databases through the WilsonTape licensing service; tapes can be loaded directly onto the institution's automation system for in-house or remote access using the same search software as for that institution's OPAC or other locally-loaded databases.

Indexing vocabulary
The Wilson indexers assign between one and five controlled subject terms per record. The databases use one subject authority file with subject terms derived from the literature itself, reference works, other Wilson indexes and the Library of Congress Subject Headings. There is no database-specific thesaurus.

Document delivery
As mentioned above, some items indexed in the Wilson databases are available as full-text documents in WILSON EDUCATION FULL TEXT.

National databases

The other important major electronic resources in education tend to be geographically-based and are essential resources for any queries relating to education in their respective countries.

AUSTRALIAN EDUCATION INDEX (AEI)

The AUSTRALIAN EDUCATION INDEX (AEI) database is a comprehensive resource for current literature relevant to Australian education. Produced by the Australian Council for Educational Research, AEI indexes and abstracts published and unpublished material at all levels of education by Australian authors or about

Australian education published in international sources. Source documents are journal articles, monographs, research and technical reports, theses, conference papers, legislation, parliamentary debates, newspaper articles, curriculum materials and tests. One hundred journals are comprehensively indexed; another 500 Australian and international journals are scanned for relevant articles about Australian education and educational research conducted by Australians. Subject coverage includes: educational research; educational history; adult and continuing education; library and information studies; curriculum and curriculum subjects; special education; management; policy administration; educational psychology; educational sociology; research and measurement techniques; teaching; teacher education; and vocational education and training.

The AEI database corresponds to the printed *Australian Education Index* and the *Bibliography of Education Theses in Australia.* All versions of AEI contain records from the VOCED database, produced by the National Centre for Vocational Education Research in Adelaide. Until the end of 1992 AEI included records from the Australian Clearinghouse for Library and Information Science (ACHLIS). From 1993 onwards only records relating specifically to library and information studies, and to education are included.

Access options
AEI is available online through Informit Online and on the INTERNATIONAL ERIC CD-ROM (see below). AEI is one of 13 databases on RMIT (Royal Melbourne Institute of Technology University) Publishing's AUSTROM disc that is issued with SilverPlatter's ERL-compliant SPIRS software. Other databases on AUSTROM of interest to educationalists are: ALISA (AUSTRALIAN LIBRARY AND INFORMATION SCIENCE ABSTRACTS), APAIS (AUSTRALIAN PUBLIC AFFAIRS AND INFORMATION SERVICE), and DELTAA (see below).

Indexing vocabulary
Search aids for the AUSTRALIAN EDUCATION INDEX include the *Australian Thesaurus of Education Descriptors* (Melbourne: Australian Council for Educational Research, 1996) which is an integral part of the INTERNATIONAL ERIC CD-ROM database.

Document delivery
Most of the documents indexed in AEI are available on interlibrary loan from the Australian Council for Educational Research's Cunningham Library. In addition, ordering information is included in many citations for indexed monographs.

BRITISH EDUCATION INDEX (BEI)

The BRITISH EDUCATION INDEX database is the equivalent of the print version of the *British Education Index* (*BEI*) plus the microfiche *British Education*

Theses Index (BETI). BEI is an authoritative index to the contents of significant journal articles in over 300 education and training journals published in the UK (many of them not indexed in ERIC), together with certain internationally published periodicals. In existence since 1961, the INDEX is developing to include more information about non-journal educational literature (reports and conferences, for example, and multi-author works). The INDEX is produced by a self-financing unit in Leeds University Library. *BETI* similarly indexes thesis literature.

The database contains *BEI* records from 1976 and *BETI* records (for all theses relevant to education accepted and deposited at UK and Irish universities and polytechnics) from 1950.

The BRITISH EDUCATION INDEX covers all aspects and fields of education from preschool to adult and higher education, usually qualified by age or educational levels. It does not normally index editorials, news items or reviews. The major subject areas are: cognitive development; management in education; computer-assisted learning; multicultural education; curriculum; physical education; educational policy; science education; educational psychology; special education; educational technology; teacher education; English as a second language; vocational education and training; and language acquisition.

Access options
The BRITISH EDUCATION INDEX is available online in the UK and internationally via DIALOG and DialogWeb. It is one of two major databases now on the INTERNATIONAL ERIC CD-ROM (see below). Members of the UK higher education community may access the BRITISH EDUCATION INDEX via BIDS Education Data Service as a Telnet, client server or World Wide Web service using an Ovid interface.

Indexing vocabulary
Earlier material in the online file (1976–1985) was indexed using the British Library's Precis system – not always a helpful one for online use. From 1986 onwards the file has been indexed with terms drawn from the *British Education Thesaurus* (Leeds University Press, 1991).

Document delivery
Recent citations in BEI include, when appropriate, the British Library Document Supply Centre Shelfmark number to facilitate ordering. In addition, some citations include the note 'online only'.

EDUCATION-LINE

The BEI office also oversees the Electronic Libraries Programme project EDUCATION-LINE to establish an electronic archive of 'grey' (report, conference, working paper) and 'pre-print' literature in the field of education and training. EDUCATION-LINE <URL http://www.leeds.ac.uk/educol> allows researchers, practitioners and policy-makers from the fields of education and training to present their work at early stages for immediate review by colleagues worldwide. It also allows them to see the latest reports, as they appear, on a daily basis and to find relevant reports and papers, in full, using the sophisticated search tools of the BRITISH EDUCATION INDEX.

CBCA FULLTEXT EDUCATION (CBCA-E)

CANADIAN BUSINESS: CURRENT AFFAIRS (CBCA) FULLTEXT EDUCATION, formerly the CANADIAN EDUCATION INDEX (CEI), is the primary source of information on Canadian education. It covers monographs and journal articles from over 200 Canadian education journals in English and French, many in full text. It also indexes book reviews but not editorials, and local news or articles of less than one page. In addition, it covers Canadian federal and provincial government research reports, 32 000 monographs from educational research communities across Canada, provincial curriculum guides, and graduate (master's theses and doctoral) dissertations in education. The database records include abstracts for monographs and reports but not for journal articles; for theses and dissertations, abstracts are included selectively. CBCA-E also incorporates the ONTERIS database of 14 000 records, covering research reports and curriculum documents originating from sources in the province of Ontario. ONTERIS documents are available up to May 1997, when ONTERIS ceased to exist.

CBCA-E covers all aspects of education, teaching and learning from preschool to higher education. The range of subjects includes, but is not limited to: educational theory; special needs education; teacher education; bilingualism and language acquisition; educational administration; multicultural education; labour and employment; educational technology; curriculum; counselling; and social problems and learners.

Access options
None of the major online vendors/hosts offers CBCA FULLTEXT EDUCATION, but it is available as a CD-ROM. As the CANADIAN EDUCATION INDEX, it was once, but is no longer, one of the databases on the INTERNATIONAL ERIC CD-ROM. In addition, the CBCA-E database is available for site licensing. Internet access is available through Micromedia's (partner-hosted) Voyageur ERL server or from a local ERL server or local network. Micromedia also supplies CBCA FULLTEXT REFERENCE, another database of interest to educationalists.

Indexing vocabulary
Indexers use terms from the bilingual (English and French) *Canadian Education Thesaurus* (Toronto: Micromedia Ltd, 1992) for CBCA FULLTEXT EDUCATION.

Document delivery

Many of the documents themselves (those prefaced with MN, ON or CD) and theses (order by ISBN) are available through Micromedia's document delivery service (order@micromedia.on.ca) or from institutions holding the Microlog Education Collection, Micromedia's full-text microfiche subscription service. Frequently CBCA-E citations include the corporate source for direct ordering.

INTERNATIONAL ERIC

INTERNATIONAL ERIC is a composite CD-ROM incorporating the AUSTRALIAN EDUCATION INDEX and the BRITISH EDUCATION INDEX. Older versions also include the CANADIAN EDUCATION INDEX (now CBCA FULLTEXT EDUCATION). Both national databases are presented independently with their own thesauri. The composite database covers all aspects of educational research and practice in Australia and the UK. It is the result of collaboration by an informal group comprising representatives from ERIC, the Australian Council for Educational Research and the *British Education Index*. The CD-ROM contains the British index back to 1976 and the *Australian Education Index* back to 1978. It also contains the *Bibliography of Education Theses in Australia* and backfiles (to its beginning in 1950) of the *British Education Theses Index*. (See also Figure 5.1, pp. 286–90)

OTHER INTERNATIONAL EDUCATION DATABASES

FRANCIS: SCIENCES DE L'EDUCATION

Available online on Questel and Orbit and on CD-ROM as FRANCIS CD-ROM, this database covers French and other European resources, with indexing in French and English, and contains citations to the literature of education on topics such as: the history and philosophy of education; education and psychology; the sociology of education; planning and economics; educational research; teaching, testing and guidance; school life; vocational training; and adult education and employment.

FRIDTJUV

FRIDTJUV contains references, in Swedish and English, to the international holdings in Sweden's National Library for Psychology and Education (SPPB). This continuously updated database, available online through SPPB, covers the period 1970 to date and also includes some older records. It is also accessible via the Internet <URL http://www.sppb.se/index.html> for the Swedish version or <URL http://www.sppb.se/welcome> for the English version.

DPBASEN (DPB)

DPB contains references to international materials acquired by the Educational Library of Denmark since 1980. It is available online through Denmark's

Pedagogiske Bibliotek and as part of Danbib, as well as through its Web site
<http://www.dhl.dk/dpb/>.

EUDISED
This database covers the whole of Europe but is limited in scope. Produced by the
Council of Europe, it corresponds to the printed *European Educational Research
Yearbook* and indexes, with summaries, ongoing and completed projects of
educational research and development. It contains more than 15 000 entries from
1975 onwards, contributed from 34 European countries, and is indexed in nine
languages.

OCLC: EDUCATION LIBRARY
A subset of OCLC WORLDCAT, this database is an international bibliography (over
685 000 records) of educational materials spanning more than 400 years.
Approximately one-quarter of the materials indexed was published after 1980
when the CD-ROM was first compiled. Subjects covered include: education in
different countries; secondary education; textbooks; literacy; teaching aids and
devices; major figures in education; and much more. It is a good source for
monographs and actual 'historical' materials, and appeals equally to academics
and practitioners. The OCLC: EDUCATION LIBRARY database is available on
a 12-month subscription with an annual update and cumulation from SilverPlatter.
There is no print equivalent.

Minor resources

Minor resources are those whose primary focus is either another subject or
discipline, or are interdisciplinary, but which cover topics related to education or
are of interest to educationalists.

Other disciplines

- AMERICA: HISTORY AND LIFE – already mentioned as a useful resource
  for education questions considered from a historical perspective. It provides
  coverage, for Canada and the USA, of interdisciplinary studies of historical
  interest and history-related topics in the social sciences and humanities.
- HISTORICAL ABSTRACTS – performs the same function for the rest of the
  world.
- PSYCINFO and its CD-ROM counterpart, PSYCLIT – important sources of
  information for educational psychology and other education topics
  approached from a psychological perspective.
- MENTAL HEALTH ABSTRACTS – covers fields such as child development
  and delinquency, and other social issues of interest to educationalists.
- SOCIOLOGICAL ABSTRACTS, WILSON SOCIAL SCIENCES

ABSTRACTS and SOCIAL SCIENCES INDEX, or SOCIAL SCISEARCH – all these databases contain relevant information on the sociological aspects of group interactions (as in a classroom or on the playground of a school) and may be better for this purpose than databases that focus specifically on education.

- PAIS (PUBLIC AFFAIRS INFORMATION SERVICE) – covers factual and statistical information in many fields, including education.
- THE PHILOSOPHER'S INDEX – a rich resource of material on the philosophy of various disciplines, such as education.
- LINGUISTICS AND LANGUAGE BEHAVIOR ABSTRACTS (LLBA) – valuable for researchers and practitioners in any discipline concerned with the nature and use of language, including language teaching. It also covers special education, learning disabilities, and other topics related to education.
- LISA (LIBRARY AND INFORMATION SCIENCE ABSTRACTS) – can satisfy requests for education-related information particularly for those with an interest in school library resource centres and/or school librarianship.
- LIBRARY LITERATURE – covers education for library and information studies, as well as many other topics (for example, automation, censorship) of interest to educationalists.

Interdisciplinary

There exists a wide range of general (that is, non-discipline-based) resources that contain information about education. They focus, for example, on particular formats such as dissertations or government documents, on particular perspectives (that is, scholarly or popular), or on particular geographic areas.

- DISSERTATION ABSTRACTS – references to more than 1.4 million doctoral dissertations and masters theses, with more than 40 000 titles added each year. Covering all disciplines and subject areas, it is the single most comprehensive source of dissertation information in the world. It includes citations for virtually every American dissertation accepted at an accredited institution since 1861, plus citations for thousands of Canadian dissertations and an increasing number of international papers – for example, British and other European dissertations from January 1988. Abstracts supplement the citations for the majority of degrees granted since 1980 and for *Masters Abstracts* from 1988. It is available online, on CD-ROM and via the Internet. ProQuest Digital Dissertations <URL http://wwwlib.umi.com/dissertations/> from UMI, with expanded search capabilities plus online ordering provides another way for searchers at institutions with a ProQuest subscription to access DISSERTATION ABSTRACTS via the World Wide Web.
- THESA – another dissertations database, available through INIST, contains descriptions of nearly 5000 theses currently in preparation or recently completed at 50 French technical, engineering, and teaching colleges in the Conférence des Grandes Ecoles.

Some of the principal education resources (for example, EDUCATION INDEX) cover book reviews and reviews of other media as a matter of course. Some (for example, the BRITISH EDUCATION INDEX) normally exclude reviews and some are selective in their coverage – including only reviews of particular types of materials or materials produced in a particular place or timeframe. The searcher, knowing that a book or other review is most likely to satisfy a client's request, may first consult BOOK REVIEW DIGEST, BOOK REVIEW INDEX, BOOKS IN PRINT WITH BOOK REVIEWS PLUS or similar resources. (See also under 'Specialized resources' below.)

Where timeliness and a non-scholarly approach are major considerations, the education searcher may forego the discipline-based resources in favour of a more current and more general resource such as those listed below:

- READERS' GUIDE [TO PERIODICAL LITERATURE] – a good source for general information relevant to education, particularly when the client is a parent or other concerned citizen rather than a practitioner or academic, and a 'popular' perspective is appropriate. It covers such general news areas as current events, business, education and politics. Indexing dates from 1983; abstracts from 1984, and full text from 1994. It is available online through WilsonWeb and DIALOG among others, on CD-ROM, and via the Internet.

- MAGAZINE ARTICLE SUMMARIES (MAS) CD-ROM – available via the EBSCOHOST. It is updated monthly and contains abstracts for more than 450 different magazines of a general-interest nature, the *New York Times*, and thousands of *Magill Book Reviews*. MAS FULLTEXT SELECT adds the full text of approximately 60 of the magazines, and MAS FULLTEXT ELITE, approximately 125 of the magazines. Topics covered by the magazines centre around medicine, sports, the arts, health, science, nutrition, business, education and politics.

- ARTICLEFIRST – from OCLC, a multidisciplinary index (dating from 1990) to articles from over 13 000 periodicals. It is an excellent resource for timely coverage of new topics and/or for material presented in a non-scholarly fashion. Since August 1999, it is to be used with OCLC's FirstSearch. Two other OCLC databases of interest to educationalists are PAPERSFIRST, which indexes conference papers presented since 1993, and PROCEEDINGSFIRST, which indexes conference publications from 1993 to the present. All are accessible online and via the Internet.

- CBCA FULLTEXT REFERENCE (Canadian Business and Current Affairs) – a more specialized regional example, dating from 1993, that combines indexing and abstracting of over 600 periodicals and nine daily news sources with direct access to the full-text content of 150 Canadian periodicals and sources of current affairs information.

Information on current topics often appears in a resource such as ARTICLEFIRST or CBCA months before it appears (if at all) in ERIC, the Wilson education databases or other discipline-based resources. In addition, ARTICLEFIRST and similar resources index periodicals that are not included in the education-specific databases' coverage. A previous search for information on 'charter schools' in British Columbia, for example, turned up a number of relevant articles from some general-interest periodicals before professional articles appeared in the (then) *Canadian Education Index.*

Other general periodical and newspaper indexes are also good sources for current awareness and news of the latest issues and trends in education They often have the added advantage of full-text availability.

- NATIONAL NEWSPAPER INDEX – combines the news from the USA's five most prominent newspapers with a wide variety of research topics.
- PERIODICAL ABSTRACTS PLUS TEXT – available on DIALOG and includes the full text (from 1988) of cited journal and magazine articles from more than 600 publications.
- CANADIAN NEWSPAPERS – available on DIALOG and includes the full text of 13 major newspapers.

Many periodical/newspaper databases (as well as the periodicals and newspapers themselves) are now accessible via the Internet – an attractive option if the searcher's institution does not have access through a vendor.

Sometimes the only resource for education information in a particular place is a national or regional database or Web site:

- AFRICA NEWS boasts full-text accessibility and frequent updates, and is an excellent source of information about current trends and issues for all topics, including some related to education, throughout Africa. It is also available as AFRICANEWS ONLINE via the Internet at <URL: http://www.africanews. org/>.

- SOUTH AFRICA ONLINE <URL http://www.southafrica.co.za/> is a comprehensive, annotated directory of information about the area, including business, education, lifestyles, government, reference, news, sports and travel.

- ASIA ROM [formerly ASIA CD-ROM] is a full-text English-language database from RMIT Publishing that is a compilation of several resources covering Asian education, social sciences and law. Available since 1995, the database is updated twice a year.

- INDEX NEW ZEALAND (INNZ) indexes and abstracts approximately 300 journals, as well as newspapers, conference papers, theses, and education resources. It is the key New Zealand database for social sciences, arts, humanities and general-interest material. It also indexes some South Pacific journals. Coverage is from 1987, updated quarterly. A list of descriptors used in INNZ can be found in the *APAIS Thesaurus* (Canberra: National Library of Australia, 1994). INNZ comprehensively indexes all articles half a page or more in length from New Zealand scholarly journals and selectively indexes articles of a half a page or more from New Zealand general-interest and international journals. INNZ does not index editorials, letters or anecdotal materials. It is available for online searching using the National Library (of New Zealand)'s TePuna service as well as on CD-ROM. Online searchers may also access INNZ via the French service CEPII.

● REPERE is a comprehensive resource for journal articles in French. Produced by Services Documentaires Multimedia Inc. (Canada), in cooperation with the Bibliothèque Nationale du Québec, the database contains more than 300 000 citations from 536 journals and is updated monthly. Publications indexed include all the major Canadian French-language titles, in addition to titles published in France, Belgium and Switzerland. REPERE corresponds to the print version of the same name. Both these resources index articles published since 1980. Subject coverage includes: art, athletics, computers, current events, education, foreign affairs, history, literature, marketing, news, political science, reference and social issues. REPERE is available on CD-ROM (except in Quebec), and via the Internet on Micromedia's Voyageur ERL server or a local ERL server (see also EDUQ below).

Specialized resources

Specialized resources include those whose primary focus is some particular aspect of education (rather than education in general). Some of these resources are specialized because of their subject matter, some because they focus on a particular type of learner, and others because they focus on a particular geographic region(s) or area(s) or language. The INTERNATIONAL ERIC CD-ROM is described earlier in this chapter. INDEX NEW ZEALAND and REPERE are other examples in this category. Another, more geographically-focused, example is EDUQ which covers all levels of education in Quebec (Canada) and contains over 15 300 references with abstracts to information on school administration, curriculum, educational psychology and philosophy, parents and community activities, and pedagogical developments and innovations. The database coverage dates from 1960 and it is updated twice yearly. The information provider and online vendor is Services Documentaires Multimedia Inc. (SDM) of Montreal.

Still other resources are specialized because they combine two or more of these attributes. THE DATABASE ON ENGLISH LANGUAGE TEACHING FOR ADULTS IN AUSTRALASIA (DELTAA), for example, combines focused subject coverage (English teaching, second language acquisition, language teaching) a particular educational level or student group (adult learners) and a specific geographic focus (Australasia). DELTAA is one of the 13 databases on the AUSTROM disc mentioned above. Also on AUSTROM is AUSTGUIDE, described under 'Resources for students' below.

The EXCEPTIONAL CHILD EDUCATIONAL RESOURCES (ECER) database, from the Council for Exceptional Children, includes citations and abstracts on all types of disabilities and giftedness, resources in all areas of special education and related services, and current policies and issues regarding exceptional children for those who study and work with them. ECER covers English-language books, dissertations, legislation, informally published print materials, commercially available non-print resources (for example, films, video, software), and over 200 journals. ECER and ERIC use the same cataloguing, indexing and abstracting rules and authorities, and the same controlled indexing vocabulary taken from the *Thesaurus of ERIC Descriptors*.

The NCBE BIBLIOGRAPHIC DATABASE (National Clearinghouse for Bilingual Education) contains more than 20 000 citations with abstracts, dating from 1978, to published and unpublished literature dealing with all aspects of the education of linguistically diverse student populations. The focus is on the USA, with some international coverage. The database is available online from the NCBE's Computerized Information Service (CIS), and is updated monthly.

For the researcher or practitioner interested in teaching and learning French as a first language in Belgium, Canada, France and Switzerland, DAF (Didactique et acquisition du français, langue maternelle) from the Université de Montréal (Canada) and INRP (Institut National de Recherche Pedagogique (Paris)) is a useful resource. DAF contains citations with abstracts to books, journals, research reports, theses and conference proceedings from 1970 to date, with 300 citations added per year. The database is available online from Services Documentaires Multimedia Inc. (SDM).

CEDEFOP is a trilingual – English, French and German – bibliographic database of approximately 26 000 citations to the international literature on vocational education and training dating from 1987. Source documents come from the member states of the European Union. The database is produced by the European Centre for the Development of Vocational Training in Thessalonika, Greece. It is available via the Internet at <URL http://www.cedefop.gr>.

The ICDL DISTANCE EDUCATION DATABASE contains information on distance education including over 3000 distance-taught programmes and courses offered by institutions in the Commonwealth countries and elsewhere, over 1000 distance-teaching institutions worldwide, and over 11 000 citations to published literature dealing with distance education. The database is available online (free to developing countries) through the (British) Open University's International Centre for Distance Learning, as well as on the Internet <URL http://www-icdl.open.ac.uk/>.

Unesco's online database, INNODATA, and its CD-ROM counterpart, UNESCO CD-ROM: KEY UNESCO DATA ON EDUCATION, each contain descriptions of hundreds of international educational innovations focusing on areas of curriculum, teaching methods and teacher education, with some information on educational administration and planning.

Some resources are specialized because they are aimed at particular groups within the discipline. Among these are resources that have been developed primarily for researchers and other academic clients. The EUDISED database has already been mentioned.

Gale Group BUSINESS A.R.T.S. (Applied Research, Theory and Scholarship) covers more than 1550 scholarly and general interest publications including the most commonly held journals in over 120 college and university libraries. Selected full-text coverage from 500 journals began in January 1993. On DIALOG, records for BUSINESS A.R.T.S. are added first to IAC NEWSEARCH which is updated daily. BUSINESS A.R.T.S. replaces ACADEMIC INDEX on DIALOG and DataStar, and has essentially the same content as SilverPlatter's Internet-accessible EXPANDED ACADEMIC ASAP.

In addition to these conventional databases, many Internet resources covering education are geared to the academic client or scholar. The World Wide Web is also a good place to search for an academic post. The searcher (or job-seeker) can go directly to such sites as THE TIMES HIGHER EDUCATION SUPPLEMENT <URL http://www.thesis.co.uk/> which includes worldwide jobs in the higher education sector or the CHRONICLE OF HIGHER EDUCATION JOB OPENINGS IN ACADEME <URL http://chronicle.com/jobs/>, or look for appropriate links from a directory-type page such as JOB HUNT <URL http://Job-Hunt.org/academia.shtml> or THE RILEY GUIDE <URL http:// www.dbm.com/ jobguide/>.

Researchers, be they academic faculty, university students or practitioners such as teachers or librarians, are constantly in need of information about sources of funding for their projects. The GRANTS DATABASE includes details on approximately 10 000 currently available grants and funding offered by federal, state, provincial and local government, commercial organizations, associations and private foundations. Subject areas encompass more than 90 academic disciplines and topics, including education. The annually updated FOUNDATION DIRECTORY describes more than 45 000 active grant makers, including foundations and corporations. The FOUNDATION GRANTS INDEX is much less comprehensive (1000 foundations) and much more specialized (grants of $10 000 and upwards only). Another useful resource in this area is the RESEARCH CENTERS AND SERVICES DIRECTORY covering thousands of non-profit organizations and institutes that currently support and conduct research worldwide. A new CD-ROM product, FC SCHOLAR, the Foundation Center's DATABASE OF EDUCATION FUNDING FOR INDIVIDUALS, enables researchers and students to search a comprehensive listing of over 3200 foundations and public charities that support a wide range of educational needs. Practitioners, as well as scholars, will find RSP FUNDING FOR POSTDOCTORATES AND PROFESSIONALS and RSP FUNDING FOR GRADUATE STUDENTS valuable sources of information on funding opportunities for study, training, professional development and travel. A complementary database for students is RSP FUNDING FOR UNDERGRADUATE STUDENTS.

Among the resources that have been developed primarily for practitioners, databases of educational materials and resources (that is, resources in all subjects, structured for use in teaching) are common. Several producers of electronic resources that are geared to students at various levels and discussed later in this chapter under 'Resources for students' also provide resources of interest to adults. For example, Bell & Howell Information and Learning's PROQUEST PROFESSIONAL EDUCATION COLLECTION provides a range of titles covering all aspects of K-12 and higher education, including more than ten years of full-text access to over 230 journals. EBSCO Publishing's line of products, available via EBSCO SCHOOL RESOURCENET <URL http://www.ebscosrn. com/>, features reference and curriculum resources for students as well as parents, teachers, librarians and administrators. The PROFESSIONAL DEVELOPMENT COLLECTION offers searchable full-text articles for over 235 education journals and an additional 90 abstracted and indexed titles. And, 'members' of EBSCO's TEACHER REFERENCE CENTER <URL http://www.teacherreference.com/> have access to a database of article summaries from approximately 300 education periodicals plus useful links to Web sites focusing on education, information literacy and related topics. The MENTAL MEASUREMENTS YEARBOOK provides descriptions and reviews of English-language psychological and educational tests. The EDUCATIONAL TESTING DATABASE is a CD-ROM product (free to school districts in Minnesota and available to others for purchase from the Minnesota Department of Education) covering ten broad subject areas and containing over 120 000 test questions, outcomes, and objectives up to the US grade 12. The experienced searcher will also be aware that the Internet is a rich source for curricular resources/instructional materials, including tests. The ERIC Assessment and Evaluation Clearinghouse's TEST LOCATOR, accessible from the ERIC Web site <URL http://www.accesseric.org> or directly at its own searchable site <URL http://ericae.net/testcol.htm>, is an excellent source for tests and information about them. Its coverage includes the following files: ETS (Educational Testing Service)/ERIC Test File; Test Review Locator; Buros/ERIC Test Publisher Locator; CEEE/ERIC Test Database; Code of Fair Testing Practices; and Test Selection Tips. The ETS Test Collection Database contains records on over 10 000 tests and research instruments encompassing all fields including education-related achievement and aptitude tests. The test descriptions are indexed with terms from the *Thesaurus of ERIC Descriptors*. In addition, the Internet is a good source for reviews of educational resources, both on the World Wide Web and in other media. Two notable examples are SCHOOLING 2001: ELECTRONIC RESOURCE EVALUATIONS <URL http://www.ged.qld.gov. au/tal/2001.erep.htm> which provides evaluative information on quality curriculum software and World Wide Web sites for preschool to grade 12, and the BRITISH EDUCATIONAL COMMUNICATIONS AND TECHNOLOGY AGENCY (BECTA) Web site <URL http://www.becta.org.uk/information/> which provides online reviews of over 1000 educational CD-ROM titles.

MICROCOMPUTER ABSTRACTS indexes and abstracts over 90 publications covering information on the latest microcomputing products and developments in business, education, libraries, the Internet, information science and technology, and the home. It includes thousands of reviews of software packages, hardware systems, peripherals and books, as well as feature articles, news, columns, new product announcements, and buyer/vendor guides. A controlled vocabulary of descriptors simplifies the task of information retrieval.

Among the major vendors offering databases of audiovisual materials for teaching is DIALOG with A-V ONLINE (also known as NICEM REFERENCE

ONLINE). A-V ONLINE provides comprehensive coverage of audiovisual media for the entire spectrum of education and training from preschool to professional and graduate school levels. The database also includes thousands of non-English-language titles. It is available online, on CD-ROM, and via the Internet. The KIDSNET ACTIVE DATABASE <URL http://www.kidsnet.org/> provides a comprehensive source of audio, video, television and radio programmes for children from preschool through high school. It is a bulletin board of information on US programmes and related teaching materials dating from 1985. Brodart's THE ELEMENTARY SCHOOL LIBRARY COLLECTION: A GUIDE TO BOOKS AND MEDIA (ESLC) on CD-ROM. It includes more than 11 000 entries for materials in 12 formats valuable for use in the USA with students pre-kindergarten to grade 6, as well as some adult materials for parents and practitioners. Each annotated entry gives suggestions for curriculum use, making ESLC a particularly helpful resource for teachers.

The new KCDL CUMULATIVE INDEX on CD-ROM is available in three versions corresponding to the print indexes for the Kraus Curriculum Development Library (KCDL) collection on microfiche. KCDL includes pre-K-12 curricula, standards, strategies, lesson plans, and teaching guides produced mainly by American and Canadian schools, school districts, departments of education, and other educational organizations and associations. The complete index provides annotations as well as subject, keyword, educational content, and grade level indexing. The next level provides references to approximately 1000 documents from the most recent five years, and the special collection to a customized version of selected recent documents. The KRAUS CURRICULUM DEVELOPMENT LIBRARY (KCDL) on CD-ROM provides a cumulative database of more than 4000 curricular frameworks and standards from 1983 to 1998.

Practitioners in the UK, or those looking for a British perspective, will do well with the TES BookFind CD-ROM. Produced by BookData and *The Times Educational Supplement*, the database provides descriptions and contents pages for books and other materials on every subject at every level from thousands of general, academic and education publishers plus more than 10 000 full-text reviews (from major educational journals) of books, software and CD-ROMs.

Access to information about courses and course vacancies is a concern of many educationalists. For example, ECCTIS 2000: THE UK COURSES INFORMATION SERVICE <URL http://www.ecctis.co.uk> provides information on courses in universities, polytechnics and colleges in the UK. It is available online or on CD-ROM.

There are many similar North American resources that counsellors and students will find useful when seeking information about career and educational opportunities. A sample of relevant CD-ROM resources includes BARRON'S PROFILES OF AMERICAN COLLEGES, COLLEGE SOURCE (also available online), DISCovering CAREERS AND JOBS, and LOVEJOY'S COLLEGE COUNSELOR. The QUALITY EDUCATION DATA <URL http://www.qeddata. com/> CD-ROM database provides current marketing information on more than

200 000 US and selected Canadian elementary and secondary educational institutions – school districts, public schools, non-public schools, colleges, state departments of education and public libraries. PETERSON'S COLLEGE DATABASE and PETERSON'S GRADLINE provide profiles of accredited baccalaureate and associate degree-granting colleges and of graduate and professional programs in colleges and universities in the USA and Canada. Both are available online, on CD-ROM, and via the Internet. These two databases are complemented by PETERSON'S: THE EDUCATION SUPERSITE <URL http://www.petersons.com/> – just one of thousands of sites on the World Wide Web offering information on courses, course vacancies and careers. The Internet is an excellent resource for those looking for lists of schools (and even details of individual schools and their programmes) and courses at all levels and in all geographic areas. For example, in Canada, SCHOOL FINDER <URL http://www.schoolfinder.com> provides information on Canadian universities, colleges and career colleges. Individual institutions almost universally have their own Web site. The Internet is also an excellent source of information about financial aid for students. More will be said about Internet resources in the separate section below.

Internet resources

Electronic resources, particularly the Internet, changed education dramatically in the last decade of the twentieth century and will continue to do so during the twenty-first. The Internet began primarily as a research-oriented tool but, today, it plays an increasingly important role in education at all levels. Indeed, one of the subject strengths of the Internet is education. Not only are faculty and other scholars pursuing their research projects on the Internet and exchanging information and databases with colleagues all around the world, but they are also using the Internet for many other innovative purposes, such as developing and delivering courses online. For example, EDNA: EDUCATION NETWORK AUSTRALIA <URL http://www.edna.edu.au/EdNA/> represents a collaboration among all sectors of the Australian education and training community to deliver education on the Internet, and EDUCAUSE's <URL http://www.educause.edu/> mission is 'to help shape and enable transformational change in higher education through ... information resources and technologies'.

The choice of online courses and the sophistication of their delivery increase daily. The development of client–server courseware enables students and instructors to connect and interact in a positive learning environment. A large number of individual courses is now available online, for many of which it is possible to transfer credit to a traditional degree programme. There is no shortage of undergraduate core courses and graduate courses in various content areas or even complete degree programmes available via the Internet. Such educational opportunities are especially appealing to a student base that is increasingly non-traditional in age, responsibilities and goals. Distance-education students can register for accredited university courses, graduate degrees or special interest non-credit classes. Even high school and elementary students can elect to learn from home. Entire universities, colleges and school districts are becoming networked, enabling students to register, take classes, submit homework, and more, over the Internet. Students are working over the Internet in all kinds of activities from international 'chat', correspondence and writing projects to collaborative and individual research projects using multimedia resources from all over the world. And, increasingly, the Internet is becoming an interactive training medium.

Advantages of the Internet … and caveats

When it comes to education resources on the Internet, however, the experienced searcher will approach and use them with caution. Although some Internet resources are updated frequently (perhaps even continuously) and regularly, others are revised so infrequently and/or so irregularly that their accuracy and reliability are suspect – a concern with Internet resources in general. Anyone or any organization with sufficient technical knowhow, the necessary contacts, and enough money (negligible amounts in some instances) can mount a Web site on the Internet. Literally thousands of these contain information about education and/or information of interest to educationalists and students. From 'Accountability' to 'Year-round Schooling', from 'At-risk Children' to 'Urban Education', from 'Inclusion' to 'Teacher Research', from 'ESL' to 'Teaching American Literature', there is a Web site to match the client's interests. One of the advantages, therefore, of choosing Internet resources for an online education search is the huge number of sources available and the enormous variety of topics covered. It is a particularly good resource for very specific or more obscure topics that may not have made it into the more traditional sources such as journal articles indexed in an online database or conference proceedings included on a CD-ROM. Furthermore, the Internet is an excellent resource for education-related information that simply is not available or as readily available in the more conventional online databases and CD-ROMs. Policy statements, position papers and other documents relating to current issues and trends in educational theory and practice are very often posted to the Internet in draft form for review and discussion. The final draft is often also 'published' on the Internet before (if ever) it becomes available in print. This is also a popular method for interested parties to preview and review conference papers and presentations. Lesson plans are another example in this category as are other curricular resources/instructional materials, including tests, lists of schools (and even details of individual schools and their programmes) and courses at all levels and in all geographic areas, and careers information. Internet resources may also be the best choice for the most recent information and/or for news stories about education.

On the downside, the constantly changing nature of the Internet and its overall lack of organization – particularly its lack of a controlled indexing vocabulary – make it more difficult and time-consuming to use than the traditional online and

CD-ROM databases. Efficient and effective searches on the Internet can be elusive. Another shortcoming of many Internet resources is that they are incomplete. They do not include links to all related sites because these site owners/developers must either pay for inclusion or make the effort to inform another site of their existence. PETERSON'S: THE EDUCATION SUPERSITE <URL http://www.petersons.com>, for example, provides links only to those schools that have paid a fee for inclusion.

Searching the Internet

The overall process of searching is the same no matter which search engine is chosen. The first steps in developing an effective strategy for Internet searches are the same as for the more traditional online and CD-ROM databases. In particular, the searcher must carefully analyse the client's request to identify key concepts and relationships. Most of what was said under 'Analysis' and 'Terminology' in the previous section of this chapter on 'Developing the search strategy' remains true for Internet searches, except that there are no thesauri for the searcher to consult, nor any widespread application of standardized indexing vocabulary to control terminology. For example, 'tracking', which is a form of scheduling and an authorized ERIC descriptor, turns up hundreds of irrelevant sites on the Internet that deal with the concept of tracking in many other contexts! Identifying key concepts and brainstorming for synonyms and more specific and/or more general terms to express those concepts is extremely important. The searcher must consider, for example:

- Who is the client and how has the query been expressed?
- How else might this client or other clients in the same category (researcher, practitioner) express it?
- How might those in other categories express it?
- How else has the client or the searcher seen the concept expressed in the education literature?
- How else has the client or the searcher seen the concept expressed in the media?

From the resulting list of terms, the searcher must choose the most important and the most specific to express the key concept in the query. A search on 'administrators', for example, retrieves too many hits in total and too many irrelevant hits if the client is specifically interested in female secondary school principals. The searcher must also use language appropriate to the client's required perspective; a popular term is inappropriate if the topic is academic and vice versa.

Many key concepts in education are best expressed as a phrase with words adjacent to one another or in a particular order. The searcher should therefore take advantage, whenever possible, of phrase or proximity searches to precoordinate terms. A search for information about planning the introduction of information technology into schools provides a useful illustration. Searching on ALTAVISTA using 'information technology' (as an exact phrase) 'AND plan*' (to include plan, plans, planning, etc.) retrieves different, and more useful, documents from 'information AND technology AND plan*'. This technique is especially useful for names, exact titles, and concepts 'built' from common terms. For example, searching LYCOS for the Australian School Library Association using 'the exact phrase' option from the pull-down menu returns the association's homepage within the first ten hits. Many key concepts in education are often expressed in terms that will turn up in dozens (if not hundreds or thousands) of Web sites. This result occurs particularly when the search engine is set to scan all portions of the documents indexed. Restricting the search to certain portions (for example, the title and/or the first few lines of the document's content) may return a more manageable number of hits but runs the risk of omitting relevant sites where the sought term(s) appears elsewhere in the document. The experienced searcher knows when it is worthwhile to restrict a search to only portions of the document and when it is necessary to attempt as comprehensive a search as possible. The latter may be necessary for a very specific topic and/or a request from a researcher requiring a good idea of everything that is available.

Executing the search

The Internet was never designed as a global information retrieval system. Consequently, there is nothing like ERIC, the Wilson education databases or the other familiar online and CD-ROM resources that index and provide access to education information for the Internet. Unlike the documents indexed in a conventional bibliographic database, the documents on the Internet are not retrievable through a controlled indexing vocabulary (see above). Instead, the searcher must rely on Internet-specific techniques for locating information about education on the World Wide Web, in Usenet newsgroups, and the like. Beyond knowledge of specific site addresses or URLs, a judicious combination of surfing, browsing subject directories, and using search engines will reward the searcher's perseverance with timely and relevant education-related information (possibly not available anywhere else).

Limiting a search for education-related information by geographic area has already been mentioned as a useful strategy. Most of the major subject directories and search engines have spawned a number of geographically specific subsets, with new countries being added all the time. Such geographically-based directories are good starting-points if the search must be confined to documents from or about a specific country.

Alternatively, the searcher can specify (when the search engine permits) a particular geographic domain in the URL. For example, limiting a search on HotBot by location using the '.uk' country code turns up sites with 'uk' in the URL (and representing sites mounted and maintained from a UK location). However, this does not necessarily mean that the information at the site pertains only to education in the UK: it could just as easily pertain to other areas as well. A more useful strategy to limit searches to sites that contain information about education in a particular place is to search for the place name or a variation on it elsewhere in the document. For example, a search using ALTAVISTA and incorporating 'canad*' turns up more relevant sites, even when the search is limited to titles only, than does a search for 'ca' in the domain.

The resources discussed in the next section are a selection only of those that may prove useful for an education search on the Internet. Because the Internet is constantly evolving, no listing of Internet resources is (or ever will be) all-inclusive, nor will it remain completely accurate over time. The discussion begins with examples of general subject directories and search engines and concludes with the more subject-specific (for education) Internet resource guides.

Subject directories and search engines

Subject directories are classified collections of Internet resources compiled by individuals or groups who have made a conscious decision to add a site to the directory. Because their subject coverage is broad rather than deep, subject directories are most useful at the outset when the searcher has only a general idea of the topic and is looking for lists compiled by experts in the field and/or wants to see what is new or 'hot'. Subject directories are good for getting an overview of the topic – when the searcher has a broad topic to investigate and perhaps wants to narrow it somewhat – and/or when he or she wants to browse. A 'pinpoint' search using narrow terms that are as likely (or more likely) to appear in the text of a document as in its title and/or headings, is best conducted on a search engine. Some subject directories/search engines treat education as a major category in its own right; some combine it with other topics (careers, for instance); still others include education as part of a larger more general category like the social sciences or a related category. The placement of education in a top-level category (or not) reflects the perspective of those who compiled the directory in the first place. The subcategories under education in the second and lower level (if included) directories further reflect the compilers' perspectives on what constitutes an education-related topic. This can be very revealing and helpful to the searcher, as well as an important factor in his or her choice of starting-point for the search.

YAHOO! <URL http://www.yahoo.com/> is currently the best known and most used of the subject directories. It covers submitted Web sites and the Usenet newsgroups (via DEJA.COM). Its 14 top-level categories include Education. YAHOO! – EDUCATION <URL http://dir.yahoo.com/Education/> is a well-organized searchable directory, including links to thousands of sites in over 30 categories and focusing on all levels of education and all subjects.

In addition, YAHOO! is searchable from its homepage and also within each category (like Education) and its subcategories and/or indices. YAHOO! also offers topic-specific directories, for example, YAHOOLIGANS! FOR KIDS (see under 'Resources for students' later in this chapter), and serves as an excellent teaching tool to illustrate how browsing works and to develop students' pointing-and-clicking skills.

GALAXY's <URL http://www.galaxy.com/> top-level categories include Social Sciences under which Education is listed. The second-level directory includes the following broad categories: Academic Institutions (including Distance Learning), Adult Education, Curriculum and Instruction (including Instructional Technology), Financial Aid (including Research Grants), Guidance and Counseling, Higher Education, K12 Education, Measurement and Evaluation, and Special Education. Sites on a 'topic page' are listed in alphabetical order by title under broad classes such as academic organizations, collections and so on. GALAXY searches only those pages actually submitted to it. The GALAXY database is searchable from its homepage and from a search window at the top of each topic page.

BUBL LINK <URL http://bubl.ac.uk/link/> uses broad Dewey Decimal classes (for example, 370 Education: general resources, 371 Schools and their activities, 374.4 Distance education, etc.) to organize its Education category. Within each broad class the selected sites are listed in alphabetical order by title. (Clicking on an accompanying icon brings up a short description of the site.) For searchers familiar with Dewey and/or those who prefer its classified approach to information, this is a useful site. It is also a useful site for those looking for a British perspective. The Search option allows the searcher to access the database using simple or advanced search techniques in addition to browsing by subject or by DDC notation.

Specialized subject directories include the LIBRARIANS' INDEX TO THE INTERNET <URL http://sunsite.berkeley.edu/InternetIndex/>, a searchable annotated subject directory (referred to by some as a 'virtual library') of more than 5500 Internet resources. Two of its top-level categories are Education and Kids, the latter including a subcategory for teachers. Search results are displayed under broad categories such as 'Directories', 'Databases' and 'Specific Resources'. Each entry in the results list includes the site's title, URL, descriptive annotation and subjects assigned. The title and subjects are hot-linked. Weekly updating of the database is another good reason for education searchers to bookmark this site, although they should be aware that it loads slowly. CANADIAN INFORMATION BY SUBJECT <URL http://www.nlc-bnc.ca/caninfo/ecaninfo.htm> is an information service developed by the National Library of Canada to provide links to information about Canada from Internet resources around the world. Its subject arrangement is based on the Dewey Decimal classification – Education is designated 370. In each of the subclasses (for example, 371 Schools) sites are listed in alphabetical order by (hot-linked) title with English and French sites interfiled (there is also a 'version française' of the site). Choosing the Title Search option from the homepage allows the searcher to locate particular keywords in the titles of the indexed sites in any subject category. The BIG EYE EDUCATION CENTER <URL http://www.bigeye.com/ educate.htm> is a browsable subject directory of selected education resources compiled for the use of students, teachers, home-schoolers and administrators, and excerpted from the overall BIG EYE site. The resources listed include virtually everything of possible interest to the education searcher from 'Academic Email and Phone Directory' to 'Learning Biology'.

Which search engines to use when

Search engines should be used when the query involves specific concepts (or a combination thereof) and/or involves proper names or phrases that are not found in the subject directories.

At one end of the spectrum are the all-purpose – powerful and fast – general search engines like ALTAVISTA and HOTBOT. At the other end of the spectrum are more specialized search engines that aim to index a smaller subset of the Internet such as Web sites that are subject- or geographically-specific. An example of such a very specialized search site is EDUCATION WEB SEARCH <URL http://www.tkm.mb.ca/education/>, a searchable database of education sites (with the emphasis on Canadian sites) found on the Internet. Among the other popular general search engines of interest to the education searcher are EXCITE, INFOSEEK and LYCOS.

ALTAVISTA <URL http://www.altavista.com/>, a very large full-text index, is an excellent teaching tool for illustrating Internet searches to students and as a 'bridge' between online and CD-ROM resources and the World Wide Web.

HOTBOT <URL http://www.hotbot.com/> or <http://hotbot.lycos.com/> does not include education among its top-level categories making it inefficient as a subject directory and/or for browsing education topics. However, HOTBOT is among the largest of the search engines and one of the best in terms of searching power. It is especially good at searching for people and other specifics.

EXCITE <URL http://www.excite.com/> is a good resource for the education searcher who requires a small number of relevant hits and a summary of contents. (The summaries are not necessarily the first few lines of the document as is usual with Internet searches, but specially written to bring dominant themes and terms to the fore.) EXCITE provides access to Web sites, as well as site reviews (written by professional journalists), newsgroup postings, or Usenet classified advertisements, and is rated highly for conceptual searching. For example, a keyword search on 'dyslexia' retrieves only documents containing that keyword, but a concept search might also select documents containing 'illiteracy'. The EXCITE Education directory, via its subcategories such as K-12 or Universities & Colleges, provides 'gateways' to various related topics. A particularly useful feature is the 'search for more documents like this one' command which allows the searcher to follow up a hit that is close to what he or she wants when it is not possible to express the query in specific terms. This is the closest the Internet comes to allowing the pearl-growing strategy discussed in the section 'Developing the search strategy' above.

INFOSEEK, now also known as the GO NETWORK, <URL http://www.infoseek.go.com/> indexes the full text of Web sites, as well as news and Usenet newsgroups, and is updated daily. It has many useful advanced search features, such as the capability to narrow a search in stages. The INFOSEEK database is searchable from its homepage and from a search window at the top of each guide page.

LYCOS <URL http://www.lycos.com/> is a good choice when a smaller number of more relevant hits is desirable. LYCOS also allows 'natural language' queries. It provides a 'Web Guide' for Education as a subdirectory under Reference. The subcategories under Education include K-12, Colleges and Universities. Another useful feature is LYCOS SEARCH GUARD <URL http://personal.lycos.com/safetynet/ safetynet.asp> that allows parents, teachers and librarians to screen possibly objectionable sites from search results.

Metasearch engines

When the query requires the searcher to discover what is available on the whole Internet for an education-related topic, metasearch engines may be a good starting point. They are useful for simpler searches where the searcher wants to ensure as comprehensive a search as possible for a more general topic at the outset. Where recall is more important than precision – in an initial search for distance education or home schooling, for example – the searcher may opt to start with a metasearch engine such as METACRAWLER <URL http://www.metacrawler.com> which sends a query to several search engines, including ALTAVISTA, EXCITE, LYCOS and YAHOO!, and searches all of them at once.

Internet resource guides

The experienced searcher will also be aware of, and will frequently want to bookmark, other subject-specific (for education) Internet resource guides.[2] As might be expected from one of the world's foremost education resources, ERIC has a presence on the Internet beyond Web-based access to its database. The previously mentioned ASKERIC is one of many services accessible through ERIC's Web site <URL http://ericir.syr.edu/>. It is an Internet-based question-and-answer service for students as well as a help and referral service for educators at all school levels – teachers, librarians, and administrators. Besides the question-and-answer service, ASKERIC also provides a Virtual Library <URL http://ericir.syr.edu/Virtual/> with many components, of which the Toolbox and the Lesson Plans are noteworthy. The Toolbox provides access to a selected number of Internet resources that the network information specialists at ASKERIC have found valuable when responding to questions. The education sites include those under the following headings: Educational Technology, Higher Education, K-12 Education, School Directories, and Subject-Specific Links. The Internet-related sites include Cool Sites for Kids.

The ARGUS CLEARINGHOUSE FOR EDUCATION <URL http://www.clearinghouse.net/> is another example of a popular subject-specific Internet resource guide. It is a deliberately selective and narrowly focused collection of topical guides on the Internet. Clicking on any one of the subcategories – adult and special education, educational institutions, higher education, instructional technology and tools, primary and secondary school, teaching and pedagogy – provides a list of guides with a URL hot link and rating (1–5 checkmarks). Instead of browsing, the searcher can identify potentially useful sites by searching the

ARGUS database that consists of information pages for each of the Clearinghouse guides – not the actual guides themselves. ARGUS indexes the titles of sites, the names of their authors and their institutions, and descriptive keywords from each information page. However, the searcher should be aware of ARGUS's quirky syntax. In searches for multiple terms AND is assumed unless one of the terms is truncated, in which case OR is assumed.

ASK JEEVES FOR TEACHERS <URL http://www.ajkids.com/Teachers.asp>, a component of ASK JEEVES FOR KIDS (see below under 'Internet resources for students'), provides links to recommended sites in three broad categories: Lesson Plans, Interactive Classroom Projects, and Glossaries, Quizzes and Science Questions. The AWESOME LIBRARY <URL http://www.neat-schoolhouse.org/> is a comprehensive directory of sites (all reviewed and judged of high quality) that grew from a US Department of Education project. Designed for teachers, students and parents, it provides 'educational resources, projects, discussions, interactions, collaborations, lessons, curricula, and standards for grades K-12'. The searcher can browse or search the site under several broad categories covering different subject areas and aspects of education or choose the Word Search option to search the World Wide Web.

Another useful library of rated learning sites for teachers and students is BLUE WEB'N <URL http://www.kn.pacbell.com/wired/bluewebn/>. This browsable/searchable database includes selected sites categorized by subject area, audience and type (lessons, activities, projects, resources, references and tools) and targeted at learners. BLUE WEB'N features 'Filamentality', a tool that turns existing Web resources into activities by prompting teachers to 'fill in the blanks' with links, instructions and questions to build a learning experience for students. CLASSROOM CONNECT is a monthly print journal for teachers with a supporting World Wide Web site <URL http://www.classroomconnect.com/>. It covers applications of the Internet in K-12 education. A similar resource, although without the print version, is Jamie McKenzie's FROMNOWON <URL http://www.fno.org>, an electronic journal focusing on the use of technology in education. Another useful resource in this category is Champelli's THE INTERNET ADVOCATE <URL http://www.monroe.lib.in.us/~lchampel/netadv.html>, a Web-based resource guide for librarians and educators interested in providing youth access to the Internet.

THE EDUCATION INDEX <URL http://www.educationindex.com/> is a non-searchable annotated directory of over 3000 reviewed sites in 66 education-related categories on the World Wide Web, sorted by subject and life stage – preschoolers, college students, continuing education and careers, to name a few. EDUCATION GATEWAY <URL http://k12.bellsouth.net/> is a commercial site navigable by browsing only.

EDUCATION RESOURCES ON THE WORLD WIDE WEB <URL http://www.uwstout.edu/lib/subjects/edpath2.htm> is another browse-only site organized in over 20 top-level categories related to education. The first category, WWW Sites, includes two subcategories:

1. General Education which provides a hot-linked list of five major subject directories/virtual libraries all of interest to the educationalist and all described in this chapter
2. 'Interesting Education Sites to Explore', which is exactly what it says and includes a very brief descriptive annotation for each site listed.

The other categories are what one would expect in an education resource and include K-12 Education, Theses/Dissertations (with a direct link to DISSERTATION ABSTRACTS), Tests, Employment Opportunities and Special Education.

THE WORLD WIDE WEB VIRTUAL LIBRARY – EDUCATION, also known as the EDUCATION VIRTUAL LIBRARY, <URL http://www.csu.edu.au/ education/library.html> is a kind of general hyperindex or subject catalogue of education-related Internet sites. It provides browsing access to the sites that it indexes in five general lists – alphabetically by site, by education level, by resources provided, by type of site and by country. The site also permits simple keyword searches to facilitate the browsing process. For example, searching for 'lesson plans' (without the quotes) results in 27 hits – all sites from the complete alphabetical listing. This approach is much quicker than browsing the long alphabetical list. The EDUCATION VIRTUAL LIBRARY provides links to related virtual libraries, including that for Distance Education <URL http://www. cisnet.com/~cattales/Deducation.html>, as well as to a number of related newsgroups. EDUCATION WORLD <URL http://www.education-world.com/> is a browsable/searchable database of over 120 000 sites. This comprehensive source for education links on the Internet includes 'Features for This Week' under categories such as Lesson Planning, Curriculum, and News for Schools and Administrators. The EDVIEW <URL http://school.edview.com/search/> Smart Zone is a searchable collection of teacher-reviewed Web sites, categorized by general educational level and then by subject, that are safe for children. The 'Teachers Tools' section includes lesson plans for a wide variety of subjects. THE GATEWAY (to Education Materials) (GEM) <URL http://www.thegateway.org/> provides access to Internet lesson plans, curriculum units, and other education materials from diverse sources. Searchers may conduct full-text, subject, keyword or title searches that can be limited by grade or educational level. Retrieved records link directly to the Internet resources that they describe. INFOMINE: SCHOLARLY INTERNET RESOURCE COLLECTIONS <URL http://lib-www.ucr.edu/> describes itself as 'comprehensive showcase, virtual library, and reference tool containing highly useful Internet/World Wide Web resources ... of relevance to faculty, students, and research staff at the university level'. INFOMINE contains links to substantive databases, guides to the Internet for most disciplines (including education), textbooks, conference proceedings, journals and directories. Separate virtual libraries or INFOMINEs exist for Instructional Resources: K-12 and Instructional Resources: University. The query page for each INFOMINE offers a number of browse features, links to featured resources and a search box. Sponsored by the School District of Philadelphia (USA), LION

(Librarians Information Online Network) <URL http://www.libertynet.org/lion/>, consists of over 30 broad category-based browsable pages of links to resources of use and interest to K-12 school librarians.

Further examples of specialized, subject-specific sites of interest to the education searcher include:

- Canada's SCHOOLNET <URL http://www.schoolnet.ca/> describes itself as a site that focuses on bringing educators and students together. With its links to the provincial educational networks and other services, this bilingual (also available in French) searchable site is which one most Canadian searchers will want to bookmark.
- EDUCATION INTERNET GUIDE: SOURCES FOR THEORY, PRACTICE, TEACHING AND RESEARCH <URL http://www.library.usyd.edu.au/Guides/Education/> is mounted and maintained by the University of Sydney (Australia) Library. It includes links to primary and secondary sources on the structure, administration and content of education, and its related systems and institutions. Its coverage is international (sites from the USA, UK and Asia) but has a distinct Australian slant. The site provides sufficient navigational aids for browsing but is not searchable.
- The MEDIA AWARENESS NETWORK <URL http://www.media-awareness.ca> provides an online, interactive clearinghouse where Canadians and others can find resources for media education, share ideas and communicate with one another. 'For Educators', at the core of the network, offers teaching units, student handouts, timely reports and background material for media education across the K-12 curriculum. Other sections of the site are geared towards students, parents and community leaders.

The following selection of personal Web sites is representative of the many available to aid the education searcher. CANADIAN EDUCATION ON THE WEB <URL http://www.oise.utoronto.ca/~impress/eduweb.html> is a non-searchable site which 'brings together everything relating to [education in] Canada that has a presence on the World Wide Web'. It lists its indexed sites alphabetically by title under several broad categories covering all levels and all types of education. KATHY SCHROCK'S GUIDE FOR EDUCATORS <URL http://www.school.discovery.com/schrockguide/> is an award-winning Web site (updated daily) that provides a classified list of Internet sites 'useful for enhancing curriculum and teacher professional growth'. SCHOOL LIBRARIAN LINKS <URL http://www.nyx.net/~rbarry/> was developed and is maintained by Kathleen Gentili, a library media specialist in Phoenix, Arizona (USA). This searchable site focuses on categories of interest primarily to school librarians but also includes 'Best Education Sites' for practitioners (other than school librarians) and 'Student Resources'.

Other useful guides to education resources on the Internet may come in the form of documents prepared by the education librarians in the searcher's own institution and mounted on the World Wide Web. A fairly typical 'GUIDE TO EDUCATION RESOURCES', including electronic resources is that prepared for the education collections at the Milton S. Eisenhower Library at Johns Hopkins University as part of Project MUSE <URL http://muse.mse.jhu.edu/research/education/education.html>.

Other useful information on the Internet

The Internet is an excellent source for current information that may not be available (or as readily available) in the more conventional online databases and CD-ROMs. Information from and about government agencies and professional associations is one example. All kinds of government agencies have their own Web sites. Many include information (and/or links to other sites that include information) of interest to educationalists. The UNITED STATES DEPARTMENT OF EDUCATION <URL http://www.ed.gov/> site, for example, provides useful and timely information about programmes, policies, people and practice that exist in the Department and elsewhere, and a fast-growing list of other educational resources available online around the world. Likewise, most education-related associations have their own Web sites. The latter include information about professional development activities, educational and professional issues such as lobbying, lists of publications, current topics and links to other references and resources. The Association for Supervision and Curriculum Development's ASCD SELECT ONLINE <URL http://www.ascd. org/ASelect/> and the International Association of School Librarianship's SCHOOL LIBRARIES ONLINE <URL http://www.hi.is/~anne/iasl.html> are just two excellent examples, among many, of such sites. (Use of the ASCD site requires the searcher to pay a subscription; use of the IASL site is free to members.) These and the government sites are often the best sources when the searcher requires the very latest information and/or a particular stance/perspective. Questions such as the following are best answered by a government or association Web site rather than a more general education database:

- What does the latest Canadian copyright bill have to say about 'fair use' in schools?
- Does my professional association (or union) have an official position on a particular issue, for example, educational qualifications for school administrators?

A professional association's Web site can be located using search-by-phrase or other techniques such as searching the URL for the association's name, abbreviated name or acronym. Most such sites are excellent resources in themselves and/or have many useful links. RESOURCES OF SCHOLARLY SOCIETIES – EDUCATION <URL http://www.lib.uwaterloo.ca/society/education_soc.html> is helpful in locating such sites. It provides links to Web sites of scholarly societies from the American Association of Higher Education to the TESL Canada Federation.

   The searcher can keep abreast of quality education sites on the Internet through a subscription to the INTERNET SCOUT REPORT, SOCIAL SCIENCES <URL

http://wwwscout.cs.wisc.edu/scout/report/> which reviews sites of interest to educators, librarians and students. The current issue annotates a number of Web sites and gives links to those described. The searcher can locate past annotations by key words or by browsing the annotations that have been assigned Library of Congress subject headings or classification. Annotations are arranged in four categories: research, learning resources, new data in the news and selected current awareness. Also useful for keeping current is the INTERNET RESOURCES NEWSLETTER <URL http://www.hw.ac.uk/libWWW/irn/irn.html>, a monthly annotated list of sites of interest to the academic community. Based at Heriot-Watt University in Scotland, it lists developments that the North American resources sometimes miss.

Periodical indexes

TIME.COM <URL http://www.pathfinder.com/> is often described as the World Wide Web's answer to the Readers' Guide. It indexes Time-Warner magazines only, but still is a worthwhile resource for education-related information. UNCOVERWEB <URL http://uncweb.carl.org/> indexes over 18 000 periodicals. These Internet multidisciplinary periodical indexes have the same advantages as their more traditional online and CD-ROM counterparts; they are excellent resources for current and 'popular' information about education for all clients, including students.

Usenet newsgroups

For a truly comprehensive search of the Internet, the searcher should be aware that Usenet newsgroups are an excellent source of advice and opinion on education-related matters, particularly as they pertain to school (K-12) education. The best way to search Usenet newsgroups is through DEJA.COM <URL http://www.deja.com/>. It permits searches by keyword, subject or e-mail address and features several power search options. As an example, a parent recently requested information from other parents about home schooling. She was considering home schooling for her children but was concerned about the potential problems that might occur because her children would not have the same chance to develop social skills as children who are interacting with others in a traditional classroom. A search using DEJA.COM for '(home school* OR homeschool*) AND social*' turned up exactly the kind of discussion in which she was interested.

Resources for students

There is a very wide range in students' abilities to use reference and research tools effectively. Consequently, there is a need for resources to accommodate the various levels of ability and the needs of this client group which ranges from primary/elementary school and secondary school into college or vocational education. The producers of electronic resources have responded by developing online encyclopedias and CD-ROM indexes, for example, geared to students at different educational levels. For students at the elementary school level, EBSCO Publishing has PRIMARY SEARCH, and the Gale Group offers INFOTRAC KIDS EDITION. Middle school/junior high students are better served by READERS' GUIDE FOR YOUNG PEOPLE (H.W. Wilson), MIDDLE SEARCH PLUS (EBSCO) or INFOTRAC JUNIOR EDITION (Gale Group). A variety of resources is suitable for secondary and tertiary/post-secondary students: from Gale Group's INFOTRAC STUDENT EDITION to H.W. Wilson's READERS' GUIDE TO PERIODICAL LITERATURE, as well as others mentioned later.

Access to information through keyword and subject searches makes the use of electronic indexes a quick and efficient way for students to research topics for assignments and to explore general interests. Librarians can teach students how to apply both basic and more sophisticated electronic searching techniques to prepare them for research and employment-related uses. Access to databases that offer abstracts or full-text articles broadens the research base for students who were previously restricted to periodicals held in their school's library. Full-text indexes also may serve as a cost-saving factor in allowing a reduction in the number of subscriptions to print periodicals. However, the librarian must consider that print images are not accessible in all full-text databases, so some duplicate print subscriptions may be required. The following discussion includes a representative sample of what the market has to offer.

Student-specific resources

Periodical and newspaper indexes

EBSCO Publishing produces and distributes PRIMARY SEARCH for elementary schools and MIDDLE SEARCH PLUS for middle/junior high schools or the upper elementary grades. Both databases are available in online and CD-ROM versions. PRIMARY SEARCH contains citations with abstracts to more than 200 000 articles published in more than 160 children's periodicals, plus the complete text, accompanying tables, charts and selected graphic images of more than 17 000 articles from over 80 children's magazines. It also provides the complete text of the *World Almanac of the U.S.A.*, the *World Almanac for Kids*, and *Funk & Wagnalls New Encyclopedia*. PRIMARY SEARCH provides international coverage in English of subjects of general interest to children, including current events, business, government, the social sciences, science and the arts. The database, first made available in 1992, has retrospective cover from 1984, with school year quarterly updates of the CD-ROM version. Both PRIMARY SEARCH and MIDDLE SEARCH PLUS include the *EBSCO Encyclopedia of Animals* and the full text of over 300 primarily health-related pamphlets. MIDDLE SEARCH PLUS contains citations with abstracts to more than 350 000 articles selected from 200 magazines. It features searchable full text, including tables, charts and selected graphic images, of more than 125 000 articles from over 100 titles. In addition, it includes the full text of some professional journals such as *Education Digest, School Library Journal, Teaching PreK-8, Arts and Activities* and *The Reading Teacher*, and indexing for others such as *The Book Report, Children's Literature in Education, Teacher Librarian Journal* and *Teaching Children Mathematics*. It also includes the complete text of *Collier's Encyclopedia*. MIDDLE SEARCH PLUS focuses on American coverage of subjects of interest to middle school students in the fields of current affairs, science, humanities and social sciences. Middle and high school students use EBSCO MAS FULLTEXT SELECT on CD-ROM. This database includes abstracts and indexing of over 470 major US news weeklies and full text of articles from over 100 K-12 magazines. It also provides charts, tables and graphs, the complete text of nearly 5000 *Magill's Book Reviews*, and abstract coverage of *The New York Times*. EBSCO databases that are suitable for high school and junior college students are MAS FULLTEXT ULTRA, MAS FULLTEXT PREMIER, MAS FULLTEXT ELITE, MAS ONLINE PLUS and MAS ONLINE (see below).

The INFOTRAC KIDS EDITION CD-ROM from the Gale Group provides kindergarten to grade-six students with indexing and full-text access to more than 35 popular children's magazines, plus newspaper articles selected for these grade levels from the Knight-Ridder/Tribune News Service, and four reference books. Coverage includes the current four years for magazines and the current two years for newspaper articles. The subscription includes updates three times during the school year for CD-ROM and daily online. Through the InfoTrac interface, elementary school students become familiar with the process of research and the search skills they will use in middle and high school. INFOTRAC JUNIOR EDITION provides indexing for over 60, and the full text of over 50, magazines suitable for middle and junior high schools. Coverage is for the current three years. The subscription includes three CD-ROM and daily online updates during the school year. INFOTRAC STUDENT EDITION is aimed at the secondary school student. It indexes 230 periodicals, with the full text of 185 titles, on the INFOTRAC Web, which also includes 14 reference books and 40 000 full-text newspaper articles, with colour maps and historical images. On the INFOTRAC CD-ROM, it includes 180 indexed titles and 136 full-text titles, as well as four reference books and 30 000 full-text newspaper articles. INFOTRAC STUDENT EDITION provides American and Canadian coverage of most subject areas for six years (periodicals) or one year (newspaper articles). The subscription includes monthly updates for the CD-ROM and daily updates for INFOTRAC Web. INFOTRAC STUDENT and JUNIOR EDITIONS also include full-text access to newspaper articles selected from the Knight-Ridder/Tribune News Service, as well as full-text access to three *Information Please* almanacs and *The Reader's Companion to American History*.

All these databases feature Boolean searching, provide a search history, and allow the searcher to print or save to disk. INFOTRAC STUDENT and JUNIOR EDITIONS give Library of Congress subject headings and cross-references when students enter their search terms. MIDDLE SEARCH PLUS does not show subject headings on the main search screen; instead, it takes the searcher directly to the citation list when keywords are entered. Students may search by entering their own terms or keywords, or by selecting terms from a subject list. They may also search a journal list. Searches may be limited by the NOT operator, date range operators, and by 'Limit to items with full text'. Results of the search may be displayed, in date order, in a brief format that includes the citation, the subject, publication name and the ISSN, or the more detailed format that includes complete bibliographic information and a brief summary about the article. Students may print or save to disk selected citations or all citations, a block of text or the complete full-text article when available. The online help function contains highlighted words or phrases that cross-reference other help screens on related subjects. There is also an online glossary of terms available from each help screen. Another useful feature is the option for the library's holdings to be entered so that students can verify whether articles not available in full text are available locally.

ProQuest databases RESOURCE/ONE SELECT FULL TEXT and RESOURCE/ONE FULL TEXT for elementary, middle and junior high school students and PERIODICAL ABSTRACTS PLUS TEXT for high school students are products of Bell & Howell Information and Learning. RESOURCE/ONE SELECT FULL TEXT covers 50 magazines. RESOURCE/ONE FULL TEXT provides indexing and abstracting for over 160 magazines and full text for over 115. Both include indexing and abstracts from *The New York Times*. PERIODICAL ABSTRACTS PLUS TEXT coverage of 200 higher-level magazines makes it suitable for college prep programmes. These CD-ROM databases are updated monthly. ProQuest online database services include KIDQUEST for elementary schools, JUNIORQUEST for junior high and middle schools, and PROQUEST for high schools. KIDQUEST offers full-text and article images for over 60 magazines plus daily full-text coverage of *USA Today*. JUNIORQUEST provides full-text coverage of over 100 magazines, seven national newspapers, and over 15 professional periodicals. There is also a JUNIORQUEST CANADA edition. ProQuest offers options of full-text coverage from 140 to 1300 titles with indexing and abstracting for an additional 1000. Each option includes the PROQUEST FULLTEXT NEWSPAPER COLLECTION's access to over 70 regional, national and regional newspapers, plus the full text of *The New York Times* and *The Wall Street Journal*. The online services are updated daily. ProQuest databases offer flexible searching and retrieval of articles.

The SIRS DISCOVERER CD-ROM, updated twice yearly, is available in three editions designed to serve specific levels: the Elementary Edition for grades 1 to 6 accesses over 650 sources; the Middle Edition for grades 5 to 9 accesses over 1000 sources; and the Deluxe Edition for grades 1 to 9 (and public library use) accesses over 1200 sources. The sources include articles (with summaries for all full-text articles) and graphics from magazines, newspapers and government publications. The resources are selected for inclusion, based on educational content, interest and readability. The reading level, determined by the Flesch reading ease scale, is indicated by a colour code designating one of three categories – easy (grades 1–4), moderate (grades 5–7), and challenging (grade 8 upwards). The software can be configured to allow access to a specific level or combination of levels. The SIRS DISCOVERER also includes the *World Almanac for Kids*, *Funk & Wagnalls New Encyclopedia* and *Country Facts*, with information on more than 100 countries, as well as individual US states and Canadian provinces. Searchers can copy and paste text into a 'notepad' for printing or saving to disk. Searchers can access source information for any article on the main database. Search options include Subject Tree searches providing access to articles categorized under one or more of 15 categories, and keyword searches using Boolean operators. The subject access points are based on the Library of Congress subject headings.

SIRS DISCOVERER ON THE WEB includes the resources available on the CD-ROM version. The dictionary, combined with a thesaurus, includes the names of many notable persons. A unique feature of the SIRS DISCOVERER ON THE WEB is the 'Spotlight of the Month', an article selected by SIRS research staff to encourage research and discussion of a specific, high-interest topic. A complementary resource, the SIRS RESEARCHER is suitable for junior and senior high school students. This full-text database of articles selected from more that 1500 US and international journals, magazines and newspapers, plus US government publications, covers social, scientific, health, historic, economic, business, political and global issues dating from 1989 to the current year. Graphics, including charts, maps, diagrams and illustrations, are available from some articles. SIRS RESEARCHER offers three search methods: the subject search accesses information indexed using Library of Congress subject headings, the topic browse search accesses articles arranged under 40 broad topics, and the keyword search can be refined using Boolean operators and truncation. The CD-ROM and Web versions include 'Maps of the World', a dictionary, a thesaurus and excerpts from the current edition of the *World Almanac and Book of Facts*. The SIRS RESEARCHER ON THE WEB includes 'Today's News' featuring top news stories of the day and the 'Spotlight of the Month' research article. Both the SIRS DISCOVERER ON THE WEB and the SIRS RESEARCHER ON THE WEB allow searchers to send full-text articles to their e-mail addresses.

H.W. Wilson's READERS' GUIDE FOR YOUNG PEOPLE indexes the headlines and abstracts from 77 periodicals for elementary to middle-school students and/or their teachers. It provides full-text coverage of 54 titles. Of the 77 periodicals, nine are selection journals such as *Bulletin of the Center for Children's Books*, *Booklist*, *Horn Book* and *School Library Journal* or professional journals such as *Education Digest*, with full-text coverage of *Media & Methods* and *Teaching PreK-8* only. It includes H.W. Wilson's *Current Biography* index and abstracts since 1995. Age-appropriate, subject-specific terms and a brief abstract for each entry make this database accessible for young students. A unique feature is the reading-level colour code. With monthly updated coverage from 1994 to date, this database has the option of monthly, nine times yearly, or quarterly subscription updates. It is available on CD-ROM for DOS or Macintosh platforms, on WilsonTape, and via the Internet on WilsonWeb.

FACTS-ON-FILE WORLD NEWS DIGEST includes the complete text of the print version, with international coverage back to 1980. Its news summaries of current events worldwide, taken from US and foreign newspapers and periodicals, cover politics, foreign affairs, government, business, economics, sports, medicine and the arts. It contains biographies of newsmakers and overviews of contemporary issues. The CD-ROM version includes over 300 maps of the USA, Canada and the world. Weekly updates are provided for the EBSCOHOST version only, and quarterly for the CD-ROM. The database is also available online. Students may search using natural language, keywords, Boolean operators, concept operators, and multiple character wildcards. They can locate highlighted search terms within the text and underlined terms as links to cross-references. They can follow the development of a topic through 'back in time' and 'forward in time' buttons and also specify the order of the results – relevance or reverse chronological.

CDJR, a product of NewsBank, Inc, is suitable for middle and junior high school students. Its quarterly updated coverage includes international news and current events through full-text news articles from more than 100 US newspapers and international and domestic wire services, plus 32 magazines. Searchers can choose an easy topic search from a preselected list of possible research topics, or keyword or customized searches for options to narrow or expand the search. NewsBank SCHOOLMATE FOR ELEMENTARY SCHOOLS and NewsBank SCHOOLMATE FOR MIDDLE SCHOOLS are available through NEWSBANK INFOWEB. Students can access more than 500 local, regional and national newspapers, over 30 magazines suitable for these levels, maps and graphics. Flexible search options include relevance ranking, Boolean logic and field searching by keyword, topic and source. CURRICULUM RESOURCE BY NEWSBANK is an integrated cross-curricular database allowing access to an expansive collection of primary source information. It is available via monthly CD-ROM delivery or InfoWeb.

A current events database, TOPICSEARCH, from EBSCO, provides coverage of social, political and economic issues, scientific discoveries and other popular classroom topics. Librarians and teachers have selected the 40 000 full-text documents. The 2500 sources include international and regional newspapers and periodicals, biographies, public opinion polls, book reviews, pamphlets, government publications, and EBSCO's Current Issues database. There are four search options: topic, subject, natural language and keyword. The database also includes a dictionary. Another special-purpose database from EBSCO, VOCATIONAL SEARCH, gives students access to information on vocational education and technical education through citations, with abstracts, to articles from nearly 500 US trade-related publications. It includes searchable full text for 140 titles, and accompanying tables and charts, and nearly 5000 *Magill's Book Reviews*. With menu-driven search and retrieval software, it provides easy-to-follow search screens for the novice searcher and truncation, wildcards or proximity/phrase searches for the advanced searcher. AUSTGUIDE provides information on general interest topics as they relate to Australia, on a level suitable for high school students. This bibliographic database covers more than 120 periodicals from 1986 to date, with semi-annual updates. While it is produced by RMIT Publishing in Melbourne, it is accessible only using SilverPlatter's SPIRS software.

General periodical and newspaper indexes

In addition to these student-specific resources, the following resources offer coverage of general periodicals and newspapers that are most likely to be of use in high schools or junior colleges, and of academic or scholarly journals that are required in colleges and universities. Many of these have already been mentioned in this chapter (see under 'Minor resources' above) as resources of which the education searcher should be aware. What follows is a brief overview; the resources are described in detail in other chapters in this *Manual*.

Available through WilsonWeb and WilsonDisc (as well as other CD-ROM vendors), the READERS' GUIDE TO PERIODICAL LITERATURE includes citations to articles from 271 popular English-language general interest periodicals published in the USA and Canada, as well as *The New York Times*. With abstracts and some full text, there are four electronic editions of the READERS' GUIDE: READER'S GUIDE ABSTRACTS, FULL TEXT MEGA EDITION, FULL TEXT MINI EDITION and the ABSTRACTS SELECT EDITION. All are available online and in CD-ROM versions, and all are suitable for senior secondary and post-secondary students.

PERIODICAL ABSTRACTS from Bell & Howell Information and Learning contains citations with abstracts to varying general-interest periodicals, depending on the edition. PERIODICAL ABSTRACTS LIBRARY covers 600 titles plus *The New York Times* and *USA Today*. PERIODICAL ABSTRACTS RESEARCH I covers 1100 titles plus *The New York Times*. PERIODICAL ABSTRACTS RESEARCH II covers 1800 journals plus *The New York Times* and *The Wall Street Journal*. PERIODICAL ABSTRACTS PLUS TEXT provides articles from 200 periodicals. With American emphasis, but selected international coverage, these databases contain information on the arts, business, current events, education, health, politics and science. The full text of articles included in the PERIODICAL ABSTRACTS database is available in microform, via the *General Periodicals* CD-ROM image database, and in paper copy, through Bell & Howell Information and Learning. ACADEMIC SEARCH INTERNATIONAL (CD-ROM and EBSCOHOST) provides access to research in the fields of social science, education, psychology and other disciplines of interest to students in international universities through full-text coverage of 630 journals and abstracts and indexing for nearly 870 periodicals from around the world. This family of databases features Library of Congress Subject Headings, full-text indexing, natural language and Boolean searching, and chronological ordering of results.

ACADEMIC ASAP provides indexing of 550 and the full text of 250 academic journals on CD-ROM and 1000/500 on the Web version, covering subjects from the arts and literature to economics and the sciences of interest to undergraduate students. It also provides indexing of the most current six months of *The New York Times*. As such, it is a smaller-scale resource than EXPANDED ACADEMIC ASAP for academic research. EXPANDED ACADEMIC ASAP indexes 1500 and has full text of 500 journals on CD-ROM and 1900/900 on the Web version. It provides international research coverage of all disciplines from the humanities, social sciences and general sciences to current events, including art, cultural studies, economics, education, environmental issues, ethics, ethnic studies, government, history, literature, politics, popular science, psychology, religion, sociology, travel and women's studies, required by large college or university library systems. Another Gale Group product, GENERAL PERIODICALS ASAP ABRIDGED, indexes 150 and includes full-text coverage of 125 academic, business, and general-interest periodicals. Articles from the Knight-Ridder/Tribune News Service are indexed and available as full text. MAGAZINE INDEX PLUS/ASAP contains citations with abstracts to articles published in more than 400 American and Canadian general interest and consumer magazines, plus *The New York Times*, *The Wall Street Journal* and articles from the Knight-Ridder/Tribune News Service. Full-text coverage applies to 300 of the periodicals. Subject coverage includes art, business, current events, economics, education, entertainment, leisure and hobbies, health and nutrition, physical fitness, social issues, and science.

EBSCO produces a wide array of databases covering general and academic subjects, from the sciences to the humanities and social sciences, of interest to students in small colleges: ACADEMIC ABSTRACTS FULLTEXT ELITE, ACADEMIC ABSTRACTS FULLTEXT ULTRA, ACADEMIC SEARCH ELITE, ACADEMIC SEARCH PLUS, ACADEMIC SEARCH SELECT and ACADEMIC ABSTRACTS (which does not provide full-text coverage). ACADEMIC ABSTRACTS FULLTEXT ELITE and ACADEMIC SEARCH SELECT are available online (EBSCO host) and on CD-ROM; the others on EBSCO host only. Coverage varies from full text for over 170 journals and abstracts and indexing of 930 publications in the FULLTEXT ELITE edition to full text of nearly 1250 journals and abstracts and indexing for nearly 2880 scholarly journals in ACADEMIC SEARCH ELITE. All include coverage of *The New York Times*, and the most comprehensive include coverage of *The Wall Street Journal* and *The Christian Science Monitor* as well. ACADEMIC SEARCH FULLTEXT INTERNATIONAL provides access to research in the fields of social science, education, psychology and other disciplines of interest to students in international universities. This family of databases features Library of Congress subject headings, full-text indexing, natural language and Boolean searching, and chronological ordering of results.

The EBSCO MAS FULLTEXT databases are available in editions suitable for high school to college libraries: MAS FULLTEXT ELITE, MAS FULLTEXT PREMIER (CD-ROMs), MAS FULLTEXT ULTRA (EBSCOHOST), MAS ONLINE PLUS and MAS ONLINE. Coverage varies from full text of 170 magazines and abstracts/indexing of 460 in the ELITE edition to 570/660 in the

ULTRA edition to full text of 300/200 respectively in the online editions. Mainly American, with some international coverage, the MAS databases include the arts, business, computers, current events, education, health, literature, politics and science from general-interest magazines, most major US news weeklies and *The New York Times*, searchable full text of nearly 5000 *Magill's Book Reviews*, and over 3000 text-searchable charts, tables and graphs. EBSCO's CANADIAN MAS FULLTEXT ELITE and CANADIAN MAS FULLTEXT SELECT provide access to the full text of over, respectively, 180 and 70 titles such as *Canadian Geographic* and *Time (Canada)*, plus abstracts and indexing for over 400 titles.

Gale Group's NATIONAL NEWSPAPER INDEX indexes the five most prominent US newspapers, plus items transmitted over PR NEWSWIRE. Coverage is updated monthly to keep the current four years on file, and is suitable for high school, college and undergraduate students. The database is available online (DIALOG and DataStar) and on CD-ROM (Gale Group). NEWSBANK NEWSFILE COLLECTION includes indexing and full-text coverage of more than 70 000 newspaper articles (updated monthly) from more than 500 US newspapers and international wire services. The database provides keyword and customized searching. NEWSBANK NEWSFILE COLLECTION is available on CD-ROM with updates or via NEWSBANK INFOWEB. PROQUEST FULLTEXT NEWSPAPERS (Bell & Howell) provides online access to 150 national and international newspapers. Subscribers have the option to select all 150 or a number of preferred titles.

Encyclopedias and reference sources

Encyclopedias and similar reference sources have long been the backbone of student research, particularly for K-12 and junior college students. They give the student the opportunity to locate information in a familiar context through recognized methods such as using indexes, cross-references and tables of contents. In some cases, such resources may even provide enough background information for a research project. On the other hand, it is preferable that such resources provide a basic understanding of a topic that, in turn, will enable the student to pursue and expand the search in other resources. Unfortunately, the coverage of some subjects may be outdated as soon as the print versions of encyclopedias and reference books are published. CD-ROM and online versions provide up-to-date coverage, plus images, sounds and animation that help to bring the information to life.

For upper elementary through middle and junior high school, there are a number of American CD-ROM choices: COMPTON'S INTERACTIVE ENCYCLOPEDIA DELUXE, ENCARTA ENCYCLOPEDIA DELUXE, GROLIER MULTIMEDIA ENCYCLOPEDIA DELUXE and WORLD BOOK MULTIMEDIA ENCYCLOPEDIA. For high school students, and junior college and undergraduate students, the two main CD-ROM choices are BRITANNICA CD DELUXE ENCYCLOPEDIA and ENCYCLOPEDIA AMERICANA. Online versions are also available for AMERICANA, BRITANNICA, COMPTON'S and GROLIER. For primary and elementary students, there are COMPTON'S INTERACTIVE ENCYCLOPEDIA, NEW BOOK OF KNOWLEDGE ONLINE and the RANDOM HOUSE KIDS' ENCYCLOPEDIA. In the UK, ENCARTA and GROLIER ENCYCLOPEDIA are available for students of all ages, as well as the BRITISH MULTIMEDIA ENCYCLOPEDIA, the HUTCHINSON EDUCATIONAL ENCYCLOPEDIA and INFOPEDIA.

COMPTON'S INTERACTIVE ENCYCLOPEDIA DELUXE contains over 40 000 articles and 8000 photographs and illustrations, plus full-motion videos, slide shows and animations. An online function enables the librarian to download updates, new articles and Web links. The student may use Boolean searching or a feature called InfoLinks that, in response to a topic or question, displays related articles and can use the Show-Maker to create multimedia presentations from the articles, pictures, video, tables and sound. The database also includes *Time Multimedia Almanac*. COMPTON'S ENCYCLOPEDIA ONLINE has many features that make it user-friendly and therefore accessible to a broad range of students from grades 4 to 12. While the default option allows the student to search the article text for keywords or query search strings, other options allow for specifying searches of articles and tables; pictures, maps, charts and sounds; or Web sites. For some Web links there may be a caution as to appropriate age level, but they are accessible if the student wishes to select them. A special search feature called the 'Search Wizard' helps students narrow or broaden their topics and understand Boolean strategies.

ENCARTA ONLINE and ENCARTA DELUXE both contain approximately 40 000 articles and include 18 months of free online updates; ENCARTA ONLINE has over 14 000 Web links. ENCARTA contains lengthy articles, videos, maps, charts, sound, pictures and animation. Students may search by browsing through the guides and 'interactivities' or use the Pin Pointer to go directly to the topic. Through the World Languages Interactivity feature, students can hear words and phrases in 60 different languages. The new 'word search' facility allows searchers to locate a name or term that does not appear in the general index.

Features of the GROLIER MULTIMEDIA ENCYCLOPEDIA DELUXE include a broad database of 59 000 quality articles, 3000 illustrations, video clips, sound clips, graphics or animations, and 900 maps, including 250 full-colour maps – some with relief features. Full-text historic documents are an additional bonus as is the Internet Index with more than 20 000 links. Search strategies can make use of keyword searches with four full lines for Boolean options, and the option to specify the scope of the search, with the most relevant hits displayed first. Recommended for grades 5–12, GROLIER MULTIMEDIA ENCYCLOPEDIA ONLINE is based on the *Academic American Encyclopedia*. It contains Internet information that is updated monthly, and articles and special features not included in the print version. Icons link to Grolier Internet Index sites, while buttons indicate maps, pictures, fact boxes and/or sounds. Cross-references, which are highlighted, are hot-linked. Bibliographies and glossaries are available for some articles. NEW BOOK OF KNOWLEDGE ONLINE (Grolier Publishing) is suitable for elementary school, ESL and inclusion students. In addition to the text of the print edition, NEW BOOK OF KNOWLEDGE ONLINE has 9000 articles, 5000 Internet links, 830 maps, 250 flags and 1000 pictures. Search options include natural keyword search, use of Boolean operators or selected subject areas. The encyclopedia articles are updated quarterly. The NEW BOOK OF KNOWLEDGE NEWS, an updated weekly feature of NEW BOOK OF KNOWLEDGE ONLINE, provides access to stories, facts and activities in six curricular areas.

The quality and currency of the print version of *World Book Encyclopedia* is carried over into WORLD BOOK MULTIMEDIA. Although the database includes only 20 000 articles, they tend to be lengthier than in some other encyclopedias, starting on a basic level and becoming more detailed for more advanced searchers. Unfortunately, many of the extensive bibliographies and discussion questions that follow the articles in the print version are not available on the CD-ROM. WORLD BOOK ONLINE provides an additional 3200 articles, plus 15 000 Web links, links to over 30 000 articles in 107 periodicals, over 8500 pictures and maps, and more than 800 videos, animation and sound clips. It also includes access to almanacs, dictionaries and an atlas. The SPEECH ENABLED EDITION is available in the WORLD BOOK ENCYCLOPEDIA component only of the WORLD BOOK PREMIER REFERENCE version which combines the latest in speech technology with other features, such as Homework Wizards, Simulations and Map Overlays.

The BRITANNICA CD ENCYCLOPEDIA has the largest database with over 83 000 articles – over 3000 more than the print version – plus 'Nations of the World' sections that include maps, flags and statistics for 191 countries and the *Merriam-Webster's Collegiate Dictionary*. The CD-ROM functions much like a Web search engine interpreting natural language questions, using Boolean search strategies and presenting hits in ranked relevance order. When a sought term is not found, a list of alternative spellings is presented. BRITANNICA ONLINE, a Web-based version of the 32-volume *Encyclopaedia Britannica*, enhanced with 130 000 Internet links and the *Merriam-Webster's Collegiate Dictionary*, features over 76 000 articles and over 10 000 illustrations. Other special features include articles on 196 nations, with flags, maps and statistics; significant articles from previous editions; *Britannica Book of the Year*; and current events and biographies of prominent people. Another of BRITANNICA ONLINE's strengths is its detailed references and bibliographies. Students can conduct a simple search by typing a word, phrase or natural language question. The frequency and proximity of keywords are used to establish the perceived relevancy of articles and to determine the order of display. The first few sentences of the article and a hot link to related Internet sites, if available, are included in the display for each hit. Caution is necessary in the use of the links by students, as BRITANNICA ONLINE acts as a pointer, not a filter. Search terms are highlighted within the articles and cross-references and links to multimedia features also are included in the articles. The student can consult the Spectrum categories for suggestions for research topics, and can refine or revise the search by using the 'Query Reports' feature. The user-friendly help section with directions for searching and a description of all features assists the novice searcher.

The CD-ROM version of the ENCYCLOPEDIA AMERICANA includes over 45 000 articles, many with extensive bibliographies. AMERICANA also includes the *Academic Press Dictionary of Science and Technology*, the *Merriam-Webster Collegiate Dictionary* and the *Helicon's Chronology of World History* that may be searched together or separately. The ENCYCLOPEDIA AMERICANA ONLINE contains the same articles as the CD-ROM version, but also includes 130 000 links to related Web sites, the *Encyclopedia Americana Journal* and *The Wall Street Journal Almanac*. Simple searches for keywords or phrases can be restricted to article titles or text; advanced searching allows for the use of standard Boolean operators, wildcard symbols and proximity operators. The student can also base a more sophisticated search on the index for articles grouped by subject or content. Combinations of the categories can produce very specific results for what may have been an obscure query. Icons connect to other topics and subtopics, maps, flags and tables of information and Web sites.

The BRITISH MULTIMEDIA ENCYCLOPEDIA contains 36 000 articles, 3500 illustrations, 14 000 dictionary entries, quotes, and video and sound clips. The HUTCHINSON EDUCATIONAL ENCYCLOPEDIA, the first British edited and produced CD-ROM encyclopedia, contains over 53 000 articles, 3300 photographs and illustrations, maps and sound clips, all fully indexed and searchable. INFOPEDIA (The Learning Co.) comprises eight reference resources, including a 29-volume encyclopedia with video, still images, animations and recordings. Eleven volumes of text, 800 photographs, video clips, animations and sound make up the HEINEMANN'S CHILDREN'S ENCYCLOPEDIA on CD-ROM. The RANDOM HOUSE KIDS' ENCYCLO-PEDIA takes a fun approach, with video characters to assist children in searching the database.

Specialized reference CD-ROMs range from the MCGRAW HILL MULTIMEDIA ENCYCLOPEDIA OF SCIENCE AND TECHNOLOGY which includes articles by scientists and engineers to EXPLORING POETRY (Gale Group) for the study of poems taught in high school. Students can conduct research on countries, people and world events using CD-ROMs such as DISCOVERING BIOGRAPHY (Gale Group), MICROSOFT ENCARTA INTERACTIVE WORLD ATLAS, SOCIAL TRENDS 1979–1995 (Office for National Statistics, UK), and EXEGY: CURRENT COUNTRY PROFILES. This latter full-text database contains an encyclopedia of current world information, including statistical information on all countries. It also covers international organizations and sports. It includes over 2000 articles written by ABC-CLIO staff, using cited sources, on over 38 000 events from the past three years; plus biographies of government officials, political leaders, cultural figures and sports personalities; and profiles of political parties, businesses, government agencies and other organizations. Students will find excerpts from, and summaries of, important documents such as speeches, judicial decisions, legislation, constitutions and treaties. Pictures and maps may be printed to accompany the text. Updates twice a year plus access to the EXEGY Web site ensure that information remains current.

The ELECTRIC LIBRARY is more than a periodical database. It is a comprehensive reference source that provides full-text access to newspapers and international newswire services, magazine articles, book chapters, television and radio transcripts, and maps, photos and images. Because the ELECTRIC LIBRARY is used by students from grade 5 to 12, it provides filtered online access to these sources. Students do not have direct access to the Internet as the articles are posted on the producer's own Web site <URL http://www.elibrary.com/>. The hundreds of periodicals available include titles for children, popular magazines, professional journals, and news magazines. Searchers can access a variety of reference sources including almanacs, a dictionary, a thesaurus, the *Concise Columbia Electronic Encyclopedia*, *The Complete Works of Shakespeare*, *Monarch Notes* and many others. Other specialized electronic reference resources which are part of the ELECTRIC LIBRARY include the ETHNIC NEWSWATCH database of over 150 international full-text ethnic publications and the CONTEMPORARY WOMEN'S DATABASE of over 100 full-text journals and newsletters that cover women's issues and studies. There are three international editions of the ELECTRIC LIBRARY: ELECTRIC LIBRARY AUSTRALASIA, ELECTRIC LIBRARY KOREA and ELECTRIC LIBRARY CANADA.

Searches on the ELECTRIC LIBRARY can be very wide-ranging: when students type in a keyword, phrase or query, the software searches all the resources by default. Alternatively, searches can be limited to specific categories of resources or to author, title, publication or time period. A spell-checker prompts students when necessary. Search results display in order of relevance determined by a weighted score, and can be sorted by date, relevancy and reading level. The display includes the author and title of the article, reading level and icons denoting the type of material. Features include a 'Best Part' icon that takes the student to the sections of the articles where the search term(s) is highlighted; a dictionary icon that takes the student to definitions of word(s) highlighted; a 'Power Setting' that enables the student to increase the number of research results displayed; and a 'Tips for Searching' icon that provides suggestions for refining searches. The availability of natural-language searching plus Boolean searching makes this a reference database for the novice to experienced searcher at many educational levels.

This is only a representative listing of research CD-ROMs and online resources for students. Funds and equipment will determine the number and variety of resources accessible in any library. To maximize the resources' cost-effectiveness and to enhance the students' learning experiences, it is important that students are taught the search skills and strategies to use the resources most effectively.

Internet resources for students

Today's school libraries encompass the full range of information resources from print to electronic including access to the World Wide Web; they also focus on a wide array of information services and information skills instruction, including use of the Internet. In addition to text, the Internet provides colourful graphics, sound and animations, as well as links to related Web sites, making it a particularly appealing resource for students. The many advantages and disadvantages of the Internet as a resource for the education searcher have already been mentioned. These apply equally to the use of the Internet by and for students. The current challenge is to use technology in general, and the Internet in particular, as a means to an end and not as an end in itself. The Internet can be viewed as a source of reference materials such as online encyclopedias and magazine indexes or as a means to gain access to information held in public or private libraries worldwide through virtual libraries. Access to the Internet also can provide a valuable learning experience in the form of a virtual field trip to a gallery, museum or science centre.

The same care and attention that go into selecting and using print, audiovisual and other electronic resources must also apply to Internet resources. Students especially must be aware of the necessity to verify the authority, accuracy and currency of the site. They must be aware that the purpose of some sites is to promote or sell products or services, rather than provide unbiased information. There are any number of useful articles, and even Web sites themselves, that aim to help students evaluate the sites from which they are gathering information. One such frequently recommended site is EVALUATION RUBRICS FOR WEB SITES at <URL http://www.siec.k12.in.us/~west/online.eval.htm>. In addition, students must acknowledge the ownership of the material retrieved via the Web, as they do from print resources. When participating in e-mail, chat rooms or discussion groups, students must follow additional guidelines regarding the provision of personal information, responding to correspondence that makes them feel uncomfortable or making personal contact with someone they have met online.

Teachers and librarians must verify the appropriateness, content and presentation of Web sites prior to sharing them with students. They must verify the curricular content and/or application of the site. They must verify that the site has all the necessary information, or additional links to it, for a particular assignment or project. They must also determine whether the reading level of the site is appropriate, as many sites are put up by and for tertiary/post-secondary students. In order to keep students focused on their task and protected from inappropriate content, teachers and librarians must investigate whether the site provides links to games, chat rooms or popular culture not associated with the assignment. Other factors that affect in-class use of Web sites are:

- reliability (is it up and running during school hours?)
- speed (is it slow due to extensive inclusion of graphics, although speed can be improved by turning off graphics or using a text-only browser
- search strategies (can a student locate additional information buried under several levels, are there indexes or search capabilities for younger/novice users?).

Sites recommended for school assignments should be previewed by teachers and/or librarians. Approved sites can be bookmarked for ready access. Students should be directed to use search engines and sites that allow access only to sites that are appropriate for young people. The sponsors of these search resources have set guidelines by which they judge the content of sites to which they allow access.

Many publications, and World Wide Web resources themselves, offer assistance in the selection and use of Web sites appropriate for students. Recommended Web sites are noted in books that deal specifically with this topic (for example, *The Best Web Sites for Teachers*, *The Busy Educator's Guide to the World Wide Web* and *The Internet Resource Directory for K-12 Teachers and Librarians*) and in others that include, as an appendix, a selection of links to curriculum resources (for example, *The Teacher's Complete & Easy Guide to the Internet*). Organizations such as the American Library Association also publish lists, for example, '50+ Great Web Sites for Kids & Parents' in THE LIBRARIAN'S GUIDE TO CYBERSPACE FOR PARENTS & KIDS and 700 GREAT SITES: AMAZING, SPECTACULAR, MYSTERIOUS, WONDERFUL WEB SITES FOR KIDS AND THE ADULTS WHO CARE FOR THEM <URL http://www.ala.org/parentspage/greatsites>. Many professional journals now include Web sites in their lists of recommended resources on specific topics. *Science Books & Films* and *Social Studies & the Young Learner*, for instance, publish articles that include Web sites, many of them with links to other sources of information on the Web. Other journals, such as *Teacher Librarian Journal* and *School Library Journal*, include regular columns that highlight recommended sites.

General resources

Internet resources for students range from subject directories such as LYCOS ZONE <http://lycoszone.lycos.com> and YAHOOLIGANS! <URL http://www.yahooligans. com> – 'hot' sites for 8–14 year olds selected by the Yahoo! Staff (see earlier under 'Subject directories and search engines' in the section on 'Internet resources') to search engine-like sites such as KIDS' SEARCH TOOLS <URL http://www.rcls.org/ksearch.htm> which provides search forms for YAHOOLIGANS! as well as for other *selected* sites by way of EDUCATION WORLD, KIDSCLICK!, and STUDYWEB. KIDS' SEARCH TOOLS also provides search forms for databases of *screened* sites: AOL NETFIND FOR KIDS, KIDFUSION, METASEARCH, ONEKEY KIDSAFE SEARCH ENGINE and SEARCHOPOLIS.

Classroom Connect's CONNECTED TEACHER <URL http//www.connectedteacher.com/library/search.usp> features A4 Web links in eight curricular groupings for grade K–6, grades 7–12 and teachers. It offers keyword and phrase searching of over 1300 selected sites. EDUCATION WORLD <URL http://www. education-world.com> is a database of over 115 000 education-related sites. KIDSCLICK! <URL http://sunsite.berkeley.edu/KidsClick!/> provides links to sites of curriculum-related subjects and popular interest topics. Searches can be limited by reading level and use of graphics. STUDYWEB <URL http://www.studyweb.com/> allows students to search over 106 000 reviewed education-oriented URLs. SAFESEARCH <URL http://www.safesearch. com/> uses relevance ranking and on-the-fly rating of documents to allow students, teachers and librarians a safe and effective way to search the Internet. ASK JEEVES FOR KIDS <URL http://www.ajkids.com/> links students to an appropriate Web page in response to a question. SUPER SNOOPER™ <URL http://supersnooper.com/> is another search engine that was designed specifically for use by children. SUPER-KIDS <URL http://www.super-kids.com/> allows students to browse by broad subject categories (for example, Animals, Countries, People, Sports), or to search by keyword, a database of over 4000 reviewed sites. A useful feature of SUPER-KIDS is its links to the Web sites of more than 12 000 schools.

In addition, there is a wide array of 'virtual libraries' on the World Wide Web that have been designed and developed for student use. Besides links to other sites, they often include information that students can use to complete assignments and research projects, as well as sections for librarians, teachers and parents. Some notable examples include:

- BERIT'S BEST SITES FOR CHILDREN <URL http://www.cochran.com/ theodore/beritsbest>.
  Provides access to over 800 reviewed and rated (out of 5) sites, accessible by browsing the listed topics or through the search form.
- Brendan Kehoe's KIDS ON THE WEB <URL http://www.zen.org/~ brendan/kids.html>.
  An ongoing list of sites that offer information for and about kids including Educational Sites. It is rated child-safe by SafeSurf.
- KIDSWEB <URL http://www.npac.syr.edu/textbook/kidsweb/>.
  Presents students with a subset of the World Wide Web. Each subject section – The Arts, The Sciences, Social Studies, Miscellaneous – contains a list of links to information suitable for K-12 students as well as links to external lists for more advanced students.
- MIDLINK MAGAZINE <URL http://longwood.cs.ucf.edu/~MidLink/>.
  An electronic magazine for the middle grades with links for 'The Honor Roll of Best Web Sites' selected by Midlink readers.
- OZ KIDZ INTERNAUT CYBERCENTRE <URL http://www.ozkidz.gil.com.au>.
  An Australian site for K-12 students and teachers providing both Australian sources and links to worldwide sites.
- SCHOOLWORK.UGH or SCHOOLWORK.ORG <URL http://www. schoolwork.org/>.
  Provides links to curriculum-related topics and references tools such as dictionaries, maps and encyclopaedias.
- KIDSCOM <URL http://www.kidscom.com>.
  Provides access to keypals, story-writing contests and other Internet projects for students in English, French, German and Spanish.
- Links to an interactive zone, children's activities, and Web connections can be

found at the ONTARIO SCIENCE CENTRE'S YOUNG PERSON'S GUIDE <URL http://www.osc.on.ca/>.

● The OzEMail Family Web Guide: 4 KIDS site <URL http://www.members. ozemail.com.au/family/4kids/index.html>.
Offers a collection of games, activities, and folklore from Australia and around the world.

● PlanetZoom <URL http://www.planetzoom.com/>.
Offers games and activities for grades K-6.

● KIDS' CORNER <URL http://kids.ot.com/>.
Offers interactive games.

● MAGELLAN INTERNET GUIDE <URL http://magellan.excite.com/ education/k 12>.
Lists links for K-12 students and resources for parents and teachers.

● ACE (Academic Center for Excellence) Kids <URL http://www.acekids.com/ kidshome.htm>.
Includes links to stories, contests, and games. SafeSurf rated.

Question answering

Some sites answer questions posed by students. For example, ASK A YOUNG SCIENTIST provides access to advanced high school chemistry students at Christiansburg High School who do research and answer questions by e-mail posed by grade 1 to 6 students <apscichs@pen.k12.va.us>. Similarly, Swarthmore College students and professors answer questions from elementary to high school students at ASK DR. MATH <URL http://forum.swarthmore.edu/dr.math/dr-math. html>. Other sites in this category are HOMEWORK CENTRAL <URL http:// www.geocities.com/> and KidsConnect <URL http://www.ala.org/ICONN/ kidsconn.html> or by e-mail <AskKC@iconnect.syr.edu>, a question answering, help and referral service for K-12 students sponsored by ICONnect, American Association of School Librarians. Part of the VIRTUAL REFERENCE DESK project, the AskA+ Locator <URL http://www.vrd.org/locator/index.html> contains over 70 quality online expert services that answer the questions of the K-12 community. There are also many sites that deal with the various curricular areas.

Curriculum resources

To give readers and searchers an idea of the range of possibilities, the following is a small representative sampling of recommended World Wide Web sites appropriate for student use and arranged in broad curricular categories.

Art
EXPLORATORIUM
<URL http://www.exploratorium.edu/>, produced by the Palace of Fine Arts in

San Francisco, provides hundreds of interactive exhibits in broad subject areas such as colour, sound, music and emotion. This site appeals to both elementary and secondary students.

Mathematics
MATHMATIC
<URL http://forum.swarthmore.edu/mathmagic/> covers a variety of math-related topics for K-12 students. MR. GOODMATH <URL http://www.safari.net/~rooneym> presents real-world mathematics problems that have been contributed by professionals.

Science
BILL NYE THE SCIENCE GUY LABS ONLINE <URL http://nyelabs.kcts.org/flash_go.html> features highlights from the recent episode of this popular American television show plus an e-mail query option. In addition, this site enables students to search for topics in the life, physical or planetary sciences.

Students can check out science information and projects at the NASA SPACELINK site <URL http://spacelink.msfc.nasa.gov/>.

The NATIONAL WILDLIFE FOUNDATION Web site <URL http://www.nwf.org/kids/> includes the table of contents for *Ranger Rick* magazine, homework help via a 'Panic' button that links to specialists and experts in the field, and covers issues such as endangered animals.

U.C. BERKELEY PHYSICS LECTURE DEMONSTRATIONS <URL http://www.mip.berkeley. edu/physics/physics.html> covers all aspects of physics from astronomy to magnetism.

SOLAR SYSTEM <URL http://www.geocities.com/CapeCanaveral/Lab/2683/> is all about the solar system.

The SCIENCE MADE SIMPLE site <URL http://www.sciencemadesimple.com/> focuses on grades 1 to 7 and describes science experiments in answer to questions such as, 'Why do leaves change colour in the autumn?'.

Social studies
CASTLES ON THE WEB: CASTLEKIDS <URL http://www.castlesontheweb.com/search/ castle_kids/> has a good selection of pictures and other information on the Middle Ages. FLAGS OF THE WORLD <URL http://fotw.digibel.be/flags/> and WHERE ON THE GLOBE IS ROGER? <URL http://www.gsn.org/roger/> are also available.

In addition to resources geared to various educational levels and curricular areas, there are also resources geared to different age and gender groups. For example, sites for young adults include LA YOUTH <URL http://www. layouth.com> which offers writing, photos and art by and about teens, and WAVE <URL http://aeropark.net/wave/> which features teen writing. TEEN ADVICE ONLINE <URL http://www.teenadvice.org/> allows teens to submit questions or browse through previous answers on a variety of topics. There are Web sites designed for girls, such as a Web index called FEMINA <URL http://www.femina.cybergrrl. com>. Other sites include AMERICAN GIRL.COM <URL http://www.americangirl. com/>, EXPECT THE BEST FROM A GIRL <URL http://www.academic.org/>, GIRL POWER! FOR GIRLS <URL http://www. health.org/gpower/>, GIRL TECH <URL http://www.girltech.com/>, A GIRLS' WORLD ONLINE CLUBHOUSE <URL http://www.agirlsworld.com/>, PLANETGIRL.COM <URL http://www.planetgirl.com> and PURPLE MOON PLACE <URL http://www. purple-moon.com/>.

Search strategies for students

As mentioned previously, there is a very wide range in the abilities of students to use reference and research tools effectively. In addition, students require different searching skills for electronic resources from those required for print sources. Using electronic resources requires more than simply loading the software and entering a search term; it requires the skill to recognize various search modes, ranging in sophistication. If the student has been taught to plan a search strategy, it is more likely that information that is more focused and specifically related to the topic will be the reward. The search strategy should begin with the identification of the topic or problem. The student can formulate a description of the general nature of the research or problem by writing it out and relating the topic to prior knowledge to put it in context. Terms that cannot be easily described can be confirmed in a dictionary or expanded by using a thesaurus. Students can brainstorm alone or with others to develop a 'mind map' or 'web', and from these determine the most relevant terms or keywords to use. Students who have been taught to use graphic organizers will be able to follow the structure of a search and the organization of the resources within a database or Web site, whether it is sequential, conceptual, hierarchical or cyclical. They will be able to develop and organize ideas and topics, see connections, patterns and relationships, classify or categorize concepts, and predict and evaluate the success of their search. They will be able to produce effective search terms and envision links between concepts. They will be able to locate additional terms and gain a better understanding of the topic from perusing hyperlinks available in electronic resources.

Students should be familiar with the browse, hierarchical and analytical search functions, and be able to develop an appropriate search strategy for each. To use the browse function, which may appear on the menu bar as an index, word list or simply 'browse', the student enters a search term or simple phrase. The student scans the resulting list of titles or subjects to identify those that are relevant and then selects them to produce the reference or full-text document. In hierarchical searching, students must employ higher-order thinking skills to formulate their search strategy. Beginning with a few broad concepts or subjects, the student must make a series of decisions while selecting subsets of the concept or subject that are most likely to contain relevant information. With each subset the topic becomes more narrowly focused. This type of search gives students a more thorough understanding of the subject because they have linked from a broad or general view to a very specific aspect of the topic. Students using analytical searching must be familiar with Boolean logic. They must also understand proximity, truncation, wildcards and search phrases, as well as the indicators used to designate them. The capacity to perform extensive searches through electronic resources can provide access to information that may have been difficult to locate within print sources. However, students must also be able to apply criteria for selecting and evaluating the most relevant information.

Encyclopedias and other reference sources on CD-ROM should be as reliable as the print editions, while full-text magazine articles and Internet resources must be examined for authority and accuracy. Students must be aware that the same rules apply as to ownership and plagiarism as for other sources, despite the ease of retrieval and ambiguity of source. Assignments that require students to analyse and synthesize information from a variety of sources will challenge them to develop and apply higher-order thinking skills.

Developing the search strategy

This section of the chapter focuses on the overall approach or strategy that ensures successful searches for education-related information. The approach outlined here assumes that the searcher is thoroughly knowledgeable about the nature of education and those who have an interest in it (see also 'Factors affecting the search' above). It also assumes that the searcher has chosen an appropriate resource and access option (where options exist) to accommodate these factors.

Analysis

The most important aspect of a successful strategy for an education search is the analysis of the client's request and, in particular, resolution of the issues regarding terminology. The purpose of this first step is to determine the basic concepts and relationships involved and to develop a shortlist of relevant search terms. Since most education topics are multidimensional; a combination of two or three search terms is most likely to yield the best results. Searching on a single term, with the possible exception of a specific name, can produce too many (and too many irrelevant) hits; searching on combinations of four or more terms can produce too few hits, or none at all. The client's input at this stage is crucial to identify and define key concepts and any relationships between them, suggest synonyms, clarify perspective and specify any delimiters. (For examples, see the searches at the end of this chapter.)

Effective searches almost always start with the most important and most specific concepts. Having worked with the client to determine the appropriate key concepts, the searcher then translates these natural language terms into the

controlled indexing vocabulary of a particular resource by consulting its thesaurus
or equivalent authority file if there is no database-specific thesaurus. Searching on
pre-coordinated index terms (or explicit free-text phrases) may be the best way to
express a relationship in some cases, but not in all. The searcher and client must
be prepared to retrieve some irrelevant results for these multidimensional
searches. For example, a search on ERIC using the Boolean AND to combine the
descriptors Media Specialists, Attitudes and Information Technology retrieves
useful and relevant documents on media specialists' attitudes to information
technology as well as irrelevant (to this specific search) documents on other
attitudes and on information technology more generally. Refining the search by
using the more specific pre-coordinated descriptor Librarian Attitudes produces
fewer and more relevant results, but still includes a document focusing on media
specialists' attitudes to something other than information technology. In this
search, the most relevant of the retrieved documents include all three key search
terms among the major descriptors. The searcher should remember to look first for
each of the most relevant search terms as a major descriptor or its equivalent, if
there is one, in databases other than ERIC. (The AUSTRALIAN EDUCATION
INDEX, for instance, indicates major descriptors with an asterisk. The BRITISH
EDUCATION INDEX and CBCA FULLTEXT EDUCATION (formerly the
CANADIAN EDUCATION INDEX) list descriptors in order of importance. The
Wilson education databases also list terms in their Subject(s) field in order of
importance.) At the same time, the searcher should quickly examine what other
search terms are high on the list or are designated as major descriptors to help
determine the potential usefulness of the retrieved document to satisfy the client's
request. This strategy for identifying relevant documents is particularly helpful
when the abstract is too brief or too vague or is missing entirely, and/or the title is
uninformative.

More general concepts, such as age or educational level, are often best left out
of the original search and used as refinements later in the process if either the
quantity or scope of the material retrieved warrants. Likewise, delimiters such as
date, language, geographic area, material/document type or target audience can be
used to further refine a search as necessary.

Terminology

Problems of terminology, as they relate to the nature of education itself, are
introduced in the section 'Factors affecting the search'. This section discusses
more specific problems of terminology as they relate to developing an effective
search strategy, and focuses on the use of a controlled indexing vocabulary.

The next step in developing an effective search strategy is to express the key
concepts, and any relevant relationships between them, using the controlled
indexing vocabulary appropriate to a particular resource. Some education
concepts require only one term to accurately describe them. Advocacy, for
example, has no real synonyms. However, many more concepts require two or

more related terms, linked by the Boolean operator OR, to express one concept, and all the aspects of it in which the client is interested, for example, Parents OR Mothers OR Fathers OR Parent–Child Relationships. Still other concepts require a very specific pre-coordinated term to express them adequately, for example, Parent–Child Relationships or Computer Uses in Education.

Controlled indexing vocabulary

At this stage, the searcher should consult a standard thesaurus if one is available. The most notable example is the *Thesaurus of ERIC Descriptors* used in the preparation of the ERIC and EXCEPTIONAL CHILD EDUCATIONAL RESOURCES databases. It is available in print form and the online and CD-ROM versions of the ERIC database, but not in the Web-based version. The AUSTRALIAN EDUCATION INDEX employs terms from the *Australian Thesaurus of Education Descriptors* which is based on the *Thesaurus of ERIC Descriptors* but modified in accordance with current Australian English usage. The *British Education Thesaurus* now underpins the BRITISH EDUCATION INDEX. It too was developed from the *Thesaurus of ERIC Descriptors* and has many terms in common with it. The bilingual (English and French) *Canadian Education Thesaurus* has been applied to CBCA FULLTEXT EDUCATION (formerly CANADIAN EDUCATION INDEX) since 1992. The latter three thesauri were each an integral part of the INTERNATIONAL ERIC CD-ROM. Now it includes only the Australian and British thesauri. There is no database-specific thesaurus for the EDUCATION INDEX, WILSON EDUCATION ABSTRACTS or WILSON EDUCATION ABSTRACTS FULL TEXT. All the Wilson education databases use one subject authority file that includes terms derived from the *Library of Congress Subject Headings*, among other sources, and an extensive cross-reference structure. Wilson indexers use the Name Authority file to verify any personal or corporate names and/or uniform titles used as subject headings. Topical subject headings and descriptor strings (subject headings with subdivisions) bring to five the types of subject access point available in the Wilson education databases. Other access points include abstract words, title words, and basic index words (that is, free-text single keywords). All the subject access points are searchable as a phrase. In addition, individual words are searchable as basic index terms (see also 'Keyword searching' below).

Keyword searching

The principal disadvantage of using a controlled indexing vocabulary is that it is always out-of-date. The compilers of a well-constructed thesaurus or authority file, such as the *Thesaurus of ERIC Descriptors* or the *Library of Congress Subject Headings*, are very good at anticipating most of the natural language terms and synonyms that clients and searchers may use to express a concept. However, the thesaurus compilers are only human and cannot be expected to anticipate *all* the terms that authors, clients and searchers may use to express a concept, particularly when that concept is a new one and/or subject to regional or temporal variations. For example, 'First Nations' has been in common usage in the literature for several years, but the term does not appear in the *Thesaurus of ERIC Descriptors* nor in the *Canadian Education Thesaurus*; both still prefer other terms – American Indians and Native Peoples respectively.

Most major database producers include procedures for regularly updating controlled indexing vocabularies. A new edition of the *Thesaurus of ERIC Descriptors*, for instance, comes out every two to three years. Proposed new descriptors in ERIC first appear in the Identifier field. Identifiers are semi-controlled retrieval terms intended to add more depth to the indexing of documents than is possible with descriptors alone. The printed *ERIC Identifier Authority List* (IAL) (Phoenix, AZ: Oryx Press, 1995) is a list of preferred identifiers and serves as a companion to the *Thesaurus of ERIC Descriptors*. Identifiers (or their equivalents, if available, in systems other than ERIC) do not appear in a thesaurus because they have not yet achieved the status of descriptors. Charter Schools and Teacher-Librarians, for example, appear in the identifier field in records retrieved in searches of the ERIC database, yet neither term appears in the thirteenth edition of the *Thesaurus of ERIC Descriptors*. Recent examples of former identifiers now in the *Thesaurus* include Active Learning, Global Education and Reflective Teaching.

Other identifiers that do not appear in the *Thesaurus of ERIC Descriptors* or similar thesauri are proper names – of geographic locations, persons, corporate bodies, tests and examinations, legislation and so forth. On the other hand, Wilson treats personal names, corporate names and uniform titles used as subjects of documents as subjects – that is, as analogous to the descriptors in a thesaurus. In addition to, or in place of, subject terms, names can make for very effective search terms. The experienced searcher will use them, whenever appropriate, to start or refine a search (see the 'Jim Cummins' example on p. 284). For new terms and others that are not yet, nor ever will be, descriptors or other authorized access points, the searcher must rely on keyword (natural-language or free-text) searches. He or she must also rely on keyword searches when searching the Internet; none of the subject directories or search engines currently utilizes a controlled indexing vocabulary.

The experienced searcher should be aware of when a particular term was authorized for use in a particular database. If the searcher has been instructed to conduct a comprehensive retrospective search and/or include a range of dates before the term achieved descriptor status or was authorized as a standard subject heading, he or she will incorporate a free-text keyword search to pick up the term in the Identifier field and/or in the titles or abstracts of the citations for those documents indexed before the term was authorized.

In those instances when a thesaurus or authority file is not available or does not provide appropriate pre-coordinated terms, the searcher should use whatever options the search software offers for phrase and/or proximity searching to avoid single-word searches. The previously mentioned search for 'charter schools' provides a useful example. Searching for 'charter AND school?' retrieves documents about charter schools in CBCA FULLTEXT EDUCATION before charter schools became an authorized descriptor. However, this search also retrieves references to documents about the Canadian Charter of Rights and Freedoms and schools. Searching on 'charter school?' or using another approach that allows the two terms to be brought into close proximity with one another (that is, within a few words) retrieves not only the exact phrase 'charter school' or 'charter schools' but also phrases where the terms are not directly adjacent to one another, such as 'charter and similar alternative schools' or 'charter-type school'.

When using ERIC the searcher should be aware that ERIC indexers may not assign descriptors and/or identifiers consistently across, or within, the two files – *Current Index to Journals in Education* and *Resources in Education*. For example, from a previously mentioned sample search, Platoon Schools appeared as an identifier in only two of three relevant records retrieved from CIJE (although all three included 'Platoon School' in the title). The RIE records did not use Platoon Schools as an identifier, nor did these words appear in the title of one relevant document. The searcher would never have found this document had she not used 'PLATOON?' in a free-text keyword search and retrieved the term from the abstract. The downside to this approach, of course, is that the search results include entirely irrelevant documents, such as, in this example, a critique of the movie *Platoon*!

The important influence of geography on terminology cannot be stressed too much. Different terms can be used to express essentially the same concept or topic. 'Mainstreaming' has already been mentioned as an example of a North American descriptor for which the British (and French Canadians as 'integration de l'enfant en difficulté') use 'integration'. ERIC also uses the related term 'inclusive schools' to express another aspect of the same concept but neither CBCA FULLTEXT EDUCATION nor the BRITISH EDUCATION INDEX do. Refining a search to address the 'inclusion' aspect through a free-text keyword search can be useful in returning more relevant documents. However, 'inclusion' is a term with many meanings beyond the very specific one intended here. A search that includes the Abstract field turns up irrelevant documents. On the other hand, a search that restricts the term to the Title field may miss relevant documents if the precise term does not appear in the title. Adding variants, such as 'inclusive education' linked with the Boolean OR is a better strategy. The search for 'charter schools' provides another example of one concept that can be described in various ways depending on where in the world one happens to be. 'Charter schools' since 1995 has been an approved descriptor in CBCA FULLTEXT EDUCATION and an identifier in ERIC. Its counterpart in the BRITISH EDUCATION INDEX is 'Grant Maintained Schools'. Interestingly, BEI also uses Charter Schools as a descriptor when the term applies to the Irish Charter Schools (an older concept) or as a current identifier when the term applies to charter schools in North America. Even though searching on 'charter schools' in BEI produces results, the results do not include relevant documents on the topic in the UK unless the document referred to covers *both* charter schools in North America and grant-maintained schools in the UK.

Local, regional, national or international perspectives can provide entirely different uses of the same term. For example, 'whole language', which originated in Australia, was comparable to the American expression 'literature-based'. While the literature now recognizes both terms, and some thesauri have incorporated Whole Language Approach as a descriptor, initially the searcher had to try a number of combinations. Educators tend to use terms and expressions as they fit their own situation. 'Multi-age grouping', 'family grouping', 'combination classes' and 'group work in education' are terms that describe the concept of students of different ages and grades working together in a classroom. Yet these terms are not linked in the thesauri. The AUSTRALIAN EDUCATION INDEX uses Multigraded Classes and Vertical Grouping as descriptors, the BRITISH EDUCATION INDEX Family Grouping and Vertical Grouping, and CBCA FULLTEXT EDUCATION Multigraded Classrooms and Split Grade Classes. As these last examples illustrate, another problem with terminology is the use of several terms to represent closely related concepts. The searcher must include all appropriate terms (linked by the Boolean OR) for a comprehensive search. A related issue – and potentially major problem – is the inclusion in a particular database's subjects lists of incorrect (for example, unauthorized or misspelled) terms. In Figure 5.1 (pp. 286–90) the searcher noted that in the AEI Subject Headings list, Academic Achievement also appears as 'Academic Achievemnt' and 'Academic Acievement' and in the Document Type list, research reports appears correctly as 'Reports – Research' and incorrectly as 'Reports Research'!

Refining the search

If an initial search strategy produces too many hits or a large number of irrelevant hits, the searcher can refine the search by adding, subtracting or substituting topical search terms and/or by introducing delimiters from a number of categories.

Educational level

In education, the first limiting factor usually is educational level or age level. The delimiter can be as specific as Grade 2, as broad as Primary Education, or as all-encompassing as Elementary Secondary Education. However, Elementary Secondary Education can itself be a limiting term if the initial search results also include many references to adult and/or post-secondary education. ERIC uses levelling descriptors to indicate either educational level or age level, sometimes both. Since it is possible to express these levels in such a variety of ways, ERIC has developed its own series of mandatory descriptors for educational levels and optional descriptors for age. Since 1975 ERIC indexers have assigned at least one (and as many as are appropriate) educational level descriptor to each document unless it is entirely inappropriate. On the plus side, the different descriptors allow for a great deal of specificity. For example, Two Year Colleges focuses a search much more than Post-secondary Education. On the negative side, documents indexed at a narrow level are usually not indexed to a broader level. An exhaustive search for a broader term, Post-secondary Education, for example, must also include the narrower terms, Higher Education and Two Year Colleges. In Figure 5.3 (pp. 309–26) the searcher achieved a more successful result by *excluding* (using the Boolean NOT) these two descriptors rather than limiting the search to Elementary Secondary Education because the educational level does not always appear as a descriptor. The other databases treat educational level differently from ERIC and from each other. CBCA FULLTEXT EDUCATION, for instance, uses an identifier to indicate educational level when it is appropriate. The BRITISH EDUCATION INDEX includes an indication of educational level, when appropriate, in the searchable Notes field along with document type. The Wilson education databases include a subject heading for educational level in the Subject(s) field in those cases where the document indexed is *about* that educational level; there is no way to indicate educational level *per se* and/or use it as a limiting factor in a search. Differences in terminology for educational level in different jurisdictions have already been mentioned (see 'Geographic factors' under 'Factors affecting the search' earlier in this chapter). The experienced searcher will be aware of all these differences concerning educational level and know when and how (or even if) to introduce it as a search refinement.

Date

After educational level, the next most relevant limiting factor is date – a particularly useful factor in education where trends tend to be cyclical. For example, should the search cover the entire database (ERIC online and on CD-ROM includes references from 1966 to the current date, the EDUCATION INDEX from 1983) or the 20 most recent documents or the years between 1970–1979? Limiting a search by date can be a very useful technique, especially in cases where the searcher has confirmed that the client is interested only in work produced before or after a particular date or within a particular range. In other cases important and relevant information on a topic may have been produced over a long period of time so that limiting the search to a narrow range may exclude useful documents from the results and/or result in too few (or none at all) hits. Such searches can be adjusted to include a broader range of dates on the assumption that there may be some relevant information in the broader group. (See also the discussion of 'Time factors' under 'Factors affecting the search' earlier in this chapter.)

As with educational level, the various databases provide different options for limiting by date, and some databases do not allow it all. When using these latter databases, the searcher must scan the results list to find a required date or range of dates – a task easily and quickly accomplished on most databases – such as those on the INTERNATIONAL ERIC CD-ROM – that list search results in reverse chronological order so that the most recent references come up first. However, some searches on the Internet return results in ranked order with what are considered the most relevant documents listed first. This seemingly useful feature can be frustrating if the client specified a particular time period and the searcher cannot limit by date.

Other delimiters

The searcher can also refine or narrow a search by specifying the language of a document, its geographic source, its document type and/or its target audience. The use of language as a limiting factor depends on the scope of the database. If there are many international documents indexed, it is worthwhile selecting only those in a language known to the searcher or client. However, in a comprehensive search, the searcher may wish to retrieve all documents and peruse those that have abstracts in the required language. In a bilingual resource such as CBCA FULLTEXT EDUCATION, the searcher may wish to limit the search to English or French documents depending on the client's language skills. ERIC includes a Target Audience field only when the authors of the document so designate and, even though 11 categories are now defined, they have not always been part of a record. In addition, not all vendors provide access to this field or access it in the same way. A search on behalf of a parent for information about current trends in educational accountability, for example, would most likely yield more useful results if it were limited to materials produced primarily for parents and/or from a parent's perspective (see also Figure 5.2(a), pp. 293–95). Materials produced for policy-makers or researchers may be totally inappropriate for the parent looking for a more popular approach and language comprehensible to the layperson.

At other times, the searcher is asked to locate education information that is research-based – for example, reports of the results of a research study/project, discussions of methodology(ies) or some kind of a case study. Incorporating authorized controlled vocabulary terms such as 'theories' or 'research' alongside subject terms may or may not prove successful in isolating those documents that are indeed research-based (see Figure 5.1 pp. 286–90). Likewise, a free-text keyword search incorporating appropriate terms may retrieve relevant documents, but it is just as likely to retrieve totally irrelevant documents where the term has merely appeared (out of context) somewhere in the citation. As might be expected, the different education databases include different options for document type. ERIC categorizes all documents by publication type using a three-digit code including 143 for research reports. One code is required; up to three are possible. Other databases provide pull-down menus or other lists from which the searcher chooses the appropriate document type. Even though a great variety of publication types is possible – and among them 'Research Reports' or 'Reports – Research' or simply 'Research' – identifying all research as such is difficult and there is frequently no easy or reliable way to isolate particular methodologies.

Executing the search

With a carefully crafted list of search terms in hand and a good idea of how they should be combined, the searcher is now ready to execute the search using the most appropriate resource and access option as determined earlier.

Interacting with the results

No matter how well-analysed the client's request and carefully planned the search strategy, uncertainties about concepts, relationships and terminology make reviewing and refining the search results an essential next step for the education searcher. A quick scan of the titles, descriptors (and identifiers) and subject(s) in the retrieved citations often reveals important terms that have been omitted and/or chosen terms with different or broader applications than anticipated. Such searches are easily revised and continued, usually by adding or subtracting search terms or introducing (or eliminating) appropriate delimiters. A search in ERIC for a special education teacher interested in information on strategies for teaching problem solving to K-12 students with learning disabilities resulted in too many hits using a strategy combining Learning Disabilities with (Boolean AND) Teaching Methods OR Learning Strategies, and with (Boolean AND) Problem Solving. Further consultation with the client led the searcher to introduce the additional free-text search terms, 'mathematics OR arithmetic' as the references to social studies were not relevant, and also to introduce educational level (see Figure 5.3, pp. 309–26).

A more problematic situation arises when the supposedly well-crafted search produces quite unexpected results. This usually happens when terms may be combined in more than one sense. Sometimes it is necessary to find the appropriate search term(s) for an implied but unstated concept or relationship in the client's request. For example, a search to retrieve information on personality characteristics of people with varying circadian rhythms (Circadian Rhythms AND Characteristics) resulted in many references to primates. Refining the search with 'AND Human Behavior' resulted in far more relevant hits.

Unexpected results are much more the norm than the exception with Internet searches. The lack of any standard indexing vocabulary for accessing documents on the World Wide Web and the sometimes quirky syntax imposed by the search engines means the searcher has far less control over an Internet search than over one on the more traditional online and CD-ROM databases. Frequently, the searcher has no alternative but to repeat the search either using the same terms and strategy with another search engine or using different terms and/or strategy on the same search engine. Few of the search engines allow the searcher to refine a search or proceed in stages as with a search on an online database or CD-ROM. Again, the client's input is crucial at this stage to ensure that the search is progressing effectively to its desired outcome.

Another strategic approach to deal with problems in educational terminology is a process some searchers call 'pearl-growing' and others refer to as 'coming in the side door'. Using this approach, the searcher first locates and displays references to a few highly relevant documents and then selects suitable terms from these records and adds them to (or uses them to replace existing terms in) the search. This method may be the only satisfactory one for searches that do not appear to conform to standard categories or terminology and may therefore defy reasonable analysis. For such an approach to be successful, the searcher must be very skilled at interpreting results online and willing to take the risk that less (but quite possibly more relevant) information will be retrieved than through a more conventional search. The lack of a controlled indexing vocabulary means that pearl-growing does not work for an Internet search. However, the 'more like this' feature on the same search engine provides an approximation.

A variation on the pearl-growing strategy is an item-specific search whereby the searcher begins with the name of the author, the title or a keyword of a reference which is known or has been recommended to the searcher as relating specifically to the topic. Suppose a client has only a reference to the name, Jim Cummins. A search under this name in CBCA FULLTEXT EDUCATION retrieves his published works. By examining the search results, the searcher can determine which descriptors and/or identifiers to use to conduct a more thorough subject search on a particular topic – for example, the use of what some call 'original' and others 'native' or 'first' language. One of the retrieved records includes the useful descriptor, Heritage Language Programs, which the searcher can now incorporate in a more comprehensive subject search. This is an effective way to focus on a specific topic, because the previous searcher or indexer has already provided the most relevant links. However, this strategy succeeds only if the known reference is indexed, if the descriptors are specific to the topic and not broad, or if the concept, as an identifier, has been used previously.

Conclusion

Successful searches for education information depend on a number of factors. First among these is a close collaboration between the searcher and the client. When clients are present during the search, they can more easily articulate their exact requirements, help plan the search, and review and assess the results as the search progresses. Where the clients do their own searching of online databases, CD-ROMs or the Internet, they bring to the exercise their own subject knowledge but lack the professional searcher's expertise and experience. Collaboration between the client and professional searcher is just as important in this scenario as when the professional performs the search for the client. The essential advice and assistance come in many forms. The experienced professional searcher may interact person-to-person with the client at the workstation, or with a group in a workshop, tutorial or other training session. Developing and delivering such training sessions may very well be an integral part of an experienced professional searcher's job, as may planning and developing printed or online 'help' for users. No matter what form the collaboration takes, the client and searcher working together throughout the search ensures success.

Searches

Search 1: Is there any research on the relationship between class size and student achievement in Australian primary schools?

The client is a primary school teacher who is also working part-time on her Master's degree in education. Her thesis has to do with factors affecting student achievement in the 'middle' grades – that is, grades 4 to 6. She prefers recent research studies but will accept older and less formal materials. She will also accept materials focusing on secondary schools. Her first choice is for Australian documents but she also would like to see references for any Canadian or British studies. If these are not available or are insufficient, she would like a search of ERIC. She also has practical reasons for wanting this information: to back up her proposal to her principal that small classes are better classes.

At the time of the request, this search was tailor-made for the INTERNATIONAL ERIC CD-ROM, starting with the AUSTRALIAN EDUCATION INDEX. The searcher begins by identifying the key topical concepts in the search as 'class size' and 'student achievement'. Verifying the authorized terms for these concepts, the *Australian Thesaurus of Education Descriptors* (available on the CD-ROM as 'AEI Subject Headings' in the search options menu) gives 'Academic achievement' and 'Class size'. While the searcher verifies these terms, she also notes the useful related terms 'Small classes' and 'Student teacher ratio'.

A quick preliminary search combining Academic achievement OR Academic achievemnt OR Academic acievement (to account for variant spellings discovered in the AEI subject headings list) with (Boolean AND) Class size OR Small classes OR Student teacher ratio results in 25 hits. These include records that deal with both class size and academic achievement, but not necessarily the relationship between them – that is, the impact of one upon the other, and not necessarily as the major focus of the document. Furthermore, the documents are not necessarily research-based. The searcher can now proceed to refine the search by limiting the document type to Reports – Research OR Reports Research (to account for the variation in the AEI subject headings list). This produces only one hit – insufficient to satisfy the client. The searcher then 'undoes' this step and limits the search another way by adding Research OR Educational research OR Research methodology OR Research reports to the initial combination. This produces a manageable list of references to ten documents, some of which are still not completely what the client requested but a few of which appear very relevant. Unfortunately, some of the apparently more relevant items have uninformative titles and/or are quite old. The searcher decided that, with a hit list of this size, there was no real need to limit any further, such as by educational level.

A very useful feature of the INTERNATIONAL ERIC CD-ROM is that it allows a search to be repeated on a new database (more than one database on the disc cannot be searched simultaneously) by saving the initial search strategy and recalling it on a second database. However, the repeated search is successful only if the search terms are generic and/or recognized as descriptors in all databases.

Repeating the search using the AEI subject headings on the CANADIAN EDUCATION INDEX (CBCA FULLTEXT EDUCATION) results in five hits, all of which list 'Class size' as the first descriptor. Two citations include 'Academic achievement' as the second descriptor, two as the third, and one as the fourth. Because CEI uses the 'research' descriptors differently from AEI, the research aspect is encapsulated in the Document Type field, in the Series field, or as a free-text keyword in the title and/or abstract. The searcher decides to omit the research aspect and to verify the other terms in the CEI subject headings list where she discovers that it is 'Teacher student ratio' (not 'Student teacher ratio') which is a related term for 'Class size', and that 'Small classes' is not used. Combining Academic achievement with (Boolean AND) Class size OR Teacher student ratio produces eight hits, five of which are the same as those retrieved on the first search of CEI and, as expected, none are the same as those retrieved in the AUSTRALIAN EDUCATION INDEX. The results include three reviews of the research literature – not reports of research *per se*, but the client has decided that they may be useful as background information for her own work.

Repeating the two-step search on the BRITISH EDUCATION INDEX results in ten hits, two of which are duplicates, but all of which are different from those in AEI and CEI. Again, a couple are reviews of the research literature and potentially useful to the client, as are a few others. Incorporating the research aspect leads to five hits, three of which appear relevant based on the position of the key search terms in the list of descriptors in each citation.

Figure 5.1 illustrates the strategy and shows sample results from the search.

S "CLASS SIZE" OR "SMALL CLASSES" OR "STUDENT TEACHER RATIO"
S S1 AND ("ACADEMIC ACHIEVEMENT" OR "ACADEMIC ACHIEVEMNT" OR "ACADEMIC ACIEVEMENT")
S S2 AND DT=("REPORTS - RESEARCH" OR "REPORTS RESEARCH")

1 of 1 Complete Record

Figure 5.1   Search (conducted November 1998) on the relationship between class size and student achievement in Australian primary schools

00061733 Australian Education Index Number: 66896 Input: ACER
The availability of baseline data on equity in Australian schools.
Robinson L; Ainley J
Publication Year: 1995
Publisher: Australia. Dept of Employment, Education and Training (DEET)
Place of Publication: Canberra
Availability: ISBN 0642229031
Document Type: Reports - Research (143)
Notes: 79p. appendices.
Issue: AEI Dec 95
Subject Category: Educational philosophy, policy and development
Descriptors: *Data; *Educationally disadvantaged; *Equal education;
 *Information sources; *Outcomes of education; Aboriginal students;
 Academic achievement; Attendance patterns; Class size; Data
 collection; Disabilities; Economically disadvantaged; Employment
 patterns; Equalisation aid; Expenditure per student; Federal
 programs; Gifted; High risk students; Information utilisation; Non

 English speaking; Participation; Postsecondary education; Rural
 students; School holding power; Student teacher ratio
Identifiers: Educational indicators; Educational equity (Finance);
 National Equity Program for Schools (Australia); Torres Strait
 Islanders

S "CLASS SIZE" OR "SMALL CLASSES" OR "STUDENT TEACHER RATIO"

S S1 AND ZZ=("ACADEMIC ACHIEVEMENT" OR "ACADEMIC ACHIEVEMNT" OR
"ACADEMIC ACIEVEMENT")
S S2 AND (RESEARCH OR "EDUCATIONAL RESEARCH" OR "RESEARCH
METHODOLOGY" OR "RESEARCH REPORTS")

 1 of 1 Complete Record

 00063884 Australian Education Index Number: 67481 Input: ACER

The contribution of IEA research to Australian education.
Keeves J P
Source: In 'Reflections on educational achievement: papers in honour of T Neville
 Postlethwaite to mark the occasion of his retirement from his chair in
 comparative education at the University of Hamburg' edited by W Bos and R H
 Lehmann, pages 137-158. Munster Germany: Waxmann
Publication Year: 1995
Document Type: Collected works - Individual papers (023)
Notes: Written in cooperation with P Lietz.
Abstract: This article considers the contribution of research undertaken as part
 of the International Association for the Evaluation of Educational Achievement
 (IEA) studies to Australian education, and in particular to educational theory,
 policy making and the conduct of research. Areas where policy making has been
 influenced include retention rates, social class differences, gender differences,

Figure 5.1   cont'd

time and school learning, and curriculum differences between Australian states.
In addition, IEA research contributed to the improvement of educational practice
by showing the significance of student attitudes and values, an emphasis on
process, opportunity to learn, time spent on homework, and class size as well as
whole group instruction.
Issue: AEI Mar 96
Subject Category: Educational psychology
Descriptors: *Academic achievement; *Educational policy; *Educational practices;
  *Educational research; *Educational theories; *Research methodology; Class size;
  Classroom environment; Comparative analysis; Cross cultural studies;
  Curriculum development; Curriculum evaluation; Homework; International studies;
  Longitudinal studies; Multiple choice tests; Multivariate analysis; Path
  analysis; Sampling; School holding power; Sex differences; Social differences;
  Student attitudes; Time on task
Identifiers: Curriculum implementation; International Association for the
  Evaluation of Educational Achievement (IEA); Lietz P

S "CLASS SIZE" OR "SMALL CLASSES" OR "STUDENT TEACHER RATIO"
S S1 AND ZZ="ACADEMIC ACHIEVEMENT"
S S2 AND (RESEARCH OR "EDUCATIONAL RESEARCH" OR "RESEARCH
METHODOLOGY" OR "RESEARCH REPORTS")

1 of 1 Complete Record

00109056 Canadian Education Index
Secondary Analyses of a Study of the Effects of Class Size in the Junior Grades
Wright, Edgar N.; FitzGerald, John; Eason, Gary
82 p.
Corporate Source: Toronto Board of Education
Sponsoring Agency: Ontario. Ministry of Education
Publisher: Toronto: Toronto Board of Education, Research Dept.
Availability: Document available from Micromedia Limited
Micromedia prices: MFx/PCa
ONTERIS Document Number: ON01608
Language: English
Document Type: Research
Geographic Source: Canada; Ontario
Notes: Data for this study is archived by OISE and is available to researchers.;
  Related records: ON00691; ON00697; Funding institution: Ontario. Ministry of
  Education. Contractual Research
Abstract: Students (Ss) and teachers (Ts) in 62 grades 4-5 classes in 11 Toronto
  schools. Data collected 1974-1975. Data collected for "The Effects of Class Size
  in the Junior Grades" were analyzed with reference to the 4 class sizes (17, 23,
  30, and 37). Secondary analyses studied: the effects of class size on Ss' scores
  in upper and lower class quarters on achievement, composition, art, and self-
  concept; class size and Ts' choice of audience; the subject of a T's speech and
  choice of audience; class conversation; the effects of subject of instruction on
  the behaviour of Ts and Ss; Ts' sex and individualization; Ss' socioeconomic
  status and behaviour; the relation between teaching technique and achievement,
  and between observation variables and Ss' academic self-concepts. Analyses of
  variance, F ratios, correlation coefficients, and means; tables and graphs. Class

Figure 5.1   cont'd

size was related to scores on the Canadian Tests of Basic Skills (CTBS) Mathematics Concepts Test for Ss in the upper quarter of the class, and to scores on the CTBS Mathematics Problem Solving Test for Ss in the lower quarter. Regardless of class size, Ts spent about the same amount of teaching time talking to individual Ss, groups of Ss, or the entire class. When Ts dealt with course content they spent approximately the same amount of time talking to individual Ss as to the class. Ss talked to other Ss 3.1% of the class time and to the T 1.5% of class time, usually in response to a question. Mathematics was 4 times as likely to be taught to the entire class (ungrouped) as was reading. The gender of the T had no correlation to the individualization of instruction. The socioeconomic status of the school community had no correlation to the measure of either Ss' behaviour or Ts' instruction. Ss' participation was shown to be related to achievement test scores; teaching technique was not. Participation by Ss and teaching techniques were not shown to have any significant correlation to Ss' academic self concept. Whether or not Ss are grouped into small groups for instructional purposes is an important variable to consider when looking at class size. Individual Ts' teaching techniques and classroom behaviour seem very stable. Furthermore, influencing Ss' participation may be more important if one wishes to affect achievement. Bibliography -- 34 items

Descriptors: Class size; Academic achievement; Students; Teaching methods; Elementaryschools

Identifiers: Toronto; Canadian Tests of Basic Skills; Indicators of Quality; NorthYork Self Concept Inventory; Toronto Class Observation Schedule; self-made art and composition measures; Grade 4; Grade 5; Grade 6; 4e annee; 5e annee; 6e annee; Junior Division; Cycle moyen

S "CLASS SIZE" OR "TEACHER STUDENT RATIO"
S S1 AND ZZ="ACADEMIC ACHIEVEMENT"

8 of 8 Complete Record

00107815 Canadian Education Index

Teacher Load, Paraprofessional Assistance and Student Performance inGrade 1
Halpern, Gerald; Cooper, Martin
47 p.
Corporate Source: Ottawa Board of Education
Sponsoring Agency: Ontario. Ministry of Education
Publisher: Ottawa: Ottawa Board of Education, Research Centre
Series: Report; 75-03
Availability: Document available from Micromedia Limited
Micromedia prices: MFx/PCa
ONTERIS Document Number: ON00182
Language: English
Document Type: Research
Geographic Source: Canada; Ontario
Notes: Funding institution: Ontario. Ministry of Education. Grants in Aid of Educational Research
Abstract: Students and teachers in 82 grade 1 classrooms. Data collected 1973-1974. Data collected on 4 teacher-load factors: ratio of student hours to adult (teacher plus assistant) hours (Fl); average class size (F2); number of student

Figure 5.1   cont'd

entrants (F3); and number of student departures (F4) during the year. Instruments measuring reading readiness, word reading, sentence comprehension, computation, mathematical understanding, attitudes toward school, values and self-worth were administered to classes. End of year and gain scores calculated and related to factors by univariate analyses of variance. 7-scale semantic differential instrument administered to teachers. Frequency distributions are tabulated. No scores were related to either F1 or F2. Sentence comprehension gain scores and final scores on reading readiness, word reading and sentence comprehension were lower in classes having 7 or more departures than in classes with 2 or less departures. Classes with fewer leavers tended to possess greater courtesy, honesty, and understanding of others. Classes with small numbers of entrants made greater gains in sentence comprehension than classes with larger numbers of entrants. Teachers had significantly more positive attitudes towards paid paraprofessionals than to unpaid paraprofessionals. The data suggest that class size, within the range represented, is not related to student learning, that unpaid assistants in the classroom did not contribute to student learning and that students who leave their grade 1 classrooms during the year are likely to be better readers.

Descriptors: Class size; Academic achievement; Self concept; Attitudes; Values; Students; Teacher aides; Paraprofessional personnel; Volunteers; Teacher workload; Elementary schools

Identifiers: Ottawa; Ottawa Board of Education, Research Centre tests for the QED Project; self-made semantic differential; Kindergarten; Grade 1; Grade 2; Grade 3; Jardin; 1re annee; 2e annee; 3e annee; Primary Division; Cycle primaire

S "CLASS SIZE" OR "SMALL CLASSES" OR "TEACHER PUPIL RATIO" OR "TEACHER STUDENT RATIO"
S S1 AND "ACADEMIC ACHIEVEMENT"
S S2 AND (RESEARCH OR "RESEARCH METHODOLOGY" OR "RESEARCH REPORTS" OR "EDUCATIONAL RESEARCH")

1 of 1 Complete Record

00186987 British Education Index (BEI)

Class size and student performance: 1984-94
Lucas, Lisa; Simonite, Vanessa; Gibbs Graham
Journal Name: Studies in Higher Education; Vol.21,no.3: Oct 96
Publication Year(s): 1996
Physical Description: p261-273
British Library Document Supply Centre Shelfmark: 8490.633000
Language: English
Country of Publication: England
Notes: Higher Education; Literature Reviews
Descriptors: Educational Trends; Academic Achievement; Class Size; Educational Research; Teacher Student Ratio
Identifiers: England and Wales; United States

Figure 5.1   concluded

Search 2: What are the pros and cons of 'accelerating' gifted elementary school students?

The client is a school counsellor who is responding to an enquiry from a parent wanting to know what has been published since she went to grade school (in the early 1970s), to determine whether her experience will be repeated for her child.

The searcher chooses ERIC as the most suitable resource in which to conduct this search. He starts with an online search using DIALOG. For interest's sake, he repeats the search on the DIALOG version of the BRITISH EDUCATION INDEX, as well as on the SilverPlatter version of ERIC and on the ERIC Web site.

The key topical concepts in this request are 'acceleration' and 'gifted students' at the elementary school level. Verifying these terms in the *Thesaurus of ERIC Descriptors*, the searcher discovers that the current term for the first concept is Acceleration (Education) and previous to November 1982 it was simply Acceleration. There are a number of related terms but none is particularly relevant to this request. The searcher also discovers that Gifted is an authorized descriptor with Academically Gifted as a narrower term.

Stage 1

The first stage in the DIALOG search is to create a set that identifies all the records in the ERIC database that include ACCELERATION (EDUCATION) OR ACCELERATION as a Descriptor (DE). The second stage is to create a set that identifies all the records that include GIFTED OR ACADEMICALLY GIFTED as a descriptor. The third stage is to combine set 1 with set 2 (S1 AND S2) to create set 3 (S3). This results in many more (and most certainly many irrelevant) hits than the client wants to peruse. What is missing from the strategy at this point is any indication of the educational level as well as the parent's perspective and anything to deal with the 'pros and cons' aspect. Incorporating the educational level descriptors Elementary Education OR Elementary Secondary Education (because materials that deal with both levels will be useful) results in the creation of set 4 (S4). Incorporating the additional descriptors Elementary Education OR Elementary School Students results in set 5 (S5). Combining these (S4 AND S5) creates set 6 (S6), which can now be combined with set 3 (S3 AND S6) to create set 7 (S7) with 45 hits. This number is still more than the client wants and includes references to many documents that are not relevant because they omit the parent's perspective and do not focus on the 'pros and cons' aspect.

At this point, the searcher can choose to review the results, focusing first on identifying those records for which the descriptors representing the key concepts are designated as major descriptors. At the same time, the searcher examines the other major descriptors to further determine the relevance of the retrieved records and looks for other clues regarding the perspective and the 'pros and cons' aspect. (Even records for which both key topical concepts are major descriptors may be irrelevant because there are still other topics that constitute a major, and more important, focus of the document.) This done, he can produce a shortlist of highly relevant references for the client.

Alternatively, the searcher can attempt further to refine the search by looking for Parents in the Target Audience field. However, as mentioned previously, as this field is not always present, he may be better advised to attempt a free-text keyword search on 'parent*' to identify records where Parents appears in the Target Audience field, if present; and/or where 'Parent' appears in a descriptor, such as Parent Materials; and/or in the title of the article, the title of the journal, or the abstract. On the other hand, the parent in question may find documents written for practitioners (such as teachers) equally useful, so it may not be necessary to limit to materials specifically for parents, but perhaps to *exclude* those intended for a highly academic audience. The searcher can also choose to refine the search further by identifying descriptors and/or free-text keywords to express the 'pros and cons' aspect. Descriptors such as Curriculum Evaluation OR Program Evaluation OR Program Effectiveness could be incorporated as could keywords such as 'benefits' OR 'advantages' OR 'disadvantages', etc, but these may narrow the search too much and result in an insufficient number of useful hits. Additional consultation with the client will determine whether or not this is so. That one very specific article could be exactly what she requires!

Including the BRITISH EDUCATION INDEX in this DIALOG search presents some challenges to the searcher, mostly derived from differences in terminology. Fortunately, in this case, the same descriptors represent the topical concepts in both the *Thesaurus of ERIC Descriptors* and the *British Education Thesaurus*, so the initial steps in the search strategy are the same. BEI uses different terms for educational level so the searcher now includes Primary Education OR Primary Secondary Education to cover the appropriate educational level, and/or Primary School Pupils OR Primary Education as descriptors in his search strategy. Interestingly, this returns few enough results that any further attempts to refine the search are unnecessary. The searcher can review the results, checking for the placement of the terms representing the key concepts in the list of descriptors (which appear in order of importance). Doing this, he notes that only one of the records includes both Academically Gifted and Acceleration (Education) among the first few descriptors. In this one case, they are the only descriptors. The article describes the acceleration of gifted students in Germany and may or may not be useful to the client. It appears the client is not going to get much transatlantic help for her query! Figure 5.2(a) illustrates the strategy and shows sample results from this search.

```
File   1:ERIC  1966-1998/Jan
       (c) format only 1998 The Dialog Corporation

    Set Items Description
    ---- ------- --------------
?S ACCELERATION/DE OR ACCELERATION(EDUCATION)/DE
          919  ACCELERATION/DE
            0  ACCELERATION(EDUCATION)/DE
    S1     919  ACCELERATION/DE OR ACCELERATION(EDUCATION)/DE
?S GIFTED/DE OR ACADEMICALLY GIFTED/DE
         8819  GIFTED/DE
         1970  ACADEMICALLY GIFTED/DE  (PERSONS WITH SUPERIOR ABILITY OR
                APTITUDE FO...)
    S2    8819  GIFTED/DE OR ACADEMICALLY GIFTED/DE
?S S1 AND S2
          919  S1
         8819  S2
    S3     431  S1 AND S2
?S ELEMENTARY EDUCATION/DE OR ELEMENTARY SECONDARY EDUCATIOIN N/DE
        57368  ELEMENTARY EDUCATION/DE  (EDUCATION PROVIDED IN
                KINDERGARTEN OR GRADE ...)
       129894  ELEMENTARY SECONDARY EDUCATION/DE  (FORMAL EDUCATION
                PROVIDED IN KINDERGARTEN OR...)
    S4  187121  ELEMENTARY EDUCATION/DE OR ELEMENTARY SECONDARY
                EDUCATION/DE
?S ELEMENTARY EDUCATION/DE OR ELEMENTARY SCHOOL STUDENTS/DE
        57368  ELEMENTARY EDUCATION/DE  (EDUCATION PROVIDED IN
                KINDERGARTEN OR GRADE ...)
        16450  ELEMENTARY SCHOOL STUDENTS/DE  ((NOTE: COORDINATE WITH
                THE APPROPRIATE MANDA...)
    S5   67601  ELEMENTARY EDUCATION/DE OR ELEMENTARY SCHOOL STUDENTS/DE
?S S4 AND S5
       187121  S4
        67601  S5
    S6   58905  S4 AND S5
?S S3 AND S6
          431  S3
        58905  S6
    S7      45  S3 AND S6
?DISPLAY S7/2/1-3
   Display 7/2/1
DIALOG(R)File  1:ERIC
(c) format only 1998 The Dialog Corporation. All rts. reserv.

EJ549021  EC616299
 Public or Private Schools: A Dilemma for Gifted Students?
 Witham, Joan H.
 Roeper Review; v19 n3 p137-41 Mar 1997
 ISSN: 0278-3193
```

Figure 5.2(a)   DIALOG search on the pros and cons of 'accelerating' gifted elementary school students

Language: English
Document Type: JOURNAL ARTICLE (080); RESEARCH REPORT (143)
Journal Announcement: CIJJAN98
Descriptors: *Acceleration (Education); *Critical Thinking; *Curriculum Design; *Educational Quality; Elementary Education; *Gifted; Integrated Curriculum; Intermediate Grades; Preschool Education; *Private Schools; Public Schools; Student Needs

- end of record -
?
    Display 7/2/2
DIALOG(R)File   1:ERIC
(c) format only 1998 The Dialog Corporation. All rts. reserv.

EJ501384   EC611016
  Serving Young Gifted Math Students: Educators Offer an Example of Implementing the Center for Talented Youth Model in Public Schools.
  Corazza, Luciano; And Others
  Gifted Child Today Magazine; v18 n2 p20-23,49,50 Mar-Apr 1995
  ISSN: 1076-2175
  Available from: UMI
  Language: English
  Document Type: JOURNAL ARTICLE (080); PROJECT DESCRIPTION (141); RESEARCH REPORT (143)
  Journal Announcement: CIJAUG95
  Target Audience: Practitioners
  Descriptors: *Acceleration (Education); *Diagnostic Teaching; Educational Diagnosis; Elementary Education; *Gifted; Individualized Instruction; *Mathematics Instruction; *Teaching Models
  Identifiers: New York (Brooklyn)

- end of record -
?
    Display 7/2/3
DIALOG(R)File   1:ERIC
(c) format only 1998 The Dialog Corporation. All rts. reserv.

EJ500465   SP523981
  The Multiple Intelligence Approach to Giftedness.
  Hoerr, Thomas R.
  Contemporary Education; v66 n1 p32-35 Fall 1994
  ISSN: 0010-7476
  Available from: UMI
  Language: English
  Document Type: PROJECT DESCRIPTION (141); JOURNAL ARTICLE (080)
  Journal Announcement: CIJJUL95
  Descriptors: Acceleration (Education); Achievement Tests; Curriculum Design; Educational Theories; Elementary Education; Elementary School Students; Evaluation Methods; *Gifted; Intelligence Quotient; *Student Evaluation; *Talent
  Identifiers: *Multiple Intelligences; Test Fairness

Figure 5.2(a)   cont'd

```
                        - end of display -
?S S7 AND PARENT?
              45   S7
           69641   PARENT?
     S8       12   S7 AND PARENT?
?S S7 AND PARENT?/AB
              45   S7
           55707   PARENT?/AB
     S9       12   S7 AND PARENT?/AB
?S S7 AND PARENT?/TI
              45   S7
           13378   PARENT?/TI
     S10       1   S7 AND PARENT?/TI
?S S7 AND TA=PARENTS
              45   S7
            3355   TA=PARENTS
     S11       2   S7 AND TA=PARENTS
?S S7 NOT TA=PRACTITIONERS
              45   S7
          112728   TA=PRACTITIONERS
     S12      33   S7 NOT TA=PRACTITIONERS
?S S7 AND (CURRICULUM EVALUATION OR PROGRAM EVALUATION OR PROGRAM
EFFECTIVENESS)
              45   S7
            5555   CURRICULUM EVALUATION  (DETERMINING THE EFFICACY, VALUE,
                   ETC. OF A S...)
           37223   PROGRAM EVALUATION  (JUDGING THE FEASIBILITY, EFFICACY,
                   VALUE, ET...)
           20652   PROGRAM EFFECTIVENESS  (DEGREE TO WHICH PROGRAMS ARE
                   SUCCESSFUL IN A...)
     S13       5   S7 AND (CURRICULUM EVALUATION OR PROGRAM EVALUATION OR
                   PROGRAM EFFECTIVENESS)
?PAUSE
>>> PAUSE started.
?
```

Figure 5.2(a)   **concluded**

Stage 2

Repeating the search on the most recent SilverPlatter CD-ROM version of ERIC involves the following steps:

1.   Identify those records that include Gifted as a descriptor.
2.   Identify those records that include Academically Gifted as a descriptor.
3.   Combine step 1 with step 2 using the Boolean OR.
4.   Identify those records that include Acceleration (Education) as a descriptor.
5.   Combine step 3 with step 4 using the Boolean AND.
6.   Identify those records that include Elementary Education as a descriptor.

7. Identify those records that include Elementary School Students as a descriptor.
8. Combine step 6 with step 7 using the Boolean OR.
9. Combine step 5 with step 8 using the Boolean AND.

This results in 13 hits – nine from CIJE and four from RIE. Interestingly, none is particularly relevant to the client even though half include both key concepts – that is, Acceleration (Education), and either Gifted or Academically gifted as major descriptors. When the searcher observes what other terms have been identified as major descriptors and what other descriptors (and identifiers) generally have been assigned, it becomes clear why the results are not always highly relevant. In most cases, another or an additional focus is evident. This serves to reinforce the importance of not only looking for required key concepts among the major descriptors but also examining the other descriptors and identifiers – both major and minor – to determine the relevance of the retrieved documents and perhaps discover ways to further refine a search. Figure 5.2(b) shows the strategy and sample records from this search.

```
No.    Records  Request


#1:     1600   GIFTED- in DE

#2:      517   ACADEMICALLY-GIFTED in DE

#3:     2073   #1 or #2
#4:      224   ACCELERATION-EDUCATION in DE
#5:      130   #3 and #4
#6:    13760   ELEMENTARY-EDUCATION in DE
#7:     5100   ELEMENTARY-SCHOOL-STUDENTS in DE
#8:    16460   #6 or #7
#9:       13   #5 and #8
                                                          1 of 13
AN: EJ549021
CHN: EC616299
AU: Witham,-Joan-H.
TI: Public or Private Schools: A Dilemma for Gifted Students?
PY: 1997
JN: Roeper-Review; v19 n3 p137-41 Mar 1997
SN: ISSN-0278-3193
DT: Journal Articles (080); Reports - Research (143)
LA: English
```

Figure 5.2(b)   ERIC search on the pros and cons of 'accelerating' gifted elementary school students (SilverPlatter disc)

DE: Elementary-Education; Integrated-Curriculum; Intermediate-Grades;
Preschool-Education; Public-Schools; Student-Needs
DE: *Acceleration-Education; *Critical-Thinking; *Curriculum-Design;
*Educational-Quality; *Gifted-; *Private-Schools
IS: CIJJAN98
AB: Twenty-four school programs were studied to investigate whether public and
private schools differed in their frequency of meeting the needs of gifted
students for acceleration, curriculum integration, and critical thinking
skills. Differences were found in the use of critical thinking skills and
acceleration but not for curriculum integration. (CR)
CH: EC
FI: EJ
DTN: 080; 143

AN: EJ501384

CHN: EC611016

AU: Corazza,-Luciano; And-Others

TI: Serving Young Gifted Math Students: Educators Offer an Example of
Implementing the Center for Talented Youth Model in Public Schools.
PY: 1995
JN: Gifted-Child-Today-Magazine; v18 n2 p20-23,49,50 Mar-Apr 1995
SN: ISSN-1076-2175
AV: UMI
DT: Journal Articles (080); Reports - Descriptive (141); Reports - Research
(143)
TA: Practitioners
LA: English
DE: Educational-Diagnosis; Elementary-Education; Individualized-Instruction
DE: *Acceleration-Education; *Diagnostic-Teaching; *Gifted-;
*Mathematics-Instruction; *Teaching-Models
ID: New-York-Brooklyn
IS: CIJAUG95
AB: This article describes the implementation in Brooklyn, New York, of the
Diagnostic Testing and Prescriptive Instruction mathematics instruction model,
which establishes the level of knowledge of each student and then offers
instruction at the student's pace. Implementation involves teacher training,
student selection, curriculum development, and program evaluation. (PB)
CH: EC
FI: EJ
DTN: 080; 141; 143

AN: EJ500465
CHN: SP523981
AU: Hoerr,-Thomas-R.
TI: The Multiple Intelligence Approach to Giftedness.

Figure 5.2(b)   cont'd

PY: 1994
JN: Contemporary-Education; v66 n1 p32-35 Fall 1994
SN: ISSN-0010-7476
AV: UMI
DT: Reports - Descriptive (141); Journal Articles (080)
LA: English
DE: Acceleration-Education; Achievement-Tests; Curriculum-Design;
Educational-Theories; Elementary-Education; Elementary-School-Students;
Evaluation-Methods; Intelligence-Quotient
DE: *Gifted-; *Student-Evaluation; *Talent-
ID: Test-Fairness
ID: *Multiple-Intelligences
IS: CIJJUL95
AB: Performance on one test captures neither the nuances of intellect nor the
criteria for giftedness. The theory of multiple intelligences (MI) greatly
enhances discourse on the nature of giftedness. The paper explains MI beyond
the linguistic and logical-mathematical traditionally esteemed in schools,
highlighting MI theory at one Missouri school. (SM)
CH: SP
FI: EJ
DTN: 141; 080

4 of 13

AN: EJ496901
CHN: SE553558
AU: Mills,-Carol-J.; And-Others
TI: Academically Talented Students' Achievement in a Flexibly Paced Mathematics
Program.
PY: 1994
JN: Journal-for-Research-in-Mathematics-Education; v25 n5 p495-511 Nov 1994
SN: ISSN-0021-8251
AV: UMI
DT: Reports - Research (143); Journal Articles (080)
LA: English
DE: Elementary-Education; Grade-3; Grade-4; Grade-5; Grade-6;
Mathematics-Education; Mathematics-Instruction
DE: *Academically-Gifted; *Acceleration-Education; *Advanced-Courses;
*Elementary-School-Students; *Mathematics-Achievement; *Teaching-Methods
ID: Johns-Hopkins-University-MD; Mathematics-Courses;
Mathematics-Education-Research
IS: CIJMAY95
AB: Third- through sixth-grade mathematically talented students (n=306)
enrolled in a flexibly paced university mathematics course far exceeded the
normative achievement gains expected over a one-year period. Restricting such
students to a rigid instructional pace may have a deleterious effect on
motivation and achievement. (64 references) (MKR)
CH: SE
FI: EJ
DTN: 143; 080

5 of 13

Figure 5.2(b)   **cont'd**

AN: EJ472629
CHN: EC607067
AU: Cramond,-Bonnie
TI: Speaking and Listening: Key Components of a Complete Language Arts Program for the Gifted.
PY: 1993
JN: Roeper-Review; v16 n1 p44-48 Sep 1993
SN: ISSN-0278-3193
AV: UMI
DT: Journal Articles (080)
TA: Practitioners
LA: English
DE: Acceleration-Education; Elementary-Education; Enrichment-Activities; Individualized-Instruction
DE: *Gifted-; *Language-Arts; *Listening-Skills; *Speech-Improvement; *Teaching-Methods
ID: Differentiated-Curriculum-Gifted
IS: CIJMAR94
AB: Differentiated instruction in speaking and listening skills for gifted students might involve an expanded range of opportunity, faster paced instruction, replacement of basic skills instruction with more advanced activities, opportunities for self-selection, individualization, and personal evaluation. Activities that emphasize cognitive and affective development are encouraged. (DB)
CH: EC
FI: EJ
DTN: 080; 120; 055

6 of 13

AN: EJ470812
CHN: EC607056
AU: Sowell,-Evelyn-J.
TI: Programs for Mathematically Gifted Students: A Review of Empirical Research.
PY: 1993
JN: Gifted-Child-Quarterly; v37 n3 p124-32 Sum 1993
SN: ISSN-0016-9862
AV: UMI
DT: Journal Articles (080)
LA: English
DE: Computer-Assisted-Instruction; Elementary-Education; Enrichment-Activities
DE: *Ability-Grouping; *Academically-Gifted; *Acceleration-Education; *Instructional-Effectiveness; *Mathematics-Instruction
IS: CIJFEB94
AB: This literature review on programs for mathematically gifted elementary students concludes that effective programs include providing an accelerated curriculum and grouping mathematically gifted students together. The long-term effectiveness of technology-based instruction needs further research as do the topics of curriculum enrichment and other non-computer-based instructional approaches. (Author/DB)
CH: EC

Figure 5.2(b)   cont'd

FI: EJ
DTN: 080; 070; 120

AN: EJ452818
CHN: EA527260
AU: Howells,-Ronald-F.
TI: Thinking in the Morning, Thinking in the Evening, Thinking at Suppertime.
PY: 1992
JN: Phi-Delta-Kappan; v74 n3 p223-25 Nov 1992
SN: ISSN-0031-7217
AV: UMI
DT: Journal Articles (080)
LA: English
DE: Elementary-Education
DE: *Acceleration-Education; *Enrichment-Activities; *Gifted-;
*Identification-; *Minority-Groups; *Pilot-Projects
ID: *Palm-Beach-County-Schools-FL
IS: CIJMAR93
AB: Concerned about the serious underrepresentation of culturally different
students in gifted programs, the Palm Beach County (Florida) Schools developed
a pilot project that established a system for identifying minority students
with potential and for designing a course of study to meet their educational
needs. The program featured enrichment, affective, and accelerated academic
components. (four references) (MLH)
CH: EA
FI: EJ
DTN: 080; 142

AN: EJ450061
CHN: EC603781
AU: Lupkowski,-Ann-E.; And-Others
TI: Mentors in Math.
PY: 1992
JN: Gifted-Child-Today-(GCT); v15 n3 p26-31 May-Jun 1992
SN: ISSN-0892-9580
AV: UMI
NT: Emphasis this issue: Mentoring.
DT: Journal Articles (080)
LA: English
DE: Ability-Identification; Elementary-Education;
Elementary-School-Mathematics; Eligibility-; Pacing-; Program-Development;
Program-Implementation; Student-Evaluation
DE: *Acceleration-Education; *Gifted-; *Individualized-Programs;
*Mathematics-Education; *Mentors-
ID: *Investigation-Mathematically-Advanced-Elem-Stu;
*Julian-C-Stanley-Mentor-Program
IS: CIJJAN93
AB: Two individualized, mentor-paced programs for elementary school students
who are extremely talented in mathematics are described--the Julian C. Stanley

Figure 5.2(b)   cont'd

Mentor Program and the Investigation of Mathematically Advanced Elementary Students. The paper discusses eligibility, level of instruction, mentor selection, student evaluation, and other program administration issues. (JDD)
CH: EC
FI: EJ
DTN: 080; 141

AN: EJ439470
CHN: EC602142
AU: Steele,-Kathleen-J.
TI: Improving the Quality of Elementary Education through Full Time Gifted Classes.
PY: 1991
JN: Gifted-Child-Today-(GCT); v14 n6 p52-55 Nov-Dec 1991
SN: ISSN-0892-9580
AV: UMI
DT: Journal Articles (080)
TA: Administrators; Practitioners
LA: English
DE: Acceleration-Education; Educational-Quality; Elementary-Education; Enrichment-Activities; Homogeneous-Grouping
DE: *Educational-Improvement; *Gifted-; *Program-Development; *Special-Classes
IS: CIJJUN92
AB: A small-town school corporation developed self-contained, full-time gifted classes for its elementary school students. This article describes program administration, acceleration and enrichment activities, staffing, and efforts to expand the benefits of the program to others. (JDD)
CH: EC
FI: EJ
DTN: 080; 141

AN: ED365758
CHN: UD029654
AU: Hopfenberg,-Wendy-S.; And-Others
TI: The Accelerated Schools Resource Guide.
PY: 1993
SN: ISBN-1-55542-545-3
AV: Jossey-Bass Inc., Publishers, 350 Sansome Street, San Francisco, CA 94104-1310.
NT: 390 p.
PR: Document Not Available from EDRS.
DT: Books (010)
CP: U.S.; New-York
TA: Practitioners
LA: English
PG: 390
DE: Academically-Gifted; Case-Studies; Educational-Cooperation; Elementary-Education; Elementary-Schools; Family-School-Relationship; Guides-; Middle-Schools; School-Community-Relationship

Figure 5.2(b)   **cont'd**

DE: *Acceleration-Education; *Educational-Change; *Learning-Strategies;
*Problem-Solving; *Resource-Materials
ID: *Accelerated-Schools
IS: RIEMAY94
AB: This resource guide represents the first comprehensive guide to the
innovative practices of accelerated schools. It is designed to be used by a
wide variety of participants as a supplement for training, as well as for
discussion and guidance in the move to transform schools nationwide. Eleven
chapters include detailed descriptions of the accelerated schools philosophy
and process, rich vignettes, case studies, and examples from actual accelerated
schools, in addition to drawings, exercises, and additional resources.
Chapters: (1) provide a rationale for having accelerated schools; (2) outline
the philosophies and processes of these schools, including getting them
started, the crucial nature of problem solving, and the inquiry process; (3)
show how accelerated schools' principles and values relate to effective
collaboration; (4) describe the changes in teaching, learning, and family
involvement that have occurred in accelerated schools as a result of using
their philosophy and process; (5) discuss the beliefs about powerful learning
strategies as presently provided to gifted and talented children; (6) offer
examples of how families and communities become involved in their accelerated
school communities; and (7) suggest tips on school assessment. An appendix
examines the inquiry process. (Contains over 150 references.) (GLR)
LV: 3
CH: UD
FI: ED
DTN: 010; 055

AN: ED364021
CHN: EC302591
TI: Visual Arts Grades Five through Eight. Black Swamp Arts Scene Course of
Study: Talented and Gifted.
CS: Defiance County Office of Education, OH.
PY: [1991]
NT: 50 p.; For related documents, see EC 302 589-590.
PR: EDRS Price - MF01/PC02 Plus Postage.
DT: Guides - Classroom - Teacher (052)
CP: U.S.; Ohio
TA: Practitioners; Teachers
LA: English
PG: 50
DE: Acceleration-Education; Beliefs-; Educational-Philosophy;
Elementary-School-Students; Enrichment-Activities; Freehand-Drawing;
Graphic-Arts; Intermediate-Grades; Junior-High-Schools;
Junior-High-School-Students; Painting-Visual-Arts; Photography-;
Public-Schools; Sculpture-; Sequential-Learning; Units-of-Study; Values-
DE: *Gifted-; *Talent-; *Visual-Arts
IS: RIEAPR94
AB: This course of study was developed for intermediate and junior high
students in the Defiance (Ohio) public schools who are talented and gifted in
the visual arts, providing for an in-depth and sequential development of skills

Figure 5.2(b)   **cont'd**

and concepts. The program's philosophy stresses that, while the products of the arts are important, a need exists to emphasize the learning process as satisfying in and of itself. It focuses on sensitizing the whole person to the arts and to developing the imagination. Options in meeting the needs of gifted students in visual arts include accelerated educational experiences in cluster groups within regular classrooms or in enriched classrooms serving gifted children. A scope and sequence chart for grades 5 through 8 lists program and subject objectives for several components of a visual arts course of study, covering drawing, graphic design, painting, photography, printmaking, and sculpture. Within each component, objectives focus on enabling students to: (1) become aware of ways society expresses values and beliefs in art and responds to art; (2) develop their abilities to respond to works of art; (3) understand how artists express themselves; and (4) understand how art critics and historians respond to art. Methods of evaluating student progress are noted. (JDD)
LV: 1
CH: EC
FI: ED
DTN: 052

AN: ED364019
CHN: EC302589
TI: Music: Grades Five through Eight. Black Swamp Arts Scene Course of Study: Talented and Gifted.
CS: Defiance County Office of Education, OH.
PY: [1991]
NT: 48 p.; For related documents, see EC 302 590-591.
PR: EDRS Price - MF01/PC02 Plus Postage.
DT: Guides - Classroom - Teacher (052)
CP: U.S.; Ohio
TA: Practitioners; Teachers
LA: English
PG: 48
DE: Acceleration-Education; Educational-Philosophy; Elementary-School-Students; Enrichment-Activities; Intermediate-Grades; Junior-High-Schools; Junior-High-School-Students; Public-Schools; Sequential-Learning; Units-of-Study
DE: *Gifted-; *Music-Appreciation; *Music-Education; *Music-Theory; *Talent-
IS: RIEAPR94
AB: This course of study was developed for intermediate and junior high students in the Defiance (Ohio) public schools who are talented and gifted in music, providing for an indepth and sequential development of the skills and concepts involved. The program's philosophy stresses that, while the products of the arts are important, a need exists to emphasize the learning process as satisfying in and of itself. It focuses on sensitizing the whole person to the arts and to developing the imagination. Options in meeting the needs of gifted students in music include accelerated educational experiences in cluster groups within regular classrooms or in enriched music classrooms serving gifted children. A scope and sequence chart for grades 5 through 8 lists program and subject objectives for several components of a music curriculum, covering

Figure 5.2(b)   **cont'd**

pitch, duration, timbre, texture, form, and style. A scope and sequence chart for music theory/appreciation addresses the same curriculum components in addition to loudness and technical objectives. Methods of evaluating student progress are noted. (JDD)
LV: 1
CH: EC
FI: ED
DTN: 052

AN: ED336465
CHN: UD028219
AU: Davidson,-Mary-E.; And-Others
TI: Monitoring Commission's Memorandum on the Admission Processes for Certain Elementary Options for Knowledge Programs.
CS: Chicago Public Schools, IL. Monitoring Commission for Desegregation Implementation.
PY: 1988
NT: 49 p.; For a complete set of Commission Reports, see UD 028 213-233.
PR: EDRS Price - MF01/PC02 Plus Postage.
DT: Reports - Descriptive (141)
CP: U.S.; Illinois
LA: English
PG: 49
DE: Competitive-Selection; Desegregation-Methods; Elementary-Education; Open-Enrollment; Racial-Composition; School-Desegregation; Urban-Schools
DE: *Academically-Gifted; *Acceleration-Education; *Achievement-Tests; *Admission-Criteria; *Magnet-Schools
ID: Iowa-Tests-of-Basic-Skills
ID: *Chicago-Public-Schools-IL
IS: RIEJAN92
AB: This document describes the procedures required for applicants to gain admission during the 1986-87 school year to certain elementary school Options for Knowledge (OFK) programs in Chicago (Illinois). Elementary magnet schools and programs that do not contain a testing requirement for admission are open to students who wish to attend by transferring from their home-school attendance and completing an application. The number of available spaces is estimated and categorized by race. Applications are categorized by race, grade, and sex to avoid in-school segregation. The enrollment of siblings and transportation needs are also considered. Applicant is interviewed to determine their potential for success. If there are more qualified applicants than available spaces, a lottery is conducted to determine which applicants will be admitted. Elementary "Classical Schools," which are sites for academically accelerated programs, and Gifted Programs require student testing for admission. The preliminary screening and the lottery process used by the magnet schools and programs is also used by the Classical Schools and Gifted Programs. In addition, applicants must meet criteria based on scores on the Iowa Test of Basic Skills (ITBS) and other standardized achievement tests in order to enter the lottery. Two administrative memoranda; descriptions of the elementary magnet schools and programs, the Classical Schools, and the Gifted Programs; and a map of OFK schools are appended. (FMW)

Figure 5.2(b)   cont'd

```
LV: 1
CH: UD
FI: ED
DTN: 141
```

Figure 5.2(b)   **concluded**

Stage 3

The searcher can also 'replicate' (to a degree) this online and CD-ROM search of the ERIC database on the Web-based version. From the homepage of the ERIC Web site <URL http://ericir.syr.edu/> the searcher chooses the 'Search ERIC Database' option. On the search page form, he types 'gifted or academically gifted' (without quotes) in the Term 1 search box, chooses Descriptor from the first pull-down Search by menu accompanying Term 1, and AND from the second pull-down menu. He then types 'acceleration (education) or acceleration' in the Term 2 search box, and chooses Descriptor and AND from the accompanying pull-down menus. Finally, he types 'elementary education or elementary secondary education or elementary school students' in the Term 3 search box and chooses Descriptor from the accompanying pull-down menu. He selects 25 as the maximum number of results to display and clicks on the Submit button. This results in 25 of 102 hits from the ERIC database for 1989 onwards displayed in ranked order with a relevance rating out of 1000. The highest rating is only 272, indicating that according to the ranking system used there are not very many documents that satisfy *all* the stated criteria. This does not mean, however, that the retrieved documents will not be relevant to the client's request. The ranking is very much an arbitrary one done by the computer and not 'evaluative' in the sense that a human ranking would/could be. The searcher (with or without the client's input) must review the hits as described above to determine their relevance and produce the final results list. Figure 5.2(c) shows the strategy and sample results from this search.

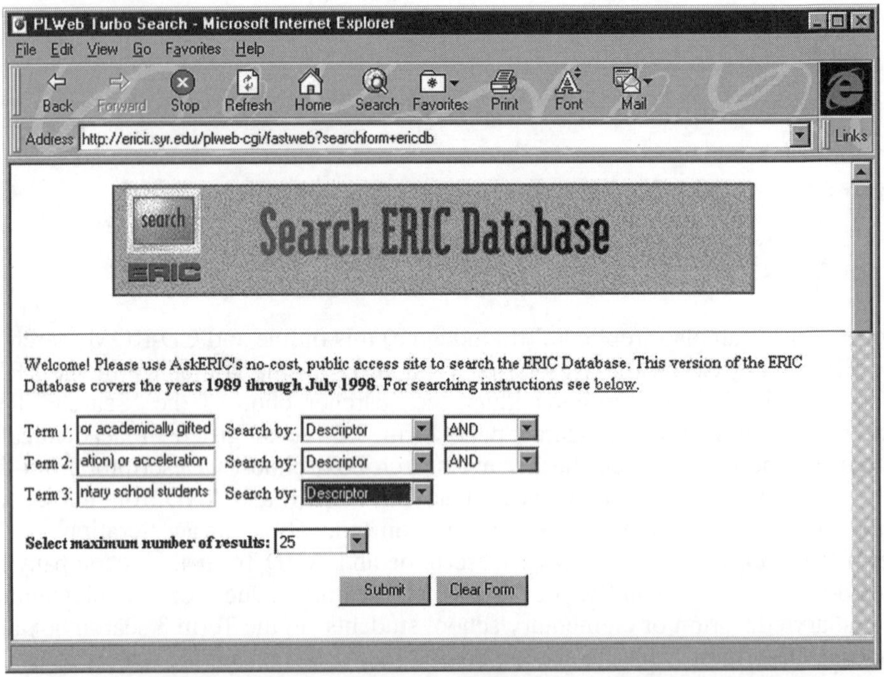

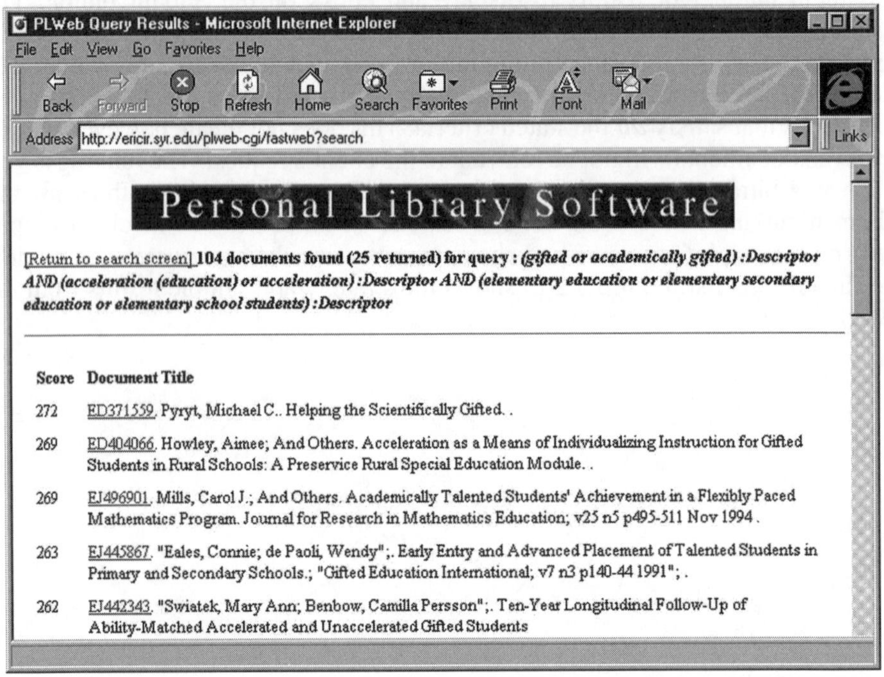

Figure 5.2(c)   **ERIC search on the pros and cons of 'accelerating' gifted elementary school students (World Wide Web)**

104 documents found (25 returned) for query : (gifted or academically gifted)
:Descriptor AND (acceleration (education) or acceleration) :Descriptor AND (elementary
education or elementary secondary education or elementary school students)
:Descriptor

Score Document   Title
272   ED371559. Pyryt, Michael C.. Helping the Scientifically Gifted.
269   ED404066. Howley, Aimee; And Others. Acceleration as a Means of
      Individualizing Instruction for Gifted Students in Rural Schools: A Preservice Rural
      Special Education Module.
269   EJ496901. Mills, Carol J.; And Others. Academically Talented Students'
      Achievement in a Flexibly Paced Mathematics Program. Journal for Research in
      Mathematics Education; v25 n5 p495-511 Nov 1994
263   EJ445867. "Eales, Connie; de Paoli, Wendy";. Early Entry and Advanced
      Placement of Talented Students in Primary and Secondary Schools.; "Gifted
      Education International; v7 n3 p140-44 1991";
262   EJ442343. "Swiatek, Mary Ann; Benbow, Camilla Persson";. Ten-Year
      Longitudinal Follow-Up of Ability-Matched Accelerated and Unaccelerated Gifted
      Students.; "Journal of Educational Psychology; v83 n4 p528-38 Dec 1991";
262   ED334217. "Titus, Janet C.; Terwilliger, James S.";. Gender Differences in
      Attitudes, Aptitude, and Achievement in a Program for Mathematically Talented
      Youth.;
260   EJ445889. "Callahan, Carolyn M.; Hunsaker, Scott L.";. To Accelerate or Not to
      Accelerate: Evaluation Gives the Answer.; "Gifted Child Today (GCT); v15 n2 p50-
      56 Mar-Apr 1992";
259   EJ445886. "Southern, W. Thomas; Jones, Eric D.";. The Real Problems with
      Academic Acceleration.; "Gifted Child Today (GCT); v15 n2 p34-38 Mar-Apr
      1992";
258   EJ434418. Harrington-Lueker, Donna;. Empty Promises.; "Executive Educator; v13
      n11 p18-25 Nov 1991";
219   EJ519832. Miller, Richard; And Others. The Appalachia Model Mathematics
      Program for Gifted Students. Roeper Review; v18 n2 p138-41 Dec 1995
207   ED343330. Rogers, Karen B.;. The Relationship of Grouping Practices to the
      Education of the Gifted and Talented Learner. Executive Summary. Research-Based
      Decision Making Series.;
207   ED343329. Rogers, Karen B.;. The Relationship of Grouping Practices to the
      Education of the Gifted and Talented Learner: Research-Based Decision Making
      Series.;
206   EJ462532. Swiatek, Mary Ann. A Decade of Longitudinal Research on Academic
      Acceleration through the Study of Mathematically Precocious Youth. Roeper
      Review; v15 n3 p120-24 Feb-Mar 1993
206   EJ494767. Gross, Miraca U. M.. Radical Acceleration: Responding to Academic
      and Social Needs of Extremely Gifted Adolescents. Journal of Secondary Gifted
      Education; v5 n4 p27-34 Sum 1994
204   EJ451480. Rogers, Karen B.; Kimpston, Richard D.. Acceleration: What We Do vs.
      What We Know. Educational Leadership; v50 n2 p58-61 Oct 1992 1992
204   ED353720. Howley, Craig. Keeping Children Gifted: How It Happens and How It
      Doesn't.
204   EJ500225. Ream, Sieglinde Kopp; Zollman, Alan. Failing the Needs of the Gifted:
      The Argument for Academic Acceleration of Extremely Gifted Mathematics
      Students. Focus on Learning Problems in Mathematics; v16 n4 p31-42 Fall 1994

Figure 5.2(c)   cont'd

203   EJ450025. Gross, Miraca U. M.. The Use of Radical Acceleration in Cases of Extreme Intellectual Precocity. Gifted Child Quarterly; v36 n2 p91-99 Spr 1992 .

203   EJ450021. VanTassel-Baska, Joyce. Educational Decision Making on Acceleration and Grouping. Gifted Child Quarterly; v36 n2 p68-72 Spr 1992

203   EJ508309. Merlin, Debrah S.. Adventures in Acceleration: A Mother's Perspective. Gifted Child Today Magazine; v18 n4 p14-17 Jul-Aug 1995 1995

202   EJ530667. Stanley, Julian C.; And Others. Educational Trajectories: Radical Accelerates Provide Insights. Gifted Child Today Magazine; v19 n2 p18-21,38-39 Mar-Apr 1996

201   EJ549068. Merlin, Debrah S.. Adventures in Radical Acceleration: A Mother's Perspective. Gifted Child Today Magazine; v20 n2 p38-41,48-49 Mar-Apr 1997

201   EJ481442. Lupkowski-Shoplik, Ann E.; Assouline, Susan G.. Evidence of Extreme Mathematical Precocity: Case Studies of Talented Youths. Roeper Review; v16 n3 p144-51 Feb 1994

201   ED370295. Lynch, Sharon J.. Should Gifted Students Be Grade-Advanced? ERIC Digest E526.

201   ED387992. White, Linda A.. Acceleration--A Viable Option for Gifted Children.

Figure 5.2(c)   concluded

Search 3: What strategies are appropriate for teaching problem-solving to K-12 students with learning disabilities?

The client is a special education teacher who is particularly interested in mathematics instruction.

As in the other searches, the searcher begins by identifying the key topical concepts in the client's request and verifying them in a standard thesaurus. The *Thesaurus of ERIC Descriptors* gives Learning Disabilities and Problem Solving as pre-coordinated descriptors sufficient to express these two important facets of the query. It also gives Teaching Methods and the related term, Learning Strategies, as likely descriptors to express the 'strategies' aspect of the query. A search on the SilverPlatter version of ERIC combining Learning Disabilities AND Problem Solving AND (Teaching Methods OR Learning Strategies) results in 43 hits – more than either the searcher or client wants to examine.

Further consultation with the client leads the searcher to introduce the free-text keywords 'mathematics' OR 'arithmetic' to limit the results to documents dealing with mathematics instruction; references pertaining to the social studies were not relevant. Finally, references to post-secondary education were excluded from the search using the Boolean NOT. This brings the hits down to a manageable 30, the most relevant of which have Learning Disabilities, Mathematics Instruction and Problem Solving among the major descriptors. Figure 5.3 shows the strategy and sample results for this search.

```
No.   Records  Request

#1:    2408   LEARNING-DISABILITIES in DE
#2:    5369   PROBLEM-SOLVING in DE
#3:   16282   TEACHING-METHODS in DE
#4:    3481   LEARNING-STRATEGIES in DE
#5:   18560   #3 or #4
#6:      43   #1 and #2 and #5
#7:   11748   MATHEMATICS
#8:     581   ARITHMETIC
#9:   11878   #7 or #8
#10:     34   #6 and #9
#11:   5366   POSTSECONDARY-EDUCATION in DE
#12:  55205   HIGHER-EDUCATION in DE
#13:  59863   #11 or #12
#14:     30   #10 not #13
```

                                            1 of 30
AN: ED410697
CHN: EC305747
AU: Jitendra,-Asha-K.; Hoff,-Kathryn; Beck,-Michelle-M.
TI: The Role of Schema-Based Instruction on Solving Multistep Word Problems.
PY: 1997
NT: 16 p.; Paper presented at the Annual Convention of the Council for
Exceptional Children (75th, Salt Lake City, UT, April 9-13, 1997).
PR: EDRS Price - MF01/PC01 Plus Postage.
DT: Reports - Research (143); Speeches /Meeting Papers (150)
CP: U.S.; Pennsylvania
LA: English
PG: 16
DE: Classroom-Techniques; Generalization-; Intermediate-Grades;
Learning-Strategies; Maintenance-; Mathematics-Instruction; Problem-Solving;
Remedial-Instruction; Teaching-Methods; Thinking-Skills
DE: *Instructional-Effectiveness; *Learning-Disabilities;
*Remedial-Mathematics; *Schemata-Cognition; *Word-Problems-Mathematics
IS: RIEJAN98
AB: This study investigated the effectiveness of a schema strategy on the
addition and subtraction word problem solving performance of four sixth and
seventh grade students with learning disabilities. Students were taught to map
features of the word problem onto problem schemata diagrams, first for one-step
problems and then for two-step problems. A multiple-baseline design across
students and across two behaviors was used. Results indicated that the schema
strategy led to increases in the percentage correct of operations and
computation solutions to word problems. Further, these results were maintained
at 2- and 4-week follow-up, and all four students' performance on two-step word
problems (mean of 86 percent correct) at the end of the study surpassed that of
the normative sample (mean of 54 percent correct). Generalization of strategy
effects was found for three of the four students. Student treatment
acceptability ratings revealed that the strategy was perceived as helpful in

Figure 5.3   **ERIC search on appropriate strategies for teaching problem-solving to K-12
students with learning disabilities (SilverPlatter disc)**

solving word problems. (Author/DB)
LV: 1
CH: EC
FI: ED
DTN: 143; 150

2 of 30

AN: EJ542706
CHN: EC616022
AU: Patton,-James-R.; And-Others
TI: A Life Skills Approach to Mathematics Instruction: Preparing Students with Learning Disabilities for the Real-Life Math Demands of Adulthood.
PY: 1997
JN: Journal-of-Learning-Disabilities; v30 n2 p178-87 Mar-Apr 1997
SN: ISSN-0022-2194
DT: Journal Articles (080); Guides - Non-classroom (055)
TA: Teachers; Practitioners
LA: English
DE: Elementary-Secondary-Education; Teaching-Methods
DE: *Daily-Living-Skills; *Learning-Disabilities; *Mathematics-Instruction; *Problem-Solving; *Thinking-Skills
IS: CIJSEP97
AB: Describes ways in which general mathematics instruction for students with learning disabilities can focus on math skills needed in daily life in the home, community, and on the job. A table charts the math skills needed for specific life demands. Also addresses life-skills math in the context of reform and curricular considerations. (DB)
CH: EC
FI: EJ
DTN: 080; 055

3 of 30

AN: EJ542705
CHN: EC616021
AU: Montague,-Majorie
TI: Cognitive Strategy Instruction in Mathematics for Students with Learning Disabilities.
PY: 1997
JN: Journal-of-Learning-Disabilities; v30 n2 p164-77 Mar-Apr 1997
SN: ISSN-0022-2194
DT: Journal Articles (080); Guides - Non-classroom (055)
TA: Teachers; Practitioners
LA: English
DE: Elementary-Secondary-Education; Instructional-Design; Junior-High-Schools; Material-Development; Metacognition-; Middle-Schools; Teaching-Methods; Thinking-Skills
DE: *Cognitive-Structures; *Learning-Disabilities; *Learning-Strategies; *Mathematics-Instruction; *Problem-Solving
IS: CIJSEP97
AB: Discusses the use of cognitive strategy instruction to improve students' performance in mathematics. The theoretical and research base for strategy

Figure 5.3   cont'd

instruction is reviewed, and developmental characteristics of students who have difficulties in mathematics are examined. A practical example of cognitive strategy instruction illustrates assessment and teaching of mathematical problem solving to middle school students with learning disabilities. (Author/DB)
CH: EC
FI: EJ
DTN: 080; 055

AN: EJ542703
CHN: EC616019
AU: Thornton,-Carol-A.; And-Others
TI: Mathematics Instruction for Elementary Students with Learning Disabilities.
PY: 1997
JN: Journal-of-Learning-Disabilities; v30 n2 p142-50 Mar-Apr 1997
SN: ISSN-0022-2194
DT: Journal Articles (080); Information Analyses - General (070); Guides - Non-classroom (055)
TA: Teachers; Practitioners
LA: English
DE: Cognitive-Processes; Cooperative-Learning; Elementary-Education; Learning-Strategies; Teaching-Methods
DE: *Learning-Disabilities; *Mathematics-Instruction; *Problem-Solving; *Thinking-Skills
IS: CIJSEP97
AB: Recent research in mathematics instruction underscores the importance of problem solving and higher-level thinking. This article presents four themes in instruction for students with learning disabilities: (1) provide a broad, balanced mathematics curriculum; (2) engage students in meaningful problem tasks; (3) accommodate diverse learning styles; and (4) encourage students to discuss and justify their problem-solving strategies and solutions. (Author/DB)
CH: EC
FI: EJ
DTN: 080; 070; 055

AN: EJ541031
CHN: EC615875
AU: Woodward,-John; Baxter,-Juliet
TI: The Effects of an Innovative Approach to Mathematics on Academically Low-Achieving Students in Inclusive Settings.
PY: 1997
JN: Exceptional-Children; v63 n3 p373-88 Spr 1997
SN: ISSN-0014-4029
DT: Journal Articles (080); Reports - Research (143); Reports - Descriptive (141)
LA: English
DE: Educational-Games; High-Risk-Students; Low-Achievement; Problem-Solving; Remedial-Instruction
DE: *Inclusive-Schools; *Instructional-Effectiveness;

Figure 5.3   cont'd

*Instructional-Innovation; *Learning-Disabilities; ^Mathematics-Instruction;
*Teaching-Methods
IS: CIJAUG97
AB: A year-long study of an innovative approach to mathematics, which
emphasized in-depth problem solving and achievement of automaticity through
math games, found such methods to be viable for students with average and above
average academic abilities, but students with learning disabilities or at-risk
students need much greater assistance if they are to be included in general
education classrooms. (Author/DB)
CH: EC
FI: EJ
DTN: 080; 143; 141

6 of 30

AN: EJ540978
CHN: EC615650
AU: Montague,-Marjorie
TI: Student Perception, Mathematical Problem Solving, and Learning
Disabilities.
PY: 1997
JN: Remedial-and-Special-Education; v18 n1 p46-53 Jan-Feb 1997
SN: ISSN-0741-9325
DT: Journal Articles (080); Information Analyses - General (070)
LA: English
DE: Difficulty-Level; Influences-; Mathematics-Achievement; Mathematics-Skills;
Middle-Schools; Problem-Solving; Student-Evaluation; Teaching-Methods
DE: *Learning-Disabilities; *Mathematics-Instruction; *Self-Concept;
*Student-Attitudes
IS: CIJAUG97
AB: Presents findings from five studies measuring students' attitudes towards
mathematics, perception of performance, perception of the importance of
mathematical problem solving, and perception of problem difficulty. The
interaction of affect and cognition and the implications for assessing and
teaching mathematical problem solving to students with learning disabilities
are discussed. (Author/CR)
CH: EC
FI: EJ
DTN: 080; 070

7 of 30

AN: ED402186
CHN: SE059452
AU: Van-Luit,-Johannes-E.-H., Ed.
TI: Research on Learning and Instruction of Mathematics in Kindergarten and
Primary School.
PY: 1994
SN: ISBN-90-75129-01-7
AV: Graviant Publishing Company, Esdoornlaan 15, 7004 BA Doetinchem, The
Netherlands.
NT: 368 p.
PR: Document Not Available from EDRS.

Figure 5.3   cont'd

DT: Information Analyses - General (070); Reports - Research (143)
CP: Netherlands
LA: English
PG: 368
DE: Academic-Achievement; Arithmetic-; Cooperative-Learning;
Early-Childhood-Education; Elementary-Education; Evaluation-; Problem-Solving;
Teaching-Methods; Word-Problems-Mathematics
DE: *Educational-Strategies; *Learning-Disabilities; *Learning-Strategies;
*Mathematics-Instruction; *Special-Education
IS: RIEAPR97
AB: Recognition of the importance of (special) children's learning of
mathematics in an active fashion has increased rapidly since the beginning of
the 1980s. This book presents current ideas and trends in the teaching of
mathematics and aims at giving an overview of new developments in the field of
(special) mathematics and showing how researchers use methodological analyses
to prove the results of their study. Sections are divided by topic as follows:
Issues on the Organization of Pupils and Schools, Knowledge and Learning in
Mental Arithmetic, Knowledge and Learning with Arithmetic Materials and Texts,
and Special Children. Chapters include: (1) "Current Trends in Research on
Learning and Instruction of Mathematics" (J.E.H. Van Luit); (2) "New Chances
for Paper-and-Pencil Tests in Mathematics Education" (M. Van den
Heuvel-Panhuizen); (3) "A Method To Diagnose Arithmetic Disabilities" (J.E.H.
Van Luit); (4) "On the Initial Learning of Mathematics: Does Schooling Really
Help?" (M. Frontera); (5) "Classrooms as Contexts To Learn How To Act in a
Conceptual Environment: An Arithmetic Word Problem Solving Case Study" (P.
Sorzio); (6) "Groups That Work: Social Factors in Elementary Students'
Mathematics Problem Solving" (L.C. Wilkinson, A. Martino, & G. Camilli); (7) "A
Vygotskian Approach To Research on Mental Addition and Subtraction Up To
Hundred: Handy Arithmetic for Primary School Students" (M. Van der Heijden);
(8) "Assessment of Flexibility in Mental Arithmetic" (T. Klein & M.
Beishuizen); (9) "Clever Rearrangement Strategies in Children's Mental
Arithmetic: A Confrontation of Eye-Movement Data and Verbal Protocols" (L.
Verschaffel, E. De Corte, I. Gielen, & E. Struyf); (10) "Exploration of
Individual Learning Processes in Mathematics" (K. Hasemann); (11) "The Use of
Counting in Numerical Reasoning" (V. Bermejo & M.O. Lago); (12) "Latino, Anglo,
and Korean Children's Finger Addition Methods" (K.C. Fuson, T. Perry, & Y.
Kwon); (13) "A Microgenetic Longitudinal Study on the Acquisition of Word
Problem Solving Skills" (E. Stern); (14) "A Cognitive Component Analysis of
Arithmetic Word Problem Solving" (H. Tajika); (15) "Reading To Learn
Mathematics: A Report on Primary School Children's Constructive Activity in
Learning From Text" (C. Desforges & S. Bristow); (16) "Cerebral Palsied
Children's Schemes To Face Quantitative Tasks" (C. Larere); (17) "The Results
of Different Treatments on Children's Weak Performance in Preparatory and
Initial Arithmetic" (B.A.M. Van de Rijt & J.E.H. Van Luit); (18) "Teaching a
Complex Counting Procedure To Improve Mathematical Word Problem Solving in
Children with Learning Difficulties" (E.C.D.M. Van Lieshout & I. Cornelissen);
(19) "Cognitive and Affective Effects of Computer-Based Arithmetic Practice on
the Lowest Achieving Students" (N. Hativa); (20) "Dealing with Learning
Difficulties Concerning Addition and Subtractions, Due to or Despite the Little
Person" (J.E.H. Van Luit); and (21) "Mathematical Word Problem Solving of
Normally Achieving and Mildly Mentally Retarded Children" (E.C.D.M. Van

Figure 5.3   cont'd

Lieshout, M.W.M. Jaspers, & B.H.M. Landewe). (JRH)
LV: 3
CH: SE
FI: ED
DTN: 070; 143

AN: EJ530769
CHN: EC614606
AU: Brigham,-Frederick-J.; And-Others
TI: Best Practices: Teaching Decimals, Fractions, and Percents to Students with Learning Disabilities.
PY: 1996
JN: LD-Forum; v21 n3 p10-15 Spr 1996
NT: Special Issue: Teaching Math to Students with Learning Disabilities: Part II.
DT: Journal Articles (080); Guides - Classroom - Teacher (052)
TA: Teachers; Practitioners
LA: English
DE: Educational-Practices; Educational-Strategies; Elementary-Secondary-Education; Problem-Solving; Remedial-Instruction
DE: *Decimal-Fractions; *Fractions-; *Learning-Disabilities; *Mathematics-Instruction; *Percentage-; *Teaching-Methods
IS: CIJFEB97
AB: Both general and specific effective strategies for teaching decimals, fractions, and percents to students with learning disabilities are presented. Information is provided on the theoretical base that underlies these curricular areas, recent research, and future trends. The need for programs to be structured around individualization and intensity is discussed. (CR)
CH: EC
FI: EJ
DTN: 080; 052

AN: EJ530768
CHN: EC614605
AU: Kelly,-Bernadette; Carnine,-Douglas
TI: Teaching Problem-Solving Strategies for Word Problems to Students with Learning Disabilities.
PY: 1996
JN: LD-Forum; v21 n3 p5-9 Spr 1996
NT: Special issue: Teaching Math to Students with Learning Disabilities: Part II.
DT: Journal Articles (080); Guides - Classroom - Teacher (052)
TA: Teachers; Practitioners
LA: English
DE: Academic-Standards; Elementary-Secondary-Education; Instructional-Effectiveness; Teaching-Methods
DE: *Learning-Disabilities; *Learning-Strategies; *Mathematics-Instruction; *Problem-Solving; *Word-Problems-Mathematics
ID: National-Council-of-Teachers-of-Mathematics

Figure 5.3   cont'd

IS: CIJFEB97
AB: Methods for teaching problem-solving strategies for word problems to students with learning disabilities are described in the context of the 1989 National Council of Teachers of Mathematics Curriculum and Evaluation Standards. Examples are given for using the specific strategies of diagrams, ratio equations, tables, and inverse operation equations. (CR)
CH: EC
FI: EJ
DTN: 080; 052

AN: EJ529409
CHN: EC614363
AU: Lock,-Robin-H.
TI: Adapting Mathematics Instruction in the General Education Classroom for Students with Mathematics Disabilities.
PY: 1996
JN: LD-Forum; v21 n2 p19-23 Win 1996
NT: Special issue: Teaching Math to Students with Learning Disabilities: Part I.
DT: Journal Articles (080); Guides - Non-classroom (055)
TA: Teachers; Practitioners
LA: English
DE: Classroom-Techniques; Computation-; Elementary-Secondary-Education; Problem-Solving
DE: *Inclusive-Schools; *Instructional-Effectiveness; *Learning-Disabilities; *Mathematics-Instruction; *Teaching-Methods
IS: CIJJAN97
AB: This article offers guidelines and suggestions for adapting mathematics instruction when teaching students with learning disabilities in the general classroom. Techniques for teaching computational skills, solving algorithms, and problem solving are offered. General techniques include increasing instructional time, varying group size, and using real life examples. (DB)
CH: EC
FI: EJ
DTN: 080; 055

AN: ED400639
CHN: EC305110
AU: Meltzer,-Lynn-J.; And-Others
TI: Strategies for Success: Classroom Teaching Techniques for Students with Learning Problems.
PY: 1996
SN: ISBN-0-89079-673-4
AV: PRO-ED, 8700 Shoal Creek Blvd., Austin, TX 78757-6897 ($29).
NT: 183 p.
PR: Document Not Available from EDRS.
DT: Books (010); Guides - Classroom - Teacher (052)
CP: U.S.; Texas
TA: Teachers; Practitioners

Figure 5.3   **cont'd**

LA: English
PG: 183
DE: Attention-Deficit-Disorders; Case-Studies; Decoding-Reading;
Elementary-Secondary-Education; Inclusive-Schools; Instructional-Effectiveness;
Learning-Problems; Mathematics-Instruction; Problem-Solving;
Reading-Comprehension; Reading-Instruction; Reading-Strategies; Spelling-;
Writing-Composition; Writing-Instruction; Writing-Strategies
DE: *Classroom-Techniques; *Educational-Strategies; *Learning-Disabilities;
*Learning-Strategies; *Teaching-Methods
IS: RIEMAR97
AB: Cost-effective classroom teaching strategies are provided for teachers
working with students with learning disabilities and attention deficit
disorders in inclusive settings from late elementary through early high school
levels. Section 1 discusses the importance of learning strategies and includes
an overview of strategic learning in the classroom and techniques for teaching
learning strategies. This section also describes how to identify students'
learning profiles, how learning difficulties and attention problems manifest in
the classroom, and how to empower students to become independent learners and
self-advocates. Section 2 provides information on selected learning strategies.
Chapters address: (1) strategies for decoding and spelling; (2) strategies for
improving reading comprehension; (3) strategies for enhancing written language;
(4) automaticity and problem solving in mathematics; and (5) strategy use
across content areas. Section 3 includes four case studies illustrating
strategy use. Appendices include brief information on reciprocal teaching and
identifying writing topics. A recommended reading list and a glossary are also
provided. (Contains 59 references.) (CR)
LV: 3
CH: EC
FI: ED
DTN: 010; 052

AN: EJ527701
CHN: EC614286
AU: Babbitt,-beatrice-C.; Miller,-Susan-Peterson
TI: Using Hypermedia to Improve the Mathematics problem-Solving Skills of
Students with Learning Disabilities
PY: 1996
JN: Journal-of-Learning-Disabilities; v29 n4 p391-401,412 Jul 1996
SN: ISSN-0022-2194
AV: UMI
NT: Special series: Technology.
DT: Journal Articles (080); Opinion Papers (120)
LA: English
DE: Cognitive-Processes; Elementary-Secondary-Education; Learning-Strategies;
Metacognition-
DE: Computer-Assisted-Instruction; *Hypermedia-; *Learning-Disabilities;
*Mathematics-Instruction; *Problem-Solving; *Word-Problems-Mathematics
IS: CIJDEC96
AB: This article reviews current knowledge about using computers to teach
problem-solving skills to students with learning disabilities (LD). It presents

Figure 5.3   cont'd

the case for use of hypermedia to improve students' mathematics problem-solving abilities. Specific suggestions are given for applying hypermedia to cognitive strategy instruction and the graduated word problem sequence. (Author/DB)
CH: EC
FI: EJ
DTN: 080; 120

AN: EJ527701
CHN: EC614286
AU: Babbitt,-Beatrice-C.; Miller,-Susan-Peterson
TI: Using Hypermedia to Improve the Mathematics Problem-Solving Skills of Students with Learning Disabilities.
PY: 1996
JN: Journal-of-Learning-Disabilities; v29 n4 p391-401,412 Jul 1996
SN: ISSN-0022-2194
AV: UMI
NT: Special series: Technology.
DT: Journal Articles (080); Opinion Papers (120)
LA: English
DE: Cognitive-Processes; Elementary-Secondary-Education; Learning-Strategies; Metacognition-
DE: *Computer-Assisted-Instruction; *Hypermedia-; *Learning-Disabilities; *Mathematics-Instruction; *Problem-Solving; *Word-Problems-Mathematics
IS: CIJDEC96
AB: This article reviews current knowledge about using computers to teach problem-solving skills to students with learning disabilities (LD). It presents the case for use of hypermedia to improve students' mathematics problem-solving abilities. Specific suggestions are given for applying hypermedia to cognitive strategy instruction and the graduated word problem sequence. (Author/DB)
CH: EC
FI: EJ
DTN: 080; 120

AN: EJ513460
CHN: EC612476
AU: Miles,-Dorothy-D.; Forcht,-Jonathan-P.
TI: Mathematics Strategies for Secondary Students with Learning Disabilities or Mathematics Deficiencies: A Cognitive Approach.
PY: 1995
JN: Intervention-in-School-and-Clinic; v31 n2 p91-96 Nov 1995
SN: ISSN-1053-4512
AV: UMI
DT: Journal Articles (080); Guides - Classroom - Teacher (052); Opinion Papers (120)
TA: Teachers; Practitioners
LA: English
DE: Algebra-; Calculus-; Classroom-Techniques; Cognitive-Objectives; Problem-Solving; Secondary-Education
DE: *Learning-Disabilities; *Learning-Strategies; *Mathematics-Instruction;

Figure 5.3   cont'd

*Mentors-; *Secondary-School-Mathematics; *Teaching-Methods
IS: CIJMAR96
AB: Deficits common among secondary students with learning disabilities or mathematics deficiencies are considered, along with a strategy to teach upper level mathematics, such as algebra or calculus. The strategy involves use of a mentor to help students to comprehend mathematics vocabulary, develop their own problem-solving strategy, and create a written model of the strategy. (SW)
CH: EC
FI: EJ
DTN: 080; 052; 120

15 of 30

AN: ED388003
CHN: EC304358
AU: Bley,-Nancy-S.; Thornton,-Carol-A.
TI: Teaching Mathematics to Students with Learning Disabilities. Third Edition.
PY: 1995
SN: ISBN-0-89079-603-3
AV: Pro-ed, 8700 Shoal Creek Blvd., Austin, TX 78757-6897 ($36).
NT: 486 p.
PR: Document Not Available from EDRS.
DT: Books (010); Guides - Classroom - Teacher (052)
CP: U.S.; Texas
TA: Teachers; Practitioners
LA: English
PG: 486
DE: Computer-Assisted-Instruction; Decision-Making; Elementary-Secondary-Education; Mathematical-Applications; Mathematics-Skills; Teaching-Methods; Thinking-Skills
DE: *Learning-Disabilities; *Mathematics-Instruction; *Problem-Solving
IS: RIEMAR96
AB: This book explores teaching techniques and adaptations that have proven effective in teaching mathematics concepts and skills to students with learning disabilities, with a focus on reasoning methods rather than algorithmic calculation. Emphasis is placed on topics that potentially can or commonly do cause the most difficulty for students with learning disabilities. Changes for this third edition include increased attention to problem solving, decision making, mental math, and the use of calculators. A chapter on problem solving provides tips and exercises on determining the correct operation to solve the problem, determining whether answers are reasonable, determining proper sequences, recognizing patterns, and comprehending the mathematical meaning of words and symbols. Guidelines for using microcomputers in mathematics instruction are provided, followed by specific methods for teaching lessons on money and time, number and place value, basic arithmetic operations, and whole number computation. Techniques for extending understanding and application of fraction and decimal concepts are provided as well. Specific strategies and adaptations are designed to fit specific learning disabilities, and include suggestions for helping students organize their mathematics worksheets and other materials. (PB)
LV: 3
CH: EC

Figure 5.3   cont'd

FI: ED
DTN: 010; 052

AN: EJ505139
CHN: EC611430
AU: Mastropieri,-Margo-A.; And-Others
TI: Reflections on "The Effects of Computer-assisted Instruction on the
Mathematical Problem Solving of Students with Learning Disabilities."
PY: 1995
JN: Exceptionality; v5 n3 p189-93 1994-95
SN: ISSN-0936-2835
AV: UMI
DT: Journal Articles (080); Opinion Papers (120)
LA: English
DE: Cost-Effectiveness; Elementary-Education; Problem-Solving; Research-Needs;
Time-on-Task; Word-Problems-Mathematics
DE: *Computer-Assisted-Instruction; *Instructional-Effectiveness;
*Learning-Disabilities; *Learning-Strategies
IS: CIJOCT95
AB: These reflections by the authors of a paper (EC 611 427) on
computer-assisted instruction of students with learning disabilities comment on
their reanalysis of the research process and their interpretations of the
unanticipated results. Implications for further research on the cost
effectiveness of learning-strategy training versus time-on-task are suggested.
(DB)
CH: EC
FI: EJ
DTN: 080; 120

AN: EJ505136
CHN: EC611427
AU: Shiah,-Rwey-Lin; And-Others
TI: The Effects of Computer-assisted Instruction on the Mathematical Problem
Solving of Students with Learning Disabilities.
PY: 1995
JN: Exceptionality; v5 n3 p131-61 1994-95
SN: ISSN-0936-2835
AV: UMI
DT: Journal Articles (080); Reports - Research (143)
LA: English
DE: Arithmetic-; Elementary-Education; Learning-Strategies;
Mathematics-Instruction; Pictorial-Stimuli; Problem-Solving; Test-Format
DE: *Computer-Assisted-Instruction; *Computer-Assisted-Testing;
*Instructional-Effectiveness; *Learning-Disabilities;
*Word-Problems-Mathematics
IS: CIJOCT95
AB: This study, involving 30 elementary students with learning disabilities,
found that students performed significantly better on mathematics tests given
using a computer than by paper and pencil. It found no differences among

Figure 5.3   **cont'd**

variations of computer-assisted instruction, with either static or animated pictures and either utilizing or not utilizing a seven-step cognitive strategy for solving arithmetic word problems. (DB)
CH: EC
FI: EJ
DTN: 080; 143

AN: EJ503149
CHN: EC611280
AU: Erenberg,-Shana-R.
TI: An Investigation of the Heuristic Strategies Used by Students with and without Learning Disabilities in Their Acquisition of the Basic Facts of Multiplication.
PY: 1995
JN: Learning-Disabilities:-A-Multidisciplinary-Journal; v6 n1 p9-12 Feb 1995
SN: ISSN-1046-6819
DT: Journal Articles (080); Reports - Research (143)
LA: English
DE: Cognitive-Processes; Computation-; Intermediate-Grades; Multiplication-; Performance-Factors
DE: *Learning-Disabilities; *Learning-Strategies; *Mathematics-Achievement; *Mathematics-Instruction; *Problem-Solving
IS: CIJSEP95
AB: Fourth-grade students (n=45) either with or without learning disabilities and achieving or not achieving at grade level in math were asked to explain strategies used to solve computational problems. Strategies were classified as reproductive or reconstructive (which varied in applicability and efficiency). Significant group differences were found. (Author/DB)
CH: EC
FI: EJ
DTN: 080; 143

AN: ED381990
CHN: EC303946
AU: Jitendra,-Asha-K.; Hoff,-Kathryn-E.
TI: Schema-Based Instruction on Word Problem Solving Performance of Students with Learning Disabilities.
PY: [1995]
NT: 17 p.; Paper presented at the Annual International Convention of the Council for Exceptional Children (73rd, Indianapolis, IN, April 5-9, 1995).
PR: EDRS Price - MF01/PC01 Plus Postage.
DT: Speeches /Meeting Papers (150); Reports - Research (143)
CP: U.S.; Pennsylvania
LA: English
PG: 17
DE: Arithmetic-; Elementary-Education; Generalization-; Instructional-Effectiveness; Learning-Strategies; Maintenance-; Teaching-Methods
DE: *Learning-Disabilities; *Mathematics-Instruction; *Problem-Solving;

Figure 5.3   cont'd

*Schemata-Cognition; *Word-Problems-Mathematics
ID: Direct-Instruction
IS: RIESEP95
AB: This study examined the effects of a schema-based direct instruction
strategy on the addition and subtraction word problem solving performance of
three third- and fourth-grade students with learning disabilities. An adapted
multiple probe across subjects design was used. The intervention involved
training students to distinguish "change," "group," and "compare" problems and
to label problem components using schemata diagrams for these problem types.
Results indicated that the intervention was successful in increasing the
percentage of correct word problems for all three students. In addition,
maintenance and generalization of word problem solving was seen 2 to 3 weeks
following the study. Student interviews also indicated that the strategy was
beneficial. Contains seven references, three figures, and two tables. (DB)
LV: 1
CH: EC
FI: ED
DTN: 150; 143

AN: EJ489564
CHN: EC609500
AU: Hutchinson,-Nancy-L.
TI: Effects of Cognitive Strategy Instruction on Algebra Problem Solving of
Adolescents with Learning Disabilities.
PY: 1993
JN: Learning-Disability-Quarterly; v16 n1 p34-63 Win 1993
SN: ISSN-0731-9487
AV: UMI
DT: Journal Articles (080)
LA: English
DE: Instructional-Effectiveness; Junior-High-Schools
DE: *Algebra-; *Cognitive-Processes; *Learning-Disabilities;
*Learning-Strategies; *Mathematics-Instruction; *Problem-Solving
IS: CIJJAN95
AB: Twelve adolescents with learning disabilities were trained to use a
cognitive strategy in algebra problem solving. The two-phase strategy (problem
representation and problem solution) was effective in improving algebra
performance on algebra word problems, and maintenance and transfer of the
strategy were evident. (JDD)
CH: EC
FI: EJ
DTN: 080; 143

AN: EJ489563
CHN: EC609499
AU: Montague,-Marjorie; Applegate,-Brooks
TI: Middle School Students' Mathematical Problem Solving: An Analysis of
Think-Aloud Protocols.
PY: 1993

Figure 5.3   **cont'd**

JN: Learning-Disability-Quarterly; v16 n1 p19-32 Win 1993
SN: ISSN-0731-9487
AV: UMI
DT: Journal Articles (080)
LA: English
DE: Cognitive-Processes; Intermediate-Grades; Junior-High-Schools;
Middle-Schools; Problem-Solving; Protocol-Analysis
DE: *Gifted-; *Learning-Disabilities; *Learning-Strategies;
*Mathematics-Achievement; *Word-Problems-Mathematics
IS: CIJJAN95
AB: This study examined the verbalizations of 90 middle school students as they
thought aloud while solving mathematical word problems. Results indicated that
students with learning disabilities (LD) and average achievers were less
strategic in approaching mathematical problem solving than gifted students, and
LD students approached problem solving in a qualitatively different manner than
their more proficient peers. (JDD)
CH: EC
FI: EJ
DTN: 080; 143

22 of 30

AN: EJ474317
CHN: EC607374
AU: Miller,-Susan-Peterson; Mercer,-Cecil-D.
TI: Mnemonics: Enhancing the Math Performance of Students with Learning
Difficulties.
PY: 1993
JN: Intervention-in-School-and-Clinic; v29 n2 p78-82 Nov 1993
SN: ISSN-1053-4512
AV: UMI
DT: Journal Articles (080)
TA: Teachers; Practitioners
LA: English
DE: Classroom-Techniques; Elementary-Secondary-Education; Problem-Solving;
Teaching-Methods; Word-Problems-Mathematics
DE: *Learning-Disabilities; *Learning-Strategies; *Mathematics-Instruction;
*Mnemonics-
IS: CIJAPR94
AB: This article describes and offers examples of acronym mnemonics in
mathematics and gives suggestions for their use with students who have learning
disabilities. The approach addresses learning the basic facts and solving word
problems. Instructional procedures for teaching mnemonics are noted. (DB)
CH: EC
FI: EJ
DTN: 080; 055

23 of 30

AN: EJ470788
CHN: EC607032
AU: Miller,-Susan-Peterson; Mercer,-Cecil-D.
TI: Using a Graduated Word Problem Sequence to Promote Problem-Solving Skills.

Figure 5.3   cont'd

PY: 1993
JN: Learning-Disabilities-Research-and-Practice; v8 n3 p169-74 Sum 1993
SN: ISSN-0938-8982
DT: Journal Articles (080)
TA: Teachers; Researchers; Practitioners
LA: English
DE: Elementary-Education; Problem-Solving; Teaching-Methods
DE: *Instructional-Effectiveness; *Learning-Disabilities;
*Mathematics-Instruction; *Sequential-Learning; *Word-Problems-Mathematics
IS: CIJFEB94
AB: This article presents a graduated word problem sequence in mathematics,
beginning with simple words; progressing to phrases, sentences, and paragraphs;
advancing to paragraph word problems with extraneous information; and finally
having students create their own word problems. Results from 67 elementary
students with learning disabilities support the strategy's use. (Author/JDD)
CH: EC
FI: EJ
DTN: 080; 055; 142

AN: EJ457374
CHN: EC604917
AU: Giordano,-Gerard
TI: Heuristic Strategies: An Aid for Solving Verbal Mathematical Problems.
PY: 1992
JN: Intervention-in-School-and-Clinic; v28 n2 p88-96 Nov 1992
SN: ISSN-0001-396X
AV: UMI
DT: Journal Articles (080)
TA: Teachers; Practitioners
LA: English
DE: Elementary-School-Mathematics; Elementary-Secondary-Education;
Metacognition-
DE: *Heuristics-; *Learning-Disabilities; *Learning-Strategies;
*Mathematics-Instruction; *Problem-Solving; *Word-Problems-Mathematics
IS: CIJJUN93
AB: Because of the importance of problem-solving skills in mathematics
instruction of children with learning disabilities, this article offers
guidance on teaching heuristic global strategies, including use of analogy,
annotating problems, detail analysis, deletion of details, detail sorting,
symbolizing operations, and designating formulas. (DB)
CH: EC
FI: EJ
DTN: 080; 055

AN: EJ450011
CHN: EC603731
AU: Mercer,-Cecil-D.; Miller,-Susan-P.
TI: Teaching Students with Learning Problems in Math to Acquire, Understand,
and Apply Basic Math Facts.

Figure 5.3   **cont'd**

PY: 1992
JN: Remedial-and-Special-Education-(RASE); v13 n3 p19-35,61 May-Jun 1992
SN: ISSN-0741-9325
AV: UMI
DT: Journal Articles (080)
TA: Practitioners
LA: English
DE: Curriculum-Development; Elementary-Secondary-Education;
Instructional-Effectiveness; Mathematics-Achievement; Problem-Solving
DE: *High-Risk-Students; *Learning-Disabilities; *Mathematics-Curriculum;
*Mathematics-Instruction; *Teaching-Methods
IS: CIJJAN93
AB: Ten research-supported instructional components are presented for promoting
mathematics achievement in students with learning problems. A curriculum
(Strategic Math Series) found to be effective in teaching students with
learning problems to acquire and understand basic facts and apply them in
problem-solving activities is described. (Author/JDD)
CH: EC
FI: EJ
DTN: 080; 141

26 of 30

AN: EJ448562
CHN: EC603389
AU: Case,-Lisa-Pericola; And-Others
TI: Improving the Mathematical Problem-Solving Skills of Students with Learning
Disabilities: Self-Regulated Strategy Development.
PY: 1992
JN: Journal-of-Special-Education; v26 n1 p1-19 Spr 1992
SN: ISSN-0022-4669
AV: UMI
DT: Journal Articles (080)
LA: English
DE: Addition-; Generalization-; Instructional-Effectiveness;
Intermediate-Grades; Maintenance-; Study-Skills; Subtraction-; Thinking-Skills
DE: *Learning-Disabilities; *Learning-Strategies; *Problem-Solving;
*Teaching-Methods; *Word-Problems-Mathematics
IS: CIJDEC92
AB: Four fifth and sixth grade students with learning disabilities were taught
a strategy for comprehending word problems and devising appropriate solutions.
Following instruction performance on mixed sets of addition and subtraction
word problems improved. Although generalization to a different setting
occurred, maintenance was mixed. (Author/DB)
CH: EC
FI: EJ
DTN: 080; 142; 143

27 of 30

AN: EJ445829
CHN: EC603158
AU: Hutchinson,-Nancy-L.

Figure 5.3   cont'd

TI: The Challenges of Componential Analysis: Cognitive and Metacognitive Instruction in Mathematical Problem Solving.
PY: 1992
JN: Journal-of-Learning-Disabilities; v25 n4 p249-52,257 Apr 1992
SN: ISSN-0022-2194
AV: UMI
DT: Journal Articles (080)
LA: English
DE: Intermediate-Grades; Junior-High-Schools; Mathematics-Instruction; Middle-Schools; Problem-Solving; Teaching-Methods
DE: *Cognitive-Processes; *Componential-Analysis; *Instructional-Effectiveness; *Learning-Disabilities; *Learning-Strategies; *Metacognition-
IS: CIJOCT92
AB: This paper comments on EC 603 157, which discusses cognitive and metacognitive strategy instruction on mathematical problem solving of middle school students with learning disabilities. The commentary analyzes the separability of cognition and metacognition and raises questions about the identifiable components that contribute to the effectiveness of process instruction. (JDD)
CH: EC
FI: EJ
DTN: 080; 120

AN: EJ445828
CHN: EC603157
AU: Montague,-Marjorie
TI: The Effects of Cognitive and Metacognitive Strategy Instruction on the Mathematical Problem Solving of Middle School Students with Learning Disabilities.
PY: 1992
JN: Journal-of-Learning-Disabilities; v25 n4 p230-48 Apr 1992
SN: ISSN-0022-2194
AV: UMI
DT: Journal Articles (080)
LA: English
DE: Intermediate-Grades; Junior-High-Schools; Maintenance-; Mathematics-Instruction; Middle-Schools; Problem-Solving; Teaching-Methods
DE: *Cognitive-Processes; *Instructional-Effectiveness; *Learning-Disabilities; *Learning-Strategies; *Metacognition-; *Word-Problems-Mathematics
IS: CIJOCT92
AB: Six students (ages 12-14) with learning disabilities received either cognitive or metacognitive strategy instruction for mathematical problem solving, followed by instruction in the complementary component. Results indicated that cognitive and metacognitive strategies were more effective than either cognitive or metacognitive strategy instruction alone. Students did not, however, maintain the strategy over time. (JDD)
CH: EC
FI: EJ
DTN: 080; 143

Figure 5.3   cont'd

AN: EJ435901
CHN: EC601787
AU: Montague,-Marjorie
TI: Gifted and Learning-Disabled Gifted Students' Knowledge and Use of
Mathematical Problem-Solving Strategies.
PY: 1991
JN: Journal-for-the-Education-of-the-Gifted; v14 n4 p393-411 Win 1991
SN: ISSN-0162-3532
AV: UMI
DT: Journal Articles (080)
TA: Researchers
LA: English
DE: Cognitive-Processes; Gifted-Disabled; Knowledge-Level; Mathematics-;
Secondary-Education
DE: *Gifted-; *Learning-Disabilities; *Learning-Strategies; *Metacognition-;
*Problem-Solving
IS: CIJAPR92
AB: Three gifted and three learning-disabled gifted students (ages 13-15)
viewed themselves on videotape solving mathematical problems and responded to
questions pertaining to their problem-solving strategies. The
non-learning-disabled students applied substantially more cognitive and
metacognitive knowledge to the problem-solving task. (Author/DB)
CH: EC
FI: EJ
DTN: 080; 143

30 of 30

AN: EJ431368
CHN: EC601405
AU: Montague,-Marjorie; And-Others
TI: Affective, Cognitive, and Metacognitive Attributes of Eighth-Grade
Mathematical Problem Solvers.
PY: 1991
JN: Learning-Disabilities-Research-and-Practice; v6 n3 p145-51 1991
SN: ISSN-0938-8982
DT: Journal Articles (080)
LA: English
DE: Comparative-Analysis; Evaluative-Thinking; Junior-High-Schools;
Learning-Strategies; Mathematics-Tests; Student-Attitudes;
Student-Characteristics; Word-Problems-Mathematics
DE: *Affective-Behavior; *Cognitive-Ability; *Learning-Disabilities;
*Mathematics-Skills; *Metacognition-; *Problem-Solving
IS: CIJJAN92
AB: This study of 60 eighth grade students found differences among students
with learning disabilities and students who were low, average, and high
achieving, on perceptions of ability and achievement; attitude toward
mathematics; knowledge of mathematical problem-solving strategies; and
knowledge, use, and control of problem representation strategies. (Author/JDD)
CH: EC
FI: EJ
DTN: 080; 143

Figure 5.3   concluded

Database details

ACADEMIC INDEX. *See* **GALE GROUP BUSINESS A.R.T.S.**

AUSTRALIAN EDUCATION INDEX (*See also* **INTERNATIONAL ERIC**)

Subject:	Education
File Size:	90 000+
Coverage:	1978–
Updates:	Semi-annually
Data Type:	Bibliographic with abstracts
Platform:	DOS; Windows; Mac
Information Provider:	Cunningham Library, Australian Council for Educational Research, Camberwell, (VIC), Australia
Online:	InformitOnline
CD-ROM:	AUSTROM, The Dialog Corporation
Internet:	Yes
Thesaurus:	*Australian Thesaurus of Education Descriptors*

A-V ONLINE *See* **NICEM REFERENCE ONLINE**

BRITISH EDUCATION INDEX (*See also* **INTERNATIONAL ERIC**)

Subject:	Education
File Size:	100 633 (December 1997)
Coverage:	BEI: 1976– ; BETI: 1950–
Updates:	BEI: quarterly; BETI: annually
Data Type:	Bibliographic
Platform:	DOS; Windows; Mac
Information Provider:	Brotherton Library, University of Leeds, Leeds, UK <URL http://www.leeds.ac.uk/bei/>
Online:	DIALOG
CD-ROM:	The Dialog Corporation
Internet:	Yes. DialogWeb, (for UK) <URL http://www.bids.ac.uk>
Thesaurus:	*British Education Thesaurus*

CBCA FULLTEXT EDUCATION (formerly **CANADIAN EDUCATION INDEX**)

Subject:	Education
File Size:	100 000+
Coverage:	1976–
Updates:	Monthly
Data Type:	Bibliographic with annotations; full text
Platform:	DOS; Windows; Mac; UNIX
Information Provider:	Micromedia Limited, Toronto (ON) Canada <URL

	http://www.mmltd.com/>
Online:	NA
CD-ROM:	The Dialog Corporation; SilverPlatter
Internet:	Yes
Thesaurus:	*Canadian Education Thesaurus*

DISSERTATION ABSTRACTS

Subject:	All disciplines, including Education
File Size:	1 400 000+
Coverage:	1861–
Updates:	Monthly
Data Type:	Bibliographic with abstracts
Platform:	DOS; Windows; Mac; UNIX
Information Provider:	Bell & Howell Information and Learning, Ann Arbor (MI) USA <URL http://www.bellhowell.com/>
Online:	DataStar; DIALOG; OCLC; Ovid
CD-ROM:	SilverPlatter; Ovid
Internet:	Yes (1981–)

EDUCATION INDEX (*See also* WILSON EDUCATION ABSTRACTS)

Subject:	Education
File Size:	454 000+ including Wilson Education Abstracts
Coverage:	1983–
Updates:	Monthly
Data Type:	Bibliographic
Platform:	DOS; Windows; Mac; UNIX
Information Provider:	H.W. Wilson Company, New York (NY) USA <URL http://www.hwwilson.com/>
Online:	Bell & Howell; DIALOG; OCLC; Ovid; WilsonWeb
CD-ROM:	SilverPlatter; WilsonDisc
Internet:	Yes (WilsonWeb)
Thesaurus:	Yes

EDUQ

Subject:	Education
File Size:	15 300+
Coverage:	1960–
Updates:	Twice yearly
Data Type:	Bibliographic; directory (full text)
Platform:	DOS; Windows; Mac
Information Provider:	Services Documentaires Multimedia Inc. (SDM), Montreal, (Quebec), Canada
Online:	SDM
CD-ROM:	NA
Internet:	NA

ERIC

Subject:	Education
File Size:	980 000+
Coverage:	1966–
Updates:	Online: monthly; CD-ROM: quarterly
Data Type:	Bibliographic; full text
Platform:	DOS; Windows; Mac; UNIX
Information Provider:	Educational Resources Information Center (ERIC), US Dept. of Education, Washington, DC, USA <URL http://www.ed.gov>
Online:	DataStar; DIALOG; OCLC; National Information Services Corporation (NISC); Ovid; SilverPlatter
CD-ROM:	EBSCO; ERIC Processing & Reference Facility; The Dialog Corporation; NISC; SilverPlatter
Internet:	Yes <URL http://www.accesseric.org/>
Thesaurus:	*Thesaurus of ERIC Descriptors*

EUDISED (European Documentation and Information System for Education)

Subject:	Educational research
File Size:	20 000+
Coverage:	1975–
Updates:	Quarterly
Data Type:	Bibliographic
Platform:	DOS; Windows; Mac; UNIX
Information Provider:	Council of Europe, Directorate of Education, Culture and Sport, Strasbourg, France; Biblioteca di Documentazione Pedagogica (BPD), Florence, Italy
Online:	European Information Network Service (EINS)
CD-ROM:	NA
Internet:	Yes <URL http://dante.bdp.it/europa/eudisedindex.htm>
Thesaurus	*European Education Thesaurus*

EXCEPTIONAL CHILD EDUCATION RESOURCES (ECER)

Subject:	Education
File Size:	100 000+
Coverage:	1966–
Updates:	CD-ROM: quarterly
Data Type:	Bibliographic with abstracts
Platform:	DOS; Windows; Mac; UNIX
Information Provider:	Council for Exceptional Children, Reston (VA) USA <URL http://www.cec.sped.org/>
Online:	NA
CD-ROM:	SilverPlatter

Internet: Ycs
Thesaurus: *Thesaurus of ERIC Descriptors*

FRANCIS: SCIENCES DE L'EDUCATION

Subject: Education
File Size: 2 000 000+
Coverage: 1972–; Research Libraries Group: 1984–
Updates: Online: monthly; CD-ROM: semi-annually
Data Type: Bibliographic
Platform: DOS; Windows
Information Provider: Centre National de la Recherche Scientifique, Institut de l'Information Scientifique et Technique, Vandoeuvre-les-Nancy, France <URL http://www. inist.fr>
Online: Questel-Orbit; Research Libraries Group (RIG)
CD-ROM: GTI Jouvre
Internet: NA

GALE GROUP BUSINESS A.R.T.S. (formerly ACADEMIC INDEX)

Subject: All disciplines, including Education
File Size: 3 060 000+
Coverage: 1976–
Updates: Weekly
Data Type: Bibliographic; full text
Platform: DOS; Windows; Mac
Information Provider: Gale Group, Foster City (CA) USA
Online: DataStar; DIALOG
CD-ROM: Gale Group
Internet: Yes

INDEX NEW ZEALAND (INNZ)

Subject: All disciplines, including Education
File Size: 200 000+
Coverage: 1987–
Updates: Online: daily; CD-ROM: quarterly
Data Type: Bibliographic
Platform: DOS; Windows; Mac
Information Provider: National Library [of New Zealand], Wellington, New Zealand
Online: National Library's TePuna
CD-ROM: National Library
Internet: Yes
Thesaurus: *APAIS Thesaurus*

INTERNATIONAL ERIC

Subject:	Education
File Size:	243 000+
Coverage:	1976–
Updates:	Quarterly
Data Type:	Bibliographic with abstracts
Platform:	DOS; Windows; Mac
Information Provider:	Australian Council for Educational Research, Camberwell, VIC, Australia; University of Leeds, Leeds, UK
Online:	NA
CD-ROM:	The Dialog Corporation
Internet:	NA
Thesaurus:	*Australian Thesaurus of Education Descriptors*; *British Education Thesaurus*

NICEM REFERENCE ONLINE (formerly A-V ONLINE)

Subject:	Education
File Size:	430 000+
Coverage:	1964– (with selected earlier coverage to 1900)
Updates:	Online: quarterly; CD-ROM: semi-annually
Data Type:	Bibliographic
Platform:	Windows; Mac; UNIX
Information Provider:	National Information Center for Educational Media (NICEM) Albuquerque, (NM) USA
Online:	DIALOG; EBSCOHOST; The Library Corporation (TLC); SilverPlatter
CD-ROM:	SilverPlatter
Internet:	Yes

OCLC: EDUCATION LIBRARY

Subject:	Education
File Size:	685 000+
Coverage:	1980–
Updates:	Annually
Data Type:	Bibliographic
Platform:	DOS; Windows; Mac; UNIX
Information Provider:	OCLC Online Computer Library Center, Inc., Dublin (OH) USA <URL http://www.oclc.org/>
Online:	NA
CD-ROM:	SilverPlatter
Internet:	NA

REPERE

Subject:	All disciplines, including Education

File Size:	310 000+
Coverage:	1980–
Updates:	CD-ROM: three times yearly; Internet: daily
Data Type:	Bibliographic with abstracts; selected full text
Platform:	DOS; Windows; Mac; UNIX
Information Provider:	Services Documentaires Multimedia Inc. (SDM), Montreal (Quebec) Canada <URL http://www.sdm.qc.ca>
Online:	
CD-ROM:	SDM; SilverPlatter
Internet:	Yes

WILSON EDUCATION ABSTRACTS (*See also* EDUCATION INDEX)

Subject:	Education
File Size:	454 000+
Coverage:	1994–
Updates:	Online: twice weekly; CD-ROM: monthly
Data Type:	Bibliographic with abstracts; selected full text
Platform:	DOS; Windows; Mac; UNIX
Information Provider:	H.W. Wilson Company, New York (NY) USA <URL http://www.hwwilson.com/>
Online:	Bell & Howell; DIALOG; OCLC; Ovid; WilsonWeb
CD-ROM:	SilverPlatter; WilsonDisc
Internet:	Yes (WilsonWeb)
Thesaurus:	Yes

WILSON EDUCATION FULL TEXT

Subject:	Education
File Size:	454 000+, including EDUCATION INDEX
Coverage:	1996–
Updates:	CD-ROM: monthly; Internet: four times per week
Data Type:	Bibliographic with abstracts and selective full text
Platform:	Windows; Mac; UNIX
Information Provider:	H.W. Wilson Company, New York (NY) USA <URL http://www.hwwilson.com/>
Online:	Bell & Howell; DIALOG; OCLC; Ovid; WilsonWeb
CD-ROM:	SilverPlatter; WilsonDisc
Internet:	Yes (WilsonWeb)
Thesaurus:	Yes

WILSON EDUCATION INDEX. *See* EDUCATION INDEX

Acknowledgements

The authors wish to acknowledge the assistance of Gillian McLean and Lynn Olson in preparation of the manuscript for this chapter.

Notes

1   This definition of education is a composite drawn from the following dictionaries: R. E. Allen, (ed.), *The Concise Oxford Dictionary of Current English*, 8th edn (Oxford: Clarendon Press, 1990); Carter V. Good, (ed.), *Dictionary of Education*, 3d edn (New York: McGraw Hill, 1973); and Gene R. Hawes and Lynne Salop Hawes (eds), *The Concise Dictionary of Education* (New York: Van Nostrand Reinhold Co., 1982); and from the homepage of the Argus Clearinghouse for Education <URL http://www.clearinghouse.net/>.

2   These subject-specific (for education) Internet resource guides are also variously referred to as home pages or homepages, indices/indexes or meta-indices/indexes or hyperindices/indexes, subject directories, subject webliographies, gateway sites, 'trailblazer' pages or virtual libraries. They are one person's or one group's collection of links in a specific field of knowledge. Unless there is a disclaimer, the searcher usually can be confident that the linked sites have been evaluated and pronounced of high quality.

Further reading

APAIS Thesaurus: A List of Subject Terms used in the Australian Public Affairs Information Service (1994), (5th edn), Canberra: National Library of Australia.

Barnett, L. and Colby, A. (1995), 'ERIC's Indexing and Retrieval: 1995 Update', in James E. Houston (ed.), *Thesaurus of ERIC Descriptors*, Phoenix, AR: Oryx Press, pp. xiv–xxiii.

Canadian Education Thesaurus (1992), (2nd edn), Toronto: Micromedia Ltd.

Glavac, M. (1998), *The Busy Educator's Guide to the World Wide Web*, London, ON: NIMA Systems.

Harris, S. and Oppenheim, C. (1996), 'Does Machine-Readable Documentation on Online Hosts and CD-ROMs Have a Role or Future?' *Journal of Information Science*, **22**, pp. 247–58.

Heide, A. (1999), *The Teacher's Complete and Easy Guide to the Internet*, (rev. and updated 2nd edn), New York: Teacher's College Press.

Houston, J. E., Weller, C. R. and Patt, C. A. (eds.) (1995), *ERIC Identifier Authority List (IAL)*, Phoenix, AR: Oryx Press.

Houston, J. E. (1995), *Thesaurus of ERIC Descriptors*, (13th edn), Phoenix, AR:

Oryx Press.

MacMillan, M. (1997), 'Insights into Internet Instruction', *Teacher-Librarian Today*, **3** (2), pp. 22–27.

Marder, J. V., and Sheffield, P. (eds) (1991), *British Education Thesaurus*, (2nd edn), Leeds: Leeds University Press.

McIntosh, C. Y. and Xu, Y. (1997), 'Educational Resources on the World Wide Web', *Teaching Education*, **8** (2), pp. 151–154.

Miller, E. B. (1997), *The Internet Resource Directory for K-12 Teachers and Librarians*, (97/98 edn), Englewood, CO: Libraries Unlimited. (Free updates are available at <URL http://www.lu.com/>.)

Miller, E. (ed.) (1996), *Australian Thesaurus of Education Descriptors*, (2nd edn), Camberwell, Vic.: Australian Council for Educational Research.

Morville, P., Rosenfield, L. and Janes, J. (1996), *The Internet Searcher's Handbook: Locating information, People & Software*, Neal-Schuman NetGuide Series, New York: Neal-Schuman.

Notess, G. R. (1997), 'On the Net: Internet Search Techniques and Strategies', *Online*, 21 (4), pp. 63–66. Available at <URL http://www.onlineinc.com/onlinemag/JulOL97/net7.html>.

Pfaffenberger, B. (1996), *Web Search Strategies*, New York: MIS Press.

Reddick, A. and King, E. (1996), *The Online Student: Making the Grade on the Internet*, Fort Worth, TX: Harcourt Brace College Publishers.

Rodrigues, D. (1997), *The Research Paper and the World Wide Web*, Upper Saddle River, NJ: Prentice Hall.

Sharp, V. F., Levine, M. G. and Sharp, R. M. (1998), *The Best Web Sites for Teachers*, (2nd edn), Eugene, OR: International Society for Technology in Education.

Taheri, B. J., Pearce, E. and Boston, C. (1996), *Directory of ERIC Resource Collections 1996*, Washington DC: US Dept. of Education, National Library of Education, Office of Educational Resources & Improvement.

Zorn, P., Emanoil, M., Marshall, L. and Panek, M. (1996), 'Advanced Searching: Tricks of the Trade', *Online*, 20 (3) pp. 14–28. Available at <URL http://www.onlineinc.com/onlinemag/mayOL/zorn5.html>.

Database index

The following index contains references to all databases and electronic resources mentioned in the text as well as to the information providers, online vendors or CD-ROM publishers that make them available. Where appropriate, file names have been linked to databases. All databases are in upper case letters as they are in the text.

700 GREAT SITES: AMAZING, SPECTACULAR, MYSTERIOUS, WONDERFUL WEB SITES FOR KIDS AND THE ADULTS WHO CARE FOR THEM 270
ABC-CLIO 129, 169–76, 176–7, 177–87, 267–8
ABM *see* ARTBIBLIOGRAPHIES MODERN
ABREN *see* AUSTRALIAN BIOLOGICAL RESEARCH NETWORK
ACADEMIC ABSTRACTS 263
ACADEMIC ABSTRACTS FULLTEXT ELITE 263
ACADEMIC ABSTRACTS FULLTEXT ULTRA 263
ACADEMIC ASAP 262–3
Academic Center for Excellence *see* ACE
ACADEMIC INDEX *see* BUSINESS A.R.T.S.
ACADEMIC SEARCH ELITE 263
ACADEMIC SEARCH INTERNATIONAL 262
ACADEMIC SEARCH PLUS 263
ACADEMIC SEARCH SELECT 263
ACE 272
ACER *see* Australian Council for Educational Research
ACHLIS *see* Australian Clearinghouse for Library and Information Science
AEI *see* AUSTRALIAN EDUCATION INDEX
AFRICA NEWS 238
AFRICANEWS ONLINE 238
AgeInfo 114
AgeLine 111
AHCI *see* ARTS AND HUMANITIES CITATION INDEX
AHL *see* AMERICA: HISTORY AND LIFE
AI *see* ART INDEX
AIFS *see* Australian Institute of Family Studies
AL IDRISI 5
ALISA *see* AUSTRALIAN LIBRARY AND INFORMATION SCIENCE ABSTRACTS
AltaVista 4, 5, 11, 18, 19, 95, 246, 248, 250, 251
AMERICA: HISTORY AND LIFE 129, 176–7, 178, 179, 180, 181–2, 186, 227, 235
American Association for School Librarians 272

American Association of Retired Persons 111
AMERICAN GIRL.COM 274
American Library Association 270
AMERICAN MEMORY PROJECT 148–9
American Psychological Association 116
American Theological Library Association 187–93
AOL NETFIND FOR KIDS 270
APA *see* American Psychological Association
APAIS *see* AUSTRALIAN PUBLIC AFFAIRS AND INFORMATION SERVICE
APPLIED SOCIAL SCIENCES INDEX AND ABSTRACTS 102, 105–6, 107, 109
ARGUS CLEARINGHOUSE FOR EDUCATION 251–2
ART ABSTRACTS 156–64
ART INDEX 129, 156–64
ART INDEX RETROSPECTIVE 159
ART LITERATURE INTERNATIONAL *see* BIBLIOGRAPHY OF THE HISTORY OF ART
ARTBIBLIOGRAPHIES MODERN 129, 169–76, 178
ARTFL Project *see* Project for American and French Research on the Treasury of the French
    Language
ARTICLEFIRST 237–8
ARTS AND HUMANITIES CITATION INDEX 25, 27, 29, 33, 34–5, 152–6
ARTS AND HUMANITIES SEARCH *see* ARTS AND HUMANITIES CITATION INDEX
ASCD *see* Association for Supervision and Curriculum Development
ASCD SELECT ONLINE 255
ASIA ROM 238
ASK A YOUNG SCIENTIST 272
ASK DR. MATH 272
ASK JEEVES FOR KIDS 252, 271
ASK JEEVES FOR TEACHERS 252
ASKA+ LOCATOR 272
ASKERIC 228, 251
ASSIA CD-ROM 105
ASSIA *see* APPLIED SOCIAL SCIENCES INDEX AND ABSTRACTS
Association for Supervision and Curriculum Development 255
ASSOCIATIONS CANADA 223
ATHENA 143
ATLA RELIGION INDEX 126, 187–93
AUSTGUIDE 239, 261–2
AUSTRALIAN BIOLOGICAL RESEARCH NETWORK 5, 7
Australian Clearinghouse for Library and Information Science 231
Australian Council for Educational Research 230–1, 234, 327, 331
AUSTRALIAN EDUCATION INDEX 217, 218, 230–1, 234, 276, 277, 280, 285–90, 327
AUSTRALIAN FAMILY & SOCIETY ABSTRACTS 114
AUSTRALIAN FAMILY RESOURCES ON CD-ROM 114
Australian Institute of Family Studies 114, 115
AUSTRALIAN INSTITUTE OF FAMILY STUDIES LIBRARY DATABASE 115
AUSTRALIAN LIBRARY AND INFORMATION SCIENCE ABSTRACTS 231
AUSTRALIAN PUBLIC AFFAIRS AND INFORMATION SERVICE 231
AUSTROM 224, 231, 239, 327
A-V ONLINE *see* NICEM REFERENCE ONLINE
AWESOME LIBRARY 252

Barnardos 112
BARRON'S PROFILES OF AMERICAN COLLEGES, COLLEGE SOURCE 243
BARTLEBY'S GREAT BOOKS ONLINE 147

Bath Information and Data Services 106–8, 232
BECTA *see* BRITISH EDUCATIONAL COMMUNICATIONS AND TECHNOLOGY AGENCY
BEI *see* BRITISH EDUCATION INDEX
Bell & Howell Information and Learning 259, 262, 328, 332
BERIT'S BEST SITES FOR CHILDREN 271
BHA *see* BIBLIOGRAPHY OF THE HISTORY OF ART
BIBLIOGRAPHY OF THE HISTORY OF ART 164–9
Bibliothèque Nationale du Québec 239
BIDS *see* Bath Information and Data Services
BIG EYE EDUCATION CENTER 249
BILL NYE THE SCIENCE GUY LABS ONLINE 273
BIOCHEMISTRY AND BIOPHYSICS CITATION INDEX 28
BIOTECHNOLOGY CITATION INDEX 28
BLAISE-LINE 223
BLAISE-Web 223
BLUE WEB'N 252
BOOK REVIEW DIGEST 237
BOOK REVIEW INDEX 237
BookData 243
BOOKS IN PRINT WITH BOOK REVIEWS PLUS 237
Bowker-Saur 105–6, 223
BRITANNICA CD DELUXE ENCYCLOPEDIA 264–6
BRITANNICA ONLINE 266
BRITISH EDUCATION INDEX 217, 218, 231–2, 234, 237, 276, 277, 279–81, 286–90, 291–5,
    327
BRITISH EDUCATIONAL COMMUNICATIONS AND TECHNOLOGY AGENCY Web 242
BRITISH ELECTION STUDIES, 1963–1992 119
BRITISH MULTIMEDIA ENCYCLOPEDIA 265, 267
BRITISH OFFICIAL PUBLICATIONS 223
BRS Online 101, 111, 224
BUBL LINK 249
Buros/ERIC Test Publisher Locator 242
BUSINESS A.R.T.S. 240–1, 330

CAB ABSTRACTS 10
Cambridge Scientific Abstracts 201
CANADIAN BUSINESS CURRENT AFFAIRS *see* CBCA FULLTEXT EDUCATION
CANADIAN EDUCATION INDEX *see* CBCA FULLTEXT EDUCATION
CANADIAN EDUCATION ON THE WEB 254
CANADIAN INFORMATION BY SUBJECT 249
Canadian MAS FullTEXT ELITE 264
Canadian MAS FullTEXT SELECT 264
CANADIAN NEWSPAPERS 238
CAREDATA 113–14
Carnegie Mellon University 146
CASTLES ON THE WEB 273
Catchword 115
CBCA FULLTEXT EDUCATION 217, 218, 233–4, 276, 277, 279–82, 284, 286–90, 327–8
CBCA FULLTEXT REFERENCE 233, 237
CBCA-E *see* CBCA FULLTEXT EDUCATION
CCEL *see* CHRISTIAN CLASSICS ETHEREAL LIBRARY
CDJr 261
CDP Technologies 224
CEDEFOP 240

CEEE/ERIC Test Database 242
Central Statistical Office *see* Office of National Statistics
Centre for Policy on Ageing 114
Centre National de la Recherche Scientifique 135, 164–9, 330
CEPII 239
Chadwyck-Healey 143
Champelli, L 252
CHEMICAL ABSTRACTS 10
Chemical Abstracts Service 23
CHEMISTRY CITATION INDEX 28
CHILD ABUSE AND NEGLECT 112
ChildData 114
CHRISTIAN CLASSICS ETHEREAL LIBRARY 146
CHRONICLE OF HIGHER EDUCATION JOB OPENINGS IN ACADEME 241
CLASSROOM CONNECT 252
CNRS *see* Centre National de la Recherche Scientifique
Code of Fair Testing Practices 242
Community Development Foundation 112
COMMUNITY MATTERS 112
Complete Works of Shakespeare 147
COMPTON'S ENCYCLOPEDIA ONLINE 265
COMPTON'S INTERACTIVE ENCYCLOPEDIA DELUXE 264–5
COMPUMATH 28
CompuServe 176, 177, 201
CONNECTED TEACHER 270
CONTEMPORARY WOMEN'S DATABASE 268
Council for Europe 235
Council for Exceptional Children 239–40, 329
Council of Europe 329
COUNSEL.LITDATABASE 121
Counselling in Primary Care Trust 121
CSA Internet Database Service 102, 111
CSA SOCIOLOGICAL ABSTRACTS 102
CSA SOCIOLOGICAL ABSTRACTS *see also* SOCIOLOGICAL ABSTRACTS
CURRICULUM RESOURCE BY NEWSBANK 261

DAF *see* DIDACTIQUE ET ACQUISITION DU FRANÇAIS, LANGUE MATERNELLE
Danbib 235
Danish Data Archive 119
DATABASE OF EDUCATION FUNDING FOR INDIVIDUALS 241
DATABASE ON ENGLISH LANGUAGE TEACHING FOR ADULTS IN AUSTRALASIA 231, 239
DataStar 5, 10, 27, 101, 105, 117–18, 152, 264, 328, 329, 330
DataStarWeb 102–3, 104, 225
DEJA.COM 248, 256
DELTAA *see* DATABASE ON ENGLISH LANGUAGE TEACHING FOR ADULTS IN AUSTRALASIA
Denmarks Pedagogiske Bibliotek 234–5
Deutsches Institut für Medizinische Dokumentation und Information *see* DIMDI
DHSS-DATA 111
DIALOG 4, 9, 10, 27, 31–2, 34–5, 36–7, 38–43, 47–8, 49–50, 51–8, 59–73, 75–83, 84–8, 89–94, 101, 102, 108, 126, 133, 135, 138, 139–40, 152, 164–9, 169–71, 176–7, 177, 179–80, 184–7, 201–2, 205, 218, 223, 226, 232, 237, 238, 241, 242, 264, 291–5, 327, 328, 329, 330, 331, 332
DIALOG Blue Sheets 135, 165

Dialog Corporation, The 7, 118, 225, 228, 327, 328, 329, 331
Dialog OnDisc 226
DialogWeb 152–6, 164, 165, 168, 169, 170, 172, 174–6, 178, 184, 201, 225, 232
DIDACTIQUE ET ACQUISITION DU FRANÇAIS, LANGUE MATERNELLE 240
DIMDI 4, 9, 23, 27
DIRECTORY OF OPEN ACCESS STATISTICAL INFORMATION SITES 120
DISCOVERING BIOGRAPHY 267
DISCOVERING CAREERS AND JOBS 243
DISSERTATION ABSTRACTS 111, 223, 236, 253, 328
DogPile 5
DPBASEN 234–5

EBSCO Publishing 187, 242, 257, 258, 261, 263–4, 329
EBSCO SCHOOL RESOURCENET 242
EBSCO TEACHER REFERENCE CENTER 242
EBSCOhost 237, 261, 262, 263, 331
ECCTIS 2000: THE UK COURSES INFORMATION SERVICE 243
ECER *see* EXCEPTIONAL CHILD EDUCATIONAL RESOURCES
Economic and Social Research Council 119, 122
EDNA: EDUCATION NETWORK AUSTRALIA 244
EDUCATION GATEWAY 252
EDUCATION INDEX 224, 229–30, 237, 252, 277, 281, 328
EDUCATION INTERNET GUIDES: SOURCES FOR THEORY, PRACTICE, TEACHING AND
    RESEARCH 254
EDUCATION RESOURCES ON THE WORLD WIDE WEB 252–3
EDUCATION VIRTUAL LIBRARY *see* WORLD WIDE WEB VIRTUAL LIBRARY –
    EDUCATION
EDUCATION WORLD 253, 270
Educational Resources Information Center 228–9, 234, 242, 329
EDUCATIONAL TESTING DATABASE 242
Educational Testing Service/ERIC Test File 242
EDUCATION-LINE 232–3
EDUCAUSE 244
EDUQ 239, 328
EDVIEW 253
EINET GALAXY HUMANITIES COLLECTION 148
EINS *see* European Information Network Services
ELECTRIC LIBRARY AUSTRALASIA 268
ELECTRIC LIBRARY CANADA 268
ELECTRIC LIBRARY KOREA 268
ELECTRONIC LIBRARY FOR SOCIAL CARE 122
ELECTRONIC TEXT CENTER 146
ELEMENTARY SCHOOL LIBRARY COLLECTION: A GUIDE TO BOOKS AND MEDIA 243
Elsevier Science 47–8
EMME 148
ENCARTA 9
ENCARTA ENCYCLOPEDIA DELUXE 264–5
ENCARTA INTERACTIVE WORLD ATLAS, SOCIAL TRENDS 1979–1995 267
ENCARTA ONLINE 265
ENCYCLOPAEDIA BRITANNICA 133
ENCYCLOPEDIA AMERICANA 264, 267
ENCYCLOPEDIA OF ASSOCIATIONS 133, 223
ENGLISH SERVER, THE 143
ERIC 102, 104, 107, 214–15, 217–20, 222, 223, 224, 225, 226, 228–9, 237, 240, 246, 247, 251,

276, 277–83, 291–308, 308–26, 329
ERIC Processing & Reference Facility 329
ERIC Web 242
ESA-IRS *see* European Information Network Services
ESLC *see* ELEMENTARY SCHOOL LIBRARY COLLECTION: A GUIDE TO BOOKS AND MEDIA
ESRC DATA ARCHIVE 119
ETHNIC NEWSWATCH 268
EUDISED 235, 240, 329
European Centre for the Development of Vocational Training 240
European Documentation and Information System for Education *see* EUDISED
European Information Network Services 329
European Union Statistical Office 120
Eurostat *see* European Union Statistical Office
EVALUATION RUBRICS FOR WEB SITES 269
EXCEPTIONAL CHILD EDUCATIONAL RESOURCES 239–40, 277, 329
EXCITE 11, 18, 250, 251
EXEGY: CURRENT COUNTRY PROFILES 267–8
EXPANDED ACADEMIC ASAP 241, 263
EXPECT THE BEST FROM A GIRL 274
EXPLORATORIUM 272–3
EXPLORING POETRY 267

FACTS-ON-FILE WORLD NEWS DIGEST 261
Family Expenditure Survey 119
FAMILY PROCESS ON CD-ROM 116
FAMILY *see* AUSTRALIAN FAMILY & SOCIETY ABSTRACTS
FAMILY STUDIES DATABASE 112
FC SCHOLAR *see* DATABASE OF EDUCATION FUNDING FOR INDIVIDUALS
FeMiNa 274
FLAGS OF THE WORLD 273
Foundation Center 241
FOUNDATION DIRECTORY 241
FOUNDATION GRANTS INDEX 241
FRANCIS CD-ROM 234
FRANCIS: SCIENCES DE L'EDUCATION 234, 330
FRIDTJUV 234
FromNowOn 252

GALAXY 249
GALE DIRECTORY OF DATABASES 133
GALE DIRECTORY OF PUBLICATIONS AND BROADCAST MEDIA 133
Gale Group 240–1, 257–8, 264, 267, 330
GALE GROUP BUSINESS A.R.T.S. *see* BUSINESS A.R.T.S.
GaleNet 133
GATEWAY TO EDUCATION MATERIALS 253
GEM *see* GATEWAY TO EDUCATION MATERIALS
GENERAL PERIODICALS ASAP ABRIDGED 263
GENOME 18
Gentili, Kathleen 254
Getty Information Institute 164–9
GIRL POWER! FOR GIRLS 274
GIRL TECH 274
GIRLS' WORLD ONLINE CLUBHOUSE 274

GO NETWORK 250
GOOGLE 95
GPO MONTHLY CATALOG 222
GPO PUBLICATIONS REFERENCE FILE 222
GRANTS DATABASE 225, 241
GREAT BRITAIN HISTORICAL DATABASE 119
GROLIER MULTIMEDIA ENCYCLOPEDIA DELUXE 264–5
Grolier Publishing 266
GTI Jouve 330
GUIDE TO EDUCATION RESOURCES 254–5

H. W. Wilson 108, 109–10, 129, 156–64, 225, 226, 237–8, 247, 257, 260, 262, 277, 328, 332
H.C. BERKELEY PHYSICS LECTURE DEMONSTRATIONS 273
HA *see* HISTORICAL ABSTRACTS
HASSET *see* HUMANITIES AND SOCIAL SCIENCE ELECTRONIC THESAURUS
HEALTH-CD 110
HEALTHGATE 111
HEINEMANN'S CHILDREN'S ENCYCLOPEDIA 267
Heriot-Watt University 256
HISTORICAL ABSTRACTS 129, 177–87, 235
HISTORICAL PSYCINFO 116
HMIC DATABASE 111
HOMEWORK CENTRAL 272
HOTBOT 95, 247, 250
HUA *see* HUMANITIES ABSTRACTS
HUMANITIES ABSTRACTS 157–64
HUMANITIES ABSTRACTS FULL TEXT 159
HUMANITIES AND SOCIAL SCIENCE ELECTRONIC THESAURUS 119
HUMANITIES INDEX 125, 157–64
HUMANITIES TEXT INITIATIVE 146
HUTCHINSON EDUCATIONAL ENCYCLOPEDIA 265, 267

IAC NEWSEARCH 241
IASL *see* Internet Association of School Librarians
IBSS *see* INTERNATIONAL BIBLIOGRAPHY OF THE SOCIAL SCIENCES
ICDL DISTANCE EDUCATION DATABASE 240
ICONNECT 272
ILO *see* International Labour Office
INDEX NEW ZEALAND 227, 238–9, 330
INFOMINE: SCHOLARLY INTERNET RESOURCE COLLECTIONS 253
INFONORDIC 225
INFOPEDIA 265, 267
INFOSEEK 11, 95, 250
INFOTRAC JUNIOR EDITION 257–8
INFOTRAC KIDS EDITION 257–8
INFOTRAC STUDENT EDITION 258
INFOTRAC Web 258
INIST *see* Institut de l'Information Scientifique et Technique
INKTOMI 4
INNODATA 240
INNZ *see* INDEX NEW ZEALAND
INRD *see* Institut National de Recherche Pedagogique
INSPEC 10, 139
Institut de l'Information Scientifique et Technique 164–9, 236

Institut National de la Langue Française 135
Institut National de Recherche Pedagogique 240
Institute for Scientific Information 6, 23–98, 117–9, 152–6
INTEGRATED DATA CATALOGUE 120
INTERNATIONAL BIBLIOGRAPHY OF THE SOCIAL SCIENCES 106–8
INTERNATIONAL ERIC CD-ROM 217, 222, 223, 224, 225, 231, 232, 234, 239, 277, 282,
    285–90, 327, 331
International Labour Office 120
INTERNET ADVOCATE 252
Internet Association of School Librarians 255
INTERNET CLASSICS ARCHIVE 146
INTERNET GRATEFUL MED 6
INTERNET RESOURCES NEWSLETTER 256

JOB HUNT 241
Johns Hopkins School of Medicine 18
Joseph Rowntree Foundation 122
JUNIORQUEST 259
JUNIORQUEST CANADA 259

KATHY SCHROCK'S GUIDE FOR EDUCATORS 254
KCDL CUMULATIVE INDEX *see* KRAUS CURRICULUM DEVELOPMENT LIBRARY
    CUMULATIVE INDEX
Kehoe, Brendan 271
KIDFUSION 270
KIDQUEST 259
KIDS' CORNER 272
KIDS ON THE WEB 271
KIDS' SEARCH TOOLS 270
KIDSCLICK! 270
KIDSCOM 271
KIDSCONNECT 272
KIDSNET ACTIVE DATABASE 243
KIDSWEB 271
Kings Fund Centre 111
Knight-Ridder/Tribune News Service 263
Kraus Curriculum Development Library 243
KRAUS CURRICULUM DEVELOPMENT LIBRARY CUMULATIVE INDEX 243

LA YOUTH 273
Labour Force Survey 119
LEXIS-NEXIS 5, 139–43
LIBRARIAN'S GUIDE TO CYBERSPACE FOR PARENTS & KIDS 270
LIBRARIAN'S INDEX TO THE INTERNET 249
LIBRARIAN'S INFORMATION ONLINE NETWORK 253–4
LIBRARY AND INFORMATION SCIENCE ABSTRACTS 236
Library Corporation, The 331
LIBRARY LITERATURE 236
Library of Congress National Digital Library Program 148
LINGUISTICS AND LANGUAGE BEHAVIOR ABSTRACTS 201–6, 215, 236
LION *see* LIBRARIANS INFORMATION ONLINE NETWORK 253
LISA *see* LIBRARY AND INFORMATION SCIENCE ABSTRACTS
LLBA *see* LINGUISTICS AND LANGUAGE BEHAVIOR ABSTRACTS
LOIS *see* AUSTRALIAN INSTITUTE OF FAMILY STUDIES LIBRARY DATABASE

LOVEJOY'S COLLEGE COUNSELOR 243
LYCOS 11, 247, 250, 251
LYCOS SEARCH GUARD 251
LYCOS ZONE 270

MAGAZINE ARTICLE SUMMARIES 237
MAGAZINE INDEX PLUS/ASAP 263
MAGELLAN INTERNET GUIDE 272
MAS FullTEXT ELITE 237, 258, 263
MAS FullTEXT PREMIER 258, 263
MAS FullTEXT SELECT 237
MAS FullTEXT ULTRA 258, 263
MAS ONLINE 258, 264
MAS ONLINE PLUS 258, 263–4
MAS *see also* MAGAZINE ARTICLE SUMMARIES
Massachusetts Institute of Technology 147
MATERIALS SCIENCE CITATION INDEX 28
MathMatic 273
MCGRAW HILL MULTIMEDIA ENCYCLOPEDIA OF SCIENCE AND TECHNOLOGY 267
McKenzie, Jamie 252
MEDIA AWARENESS NETWORK 254
MEDLINE 5, 10, 20, 139, 140, 141
MENTAL HEALTH ABSTRACTS 235
MENTAL MEASUREMENTS YEARBOOK 242
MetaCrawler 5, 251
MetaSearch 270
MICROCOMPUTER ABSTRACTS 242
Micromedia 224, 233–4, 327–8
MICROSOFT ENCARTA *see* ENCARTA
MIDDLE SEARCH PLUS 257–9
MIDLINK MAGAZINE 271
Milton S. Eisenhower Library, Johns Hopkins University 254–5
MLA INTERNATIONAL BIBLIOGRAPHY 125, 129, 193–201
MLAIB *see* MLA INTERNATIONAL BBLIOGRAPHY
Modern Language Association of America 129, 193–201
MR. GOODMATH 273
MULTIMEDIA ENCYCLOPEDIA (World Book) 9
MUSIC LITERATURE INTERNATIONAL 126

NASA SPACELINK 273
National Association of Social Workers 111
National Center for Child Abuse and Neglect *see* US National Center for Child Abuse and Neglect
National Centre for Vocational Education Research 231
NATIONAL CHILD ABUSE CLEARING HOUSE 114, 115
National Children's Bureau *see* UK National Children's Bureau
National Clearinghouse for Bilingual Education 240
NATIONAL ELECTRONIC LIBRARY FOR HEALTH 122
National Information Center for Educational Media 331
National Information Services Corporation 112, 329
National Institute for Social Work *see* UK National Institute for Social Work
National Library for Psychology and Education (Sweden) 234
National Library of Education 228–9
National Library of Medicine 6, 10
National Library of New Zealand 238–9, 330

NATIONAL NEWSPAPER INDEX 238, 264
NATIONAL WILDLIFE FOUNDATION 273
National Youth Agency *see* UK National Youth Agency
NCBE BIBLIOGRAPHIC DATABASE 240
NCBE Computerized Information Service 240
NCBE *see* National Clearinghouse for Bilingual Education
NESSTAR *see* NETWORKED SOCIAL SCIENCE TOOLS AND RESOURCES
NETWORKED SOCIAL SCIENCE TOOLS AND RESOURCES 119–20
NEUROSCIENCE CITATION INDEX 28
NEW BOOK OF KNOWLEDGE ONLINE 265–6
NEWSBANK 261
NEWSBANK INFOWEB 261, 264
NEWSBANK NEWSFILE COLLECTION 264
NHS NATIONAL RESEARCH REGISTER 122
NICEM REFERENCE ONLINE 242–3, 331
NISC *see* National Information Services Corporation
NLM *see* National Library of Medicine
NNCAN *see* US National Center for Child Abuse and Neglect
NORTHERN LIGHT 5, 11
Norwegian Social Science Data Services 119
Nuffield Institute for Health 111
NZ EXPLORER 5

OASIS *see* DIRECTORY OF OPEN ACCESS STATISTICAL INFORMATION SITES
OCLC 27, 152, 156, 157, 187, 193, 224, 230, 328, 329, 331, 332
OCLC FIRSTSEARCH 5, 194, 237
OCLC WORLDCAT 235
OCLC: EDUCATION LIBRARY 235, 331
OED *see* OXFORD ENGLISH DICTIONARY ON COMPACT DISC
Office of National Statistics 119
OMNI *see* ORGANISING MEDICAL NETWORKED INFORMATION
ONEKEY KIDSAFE SEARCH ENGINE 270
ON-LINE BOOKS PAGE 143
ONTARIO SCIENCE CENTRE'S YOUNG PERSON'S GUIDE 272
ONTERIS 233
Open University International Centre for Distance Learning 240
Orbit 10
ORGANISING MEDICAL NETWORKED INFORMATION 20
Ovid Technologies 5, 9, 111, 156, 157, 187, 193, 224, 225, 230, 232, 328, 329, 332
Ovid Web Gateway 226
OXFORD ENGLISH DICTIONARY ON COMPACT DISC 135, 136–7
OZ KIDS INTERNAUT CYBERCENTRE 271
OZEMAIL FAMILY WEB GUIDE: 4 KIDS 272

PAIS *see* PUBLIC AFFAIRS INFORMATION SERVICE
Palace of Fine Arts, San Francisco 272–3
PERIODICAL ABSTRACTS 262
PERIODICAL ABSTRACTS LIBRARY 262
PERIODICAL ABSTRACTS PLUS TEXT 238, 259, 262
PERIODICAL ABSTRACTS RESEARCH I 262
PERIODICAL ABSTRACTS RESEARCH II 262
PETERSON'S COLLEGE DATABASE 244
PETERSON'S GRADLINE 244
PETERSON'S: THE EDUCATION SUPERSITE 244, 246

PHILOSOPHER'S INDEX 128–9, 207–10, 236
Philosopher's Information Center 128–9, 207–10, 236
PLANETGIRL.COM 274
PLANETZOOM 272
PR NEWSWIRE 264
PRIMARY SEARCH 257
PROFESSIONAL DEVELOPMENT COLLECTION 242
Project for American and French Research on the Treasury of the French Language 135–6
PROJECT GUTENBERG 143–4
PROQUEST 259
PROQUEST DIGITAL DISSERTATIONS 236
PROQUEST FULLTEXT NEWSPAPER COLLECTION 259, 264
PROQUEST PROFESSIONAL EDUCATION COLLECTION 241–2
PSYCINFO 10, 102, 107, 116, 227, 235
PSYCLIT 10, 235
PUBLIC AFFAIRS INFORMATION SERVICE 236
PUBMED 5, 139, 140, 141
PURPLE MOON PLACE 274

QUALITY EDUCATION DATA 243
Questel-Orbit 164, 234, 330
QUOTATIONS DATABASE 135, 137, 138

R•CADE 120
RANDOM HOUSE KIDS' ENCYCLOPEDIA 265, 267
RDB *see* ATLA RELIGION DATABASE
READERS' GUIDE ABSTRACTS 262
READERS' GUIDE ABSTRACTS SELECT EDITION 262
READERS' GUIDE FOR YOUNG PEOPLE 257, 260
READERS' GUIDE FULL TEXT MEGA EDITION 262
READERS' GUIDE FULL TEXT MINI EDITION 262
READERS' GUIDE TO PERIODICAL LITERATURE 237, 257, 262
REGARD 122
REPERE 239, 331–2
RESEARCH CENTERS AND SERVICES DIRECTORY 241
RESEARCH CENTERS DIRECTORY 133
Research Libraries Group 164, 330
Resource Discovery Network 120
RESOURCE/ONE SELECT FULL TEXT 259
RESOURCES OF SCHOLARLY SOCIETIES – EDUCATION 255
RILA *see* BIBLIOGRAPHY OF THE HISTORY OF ART
RILEY GUIDE 241
RILM *see* MUSIC LITERATURE INTERNATIONAL
RMIT Publishing 114, 224, 231, 238, 262
RSP FUNDING FOR GRADUATE STUDENTS 241
RSP FUNDING FOR POSTGRADUATES AND PROFESSIONALS 241
RSP FUNDING FOR UNDERGRADUATE STUDENTS 241

SAFESEARCH 271
School District of Philadelphia 253–4
SCHOOL FINDER 244
SCHOOL LIBRARIAN LINKS 254
SCHOOL LIBRARIES ONLINE 255
SCHOOLING 2001: ELECTRONIC RESOURCE EVALUATIONS 242

SCHOOLMATE FOR ELEMENTARY SCHOOLS 261
SCHOOLMATE FOR MIDDLE SCHOOLS 261
SCHOOLNET 254
SCHOOLWORK.UGH (SCHOOLWORK.ORG) 271
Schrock, Kathy 254
SCIENCE CITATION INDEX 27, 29, 31–2, 46, 47–8, 49–50, 51–8, 74, 75–83, 84–6
SCIENCE MADE SIMPLE 273
SCISEARCH *see* SCIENCES CITATION INDEX
SCOUT REPORT FOR SOCIAL SCIENCES 121, 255–6
SDM *see* Services Documentaires Multimedia 329
SEARCHOPOLIS 270
SEARCHUK 5
Services Documentaires Multimedia (Canada) 239, 240, 328, 331–2
SilverPlatter 5, 10, 102, 108, 111, 114, 156, 157, 187–93, 193–201, 203–6, 207–10, 223, 224, 226,
    230, 231, 235, 241, 262, 295–305, 308–26, 328, 329, 331–2, 332
SIRIS *see* Smithsonian Institution Research Information System
SIRS DISCOVERER CD-ROM 259–60
SIRS DISCOVERER ON THE WEB 260
SIRS RESEARCHER 260
SIRS RESEARCHER ON THE WEB 260
Smithsonian Institution Research Information System 150–1
SOCIAL PLANNING AND DEVELOPMENT ABSTRACTS 104
SOCIAL POLICY VIRTUAL LIBRARY 121
SOCIAL SCIENCE CITATION INDEX 27, 29, 36–7, 38–43, 59–73, 86–8, 89–94, 117–19
SOCIAL SCIENCE INFORMATION GATEWAY 5, 8, 20
SOCIAL SCIENCE INTERNET GATEWAY 120
SOCIAL SCIENCES ABSTRACTS FULL TEXT 108, 109–10
SOCIAL SCIENCES CITATION INDEX 235–6
SOCIAL SCIENCES INDEX 125
SOCIAL SCISEARCH *see* SOCIAL SCIENCE CITATION INDEX
SOCIAL SERVICES ABSTRACTS 111
SOCIAL SERVICES ABSTRACTS *see* also SOCIAL PLANNING AND DEVELOPMENT
    ABSTRACTS
SOCIAL TRENDS CD-ROM 119
SOCIAL WORK ABSTRACTS+ 111, 114
SOCIOFILE 104, 111
SOCIOFILE *see also* SOCIOLOGICAL ABSTRACTS
SOCIOLOGICAL ABSTRACTS 102–4, 109, 111, 201–6, 235–6
SOCIOLOGICAL ABSTRACTS *see also* CSA SOCIOLOGICAL ABSTRACTS; SOCIOFILE;
    SOCIAL SERVICES ABSTRACTS
SOLAR SYSTEM 273
SOPODA *see* SOCIAL PLANNING AND DEVELOPMENT ABSTRACTS; SOCIAL
    SERVICES ABSTRACTS
SOSIG *see* SOCIAL SCIENCE INFORMATION GATEWAY
SOUTH AFRICA ONLINE 238
SPPB *see* National Library for Psychology and Education (Sweden)
SSCI *see* SOCIAL SCIENCE CITATION INDEX
STATBANK 223
STATEWATCH DATABASE 120–1
STATIONERY OFFICE'S PUBLICATIONS DATABASE 223
STN International 4, 10, 27
STUDYWEB 270–1
SUPER SNOOPER 271
SUPER-KIDS 271

TEEN ADVICE ONLINE 273
TePuna 239, 330
TES BOOKFIND 243
TEST LOCATOR 242
Test Review Locator 242
Test Selection Tips 242
THESA 236
TIME.COM 256
TIMES HIGHER EDUCATION SUPPLEMENT 241, 243
TLC *see* Library Corporation, The
TOPICSEARCH 261

UK Department of Health 122
UK Department of Health and Social Security 111
UK National Children's Bureau 114
UK National Institute for Social Work 113–14
UK National Youth Agency 112
UMI 111, 236
UNCOVER 115
UNCOVERWEB 256
UNESCO CD-ROM: KEY UNESCO DATA ON EDUCATION 240
UNESCO *see* United Nations Education, Scientific and Cultural Organization
UNIDO *see* United Nations Industrial Development Organization
United Nations Education, Scientific and Cultural Organization 120, 240
United Nations Industrial Development Organization 120
Université de Montréal 240
University of Chicago, Divisions of the Humanities and Social Sciences 135
University of Leeds, Brotherton Library 231–3, 327
University of Michigan 146
University of North London 112
University of Pennsylvania 143
University of Sydney Library 254
UNIVERSITY OF TORONTO ENGLISH LIBRARY 147
University of Virginia 146
US Department of Education 228–9, 252, 329
US DEPARTMENT OF EDUCATION Site 255
US National Center for Child Abuse and Neglect 112

VIRTUAL REFERENCE DESK 272
VOCATIONAL SEARCH 261
VOCED 231
VOLNET 112–13
Volunteer Centre 112

WAITER.COM 5
WAVE 273
WEB OF ONLINE DICTIONARIES 134
Web of Science 28, 29–30, 152
WEBCRAWLER 11
WEBMUSEUM NETWORK 148–9
Western Michigan University, English Department 147
Wheaton College, Illinois 146
WHERE ON THE GLOBE IS ROGER? 273

WILSON EDUCATION ABSTRACTS 218, 224, 226, 229–30, 277, 332
WILSON EDUCATION ABSTRACTS FULL TEXT 277
WILSON EDUCATION FULL TEXT 224, 229–30, 332
WILSON EDUCATION INDEX *see* EDUCATION INDEX
WILSON SOCIAL SCIENCES ABSTRACTS 235–6
Wilson, H. W. *see* H. W. Wilson
WilsonDisc 156, 157, 194, 230, 262, 328, 332
WilsonLine 156, 157, 328
WilsonTape 230, 260
WilsonWeb 156, 157, 230, 237, 260, 262, 328, 332
WORLD BOOK MULTIMEDIA ENCYCLOPEDIA 264, 266
WORLD BOOK PREMIER REFERENCE 266
WORLD WIDE WEB VIRTUAL LIBRARY – EDUCATION 253
WWWEBSTER DICTIONARY 133–4

YAHOO! 5, 6, 133, 248, 251
YAHOO! – EDUCATION 248
YAHOOLIGANS! 270
YAHOOLIGANS! FOR KIDS 248
YEARBOOK OF INTERNATIONAL ORGANIZATIONS ON CD-ROM 223

Subject index

Academic American Encyclopedia 265
Academic Press Dictionary of Science and Technology 267
Adobe Acrobat 109, 115
advertising 150, 156
Africa 238
aging see senior citizens
agriculture 138
America: History and Life 177
American Library Association 270
American Psychological Association 116
American Theological Library Association 187–8
American Verse Project 146
animation 10
anthropology 150, 201, 207
APAIS Thesaurus 238, 330
archaeology 152, 156, 157
architecture 33, 152, 156, 164, 170
archives 150, 177, 178
Archives and Manuscripts Catalog 150–151
Archives of American Art 150
Archives of American Gardens 150
art 33, 34–5, 137–8, 140, 143, 148, 150, 152, 156–76, 237, 239
Art Index 157
Art Inventories Catalog 150
ARTBibliographies Modern 170
ARTFL 135
artificial intelligence 201
artificial languages 135
Arts see Humanities
Arts & Humanities Citation Index 152
Asia 238
astronomy 273
audiovisual materials 242
Australia 114–15, 217, 218, 224, 230–1, 234,

239, 244, 254, 261–2, 268, 272, 327
Australian Biological Research Network 5
Australian Clearinghouse for Library and Information Science 231
Australian Council for Educational Research 231, 234, 327, 331
Australian Education Index 231, 234
Australian Family Profiles: Social and Demographic Patterns 115
Australian Institute of Family Studies 114
Australian Journal of Marriage and Family 114
Australian Journal of Social Issues 114
Australian Thesaurus of Education Descriptors 231, 277, 285, 327, 331

Bartlett's Familiar Quotations 137
Bath Information and Database Service (BIDS) 106–7, 232
behavioural sciences see social sciences
Belgium 239, 240
Best Web Sites for Teachers 270
Bibliographie d'Histoire de l'Art 165
Bibliography of Education Theses in Australia 231, 234
Bibliography of the History of Art 165
Biblioteca di Documentazione Pedagogica 329
Bibliothèque Nationale du Québec 239
biochemistry 28
biophysics 28
biosciences 18
biotechnology 28
blocking software see filtering
Book List 260
Book Report 258
book reviews 109, 157, 177, 188, 202, 230, 233, 237, 243, 258, 261

Britain *see* UK
Britannica Book of the Year 266
British Education Index 231, 234
British Education Thesaurus 220, 232, 277, 292, 327, 331
British Education Theses Index 231–2, 234
British Journal of Social Work 109
British Medical Journal 119
browsing 9–10, 28, 29
Bulletin of the Center for Children's Books 260
business 105, 237, 238, 242, 261, 262, 267
Busy Educator's Guide to the World Wide Web 270

Canada 177, 188, 220, 225, 233–4, 235, 236, 237, 238, 239, 240, 243, 244, 249, 250, 254, 262, 263, 264, 268, 327
Canadian Education Index 238
Canadian Education Thesaurus 220, 233, 277–8, 328
Canadian Geographic 264
Carnegie Mellon University 146
catchword 115
censorship 236
Central Statistical Office *see* Office of National Statistics
Centre for Policy on Ageing 114
Centre National de la Recherche Scientifique (CNRS) 135, 164, 330
Chemical Abstracts Service (CAS) 23
chemistry 23, 28, 74, 272
children 3, 19, 112, 113–15, 216–17, 248, 256–60, 264, 269–74
Children and Society 114
Children's Literature in Education 258
Christian Science Monitor 263
citation indexes 23–96, 117–19, 152–6
    co-citations 33–44, 83, 86–8
    cycling 45–46
    history 26–27
    principles 24–26
    research assessment 26
citation studies 128
Clearing House Newsletter 115
Clever Project 95
Collier's Encyclopedia 258
communication studies 157, 201
computer science 28, 156, 201, 239
conferences 121, 152, 165, 188, 202, 228, 230, 231, 232, 237, 238
controlled- vs natural-language searching 11–13, 126, 132, 183–4, 194, 247, 275–80, 292–3, 308
copyright 211

Council for Exceptional Children 239, 329
Council of Europe 329
Counselling in Primary Care Trust 121
Country Facts 260
crafts 156
Cranfield Projects 14–15
cross-file searching 11
current awareness 88, 121, 123
Current Biography 260
Current Contents/Social and Behavioral Sciences 117
Current Index to Journals in Education 228, 279

Danbib 234
dance 152, 157
Danish Data Archives 119
database evaluation 10–11, 17–20, 114, 222–7, 245–6, 269–70, 275
DBWebPublisher 113
Denmark 119, 234–5
descriptors *see* controlled languages
design 156, 164, 169, 170
dictionaries 133–7, 138, 260, 267
Dictionnaire de l'Académie Française 135
direct manipulation 7–8
directories 138, 223
    Directory of ERIC Information Service Providers 229
    Directory of ERIC Resource Collections 229
Disability & Society 115
dissertations 11, 165, 170, 177, 178, 188, 202, 230, 231, 232, 233, 236, 238, 240, 328
distance education 244–245
document delivery 11, 227, 229, 230, 232, 233, 234
drama 147, 157, 162,
Dyna Text 116

Economic and Social Research Council 119, 122
economic history 177, 178
economics 138, 234, 261
education 107, 138, 178, 207, 213–33
    terminology 219–21, 280–1
Education Digest 258, 260
Education Index 229
Educational Library of Denmark 234
EINET Galaxy Humanities Collection 148
Elders 113
Electronic Libraries Project 232
Eliot Elisofon Photographic Archives 150
EMME 148
Encyclopedia Britannica 148

Encyclopedia of Animals 257
encyclopedias 133, 223, 258, 260, 264–8
engineering 138
England *see* UK
English server 143, 146
ERIC Identifier Authority List 278
ERIC *Thesaurus see* Thesaurus of ERIC
    Descriptors
e-texts 143
ethics 187, 207
European Centre for the Development of
    Vocational Training 240
European Education Thesaurus 329
European Educational Research Yearbook 235
European Parliament 121
European Union Statistical Office (Eurostat)
    120
exhibitions 162, 165, 166, 168, 170, 172, 173,
    174–5
Explode 195–7

Family Expenditure Survey 119
family history 177
Family Matters 114
film studies 152, 156, 157
films *see* motion pictures
filtering 19
folklore 139, 156, 157, 177, 193, 196, 272
foreign affairs *see* international relations
France 135, 234, 236, 239, 240, 330
Funk & Wagnell's New Encyclopedia 257, 260

Gale Directory of Databases 152, 165
General Election surveys 119
Getty End-User Online Searching Project 133
Getty Information Institute 164
girls – Web sites 273–4
grants databases 241, 249
graphics 10
Great Britain *see* UK
Greece 240

health *see* medicine
Helicon's Chronology of World History 267
Heriot-Watt University 256
Higher Education Funding Council for England
    106–7
Higher Education Funding Council for Wales
    106–7
Historical Abstracts 178
history 138, 143, 148, 150, 152, 157, 177–87,
    188, 201, 207, 234, 235, 239
history of science 177, 178
Horn Book 260

House of Commons 121
House of Lords 121
Human Studies Film Archives 150
humanities 23, 24–5, 27, 125–211, 238, 261,
    262
    research behaviour 127–129
    information seeking 126–7, 129–32
Humanities Index 157
hypertext 9–10, 29, 95, 126, 133, 211

images 10, 143, 148, 211
Index to Book Reviews in Religion 188
Index to Religious Periodical Literature 188
infometrics 96
Information Please 258
information seeking 1–4, 29, 99, 100–1, 126–7,
    129–32, 210–11, 214–19, 226, 246–51,
    274–326
information technology 230, 242
Inmagic 113
Institut National de Recherche Pedagogique
    240
Institute for Scientific Information (ISI) 23, 27,
    28, 29–30, 44, 152
Institute of Race Relations 121
Interfaces 3, 7–8, 13, 18, 20, 29, 102–3, 105–6,
    107, 108, 112, 226
intermediaries *see* information seeking
International Association of School
    Librarianship 255
International Labour Organization 120
international relations 177, 178, 239, 261
International Social Work 109
*Internet Resource Directory for K-12 Teachers
    and Librarians* 270

Java 107
Johns Hopkins University 18, 255
Joint Information Systems Committee (JISC)
    100, 106–7, 120
Joseph Rowntree Foundation 122
Journal of Family Studies 114
Journalism 157
Juley Photographic Collection 150

Kings Fund Centre 111
Korea 268
Kraus Curriculum Development Library 243

Labor Force Survey 119
law 23, 26, 105, 139–43, 207, 230, 238, 267
Leeds University 232, 327, 331
librarians 216, 241, 254–5, 257
libraries 127, 128, 148, 236

library and information studies 177, 178, 231, 236, 242
Library of Congress 148
Library of Congress Subject Headings 115, 158, 160–61, 230, 260, 277
linguistics 152, 193, 196, 201–206, 230, 236
Linguistics and Language Behavior Abstracts 202
literacy 242
literature 140, 143, 146, 147, 148, 152, 157, 193–201, 239, 262–3

Magill's Book Reviews 237, 258, 261, 264
management 138, 231
manuscripts 148, 150, 164
maps 148, 187, 260, 261, 265, 267–8
marketing 239
Massachusetts Institute of Technology 147
materials science 28
mathematics 28, 201, 273
Media and Methods 260
medicine 28, 96, 138–1, 177, 178, 237, 261, 262
Merriam-Webster's Collegiate Dictionary 133, 266, 267
MeSH 122, 139
metasearch engines 5, 251
Methodist Reviews Index 188
Michigan Early Modern English Materials 146
Microlog Education Collection 234
Middle English Collection 146
MLA Bibliography Thesaurus 194
MLA International Bibliography of Books and Articles on the Modern Languages and Literature 194, 195
motion pictures 148, 163, 177, 230, 240
movies *see* motion pictures
multifile searching 226
multilingual aspects 18–19
multimedia 10, 148, 211, 264–8
museums 150, 156–7, 164, 170, 269
music 33, 141–2, 143, 152, 153, 157, 163

names – searching 130, 132, 155, 158, 167, 172, 185–6, 189, 196, 197, 205, 209–10, 278
National Anthropological Archives 150
National Association of Retired Persons 111
National Center for Child Abuse and Neglect 112
National Children's Bureau 114
National Clearinghouse for Bilingual Education 240
National Digital Library Program, Library of

Congress 148
National Electronic Library for Health 122
National Information Center for Educational Media 331
National Institute for Social Work 113
National Library of Australia 238
National Library of Canada 249
National Library of Education 228
National Library of Medicine 6, 139
National Library of New Zealand 239, 330
National Museum of American Art 150
natural languages *see* controlled- vs natural-language searching
netskills 100
networking 29, 101
neuroscience 28
New Technology in the Human Services 113
New York Times 237, 258, 259, 262, 263, 264
New Zealand 227, 238–9, 330
newspapers 140–1, 143, 231, 237–8, 258–64, 268
NLM *see* National Library of Medicine
Northern Ireland *see* UK
Northern Ireland Department of Education 107
Norway 119
Norwegian Social Science Data Services 119
NSPCC 112
Nuffield Institute for Health 111

Office of National Statistics 119
OPACs 3, 4, 13, 100, 102, 148, 211, 225
Open University 240
Organising Medical Networked Information Consortium (OMNI) 20
Oxford Dictionary of Quotations 135
Oxford English Dictionary 135

Palace of Fine Arts 272–3
patents 23, 27
pearl growing (search technique) 284
Philosopher's Index 131, 208
Philosopher's Index Thesaurus 208
philosophy 131, 143, 148, 152, 157, 187, 201, 207–10, 234, 236, 239
photographs 148, 150, 187
photography 33, 156, 157, 164, 170
physics 273
planning 156
plays *see* drama
poetry 146, 147, 152, 162, 267
political science 239
politics 105, 177, 237, 261, 262, 267
Practice 113
precis 232

precision 14–17, 26, 198–9
pricing 8–9, 10, 20, 100–1, 224–6, 257
psychology 105, 107, 116, 188, 215, 230, 231,
    234, 235, 239, 263

quotations 135, 137–8

radio 152, 243, 268
Ranger Rick 273
ranking 9
Reader's Companion to American History 258
Reading Teacher 258
recall 14–17, 26, 198–9
reference databases 133–8, 239
Religion Index 188
Religion Indexes Thesaurus 189
religious studies 146, 148, 152, 157, 177,
    187–93, 207
Research in Ministry 188
Research Policy and Planning 113
Resources in Education 228, 279
Roget's Thesaurus 135
Royal Melbourne Institute of Technology
    University (RMIT) 231, 261

School Library Journal 258, 260, 270
science 23, 27, 143, 177, 178, 207, 237, 262,
    267, 273
Science Books & Films 270
Scotland *see* UK
Scottish Higher Education Funding Council
    106
search evaluation 14–17
searching *see* information seeking
senior citizens 3, 111
Services Documentaires Multimedia Inc. 239,
    240, 328, 332
Shakespeare, William 147–8, 268
Shepard's Citations 26
Smithsonian Chronology Catalog 150
Smithsonian Institution Research Information
    System (SIRIS) 150–1
Social Science Information Gateway 5, 20
social sciences 23, 27, 99–123, 188, 238, 263
Social Sciences Citation Index 117
Social Services Abstracts 111
Social Studies & the Young Learner 270
social welfare 110–15
social work 109
Social Work 109
Social Work in Europe 113
sociology 102–4, 105, 188, 201, 231, 234,
    235–6
sound 10, 148, 211, 264, 265

South Pacific 238
Southern California Online User Group 20
spamming 11
sport 237, 238, 239, 261, 267
SPSS 119
Statewatch 121
statistics 26–7, 119–20, 223, 267
Sweden 225, 234
Swedish National Library for Psychology and
    Education (SPPB) 234
Switzerland 239, 240
synonyms 3, 101
Systran 19

Teacher Librarian Journal 270
*Teacher's Complete & Easy Guide to the
    Internet* 270
Teaching Children Mathematics 258
Teaching PreK-8 258, 260
technology 23, 150, 177, 178, 267
television 152, 156, 163, 242, 268
TePuna 239, 330
textiles 156, 170
theatre 152
theology *see* religious studies
Thesaurus of Aging Technology 111
Thesaurus of ERIC Descriptors 220, 229, 240,
    242, 277–8, 291, 292, 308, 329, 330
Thesaurus of Linguistic Indexing Terms 202,
    204–5
Time (Canada) 264
time periods – searching 130–1, 164, 167, 169,
    178, 186–7, 221–2, 281–2
Time Warner 256
Times Educational Supplement 243
training 4, 20
transliteration 129–30, 180, 189, 197, 203, 208
travel 238
Trésor de la langue française 135

UK 100, 105, 106–7, 110, 111, 112–13, 115
    119, 120, 121, 122, 217, 218, 220–1, 223,
    232–3, 234, 236, 243, 249, 265, 327
UK Department of Health and Social Security
    110, 111, 122
UN Industrial Development Organization
    (UNIDO) 120
UnCover 115
Unesco 120, 240
Université de Montréal 240
University of Chicago 135
University of Leeds *see* Leeds University
University of Michigan 146
University of North London 112

University of Pennsylvania 143
University of Sydney 254
University of Toronto English Library 147
University of Virginia 146
urban studies 177
US Department of Education 228, 252, 255, 329
USA 100, 105, 111, 112, 116, 135, 150, 177, 188, 218, 219, 222, 228, 235, 236, 238, 240, 242, 243–4, 262, 263, 264
USA Today 259, 262
Usenet 256
user studies 3–4

video 10, 156, 170, 177, 240, 243, 265

Wall Street Journal 259, 262, 263
Web of Science 28, 29–30, 152
Web site evaluation *see* database evaluation
WebMuseum Network 148–9
WebPacs *see* OPACs
Webster's Revised Unabridged Dictionary 135
Western Michigan University 147
Wheaton College 146
women's studies 177, 268
World Almanac and Book of Facts 260
World Almanac for Kids 257, 260
World Almanac of the USA 257
World Book Encyclopedia 266

Italicized entries are journal titles.